**IET COMPUTING SERIES 29**

# Blockchains for Network Security

# Series Page for front matter

## IET Book Series on Big Data – Call for Authors

Editor-in-Chief: Professor Albert Y. Zomaya, University of Sydney, Australia

The topic of big data has emerged as a revolutionary theme that cuts across many technologies and application domains. This new book series brings together topics within the myriad research activities in many areas that analyze, compute, store, manage, and transport massive amounts of data, such as algorithm design, data mining and search, processor architectures, databases, infrastructure development, service and data discovery, networking and mobile computing, cloud computing, high-performance computing, privacy and security, storage, and visualization.

Topics considered include (but not restricted to) IoT and Internet computing; cloud computing; peer-to-peer computing; autonomic computing; data center computing; multicore and many core computing; parallel, distributed, and high-performance computing; scalable databases; mobile computing and sensor networking; green computing; service computing; networking infrastructures; cyberinfrastructures; e-Science; smart cities; analytics and data mining; big data applications, and more.

Proposals for coherently integrated International coedited or coauthored handbooks and research monographs will be considered for this book series. Each proposal will be reviewed by the Editor-in-chief and some board members, with additional external reviews from independent reviewers. Please email your book proposal for the IET Book Series on Big Data to: Professor Albert Y. Zomaya at albert.zomaya@sydney.edu.au or to the IET at author_support@theiet.org.

# Blockchains for Network Security

## Principles, technologies and applications

Edited by
Haojun Huang, Lizhe Wang, Yulei Wu
and Kim-Kwang Raymond Choo

The Institution of Engineering and Technology

**British Library Cataloguing in Publication Data**
A catalogue record for this product is available from the British Library


**ISBN 978-1-78561-873-4 (hardback)**
**ISBN 978-1-78561-874-1 (PDF)**


Typeset in India by MPS Limited
Printed in the UK by CPI Group (UK) Ltd, Croydon

# Contents

# About the editors

**Haojun Huang** is an associate professor at the School of Electronic Information and Communications, Huazhong University of Science and Technology, Wuhan, China. His current research interests include Internet of Things, Network Function Virtualization, Software-Defined Networking, and Artificial Intelligence for networking. He holds a Ph.D. degree in Communications Engineering from the University of Science and Technology of China.

**Lizhe Wang** is the dean and "ChuTian" chair professor at the School of Computer Science, China University of Geosciences (CUG), and a professor at the Institute of Remote Sensing and Digital Earth, Chinese Academy of Sciences (CAS), China. His research interests include cloud computing, HPC, e-science, and spatial data processing. He is a fellow of the British Computer Society and the IET and a series board member of the IET Book Series on Big Data.

**Yulei Wu** is a senior lecturer with the Department of Computer Science, College of Engineering, Mathematics and Physical Sciences, University of Exeter, United Kingdom. His main research focuses on computer networks, networked systems, software-defined networks and systems, network management, and network security and privacy. He is an associate editor of IEEE Transactions on Network and Service Management and an area editor of Computer Networks (Elsevier).

**Kim-Kwang Raymond Choo** holds the Cloud Technology Endowed Professorship at the University of Texas at San Antonio, United States. He is the recipient of various awards, including the 2019 IEEE Technical Committee on Scalable Computing (TCSC) Award for Excellence in Scalable Computing (Middle Career Researcher).

*Chapter 1*

# Introduction to blockchains

*Haojun Huang[1], Jialin Tian[1], Geyong Min[2] and
Wang Miao[2]*

In the current information age, we are constantly exchanging and sharing information with each other, in which some networks such as Internet, 5G, and Internet of Things (IoT) have become indispensable parts. Most of these networks are centralized, meaning that the important data required for communication is stored in centralized servers and maintained by specific organizations. Such centralized storage requires high security for centralized organizations and network infrastructure, and the data therein could be tampered and forged in the storage, transmission, management and use, causing serious privacy and security issues. (In addition, such fully centralized data storage and sharing systems are generally less fault tolerant. If the centralization organization is attacked or a critical part fails, the entire network interaction system will be deeply affected.)

In response to the previous challenges, blockchain characterized by decentralization is considered to be a promising technology that can effectively resolve those challenges and improve network security. A blockchain is a distributed database or ledger that maintains an ever-growing list of data records in opposition to tampering and revision. It provides immutable data storage over a distributed network and supports a large number of encrypted and coded interactions, which improves the reliability of the entire network interaction system and reduces the need for trust. Even if some nodes in the blockchain are hacked and fail, the system can run as usual. (In such a scenario, users are enabled to form a distributed peer-to-peer (P2P) network in which they could interact with each other in an efficient manner without a trusted intermediary.) What the decentralized blockchain has effectively improved in terms of network security has aroused widespread concern in both academia and industry.

In this chapter, in order to better understand the blockchain technology, there will be a brief introduction to blockchain, including its overview referring to

[1]Department of Information Engineering, Huazhong University of Science and Technology, Wuhan, China
[2]Department of Computer Science, University of Exeter, Exeter, UK

characteristics and classifications, structure, key technologies involved, evolution and typical applications.

## 1.1    Overview

Blockchain was originally known around the world for its success as an underlying technology for Bitcoin, which was the first prototype of cryptocurrency. In 2008, a person named Satoshi Nakamoto proposed a P2P version of the electronic cash, Bitcoin, in his paper titled "Bitcoin: A Peer-to-Peer Electronic Cash System" [1]. He defined a cryptographic guarantee rather than the current "trust-based" electronic payment system and described that it allows electronic cash transferring directly from one party to another without relying on intermediaries. What supports such a new type of cryptocurrency is exactly blockchain.

However, Nakamoto did not directly give the term "Blockchain" and its exact definition in that paper. He described the underlying technology through "block" and "chain" as a data structure based on a distributed P2P network. A blockchain is sequentially linked by a number of chronological "blocks" containing transaction information, forming an ongoing "chain." Each block contains all the information in the current block's constituent time and is encapsulated by a hash value and pointed to the previous block. Moreover, the transactions recorded therein are verified by consensus of most participants in the system and cannot be modified once they are recorded.

In 2009, the first open-source project based on this new protocol was released and produced Genesis block of 50 coins. Since then, the blockchain has continued to attract attention and evolve. Nowadays, blockchain technology has evolved more beyond finance than just the underlying technology of Bitcoin.

### 1.1.1    Characteristics of blockchain

In addition to being famous for decentralization, blockchain has shown other significant characteristics during its development, such as reliability, anonymity, transparency, auditability and programming [2,3]. A more detailed explanation of them follows next.

#### 1.1.1.1    Decentralization

In blockchain, the verification, accounting, storage, maintenance and transmission of data are all carried out at each node based on the distributed system. The trust between nodes is established by cryptographic guarantee rather than the central institution, thus forming a decentralized trusted system. Each device can participate in the P2P network of blockchain as a node, and each node is an independent and autonomous entity, cooperating with each other and reaching a consensus under consensus mechanism. In traditional centralized systems, any transaction needs to be verified by the centralized trusted institution, which results in increased communication costs, heavy load on the central server and collapse of network once the central node was attacked. In comparison, the data storage and update in distributed blockchain can effectively reduce the cost of servers, and the damage to one or even several nodes will not affect the operation of entire system, which has strong robustness.

### 1.1.1.2  Reliability

In the distributed database of blockchain, each transaction needs to be verified, recorded in the block and reserved permanently by each node. Nodes in the P2P network can form powerful computing power through consensus algorithms such as proof-of-work (PoW), the block hashes derived from all transactions and the hash of its previous one. Unless the attacker has controlled more than 51% nodes of the whole network at the same time, the data cannot be easily tampered or forged. Therefore, the stability and reliability of data in blockchain are extremely high.

### 1.1.1.3  Anonymity

In the distributed P2P network of blockchain, each user can join and exchange data with others through a meaningless address linked with the users public key. The only thing that can identify the user is such an address that can be randomly generated at any time. There will be no other privacy information about the user expect his address. Besides, a user can even apply for multiple addresses and constantly change among them. Therefore, transactions in blockchain are not linked to the real identity of users, but only to the address of them, which guarantees the anonymity of transactions.

### 1.1.1.4  Transparency

In the decentralized blockchain, each transaction needs to be recorded by each node after verification, that is, all nodes need to share data across the network and synchronize one database or ledger. Therefore, the generation, recording and updating of data in blockchain are transparent to all nodes of the whole network. Users can get the status of the current blockchain through any node.

### 1.1.1.5  Auditability

Since the creation of Genesis block, each newly generated "block" will be connected with the previous block and added to the "chain," forming the blockchain. Thus, blockchain stores all the transaction data in the blocks from the time it was created. In addition, each block was printed a timestamp to prevent tampering when it was generated. Combining transaction data with the timestamp in a block, the time, participating nodes and content of transactions can be well proved. Therefore, blockchain performs well in terms of auditability and can track each transaction data.

### 1.1.1.6  Programming

As stated earlier on transparency, not only is the transaction data in blockchain open source but the code of it is also highly transparent. The blockchain platform has offered a flexible scripting system that allows users to programmatically produce currencies, advanced smart contracts and decentralized applications. The

Ethereum platform in blockchain, for example, provides a Turing complete scripting language that allows users to build any type of smart contracts or transaction that can be precisely defined.

## 1.1.2    Classifications of blockchain systems

According to the different degree of openness and coverage, the current blockchain can be classified into three categories: public blockchain, consortium blockchain and private blockchain [4,5]. Their characteristics are somewhat different on consensus participant, read permission, decentralization, access permission, immutability and efficiency. Details are as follows and the comparisons of their characteristics are listed in Table 1.1.

### 1.1.2.1    Public blockchain

It refers to a blockchain that anyone in the world can access the system at any time to read data, send transactions and take part in creating new blocks. The public blockchain, which is also called permissionless blockchain, allows each node take part in the consensus determination process. All the transactions and data are highly transparent and available to the public. Its most prominent feature is completely decentralized and not controlled by any organization, relying on encryption technology to ensure security. In such a highly decentralized system, transactions and data are stored in each node; thus, they are almost impossible to be tampered, which shows great immutability. However, the participation of too many nodes in the public blockchain makes the propagation of transactions, the synchronization of data and reaching a consensus particularly time-consuming and inefficient.

### 1.1.2.2    Consortium blockchain

It is a blockchain with several preselected organizations rather than one public entity participating in management. Each organization runs one or more nodes. Different with public blockchain, the consortium blockchain is obviously a partially decentralized blockchain, where there are only a small part of nodes selected to participate in the consensus determination. For a new node, it needs to be verified to participate in the consensus process, which shows that the consortium

Table 1.1    *Comparisons among public blockchain, consortium blockchain and private blockchain*

| Property | Public blockchain | Consortium blockchain | Private blockchain |
|---|---|---|---|
| Access permission | Permissionless | Permissioned | Permissioned |
| Consensus participant | All nodes | Selected set of nodes | Single organization |
| Read permission | Public | Public or restricted | Public or restricted |
| Decentralization | Yes | Partial | No |
| Immutability | Impossible to tamper | Possible to tamper | Possible to tamper |
| Efficiency | Low | Medium | High |

blockchain is permissioned. As for the read permission, the stored information can be public or restricted depending on the determination of decision-makers. Besides, due to the reduction of the size of nodes participating in the consensus, it is easier to reach more than 50% of nodes that want to reverse or tamper with the data in consortium blockchain, which performs worse than public blockchain in immutability. Meanwhile, with fewer validators, transaction throughput and the latency in consortium blockchain could perform better.

### 1.1.2.3 Private blockchain

It refers to a blockchain whose permissions are controlled by one single organization and institution to build, maintain and manage. The qualifications of participating nodes are strictly restricted; thus, the private blockchain is also called a permissioned blockchain. However, not all nodes can participate in the consensus process. Same as the consortium blockchain, the stored information and transactions of it can be public or restricted to public. In addition, because it is entirely controlled by one organization, it is almost centralized and is the easiest one to be reversed or tampered, which performs worst of the three in decentralization and immutability. Meanwhile, with almost the fewest nodes, the validation of transaction and the synchronization of block can be fast.

The previous three blockchains can apply to different scenarios depending on their features. As the most decentralized and public blockchain, public blockchain attracts many users. It is mainly used in Bitcoin, Ethereum and Hyperledger Fabric, among which the ancestor of public blockchain is Bitcoin blockchain. As for the consortium blockchain, represented by R3, Hyperledger Sawtooth and FISCO, it emphasizes the strong correlation of values and synergies between institutions or organizations in the same industry or across industries, as well as the weak centralization within the alliance. In practice, the private blockchain is often used for internal auditing because it is faster, cheaper and respects a company's privacy.

## 1.2 Structure of block and chain

As initially described by Nakamoto [1], blockchain is a chain of blocks, each of which stores a complete list of transaction information. Figure 1.1 illustrates an example of a blockchain [6]. It is the hash value that implements the connection between blocks, which usually takes the form of a hash pointer to the previous block. Each block stores not only its own hash value in its block head but also the hash value of the previous block, so as to indicate the logical relationship to realize connection. It is a prominent characteristic of blockchain to connect all the blocks containing transactions in an orderly manner and keep the same current state of blockchain in all the nodes.

### 1.2.1 Block

Blockchain can be defined as a linked list, and the block is the data element of it. A block contains information about the transactions occurring over a period of time,

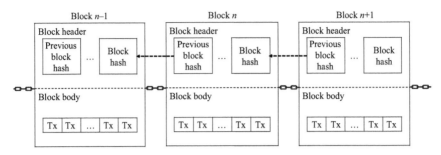

*Figure 1.1    The chain and connections between blocks*

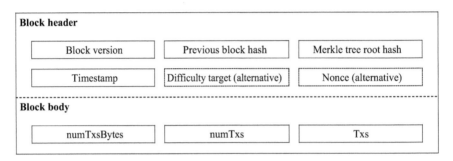

*Figure 1.2    An example of block structure under PoW mechanism. The difficulty target and nonce exist only when the consensus mechanism is PoW*

and it is usually generated by a node that eventually acquired the accounting rights in consensus process. In addition, those transactions stored in the block are generally encoded with hash values. Typically, a block is composed of a block header and block body. The details of the block structure can be different when different consensus mechanisms are chosen. In this section, we mainly take PoW as an example to introduce the block structure, as illustrated in Figure 1.2.

In the block header, there are block version, timestamp, previous block hash, Merkle tree root hash of that block and some alternative fields, which vary with the consensus mechanism [7]. PoW takes difficulty target and nonce as options. Detailed explanations are shown next and summarized in Table 1.2

- Block version. With the growing of blockchain, its protocols are also evolving, producing many versions. Therefore, the block version is used to indicate the version number of protocols for later verification. It is 4-byte long.
- Timestamp. It identifies the specific time when the block was generated by miners, ensuring that all blocks containing transactions are recorded in chronological order. To some extent, this helps one to ensure the transparency and auditability of blockchain. It is in the form of year, month, day, hour and second and is 4-byte long. It is the total number of seconds since 00:00 G.M.T. (Greenwich Mean Time) on January 1, 1970 and is 4-byte long.

Table 1.2   *Fields in the block header*

| Field | Size (bytes) | Description |
|---|---|---|
| Block version | 4 | The version number of the block |
| Timestamp | 4 | The time the block was generated in seconds |
| Merkle tree root hash | 32 | Hash value of the root of the Merkle tree |
| Previous block hash | 32 | Hash value of the previous block |
| Difficulty target (alternative) | 4 | The target value of PoW algorithm for the block |
| Nonce (alternative) | 4 | A counter for the PoW algorithm |

- Merkle tree root hash. All the transactions contained in the block form a Merkle tree in the block body and its root is stored in the block header in forms of hash value, which is what this section is recording. It can be used to verify the correctness of the transactions stored in this block and is 32-byte long. What is more, it is the block hash indicated in Figure 1.1. Details about Merkle tree will be described in a later section.
- Previous block hash. It represents the hash value of the previous block and also is 32-byte long. Considered to be a hash pointer stored in this block, it is what makes the connection between the two blocks. In addition to forming the chain, it also strongly guarantees the tamperability of blockchain. This is because when a new block is created, the hash value of the old block is quickly passed on and constantly indirectly cited, making it difficult to tamper with it.
- Difficulty target. It exists only if the consensus mechanism is PoW and is the target value of PoW. It controls the difficulty of mining by its value, which means the higher the value, the easier the calculation.
- Nonce. It is actually a 4-byte counter and also exists only in the consensus mechanism of PoW. In order to generate the hash less than the target, it starts with 0 and increases with each hash calculation until the most appropriate hash value is found.

On the other hand, the block body includes numTxs, numTxsBytes and Txs in the form of hash. Obviously, numTxs identifies the number of transactions that the block contains and is limited by the size of the block and each transaction, whose byte size can range from 0 to 8. In order to save storage space, it often adopts the compressed storage with the help of numTxsBytes. The numTxsBytes, 1-byte long, exists to indicate where numTxs exists in the block, in preparation for reading the number of transactions. Therefore, the numTxsBytes should be read first, and the position of the numTxs will be determined according to the value of this field as follows:

$$Position \ of \ numTxs = \begin{cases} where \ numTxsBytes \ is & numTxsBytes < 253 \\ 2 \ bytes \ after \ numTxsBytes & numTxsBytes = 253 \\ 4 \ bytes \ after \ numTxsBytes & numTxsBytes = 254 \\ 8 \ bytes \ after \ numTxsBytes & Otherwise. \end{cases}$$

What is more, transactions are stored as hash values and a Merkle tree in the block body and can be validated through asymmetric cryptography mechanism and digital signature. Designed for different applications, the block body could be changed as the application changes.

There are two special blocks, genesis block and uncle–nephew block, in the blockchain. As mentioned earlier, the genesis block is the first block created in a blockchain, which is the ancestor of all blocks and deservedly has no previous block. Therefore, the previous block hash does not actually exist and is usually set to some special value such as zero. As for the uncle–nephew block, it is actually a name for a particular set of blocks, which includes an uncle block and nephew blocks. Usually, there is only one parent block and one child block, which means that each block usually has only one previous block and one successor block. However, in some blockchain systems, a block may create multiple successor blocks. In such a scenario, the preceding block is called uncle block and its successor blocks are called nephew blocks, both of which can continue to create new blocks.

### 1.2.2  Fork

After the block described earlier is packaged and generated in a node, it will be verified by some other nodes and reach a consensus according to the consensus mechanism [8]. The verified block will be broadcasted to each node in the entire P2P network, thus synchronizing the same blockchain across each node. However, in the process of negotiation of such distributed nodes, it may occur that not all nodes are consistent due to time difference or other reasons, that is, different nodes support different new blocks that should be linked to the chain. Thus, there will be a fork occurred, which means that a blockchain is potentially diverged into two different paths forward. According to different reasons, the fork can be divided into two categories: temporary and persistent; and the latter can be divided into hard and soft forks as shown in Table 1.3.

Among them, temporary fork is generated when the latest block is different on different nodes. It may be that two independent blocks are generated and broadcasted at about the same time, or that verified blocks are limited by network latency during the broadcast process, resulting in that new blocks have been generated when that block propagated to some nodes. Thus, two (or more) different versions of the blockchain can appear in different nodes. From the perspective of the overall blockchain, the temporary fork shown in Figure 1.3 will appear, which potentially include different sets of transactions.

*Table 1.3  Categories and cause of fork in blockchain*

| Categories | | Cause |
|---|---|---|
| Temporary fork | | The difference in latest accepted block on different nodes |
| Persistent fork | Hard fork | Blockchain software upgrade not compatible with the older |
| | Soft fork | Blockchain software upgrade compatible with the older |

As a result, nodes will support one choice over the other and miners will continue to work on the branch they believe in. In general, it is very unlikely that two chains will produce a new block at the same time. Therefore, the first branch to be extended will become the longer branch and is considered to be the main chain by PoW protocol. The other branch will be no longer increased and the block of it will become an orphan block. Miners on the abandoned chain will switch to the main chain and the nodes of entire network continue to agree on the main chain.

Taking the temporary fork shown in Figure 1.3 as an example, as block $B_{I4}$ and block $B_{II4}$ are created and validated simultaneously, the blockchain forks to chains 1 and 2. Then with the production of block $B_{II5}$ that is added to block $B_{II4}$, the chain 2 becomes the longer one and will be considered to be the correct chain with all miners going back to work on it.

The persistent fork results from an update to the blockchain software that updates the block version to optimize the block structure. However, for the distributed P2P network of blockchain which contains many distributed users around the world, synchronous updates of all nodes are extremely difficult. Therefore, the difference in block verification between updated and non-updated nodes will be resulted in, which can lead to forking. For the soft fork, the update is backward compatible with those non-updated nodes, that is, the changed rules still apply to them. On the contrary, those non-updated nodes will reject the changed rules and flowing blocks for the hard fork.

A soft fork, illustrated in Figure 1.4, is a software upgrade that is backward compatible. We call the blocks generated by the new rule as updated blocks, and those that do not follow the new rules as non-updated blocks. Furthermore, we assume that the new rule is to reduce the maximum size of the block from

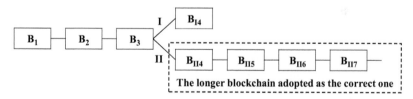

*Figure 1.3   An example of temporary fork*

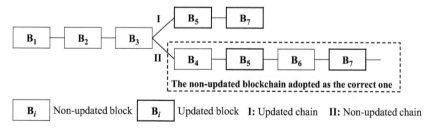

*Figure 1.4   An example of soft fork*

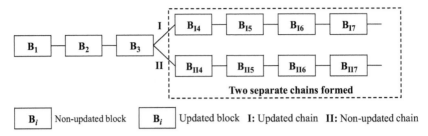

*Figure 1.5    An example of hard fork*

1.0 to 0.5 MB. For the soft fork, the updated blocks whose size is less than 0.5 MB can be accepted by those non-updated nodes on non-updated chain 2, because the update made does not break their old rules of 1.0 MB. Of course, those non-updated blocks can also be accepted. Therefore, the chain 2 contains almost every block. On the contrary, the non-updated blocks cannot be accepted by updated nodes on the updated chain 1, thus there will not be non-updated blocks on chain 1. As a result, when an update is followed by only a minority of nodes in the network, the soft fork could make the updated chain to be the shortest one and get orphaned.

A hard fork, illustrated in Figure 1.5, is a software upgrade that is not backward compatible. Usually, all involved nodes will need to update to the updated protocol and switch to use it. However, if there are some nodes reject to the update, all of them will be divided into updated and non-updated nodes, and updated and non-updated blocks will be generated as defined in the soft fork. Because the updated and the non-updated versions are incompatible, the non-updated nodes cannot accept the updated ones and transact on the updated chain such as chain 1. The updated nodes face the same situation and cannot transact on the non-updated chain such as chain 2. As a result, the updated and non-updated blocks will parallelly develop, and two versions of the blockchain will exist simultaneously as shown in Figure 1.5. Therefore, hard fork is often considered to be one of the causes of blockchain splitting. The hard fork of Ethereum DAO is a case of how a blockchain can split over rules where the majority of nodes moved to the new fork while the old fork, Ethereum Classic, continued operating.

## 1.3    Key technologies involved in blockchain

The seemingly complex blockchain technology is actually composed of several technical components [9]. This section introduces several key technologies, including hash algorithm, Merkle tree, asymmetric cryptography and digital signature, and some consensus mechanisms.

### 1.3.1    Hash algorithm and Merkle tree

Hash algorithm is a typical encryption algorithm applying cryptographic hash function, which plays an important role in modern cryptography and is a significant component of blockchain technology. It is often used to achieve data integrity and entity authentication, constituting the security guarantee of various cryptography systems and protocols. The function of the cryptographic hash function is to compress messages of arbitrary length into binary strings of fixed length in a limited reasonable time, and its output is called a hash value [9]. It is worth noting that the mapping from the input value to the output value in the hash computation is unique. It allows users to prove whether the original data has been changed by verifying the hash value. To support it, cryptographic hash functions have some security properties as follows.

- Fast forward mapping. Given the plaintext (e.g., $x$) and hash algorithms, hash values (e.g., $hash(x)$) can be calculated quickly in limited time and resources.
- Hard reverse mapping. The calculations of hash functions are preimage resistant and one-way, which means that they can only map from $x$ to $hash(x)$. Given a hash value (e.g., $hash(x)$), it is almost impossible to reversely derive plaintext (e.g., $x$) in a finite amount of time.
- Sensitive input. The hash function is sensitive to changes in the input. Even if the original input changes a little bit or even just a single bit, the resulting hash value can be quite different.
- Strong collision resistance. Collision is an important concept related to hash function, which reflects the security of hash function. It means that two different messages have the same hash value under the action of the same hash function. The collision resistance of hash function is so strong that no one can find any two different inputs (e.g., $x$, $y$ and $x \neq y$) that have the same hash value output (e.g., $hash(x) = hash(y)$).

Two cryptographic hash functions are used in the Bitcoin blockchain system, one is SHA256 and the other is RIPEMD160. The former is used in many blockchain systems and is the main cryptographic hash function used to construct blockchain. SHA256 is one of the Secure Hash Algorithm (SHA) [10] and its output size is 256 bits which is equivalent to an array of 32 bytes in length and displayed as a hexadecimal string of 64 characters. In the blockchain, the SHA256 is used for many tasks as following [7]:

- Generating the address. Some blockchain systems use addresses to identify nodes in transactions as the from and to endpoints. An address is a short alphanumeric string generated by a public key and cryptographic hash function. Specifically, a user creates a public key then applies a hash function to it and converts the resulting hash value to text to get the address. It is not secret and is shorter than the corresponding public key.
- Simplifying unique identifiers. The hash value of blockchain can uniquely and accurately identify a block and any transaction. In addition, it will save storage space for the entire network and improve block efficiency. Any node in the blockchain can obtain the hash value of this block through simple hash calculation.
- Securing the block data. The transactions in each block are stored as hash values calculated by cryptographic hash function. The hash values of

transactions are added to a Merkle tree as leaves, whose root is stored in the block header also in the form of a hash value. In this way, instead of saving all the transaction information, nodes can know whether the transaction has been tampered by verifying the hash value of the root in the block header, effectively protecting the transaction data. What is more, the hash value of one block header is also stored in its subsequent blocks header by a hash pointer, which will secure block data very well.

- Used for PoW consensus algorithm. If the consensus mechanism utilized in the blockchain is PoW, the hash algorithm is used to dig the block. After the hash value of the Merkle tree root has been worked out, the block header needs to be continually hashed as nonce changes until the hash value of block header is less than the target hash, which marks the generation of a block.

Merkle tree is a typical application of the previous hash algorithm in the block-chain. It is used to store the hash value of the transaction in the block body and store the root of the tree in the block header for easy transaction validation. In essence, a Merkle tree is a binary or multi-fork tree with multiple nodes, where the value of a leaf node is usually data's hash value, while that of other nodes is the hash value of the combination of its child nodes. The combination and calculation of the hash value keep going on until the root hash is generated which can represent the entire tree structure and information contained [11]. Suppose a block contains eight transactions, as shown in Figure 1.6, whose hash values are stored as leaf nodes in the Merkle tree. Taking Hash1 and Hash2 as example, their hash values are combined and sent up and then hashed and stored in the node Hash (1&2). Such a combination and hash operation occurs on two adjacent nodes at each level, resulting in a Hash (1&2&3&4&5&6&7&8), which is the root of the tree and contains all information. In the blockchain, the root node is stored in the block header to save space and help to validate transactions.

Since the input to the hash algorithm is sensitive, any tampering with the transaction will cause the leaf node to change, which will be reflected in the tree. When data is transferred from A to B, in order to verify the integrity of data, it is

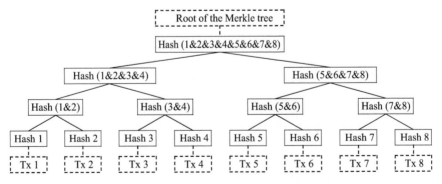

*Figure 1.6   An example of Merkle tree that contains eight transactions*

only necessary to verify whether the root of Merkle tree contained in the block of A and B is consistent. If so, the data has not changed during transmission, or else the data has been modified during transmission. Furthermore, the user can verify whether a transaction is included in the block by checking the Merkle tree root in the block header [12] and the list of intermediate hash values provided by other users.

In Bitcoin blockchain, there is a Simplified Payment Verification that takes advantage of Merkle trees [13] for its lightweight nodes. After merging the transaction into a block and validating the block, the network will discard all hash values in the tree except the root hash contained in the block header. Instead of keeping the entire transaction record, nodes keep only the block headers in the longest chain.

## 1.3.2 Asymmetric cryptography and digital signature

Asymmetric cryptographic algorithm is a key part of the cryptographic primitives used to protect the security of data and process in such a publicly distributed blockchain [9]. As one of the modern cryptographic algorithms, its typical components include encryption and decryption algorithm, public key and private key. In the process of encryption, the plaintext is encrypted by encryption algorithm and public key to obtain the ciphertext. In contrast, the decryption process applies decryption algorithm and private key to convert ciphertext into plaintext. In asymmetric cryptographic algorithm, the public key and keys are different, and each user has both of them [14]. In general, the public key is public without reducing the security, while the private key is kept secret for data security. Even if they are mathematically related, the private key cannot be deduced from public key.

This contrasts with symmetric cryptographic algorithm in which the public key is the same as the private key. With symmetric cryptographic algorithm, the communicating parties must establish a trust relationship and exchange the pre-shared key before formally transmitting data. If one party's private key is compromised, the whole communication will be cracked. Therefore, it is obvious that asymmetric cryptographic algorithm has better security than symmetric one. The separation of public and private keys makes it easy to manage and distribute the two keys. Besides, asymmetric cryptographic algorithm works better on distributed networks, such as blockchain, where trust is not required.

In blockchain, the asymmetric cryptographic algorithm can be used for digital signatures in transactions [9], generation of the address mentioned earlier and the ability to verify that one user who transfers value to others is able to sign transactions. Among them, digital signature is an extremely important application for so many transactions in the blockchain, whose typical process is shown as Figure 1.7.

Digital signatures are used to verify the integrity and source of data, which are used as authentication mechanism in the transaction process of blockchain [4]. It is usually carried out in two processes, as shown in Figure 1.7, the signature process and the verification process. In the signature process, the sender hashes the data to get the information summary and encrypts it with its private key to get the

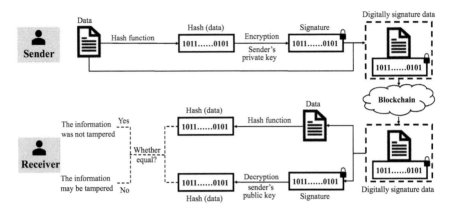

*Figure 1.7    The process of digital signature*

signature. The signature combined with the data is the digital signature, which is sent to the blockchain network. However, the verification process is that the receiver uses the sender's public key to verify the authenticity of the signature [15]. The receiver divides the information received from blockchain into the data file and the encrypted digital signature and then hashes the data file to get the hash value and decrypts the digital signature with the sender's public key to get the hash value. The two hash values are then verified, and if they are identical, the data is complete and the signature is valid.

## 1.3.3    Consensus mechanism

Blockchain is an asynchronous system based on distributed P2P network where nodes do not trust each other. Without the help of a trusted third party, updating and keeping these untrusted nodes in the same state is a big issue. To solve it, they work together relying on overall agreements among most of them, that is, a mechanism is adopted so that the state of each node finally reaches an agreement. This is what we called consensus [8]. In addition, how to ensure that only one node is allowed to generate a legitimate block over a period of time, how nodes agree with the validity of transactions and maintain consistent records is called "reaching consensus." There are several common approaches for reaching consensus in the blockchain and we will outline some of the typical one, shown in Table 1.4, as follows.

### 1.3.3.1    Proof-of-work

PoW is the earliest consensus mechanism and used in Bitcoin network [16]. Its certification is based on workload, which means that nodes with more work and higher hash rate are more likely to add new blocks to the chain and earn the PoW reward. Its most significant feature is that complex calculations are required on a work node to get a result, while the validation process is easy. In Bitcoin blockchain, PoW algorithm is implemented on the basis of nonce and difficulty target mentioned earlier.

Table 1.4 *Comparisons among typical consensus algorithms*

| Property | Node permission | Certification object | Error-tolerant (%) | Example |
|---|---|---|---|---|
| PoW | Permissionless | Computing power | 25 | Bitcoin |
| PoS | Permissionless | Stake | 51 | Peercoin |
| DPoS | Permissionless | Stake of validators | 51 | BitShares |
| PBFT | Permissioned | Replicas of state machines | 33.3 | Fabric |

When a miner packages a number of transactions into a block, the packaged result is connected with a randomly generated integer value string, nonce, and SHA256 hash operation is performed on them. If the hash result obtained (expressed in hexadecimal form) starts with $n$ zeros, the verification is passed, where $n$ represents the difficulty of the calculation, which is controlled by difficulty target in the block header. In order to achieve this goal of PoW, the nonce value needs to be continuously increased, and the corresponding hash value is calculated until the verification is passed. According to this rule, if $n = 3$, it takes 2,688 computations to find the hash value in which the first three digits are 0. Obviously, this is a huge amount of work. The first miner to complete such work has the right to produce a new block and broadcast it to other nodes for verification.

### 1.3.3.2 Proof-of-stake

Proof-of-stake (PoS) is an energy-efficient alternative to PoW. Different form the workload in PoW, the certification in PoS is based on the priority in hash calculations, which is determined by the ratio of virtual currency held by nodes. Instead of finding the right nonce, nodes need to prove the ownership of their virtual currencies quantity [17]. It is based on the thought that the more currencies a node has, the less likely it is to attack the network, which is because its dishonest act reduces the value of its currency. To some extent, this can also motivate any node to avoid dishonest act.

There is a special measure in PoS: coin age, which is defined as the product of tokens held by nodes and the holding time. According to the coin age of nodes, the corresponding interest will be allocated to them. Suppose a node holds 100 coins for a total of 30 days, then its currency age is 3,000. The node with the largest coin age can be a candidate for generating the next new block. Once it has successfully created a new block, its coin age will be reset to zero and cannot generate any new block for some time. What is more, each time a certain amount of coin ages (e.g., 365 coin ages) of the node is cleared, it will receive a certain amount of interest in the form of coins (e.g., 0.05 coins). Obviously, rich nodes in PoS have great advantages. Compared with the PoW, PoS relies not only on computing power, but also on cumulative qualifications for the ability to generate new blocks on the blockchain. It is currently applied in virtual currencies such as Peercoin, Blackcoin and ShadowCoin.

### 1.3.3.3 Delegated proof-of-stake

Delegated PoS (DPoS) is an improvement on PoS. Similarly, miners get their priority in the hash calculation based on their stake and then generate new blocks.

Unlike PoS, nodes with stake in DPoS will vote for some representatives to create and validate new blocks. Besides, if there are representatives becoming dishonest or failing to perform their duties, such as generating a block, when it is their turn, they will be removed and new representatives will be chosen. With fewer nodes participating in validation, the generation of new blocks and the verification of transactions will be faster. Currently, DPoS has been implemented in BitShares.

### 1.3.3.4    Practical Byzantine fault tolerance

Practical Byzantine fault tolerance (PBFT) [18] is an algorithm to solve a Byzantine fault, which comes from the Byzantine Generals Problem (BGP) [19]. A group of troops from the Byzantine Empire wanted to attack a powerful enemy, and they divided into several groups. However, these troops that are in separate encirclement situations need to attack at the same time, and any army alone has no chance of winning. Therefore, the generals need to communicate in order to reach an agreement on whether to launch an attack. Meanwhile, there may be traitor generals attempting to disrupt the agreement. Such the decentralized distributed environment is much like blockchain, and PBFT is the first solution to BGP for blockchain.

It works with a three-phase protocol based on the Byzantine fault-tolerant method, where consensus is reached through the pre-prepare phase, prepare phase and commit phase. When there are $f$ fault nodes, it can guarantee the reliability of network which contains at least $3f + 1$ nodes in which there are $2f + 1$ reliable nodes. Unlike previous consensus agreements, PBFT relies on an important leader. Each incoming block is proposed by the leader and broadcast to other nodes in the network. After receiving the broadcast, the other nodes perform the three-phase consensus process to verify and return the message to the leader. Once $2f + 1$ confirmation messages are received, the leader will announce the result to all participating nodes and they will record it in their ledgers, which marks the creation of a new block. Based on the previous characteristics, PBFT is more suitable to use in permissioned blockchain such as the consortium blockchain. It has been adopted in Ripple and Stellar.

## 1.4    Evolution

Originating from Bitcoin, blockchain technology has developed well in both academia and industry. With the technological development of digital economy, communication interconnection and public service, blockchain has become a promising technology far beyond currency. It is considered to be the fifth disruptive computing paradigm after mainframes of the 1970s, personal computers of the 1980s, the Internet and mobile networks, reconfiguring almost every aspect of society and its functioning. In this process, the evolution of blockchain has gone through three processes: blockchain 1.0, 2.0 and 3.0 [20,21]. It is worth noting that they are not carried out in chronological succession but exist in cross parallel and have different representative characteristics in different stages as shown in Figure 1.8.

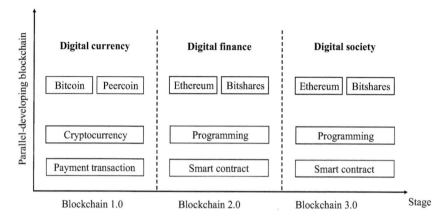

*Figure 1.8 Evolution of blockchain*

## 1.4.1 Blockchain 1.0—digital currency

Blockchain 1.0, known as digital currency stage, is strongly related with the decentralization and payment of cryptocurrencies. It represents a store and exchange of value, whose core functionality is to support any transaction sourced and completed directly between two participants over P2P networks. There are mining, hashing and public ledger as underlying technology platforms, overlying protocols to support transactions and digital currencies to complete payments. In blockchain 1.0, its main goal is to apply cryptocurrencies to cash transactions such as currency transfers, remittances and digital payment systems.

Taking the Bitcoin [1] blockchain as a typical example, it has become the most effective decentralized transnational circulation system in many countries in the world. In addition to Bitcoin, more than 600 virtual currencies have been produced, such as Litecoin which is similar to Bitcoin, Peercoin which is mixed with PoW and PoS [22] and so on.

## 1.4.2 Blockchain 2.0—digital finance

Blockchain 2.0, known as digital finance stage, introduces economic, financial and market applications by programming far from simple currency transactions. To be specific, the applications can include traditional banking operations such as ordinary loans, mortgages and trade financing, complex financial operations such as stocks, futures and bonds, as well as market operations such as property rights, contracts and smart property. These characteristics make this era considered as the second layer of blockchain application in industry and market from 2014. There are many classifications and definitions of blockchain 2.0 still in their formative stages, with some representative terms such as smart property, smart contracts, decentralized applications and decentralized autonomous organizations. Among them, the most significant features of blockchain 2.0 are the introduction and application of smart contracts.

Smart contract [23] is a computer protocol designed to disseminate, verify or execute contracts in an informational manner, which will behave in a transparent way when certain preconditions are met. Besides, they allow for trusted transactions that are traceable and irreversible without a third party. They can apply to a variety of situations, which could be financial services, crowdfunding agreements, insurance premiums, default contracts, credit enforcement, etc. It is worth noting that smart contracts are not necessarily realized relying on blockchain, but the decentralization and data's tamper-proof of blockchain provide a more appropriate environment for smart contracts, which solve the trust problem of them. In blockchain 2.0, smart contracts are usually expressed as a piece of code and implemented programmatically [24]. In this way, several transparent and trusted financial applications can be deployed in the form of smart contracts on the blockchain. What is more, new organizational types such as decentralized autonomous organizations can also be created.

The representative of smart contracts is Ethereum [25], which is a platform that provides various modules for users to build types of decentralized blockchain applications. It provides a powerful Turing-complete virtual machine that can perform coding of any algorithmic complexity. Platform applications implemented programmatically, smart contracts, are the core of Ethereum technology. Through the development of smart contracts, Ethereum can implement complex logic in a variety of commercial and noncommercial environments, so that blockchain technology can provide more application scenarios far than just issue tokens.

## 1.4.3    Blockchain 3.0—digital society

Blockchain 3.0, known as digital society stage, provides decentralized solutions for a variety of industries beyond just financial scene. There are some possible applications over networks, including but not limited to government, health, science, education, culture, public goods, social networks, communication and various aspects of our lives [26]. Its most obvious feature is that it no longer relies on a third party or organization to gain trust or establish credit. Meanwhile it not only greatly saves labor and time cost but also improves efficiency. This is exactly how blockchain changes the production relations. Blockchain 3.0 makes blockchain's high scalability, adaptability, sustainability, interoperability into a reality. There are many application scenarios as following:

- Machine-to-machine (M2M). It is possible to successfully employ the blockchain technology to facilitate M2M interactions [27–30] and establish an M2M electricity market in the context of the chemical industry via the IoT, where electricity producers and electricity consumers trading with each other over a blockchain.
- Electronic medical records (EMRs). Leveraging the blockchain technology, the concept of decentralization might be applied to large-scale data management in an EMR system [31], providing auditability, interoperability and accessibility via a comprehensive log.

- Digital identity. Digital identity enabled by the blockchain technology has the potential to change lives [32]. With the benefit of digital identity, many of the world's 2 billion unbanked individuals could store their identities on a blockchain, permission banks to fulfill regulatory requirements such as know your customer, and gain access to bank accounts, loans and other financial services previously inaccessible to them.
- Reputation systems. In the cyberworld, people often make transactions with others that they have not met with. Reputation systems have been widely used in the cyberspace as an effective way to allow people to evaluate the trustworthiness of a potential seller. However, current reputation systems are vulnerable to fraud rating and the detection of fraudulent raters is difficult, since they can behave strategically to camouflage themselves. The blockchain technology provides new opportunities for redesigning the reputation system [33].
- Improve transparency and regulatory efficiency to avoid fraud. Because blockchain technology can better monitor all transactions and smart contracts in real time and can retain all transactions in an irrevocable, non-repudiation and non-tampering manner, it is greatly convenient for regulators to realize real-time monitoring and supervision [34]. As a result, transparency is greatly improved, fraud is avoided and regulation is implemented more efficiently.

The most innovative feature of blockchain lies not in the single point technology, but in the combination of a package of technologies, in the systematic innovation, in the innovation of thinking. Because blockchain is a rock-bottom and systematic innovation, blockchain technology, together with emerging technologies such as cloud computing, big data, artificial intelligence and quantum computing, is regarded as one of the most transformative emerging technologies.

# References

[1] Nakamoto S. Bitcoin: A peer-to-peer electronic cash system; 2008.
[2] Zheng Z, Xie S, Dai HN, *et al.* Blockchain challenges and opportunities: A survey. International Journal of Web and Grid Services. 2018;14(4):352–375.
[3] Viriyasitavat W and Hoonsopon D. Blockchain characteristics and consensus in modern business processes. Journal of Industrial Information Integration. 2019;13:32–39.
[4] Zheng Z, Xie S, Dai H, *et al.* An overview of blockchain technology: Architecture, consensus, and future trends. In: 2017 IEEE International Congress on Big Data (BigData Congress). IEEE; 2017. p. 557–564.
[5] Xu X, Pautasso C, Zhu L, *et al.* The blockchain as a software connector. In: 2016 13th Working IEEE/IFIP Conference on Software Architecture (WICSA). IEEE; 2016. p. 182–191.
[6] Bahga A and Madisetti VK. Blockchain platform for industrial internet of things. Journal of Software Engineering and Applications. 2016;9(10):533.
[7] Gupta SS. Blockchain. John Wiley & Sons, Inc; 2017.

[8]     Baliga A. Understanding blockchain consensus models. In: Persistent; 2017.

[9]     Yaga D, Mell P, Roby N, *et al.* Blockchain technology overview. arXiv preprint arXiv:190611078. 2019.

[10]    Crosby M, Pattanayak P, Verma S, *et al.* Blockchain technology: Beyond bitcoin. Applied Innovation. 2016;2(6–10):71.

[11]    Tschorsch F and Scheuermann B. Bitcoin and beyond: A technical survey on decentralized digital currencies. IEEE Communications Surveys & Tutorials. 2016;18(3):2084–2123.

[12]    Lin IC and Liao TC. A survey of blockchain security issues and challenges. International Journal of Network Security. 2017;19(5):653–659.

[13]    Vujicic D, Jagodic D, and Rani S. Blockchain technology, bitcoin, and Ethereum: A brief overview. In: 2018 17th International Symposium INFOTEH-JAHORINA (INFOTEH). IEEE; 2018. p. 1–6.

[14]    Lee B and Lee JH. Blockchain-based secure firmware update for embedded devices in an Internet of Things environment. The Journal of Supercomputing. 2017;73(3):1152–1167.

[15]    Zyskind G, Nathan O, and Pentland A. Decentralizing privacy: Using blockchain to protect personal data. In: 2015 IEEE Security and Privacy Workshops. IEEE; 2015. p. 180–184.

[16]    Vukolić M. The quest for scalable blockchain fabric: Proof-of-work vs. BFT replication. In: International Workshop on Open Problems in Network Security. Springer; 2015. p. 112–125.

[17]    Saleh F. Blockchain without waste: Proof-of-stake; 2020. Available at SSRN: http://dx.doi.org/10.2139/ssrn.3183935.

[18]    Castro M and Liskov B. Practical Byzantine fault tolerance and proactive recovery. ACM Transactions on Computer Systems (TOCS). 2002;20 (4):398–461.

[19]    Rabin MO. Randomized byzantine generals. In: 24th Annual Symposium on Foundations of Computer Science (SFCS 1983). IEEE; 1983. p. 403–409.

[20]    Zhao JL, Fan S, and Yan J. Overview of business innovations and research opportunities in blockchain and introduction to the special issue. SpringerOpen; 2016.

[21]    Efanov D and Roschin P. The all-pervasiveness of the blockchain technology. Procedia Computer Science. 2018;123:116–121.

[22]    Vasin P. Blackcoin's proof-of-stake protocol v2. URL: https://blackcoin co/ blackcoin-pos-protocol-v2-whitepaper pdf. 2014;71.

[23]    Luu L, Chu DH, Olickel H, *et al.* Making smart contracts smarter. In: Proceedings of the 2016 ACM SIGSAC Conference on Computer and Communications Security. ACM; 2016. p. 254–269.

[24]    Atzei N, Bartoletti M, and Cimoli T. A survey of attacks on Ethereum smart contracts (SoK). In: International Conference on Principles of Security and Trust. Springer; 2017. p. 164–186.

[25]    Wood G. Ethereum: A secure decentralised generalised transaction ledger. In: Ethereum project yellow paper. vol. 151(2014); 2014. p. 1–32.

[26]  Aste T, Tasca P, and Di Matteo T. Blockchain technologies: The foreseeable impact on society and industry. Computer. 2017;50(9):18–28.

[27]  Sikorski JJ, Haughton J, and Kraft M. Blockchain technology in the chemical industry: Machine-to-machine electricity market. Applied Energy. 2017;195:234–246.

[28]  Li R, Song T, Mei B, *et al.* Blockchain for large-scale Internet of Things data storage and protection. IEEE Transactions on Services Computing. 2019;12 (5):762–771.

[29]  Coutinho RW and Boukerche A. Modeling and analysis of a shared edge caching system for connected cars and industrial IoT-based applications. IEEE Transactions on Industrial Informatics. 2019.

[30]  Yao H, Mai T, Wang J, *et al.* Resource trading in blockchain-based industrial Internet of Things. IEEE Transactions on Industrial Informatics. 2019.

[31]  Dubovitskaya A, Xu Z, Ryu S, *et al.* Secure and trustable electronic medical records sharing using blockchain. In: AMIA Annual Symposium Proceedings. vol. 2017. American Medical Informatics Association; 2017. p. 650.

[32]  Jacobovitz O. Blockchain for identity management. The Lynne and William Frankel Center for Computer Science Department of Computer Science Ben-Gurion University, Beer Sheva Google Scholar. 2016;1:9.

[33]  Dennis R and Owen G. Rep on the block: A next generation reputation system based on the blockchain. In: 2015 10th International Conference for Internet Technology and Secured Transactions (ICITST). IEEE; 2015. p. 131–138.

[34]  Hyvärinen H, Risius M, and Friis G. A blockchain-based approach towards overcoming financial fraud in public sector services. Business & Information Systems Engineering. 2017;59(6):441–456.

*Chapter 2*

# Blockchain system architecture, applications and research issues

*Wang Miao[1], Geyong Min[1], Haojun Huang[2] and Haozhe Wang[1]*

Blockchain technology is a new distributed computing paradigm, which is characterized by the structure of blockchain for storing data, the distributed node consensus algorithms for generating and updating data, advanced cryptography algorithms for securing and validate data and smart contracts for programming and manipulating the data. In each time slot, all transactions generated by the blockchain participants are packaged into a single data block. A point is created in each block to record the address of the block generated in the previous time slot. All blocks are connected in the sequential order, therefore, forming the data structure of blockchain. Within the blockchain network, each participant maintains the same blockchain. In each time slot, the new transactions or data can be added in blockchain, the previous blocks cannot be changed unless the consent of the majority of the participants is achieved. Due to the non-temperable and transparent features, blockchain has been widely used for the scenarios of information sharing or decision-making among multiple parties. Built on the technologies of consensus algorithms, peer-to-peer (P2P) communication, cryptography, database technology and virtual machines, compared with the traditional centralized computing paradigm, blockchain has the following key features:

- Shoring data: driven by the development of database technology and hardware storage computing power, blockchain makes it possible for multiple entities to store the same data at the same time. In addition, with the accumulation of time, the size of blockchain is also rising, more and more blocks are linked into the blockchain accessed by multiple entities.
- Sharing data: various consensus algorithms are used in blockchain to enable multiple entities to reach consensus, making it possible for multiple entities to share the same trusted data ledger.

[1]Department of Computer Science, University of Exeter, Exeter, UK
[2]Department of Information Engineering, Huazhong University of Science and Technology, Wuhan, China

- Distributed architecture: instead of using centralized network architecture, blockchain is built on P2P communication technology, which provides a point-to-point information transmission for multiple entities in blockchain.
- Anti-tampering and protection of privacy: exploring the cryptography technologies, such as public and private keys, hash algorithm and other cryptography tools, the identity of each subject and the security of common information are well protected in blockchain system.
- Digital contracts: enabled by virtual machine technology, the cross-entity digital smart contract is created in the evolved version of the blockchain system. In digital contact, the execution of digital contracts will be triggered once the preset conditions are satisfied.

In this chapter, we will first introduce the system architecture of blockchain system, followed by the detailed explanation of the basic components in the architecture. In order to demonstrate the usage of blockchain system, we also give the practical implementation of blockchain system. We will also discuss the potential challenges that blockchain system meets in the large scale of practical deployment. This chapter will serve as the foundation for the remaining chapters.

## 2.1    System architecture

Although various blockchain applications appeared and have different implementations, for instance, from the earliest blockchain application called the Ethereum, which is the first to introduce smart contracts in the blockchain, to the most widely used alliance chain, Hyperledger Fabric, they share the similar system architecture, as shown in Figure 2.1. The blockchain platform consists of five layers: physical infrastructure layer, data layer, consensus layer, smart contract layer and application layer. Physical infrastructure layer is responsible for providing the communication, computing and storage materials and related software systems for the overall blockchain platform. Data layer is responsible for managing the data related work, e.g., user account mode, data search structure and data storage. Consensus layer provides various consensus algorithms, such as proof-of-stake (PoS) or proof-of-work (PoW), to make multiple entities to reach the consensus for decision-making. Smart contract layer is created to embed the smart contract feature in the blockchain system, which includes smart contracts, program language and virtual machine. Finally, the application layers include various implementations and services driven by blockchain technology, such as electric invoice, financial service, energy transaction, credit check and copyright protect. Before giving the detailed explanation of each layer, we provide a classification of blockchain system.

### 2.1.1    Classifications of blockchain system

Blockchain can be divided into three categories according to degree of the decentralization, including public chain, alliance chain and private chain:

- Public chain: there is no official organization and management agency in the public chain. The nodes participating in the public chain can freely access the

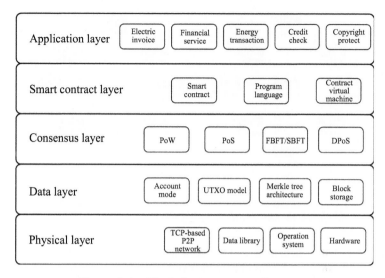

*Figure 2.1 Blockchain system architecture*

network according to the rules of the system. Bitcoin is a typical example of public chain. The public chain applies to scenarios where trust is difficult to build among multiple entities, and all users can enter the public chain to become one of the nodes.

- Alliance chain: the alliance chain is jointly initiated by several institutions. It is a mix of the public chain and the private chain, with the characteristics of partial decentralization. The participating members of the alliance chain are predefined. It is suitable for the scenario of connecting multiple companies or centralized organizations, such as interbank clearing.
- Private chain: the private chain is generally established in an enterprise. The management and operation of the system (modification and read permissions) are owned by few entities. Private chain still retains the authenticity of the blockchain and partially decentralized features.

For the previous three types of blockchains, only the public chain fundamentally solves the issue of the trust problem. As the alliance chain and the private chain are still using certain features of centralized system to realize the system management, through exploring the incentive or proof mechanism, such as the mining, public chain remove the trust mechanism of the centralized system and could reach the trust among different entities. However, the additional proof mechanism causes some practical issue, such as huge amount of power consumption in Bitcoin mining. The performance of the public chain is the lowest in these three types of blockchain, especially, for the process of reaching consensus among multiple entities.

## 2.1.2 Physical layer

Physical infrastructure layer includes the various computation, communication and storage hardware devices and the related software. In comparison with the

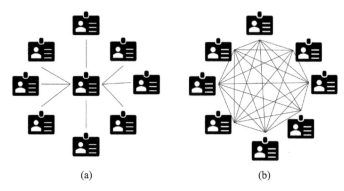

(a)                              (b)

*Figure 2.2    Network architecture of blockchain system: (a) centralized network
architecture and (b) distributed network architecture*

centralized system, blockchain uses the same hardware devices for the computation
and storage, however, utilizing a different network strategy. As shown in Figure 2.2,
we demonstrate both the centralized network architecture and distributed network
architecture. In order to eliminate the centralized control, blockchain utilizes the P2P
network architecture in Figure 2.2(b). In 2001, Gribble *et al.* [1] proposed P2P technology and conducted a measurement study to investigate the performance of P2P
architecture. This joint research was conducted according to the file sharing system.
The P2P-based blockchain could support the financial application of digital asset
transaction. There is no central node in the blockchain network, and any nodes can
directly trade with each other. At any time, each node can join or exit the network
freely. The blockchain platform usually selects a P2P protocol that is completely distributed and can tolerate single point of failure. Blockchain network nodes have the
characteristics of equality, autonomy, distribution, etc. All nodes are connected in a flat
topological structure as shown in Figure 2.2(b). There are no centralized authority
nodes and hierarchical structures. Each node has route discovery, transactions broadcast, blocks broadcast, new nodes discovery and other functions.

The P2P protocol of the blockchain network is mainly used to transmit transaction data among different nodes. The P2P protocol of Bitcoin and Ethereum is
based on the Transmission Control Protocol (TCP) protocol. The P2P protocol of
Hyperledger Fabric is implemented based on the HTTP/2 protocol. In a blockchain
network, a node listens to data broadcast. When receiving new transactions, it first
verifies whether the transactions and blocks are valid, including the digital signature in the transaction, the proof of the workload in the block. Only the transactions and blocks passed by the verification will be processed (new transactions
are added to the block being built, the new block is linked to the blockchain). The
invalid data will not be forwarded to prevent the propagation of invalid data.

Ripple is an Internet protocol that supports P2P financial transactions. Internet
protocols consist of a set of rules that P2P network node should obey in order to
facilitate communication with each other. The Ripple protocol supports the following operations for financial system, the communications among different

payment systems, standardization of data transmission and the verification for the block generated. Ripple brings quick and immediate transactions, and the reduction of transmission costs. Ripple creates a shared standard environment for financial payment. Ripple is not managed by any centralized department or institute, making it less risky for attacks. With a standard protocol for financial transactions, payments become as fast, cheap and instant. Ripple has been regarded as a practical network protocol in blockchain system.

### 2.1.3   Data layer

In the design of the data layer, the most of the existing blockchain platforms mainly refer to the research work conducted by Haber and Stornetta [2]. They designed a digital notarization service by leveraging the document time stamp to prove the creation time of various electronic documents. The time stamp server signs the newly created document, the current time, the hash pointer that points to the previous document signature and the subsequent document that signs the current document signature, thus forming a time-stamp-based certificate chain. This reflects the file creation sequence. Because of the feature of hash function, the time stamp in the chain cannot be tampered with. In addition, Haber and Stornetta also proposed the solution of how to group multiple documents into a block and how to sign this block. The method to organize the in-block documents is Merkle trees [3,4].

There are two parts in each block in the blockchain: a block header and a block body, shown as Figure 2.3. The block header stores data of a Merkle root, a previous block hash, and a time stamp and the block body stores batch transaction data. The Merkle tree that stores the intra-block transactions uses hash implementation at each node to realize the unfortunate modification of the intra-block transactions and also provide the simple payment verification. The previous block hash is used to point to the former block content, which connects the blocks together and form the chain. Hash function plays a critical role in the development of blockchain system. Therefore, we give a short description of the function and mechanism of hash function. A hash function could map binary values with arbitrary length to shorter fixed-length binary values. This small binary value is called a hash value. Generally, the hash function satisfies the following relationship. With

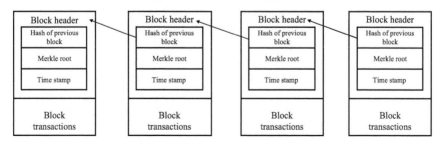

*Figure 2.3   Data structure of blockchain system*

the input of arbitrary data, hash function outputs a fixed-length data key by using the hash algorithm. This conversion is a compression progress, which means the space of the hash value is smaller than the input space. It is a unique numerical representation of a piece of data. Even if a piece of data is slightly modified, hash functions will produce quite different hash values. In addition, it is computationally impossible to find two different inputs with the same hash value.

The time stamp indicates the creation time of the block. Bitcoin [5], Ethereum [6] and Hyperledger Fabric [7] each has unique features in blockchain data structures, data models and data storage. For instance, Bitcoin's block header also contains data such as difficulty targets and nonce to support mining operations in the PoW consensus mechanism. In addition, in the design of the data model, Bitcoin uses a transaction-based data model. Each transaction consists of an input indicating the source of the transaction and an output indicating the direction of the transaction. All transactions are linked through input and output so that each transaction is traceable. Ethereum and Hyperledger Fabric need to support feature-rich of universal applications, so an account-based model is used to quickly query current balance or status based on the account.

In the design of data storage, the blockchain data is similar to the pre-written log of the traditional database. It is normally stored in the format of log file. Furthermore, because the system requires a large number of hash-based key–value (KV) retrieval, such as transaction-based hash retrieval transactions and block-based hash check. The data and state of the block are usually stored in the KV database. For example, all Bitcoin, Ethereum and Hyperledger Fabric store the index data in the LevelDB1 database.

## 2.1.4   Consensus layer

Paxos [8,9], Zab [10] and Raft [11] protocols are mainly used in distributed databases to achieve consistency among multiple distributed nodes. However, these algorithms are mainly used in the datacenter or private cloud environment, which are managed and maintained by a logically centralized department or organization. There are no fault nodes in the network, and the central management system only needs to support the crash fault tolerant. This is quite different from the scenario of the blockchain system, which is located distributively and managed by multiple network nodes. The number of nodes can be changed anytime and some nodes may not be credible. The consensus among the nodes forms the problem of complex Byzantine Fault Tolerance (BFT) [12]. According to the work conducted by Vukolić in [13], let $n$ denote the number of the total nodes in the blockchain system and $f$ denote the number of the untrusted nodes. For a synchronous and reliable network, the Byzantine general problem can be solved under the condition of $n >= 3f + 1$. Fischer *et al.* demonstrated that a deterministic consensus cannot achieve in the present of any node failure in the case of asynchronous communication. In [14], practical BFT (PBFT) was proposed with the aim of reducing the complexity of the Byzantine protocol from exponential to polynomial, making it possible to apply Byzantine protocols in distributed systems. Following [14], in order to improve the performance of PBFT, an improved version of PBFT, named speculative BFT, was proposed in [15]. There is a reasonable assumption in the advanced version that at the most of the time, the nodes in the network are normal. This assumption reduced the times of execution and significantly decreased the algorithm complexity. In the practical blockchain system, such as Bitcoin, the work conducted by Kwon *et al.* in [16] played a critical part, which assigns different weights to each vote on the basis of node counting. The more importance of the nodes and the higher weight will be assigned to this node. A consensus is reached, once the voting weight exceeds two-thirds of the overall nodes. This kind of design could reduce the number of messages broadcast within the P2P network. In digital-currency-based applications, such as Bitcoin, the weight can be mapped into the amount of the currency of each node. Furthermore, the work in [17] proposed a new method of building distributed systems that tolerate Byzantine faults. The authors assumed that it is impossible for a single node to control the entire network and Byzantine nodes at the same time. This assumption could significantly simplify the BFT message. This work demonstrated that under the given assumption, Byzantine general problem could be solved under the condition of $n \geq 2f + 1$. Furthermore, the Ripple payment discussed in network layer also proposes a Ripple Protocol consensus algorithm based on a set of trusted authentication nodes.

In the consensus layer, Bitcoin system applies the PoW mechanism to address the problem of Sybil attack [18], which introduces the issue of the free entry and exit. PoW is derived from the anti-spamming technique developed by Dwork and Naor in [19]. It proposed that only mail that has completed a certain calculation and provided proof-of-task accomplishment can be received. Following the idea of anti-spamming technique, Bitcoin applies that only nodes that complete a certain amount of computational task and provide the proof-of-task accomplishment can generate blocks. Each network node needs to use its own computing resources to solve the problem of hash operations. The problem of PoW is that a huge amount of energy resources are used to solve the hash problems. In order to avoid relying heavily on the power consumption of node computing power, the researchers proposed some mechanisms that can achieve consensus without consuming large amount of computational power. In this context, PoS was proposed, which transfers the block generation difficulty to the share of the node [20]. Further improved versions of PoS include delegated PoS (DPoS) mechanism [21], Hyperledger Sawtooth based on Intel SGX2 trusted hard [22] and proof-of-elapsed-time mechanism. Different blockchain applications apply different consensus mechanism. The consensus based on the proof mechanism is usually applied to the public chain with free nodes. For instance, Bitcoin and Ethereum use the PoW mechanism. The consensus based on voting mechanism is usually applied to the alliance chain, which is managed by a management system, and the Hyperledger Fabric uses the PBFT algorithm.

One important aspect of consensus layer is the incentive mechanism that encourages the network nodes to participate in the management and operation of the blockchain system. For the demonstration, we use Bitcoin as an example to show how incentive mechanism works. Bitcoin is used by the blockchain system to reward the miners who create new blocks. The amount of the Bitcoin is halved every 4 years. In the Bitcoin system, a new block is generated every 10 min, which means a new Bitcoin is awarded to the miners every 10 min. This is the way how the currency is issued. Based on the simple calculation, by the year 2140, the newly created block would not be rewarded by the system anymore. At that time, the total amount of Bitcoin will be about 21 million. This is the total amount of Bitcoin, so there is no indefinite issue in Bitcoin system. Another source of incentives is the transaction fee. Once there is no reward for the newly created block, the miner's income will be from the system reward to the transaction fee. For example, network node can specify a certain amount of Bitcoin, e.g., 0.5% of transaction, to the miners who record block when transferring money. Therefore, the incentive mechanism includes two parts, mining reward and transaction fee, which drive the operation of the overall Bitcoin system.

## 2.1.5   Smart contract layer

A smart contract is a series of programming rules defining the contract content, trigger condition and the related actions. It is implemented through trusted shared script code deployed on a blockchain. Once the smart contract is created and signed by the related parties, this contract will be attached to a blockchain data in the form of program code. After the validation, this blockchain data would be stored as a specific block in the blockchain. Within the smart contracts, it contains a number of predefined states, transition rules, scenarios that trigger contract execution and response actions when the conditions are satisfied. The blockchain system would check the status of the smart contract in real time and activate and execute the contract by checking the external data source once certain trigger conditions are met.

Smart contracts are important for blockchain technology. On the one hand, smart contracts increase the flexibility of the blockchain, providing the programmable mechanisms and algorithms for static blockchain data, and laying the foundation for building programmable financial systems and social systems basis. On the other hand, the automation and programmability of smart contracts make it possible to encapsulate the complex behavior of nodes in a distributed blockchain system. The application of chain technology in various distributed artificial intelligence systems makes it possible to construct various decentralized applications, decentralized autonomous organizations, decentralized autonomous companies and even decentralized autonomous societies based on blockchain technology. Compared with the traditional contract, blockchain smart contract by using a program algorithm avoids relying on a specific person to execute the contract, reducing the risk of personal effects and guaranteeing the reliability and safety of contract execution. The normal operation of smart contracts requires the automated integration and coordination of blockchain systems, components and multiple nodes. Herein, we summarize the characteristics of blockchain-based smart contract as follows:

● Data transparency: all data on the blockchain is publicly transparent and can be accessed by any blockchain nodes. Smart contracts are part of blockchain system. Therefore, the data processing of smart contracts is also transparent, which means any blockchain node can view the code and data of smart contract at runtime.

- Not tampering: all data in the blockchain itself cannot be tampered with. So the smart contract code deployed on the blockchain and the output of the data generated by the execution are not tampered. The parties creating the smart contracts do not need to worry about the contract safety.

- High reliability: because the blockchain system is implemented in the distributed manner, each node owns the full version of the blockchain. Therefore, the failure or non-function of certain nodes cannot stop the execution of the smart contracts, which provides the high reliability and trustability for smart contracts. Once the contract is created and validated, the data of the smart contract cannot be deleted, modified, can only be added, and the history of the smart contract can be traced, and the cost of falsifying the contract or default will be high. Therefore, a single party cannot manipulate the contract, which provides high reliability in smart contracts.

- No credit check: before the traditional contract is reached, the participants must first understand the credit background of each party to select the appropriate target. The stage after the contract is reached must also rely on the honesty and credit of the parties, or introduce a third party to guarantee the performance of the contract. Smart contract does not need the strict credit check. The contract can be signed among multiple unreliable parties and does not need the third party to monitor the contract execution.

## 2.1.6   Application layers

Driven by the advantages of blockchain technology, various blockchain-based applications are emerging to improve the security, reliability and efficiency of service provisioning, such as cross-border payment, copyright protection, healthcare, charity, Internet advertisement, voting activity and food tracking.

- Cross-border payment: the financial industry plays an important role in the economic and is regarded as the first driving force for global economic development. Payment is one of the key components in finance field, especially cross-border payments. However, the current cross-border payment efficiency suffers from high transmission rate and low efficiency. This is the biggest problem for the traders who do cross-border business. The essence of blockchain design is point-to-point transmission. When the underlying technology blockchain is applied to the payment field, the advantages of point-to-point transmission assist financial industry to solve the issues of cross-border payment. For instance, the blockchain is characterized by the non-tamperable and intelligent contracts. In the process of blockchain-based cross-border payment, the remittance channel is transparent and traceable, and the remittance party and the payee have reliable guarantees, making the payment safer and more reliable.

Cross-border payment has always been a global concern. There have been several blockchain companies that have been working in this direction. Ripple has begun to implement practical applications of blockchain-based cross-border payment. The blockchain enables the convenience and efficiency of cross-border payments, which will be beneficial for the global economy.

- Copyright protection: for the copyright protection, there are some issues, e.g., high registration fee and long approval time, that affect the development of content publication. With blockchain as a key technology, coupled with a variety of advanced technologies such as big data and artificial intelligence, the data of producers and products can be stored and explored in the distributed manner to realize the traceability of ownership and improve the efficiency of the copyright protection. For instance, Huitie.com launched a commercial product Huicai Digital Intellectual Property Application Platform (IP Chain) with the aim of providing a series of copyright services. Through their copyright registration certificate service based on blockchain technology, users can obtain blockchain certificate within several minutes.

- Healthcare: with the advancement of science and technology, huge successes have been achieved in the area of healthcare. However, there are still some problems that need to be addressed for providing better health-care services for the public. For example, hospitals do not want to share their data, and the health-care information or data is locked in individual datacenter. With the technology of blockchain, a shared medical platform could be established to enable medical-related data online and accessed by related persons from different organizations. In addition, any medical research and development breakthroughs in one hospital can also be quickly shared with other medical treatments. From a macro perspective, this will enable a closer collaboration of major medical institutions to promote the development of our medical industry. There have been some industry implementations of blockchain-based health-care platform. For example, Korean technology company Mark Long developed a blockchain-based data ecosystem for storing personally relevant medical information such as genes. It is believed that the exit of these blockchain medical projects will reshape the global medical landscape and bring the faster and better medical progress.

- Charity: charitable donations have always been a public welfare field. For a successful donation system, the transparence and fairness are critically important to make the people aware that their donations are managed and distributed in a fair way. Blockchain can be used to improve the transparency of information in donations and provide donors the feedback of their kind activity, forming a virtuous circle for the entire donation system. For example, blockchain technology can be used to track the source and the flow of money, confirm the identity of the donor and establish an accountability mechanism in the charity field, which can also improve the organizational efficiency.

In the field of blockchain-based charity service, BitGive Foundation uses distributed ledger technology to enable donors to have a clearer understanding of the fund's circulation. Currently, the blockchain platform has released blockchain-based charity service in the version of beta, providing services such as tracking and permanently recording charitable donations around the world.

- Voting activity: voting has been a solution that ultimately allows the public to reach a consensus. For example, the leader of a country is chosen through the voting in the state. However, the transparency of the entire voting system plays a critical role that may result in serious issues, such as violence and war. It is always difficult to avoid black-box operations and, for some profit targets, the number of fake votes. Even if the relevant work parties take various measures to prevent fraud, it is still difficult to eradicate such false votes. Therefore, how to build a fair and transparent voting is a challenging issue. In this area, the blockchain has the characteristics of distribution. The data recorded on the chain is recorded by the nodes. Therefore, the data is not easily falsified, and each step is transparent. When the blockchain is placed on the vote, it could make the voting more transparent, authentic and reliable.

In the area of distributed voting system, Sierra Leone in Africa has developed a voting electoral system based on blockchain technology [23]. This system is processed and calculated by Swiss-based start-up Agora using blockchain technology. On March 7, 2018, the people of Sierra Leone use the new system to select their president. In addition, a voting application named My Number Card is developed in the Tsukuba City of Japan, which is used to vote for the community issues.

- Food tracking: from the raw materials to final product in the supermarket, the food products experience a series of processes, including production, wholesale, transportation and sales. There are various issues in the overall process. For example, the incorporation of fake products makes the quality or the cost of the products obtained by consumers may not be the best. Although there are some tracking methods in the traditional food tracking, the performance of the food tracking cannot be guaranteed. Transparency is one of the basic characteristics of blockchain system. By using distributed ledger technology, all data in the food supply chain is recorded on this distributed ledger, which is maintained by all nodes in the network to ensure that the data is true and non-tamperable. For a blockchain traceability chain, every step from production to consumer can be trackable and is transparent for the customers.

Blockchain-based food tracking system has attracted significant attentions for the industry. For instance, IBM has made great efforts in the traceability chain. To address the food safety issue, IBM has developed a food traceability application named IBM Food Trust. The IBM Food Trust [24] is a decentralized network, the participants of which include growers, processors, wholesalers, distributors, manufacturers, retailers and consumers. Based on the IBM blockchain platform, IBM Food Trust permanently records the food details and processing data, improving visibility and reliability at every stage of the food supply. This product has been adopted by Walmart to track their products.

## 2.1.7    Potential issues

Although the advantages of blockchain-based application have been widely recognized, there are still some issues that need further investigation to fully exploit the potentials of blockchain system. For example, blockchain transaction concurrency capacity, data storage capacity, universality and security are still obviously inadequate.

• Transaction concurrency capabilities: currently, the capabilities of transaction concurrency within the blockchain system are not enough for continuously support the huge amount of the concurrency transmission. This is mainly because of the low efficient consensus algorithm. The typical consensus algorithms used in blockchain include PoW, PoS, DPoS and PBFT. A powerful consensus algorithm is needed to improve the capacities of transaction concurrency in blockchain system. Furthermore, the ledger structure is another factor that affects the transaction concurrency performance of blockchain system. The typical blockchain ledger is designed as a single-chain structure of blocks, meaning that all transactions can only be processed sequentially from a global perspective. Compared with the traditional centralized system, the lack of parallelism in transaction processing makes it difficult to achieve the similar performance as that of centralized system.

In the enterprise scenario, the transaction concurrency requires the blockchain system to process hundreds of thousands of transactions per second (TPS), such as Amazon Prime Day. The requirement of concurrency performance is much higher than that of the current blockchain system. The new blockchain system with high transaction concurrency capabilities needs to scale dynamically as the business grows. And the potential solutions to this new system include new consensus algorithms, the evolved ledger structure as well as the continuous optimization of overall blockchain system.

• Data storage capabilities: because the data can be added into blockchain to form new block and the data cannot be modified or removed; therefore, the size for storing the blockchain data should be increase to meet the requirement of data storage. This introduces the issue of data storage capacities in blockchain system.

In the case of the e-commerce supply chain, the daily data record of the main e-commerce business can be on the scale of million or tens of millions. Currently, the typical blockchain system in the implementation of the storage of ledger data is based on the file system or simple KV database storage, without the consideration of distributed storage and huge amount of data storage in each node. Therefore, how to meet the requirement of a huge amount of data storage is a challenging issue in blockchains system and need more research efforts to achieve a high-performance blockchain system.

• Universality: blockchain needs to adapt to diverse business needs and meet the requirements of data sharing across multiple business chains, which means the data should be recorded in the blockchain in a way that is sufficiently common and standard to represent a variety of structured and unstructured information and to meet the cross-chain requirements for business grows. At present, most of the blockchain systems use specific consensus algorithms, encryption algorithms, account models, ledger models and storage types, lacking pluggable and transferable ability, which is difficult to support different application scenarios. In addition, for the existing blockchain platform, it is difficult to adapt to the requirements of the rapid development of business such as the capability of conducing user authentication and multilevel authorization.

- Scalability: whether used as a virtual currency or a generalized database, the data services on the blockchain are completed in the form of transaction. Due to the distributed nature of the blockchain, transactions are always generated concurrently. Blockchain system suffers from the scalability issue in the practical implementation. Herein, the scalability of a blockchain generally refers to the maximum number of concurrent transactions that can be supported per unit of time. In general, the blockchain throughput is characterized by TPS, which is determined by the size of the block, the time the consensus algorithm is running and the time of broadcast and verification. Because the blockchain uses decentralization to verify transactions, it is necessary to form a consensus on most nodes before verification can be completed. The consequence is that the current blockchain will inevitably decrease in transaction speed with the increase of network nodes. Bitcoin's throughput rate is estimated between 3.3 and 7 TPS, and Ethereum is slightly higher around 30 TPS. In contrast, VISA credit cards that use a centralized approach to verify transactions can have a sustained throughput rate of more than 1,700 TPS [25]. Therefore, how to improve the scalability or performance of the distributed blockchain system to achieve the similar performance of the traditional centralized system is a challenging issue.

- Security and privacy: the blockchain adopts a decentralized consensus mechanism, which provides high security. However, blockchains are implemented by the network, the network protocols are likely to be attacked and cause serious problems. For example, the Mt Gox exchange was stolen due to a security hole of the wallet for $360 million, which directly led to the bankruptcy of the exchange.

In addition, the mechanism of smart contracts can also be attached. Because smart contracts are Turing-complete programs in blockchain system, and the potential risks are greatly increased when the code is run on a distributed network environment. In addition, the smart contract programming is mainly based on the Solidity language, which is far from real maturity, so although the code is executed by the virtual machine, the attacker can use the overflow and other conditions to invade the host computer. Furthermore, in the latest version of the blockchain system, the introduction of cross-contract program calls is vulnerable to re-entry attacks. The typical case is an attack to distributed autonomous organization (DAO) [25], which is a crowdfunding project on Ethereum. DAO system was attacked in 2017, and more than $60 million worth of DAO was stolen in this attack.

In addition, the data on the blockchain public chain is generally completely open for public chain. Therefore, with the continuous expansion of blockchain application and the increase of the proportion of its database applications, how to introduce a complete privacy protection mechanism in the blockchain has become an urgent problem to be solved.

## 2.2   Conclusion

Blockchain is a technological revolution from the centralized system to securely distributed system. It covers multiple scientific domains, including cryptography, distributed storage, consensus mechanisms, smart contracts and other technologies, establishing a new type of trust and incentive system, which greatly enhances transparency and reduces credit risk. In this chapter, our aim is to demonstrate a system architecture of blockchain system to provide a whole view of the blockchain system. Then we presented the function of each layer in the system architecture with details of how each layer contributes to the key features of the blockchain system. Furthermore, we provide some key blockchain applications to show its potential in improving the efficiency and security of social service provisioning. Finally, we discussed some key challenges that blockchain meets due to its inherent design. The solutions to address these problems require the active exploration and cooperation of all parties to jointly build a new digital society that is convenient and reliable.

## References

[1]   Saroiu S, Gummadi PK, and Gribble SD. Measurement study of peer-to-peer file sharing systems. In: Multimedia Computing and Networking 2002. vol. 4673. International Society for Optics and Photonics; 2001. p. 156–170.

[2]   Haber S and Stornetta WS. How to time-stamp a digital document. In: Conference on the Theory and Application of Cryptography. Springer; 1990. p. 437–455.

[3]   Rogers B, Chhabra S, Prvulovic M, *et al.* Using address independent seed encryption and bonsai Merkle trees to make secure processors OS- and performance-friendly. In: 40th Annual IEEE/ACM International Symposium on Microarchitecture (MICRO 2007). IEEE; 2007. p. 183–196.

[4]   Becker G. Merkle signature schemes, Merkle trees and their cryptanalysis. Tech Rep. Ruhr-University Bochum; 2008.

[5]   Gandal N, Hamrick J, Moore T, *et al.* Price manipulation in the Bitcoin ecosystem. Journal of Monetary Economics. 2018;95:86–96.

[6]   Antonopoulos AM and Wood G. Mastering Ethereum: Building Smart Contracts and DApps. O'Reilly Media; 2018.

[7]   Androulaki E, Barger A, Bortnikov V, *et al.* Hyperledger Fabric: A distributed operating system for permissioned blockchains. In: Proceedings of the 13th EuroSys Conference; 2018. p. 1–15.

[8]    Ailijiang A, Charapko A, and Demirbas M. Consensus in the cloud: Paxos systems demystified. In: 2016 25th International Conference on Computer Communication and Networks (ICCCN). IEEE; 2016. p. 1–10.

[9]    Wilcox JR, Sergey I, and Tatlock Z. Programming language abstractions for modularly verified distributed systems. In: 2nd Summit on Advances in Programming Languages (SNAPL 2017). Schloss Dagstuhl-Leibniz-Zentrum fuer Informatik; 2017.

[10]   Botelho F, Ribeiro TA, Ferreira P, *et al.* Design and implementation of a consistent data store for a distributed SDN control plane. In: 2016 12th European Dependable Computing Conference (EDCC). IEEE; 2016. p. 169–180.

[11]   Ongaro D and Ousterhout J. In search of an understandable consensus algorithm. In: 2014 USENIX Annual Technical Conference (USENIX ATC '14); 2014. p. 305–319.

[12]   Cachin C. Architecture of the Hyperledger blockchain fabric. In: Workshop on Distributed Cryptocurrencies and Consensus Ledgers. vol. 310; 2016.

[13]   Vukolić M. The quest for scalable blockchain fabric: Proof-of-work vs. BFT replication. In: International Workshop on Open Problems in Network Security. Springer; 2015. p. 112–125.

[14]   Castro M and Liskov B. Practical Byzantine fault tolerance. In: OSDI. vol. 99; 1999. p. 173–186.

[15]   Kotla R, Alvisi L, Dahlin M, *et al.* Zyzzyva: Speculative Byzantine fault tolerance. In: Proceedings of 21st ACM SIGOPS Symposium on Operating Systems Principles; 2007. p. 45–58.

[16]   Kwon J. TenderMint: Consensus without mining. Draft v. 0.6, fall. vol. 1; 2014. p. 11.

[17]   Liu S, Viotti P, Cachin C, *et al.* XFT: Practical fault tolerance beyond crashes. In: 12th USENIX Symposium on Operating Systems Design and Implementation (OSDI'16); 2016. p. 485–500.

[18]   Eyal I and Sirer EG. Majority is not enough: Bitcoin mining is vulnerable. In: International Conference on Financial Cryptography and Data Security. Springer; 2014. p. 436–454.

[19]   Dwork C and Naor M. Pricing via processing or combatting junk mail. In: Annual International Cryptology Conference. Springer; 1992. p. 139–147.

[20]   King S and Nadal S. PPcoin: Peer-to-peer crypto-currency with proof-of-stake. Self-published paper. 2012;19:1.

[21]   Larimer D. Delegated proof-of-stake (DPOS) [BitShare Whitepaper]; 2014.

[22]   Androulaki E, Barger A, Bortnikov V, *et al.* Hyperledger Fabric: A Distributed Operating System for Permissioned Blockchains; 2018. p. 30.

[23]   Kshetri N and Voas J. Blockchain-enabled e-voting. IEEE Software. 2018;35(4):95–99.

[24]   Galvin D. IBM and WALMART: Blockchain for food safety [PowerPoint Presentation]; 2017.

[25]   Mehar M, Shier CL, Giambattista A, *et al.* Understanding a revolutionary and flawed grand experiment in Blockchain: The DAO attack. Journal of Cases on Information Technology. 2019;21(1):19–32.

*Chapter 3*

# Blockchain consensuses and incentives

*Meijun Li[1], Gaoyang Liu[1], Jialin Tian[1], Chen Wang[1],*
*Yang Yang[2] and Shaohua Wan[3]*

As the core of a blockchain system, the consensus mechanism not only helps to maintain the consistency of nodes' data but also gets involved in issuance of tokens and prevention of attacks. Since the first blockchain system was born in 2009, it has been continuously improved with the development of the blockchain technology and evolved into multiple new branches. Starting with the basic introduction of the consensus and the classic Byzantine Generals Problem in distributed computing area, this chapter proposes a thorough classification of current consensus protocols in blockchain system, enumerates the characteristics of mainstream protocols (proof-of-work (PoW), proof-of-stake (PoS), delegated PoS (DPoS), practical Byzantine fault tolerance (PBFT), etc.) and analyzes the strengths and weaknesses of them. Then we compare the performances of them from the number of nodes to the degree of scalability and other aspects. In the end, we introduce the incentive mechanism in the design of a consensus and summarize the future directions of developing more practical consensus schemes.

## 3.1 Blockchain consensuses

A blockchain system is essentially an asynchronous distributed system that can be analyzed as a set of state machine replications (SMRs) [1]. Each blockchain node involved in recording data is an SMR, and the data it records is the current state. Appending a verified block to the system by each node is equivalent to an operation that changes the current state. To achieve a consistent state for all nodes in the system, it acquires the consistent initial state of each node, and the consistent operation adding to the system each time. This process/algorithm of achieving the consistency of distributed nodes is the consensus [2].

[1]Department of Communication Engineering, Huazhong University of Science and Technology, Wuhan, China
[2]School of Computer Science and Information Engineering, Hubei University, Wuhan, China
[3]School of Information and Safety Engineering, Zhongnan University of Economics and Law, Wuhan, China

In a distributed system, the consistency problem is an important and classic problem studied since the 1970s. There is a basic assumption that the nodes participating in the calculation are not reliable and may fail. Normally, the failures come in two types: crash failures and Byzantine failures [3]. The difference is that the former ones only lose normal functions, while the latter ones not only work improperly but also could maliciously interfere with normal nodes' work. The term "Byzantine failure" is derived from the Byzantine Generals Problem described by Leslie Lamport [4]: due to the vast territory of the Byzantine Roman Empire, each royal army is separated far apart for defense, and the generals of different armies can only rely on the messengers to exchange information. Before each action, it is necessary for them to agree on whether to attack or retreat. But there could be traitors among all the generals, and they may send wrong messages intentionally to interfere with others. In that case, how can a loyal general unify his plan of war with the knowledge of a traitor? This is the Byzantine Generals Problem. In a blockchain system, each node can be seen as a general who wants to ensure the consistency of the blockchain ledger. However, there may be malicious nodes trying to tamper with the content of the ledger and obtain greater economic revenues. How to deal with the problem depends on the design and implementation of the consensus mechanisms.

In most mainstream blockchain consensus mechanisms, the process of reaching consensus can be divided into four phases as leader election, block generation, data validation and chain updation. The input to the consensus process is the data generated and verified by the nodes, and the output is the encapsulated data block and the updated blockchain. For more details, we give the description next.

*Phase 1:* Leader election. It is the process of electing the leader node $A$, which submits the new block, from the entire node set $M$. We can use the formula $f(M) \rightarrow A$ to represent this phase, where $f$ represents the specific implementation of the consensus algorithm. In general, $|A| = 1$, meaning there is only one node to be the leader ultimately.

*Phase 2:* Block generation. The leader node elected by Phase 1 packs the transactions or data generated by all nodes in current period into a block according to a specific strategy and broadcasts the generated new block to the entire nodes or delegate nodes. These transactions or data are usually packed into new blocks by the order according to the block capacity, transaction fees, transaction time and other factors. The strategy of block generation is a key factor in the performance of a blockchain system.

*Phase 3:* Data validation. After the other nodes receive the broadcasted new block, they will verify the correctness and rationality of the transactions or data encapsulated in the block. If the new block is approved by most of the validator/delegate nodes, it will be updated to the blockchain as the next block.

*Phase 4:* Chain updating. The leader adds the new block to the main chain, forming a complete, longer chain from the genesis block to the latest block. If there are forks in the main chain, it is necessary to select one of the appropriate forks as the main chain according to the main chain criterion specified by the consensus algorithm.

### 3.1.1    Consensus classification

Based on whether the number of nodes in the calculation is certain or not, and whether the nodes have malicious behaviors, we can divide the current consensus protocols into four cases. Considering the assumption that the number of nodes is uncertain and the nodes do not have malicious behaviors is too ideal, we only talk about the other three practical cases shown in Figure 3.1. Note that in practice the blockchain is more considered about the consensus among untrusted nodes, so the "non-BFT (Byzantine fault tolerance) consensus with limited nodes" in the dashed box in Figure 3.1 only exists in theory. Moreover, such kinds of blockchain systems, as far as we know, have not yet emerged. Even if such systems exist, they are only suitable for highly trusted private networks. In the following subsections, we will introduce the different consensus protocols mentioned in this classification.

### 3.1.2    Proof-of-work

The PoW consensus is the first and the most widely adopted consensus protocol in current blockchain systems. Simply speaking, PoW is a proof to confirm that you have done a certain amount of work. Its concept was first proposed by Cynthia Dwork and Moni Naor in 1993 to resolve the problem of spam mail [5]. The basic idea is that, before sending a mail message, the user is required to send a PoW related to the message. This PoW is usually a process that aims to solve a mathematical problem and the problem should meet the following conditions:

- Be related to the messages to defend replay attacks against PoW.
- Be difficult enough to prevent being cracked by the third party.
- Be easy enough to verify the recipient, so as to avoid excessive computing overhead.

In [6], another anti-spam system used PoW for Hashcash. After that, Nakamoto adopted this innovative mechanism to achieve the consistency of nodes in Bitcoin

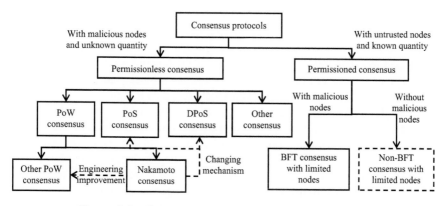

*Figure 3.1    Consensus protocols in blockchain systems*

in 2008, laying a foundation for various blockchains and consensuses in others' later work.

For Bitcoin network, Nakamoto has improved the traditional PoW consensus. To distinguish it from the earlier one, we call it Nakamoto Consensus here. The mathematical puzzle that Nakamoto Consensus adopted is to solve a 256-bit integer *Nonce* as a so-called "lucky number," ensuring the hash value of it and the created block header is less than a "difficulty," i.e.,

$$H(B) \leq m \tag{3.1}$$

where $B$ is the block to submit, $H$ is a hash function and $m$ is the difficulty, a very small real number determined by the nature of the hash function.

If a required *Nonce* is found and approved in the Bitcoin system, the discoverer can receive a corresponding amount of Bitcoins as a reward. Because violently seeking *Nonce* requires a lot of calculations, the process of calculating is thus vividly called "mining." In order to adapt to the dynamic changes of the computing power of entire system, it is ensured that the system generates blocks roughly at a predetermined rate (about one block every 10 min), the difficulty is dynamically adjustable, and the adjustment is also based on the consensus. The adjustment period is approximately 1 week (i.e., adjust the difficulty per $24 \times 6 \times 7$ blocks). In the PoW mechanism, since the expected time to find the *Nonce* can be adjusted, a mechanism of decentralized time series is constructed. At the same time, the decision problem of the decentralized multiple nodes is also solved, that is, the entire network uses the data submitted by the node that first finds the legal *Nonce*.

Next, let us see how to reach the consensus. After any honest node generates a new block, it broadcasts the block to the entire network. For other honest nodes, they verify the correctness of the newly received block. If the block is proved to be valid, they will abandon their ongoing block calculations, then reselect the transaction not added to the blockchain from the received list of transactions based on the received new block, generate a new block header and perform a new round of *Nonce* calculation.

Since the transactions received by different nodes have precedence, it may cause one node to receive two or more legitimate blocks, which leads to a temporary fork, like Figure 3.2(a). After the fork occurs, each node can only continue to generate new blocks based on one of the new blocks, until one of the forks wins the competition. The fork is only temporary; as the time grows, it will be replaced by the longest chain, as Figure 3.2(b) shows. Once a blockchain node decides to generate a new block based on a certain block, it means that the node permits the block and all other previous records. This permission is based on probability. If the chains published by other nodes are longer, the node will abandon the former consensus. Although the consensus is based on probability, it can be proved when the total computing power of the nodes participating in block generation is not dominant, that is, when the computing power is lower than 51% of the total computing power in the entire network [7], the probability that the $n$th block before the current block is discarded is exponentially negatively correlated with $n$, i.e., the

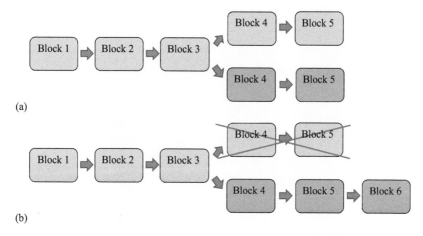

*Figure 3.2 The fork forms and disappears in the PoW blockchain: (a) temporary fork and (b) final fork*

larger *n* is, the lower the probability of the *n*th preceding node in the current block is discarded. Generally speaking, in Bitcoin system, the transactions on the six blocks before the current block are basically considered to be accepted by the entire system in terms of probability.

The biggest feature as well as advantage of PoW is reflected in the fairness of the protocol, which is if a miner's computing power accounts for *p%* of the network's total computing power, there is a corresponding *p%* possibility to generate blocks and get paid. That also illustrates the difficulty of the attack. The attacker's computing power needs to compete with other honest nodes in the whole network to generate the blocks that are "beneficial" for him. The PoW algorithm has successfully guaranteed the safety of the Bitcoin network from birth.

However, as more and more people use Bitcoin for trading, its defects are gradually manifested. The original intention of PoW is to achieve a decentralized democratic consensus through "one-CPU-one-vote," which is a time-consuming process to reach consensus. In addition, due to the fast increase in Bitcoin prices, the professional mining equipment appears on the market. The increase in the number of users purchasing mining equipment leads to the loss of more and more ordinary miners. The foundation of democracy is damaged, and monopoly issues are also highlighted [8]. As more and more users participate in Bitcoin mining, not only in order to reduce the mining threshold but also to improve the stability of mining, many commercial mining pools occur in the system. A mining pool is an opening mining server that forces many users' computing power to a team to mine, such as BTC.COM, AntPool and SlushPool.*

As shown in Figure 3.3, over the past 24 h of April 9, 2019, more than 50% of the blocks were mined by the top three mining pools. It is undeniable that the

---

*Global computing power distribution [Online], available: https://btc.com/stats/pool, April 9, 2019.

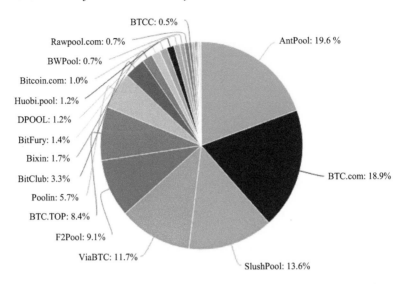

*Figure 3.3    Computing power distribution of current mining pools*

*Table 3.1    The energy consumption statistics of the Bitcoin network*

| Description | Value |
| --- | --- |
| Bitcoin's current estimated annual electricity consumption (TWh) | 54.27 |
| Bitcoin's current minimum annual electricity consumption (TWh) | 41.98 |
| Annualized global mining revenues | $3,855,324,810 |
| Annualized estimated global mining costs | $2,713,725,581 |
| Current cost percentage | 70.39% |
| Estimated electricity used over the previous day (KWh) | 148,697,292 |
| Implied Watts per GH/s | 0.117 |
| Total Network Hash rate in PH/s (1,000,000 GH/s) | 52,757 |
| Electricity consumed per transaction (KWh) | 413 |
| Number of US households that could be powered by Bitcoin | 5,025,418 |
| Number of US households powered for 1 day by the electricity consumed for a single transaction | 13.95 |
| Bitcoin's electricity consumption as a percentage of the world's electricity consumption | 0.24% |

mining pools have mastered enormous computing power. If a single mining pool exceeds 50%, or several large mining pools make an alliance privately, it is easy to launch a 51% attack on the Bitcoin system.

Second, the problem of energy waste has been criticized for a long time. Numerous mining rigs waste a lot of electric power day and night but have no other

---

[†]Energy consumption statistics [Online], available: https://digiconomist.net/bitcoin-energy-consumption, April 9, 2019.

effect except generating Bitcoins. Table 3.1[†] indicates the energy consumption statistics of the Bitcoin network currently. It is estimated that the Bitcoin system has consumed at least 54.27 TWh of electricity annually, making it comparable with the amount of a country such as Bangladesh [9].

In addition, the PoW consensus mechanism has some other problems such as long confirmation cycle, and low throughput. Regarding the problems of Nakamoto Consensus, blockchain systems have conducted different improvements based on specific conditions. There are two ways of improvement. One is the engineering improvement, e.g., the improvement of Primecoin[‡] is an algorithm to turn meaningless hashing into a meaningful search for large prime numbers when seeking *Nonce*. It is expected to bring some scientific contributions to the mathematical academia. Focusing on the increasing centralization of computing power caused by ASIC (application specific integrated circuit) mining rigs, Tromp [10] proposed an anti-ASIC mining rig algorithm based on memory consumption. The other venue of improvement is to change the consensus mechanism, such as the PoS and DPoS, which are mostly adopted and will be discussed next.

### 3.1.3 Proof-of-stake

Owing to the vulnerabilities like serious waste of computing power and the 51% attack in the PoW mechanism, researchers have put forward a new kind of consensus mechanism known as PoS [11]. What is the "stake"? In early versions of PoS, it has another commonly used name "coin age," i.e., a number derived from the product of the number of coins multiplied by the number of days the coins have been held. For example, if user Alice receives two coins from user Bob and holds them for 50 days, then Alice can collect 100 coin age (2×50). And when Alice spends the money, the collected coin age will be eliminated. Nodes with a positive stake are called stakeholders. In contrast to PoW's ability to compete for record data in accordance with the ability of each node, PoS has more ability to have record data for those nodes that with more stakes (or coin age). The manifestation of this ability is that for a node with a long coin age, its ledger recording difficulty is relatively smaller.

In order to generate blocks faster, the PoS mechanism replaces the process of exhaustively seeking *Nonce* with the next algorithm:

$$H(H(B_{prev}, A, t)) \leq balance(A)m \qquad (3.2)$$

where $H$ is still a hash function, $t$ is the UTC timestamp, $B_{prev}$ refers to the previous block, $balance(A)$ is the coin age of the account $A$ and $m$ is a fixed real number.

PPCoin (PPC) [11] is the first to introduce the PoS mechanism into the blockchain system in 2012. In PPC, in addition to processing classical PoW-based transactions, the system also deals with a transaction called coin-stake in which each transaction will consume the coin age of the data record. In the coin-stake transaction, the stakeholder is required to send the coins to himself (to ensure that the coin age clears to zero after the stake block is generated), which is used to

---

[†]Primecoin Website [Online], available: http://primecoin.io/, April 9, 2019.

generate the PPC block and obtain partial revenue. The price of gaining revenue is the consumption of coin age. Similar to the Bitcoin system, the PPC block also requires participants to look for random numbers to make the hash value of block header meet the target difficulty, except that the target difficulty to generate a block in PPC system is different for various participants. The target difficulty is inversely proportional to the coin age consumed in coin-stake. The more coin age accumulated by the participants, the lower the difficulty of recording the ledger, and the greater the probability of generating blocks. In other words, the concept of coin age in PoS can be imagined as the computing power in PoW. If someone holds a large sum of currency for a long time, then he will have the opportunity to use a powerful ASIC mining rig once in the next mining process. But this opportunity does not depend on the consumption of hardware and electricity, it only depends on the user's deposit in the system and the time of saving the currency. Unlike the competition in PoW mining, PoS mining is more like a lottery. The more accumulated the coin age, the more chance there is to win. Once the winning is already, the coin age will be consumed, and the probability of the second win will be reduced [12].

The transformation of the design basis brings PoS the following advantages.

First, PoS alleviates the waste problem of PoW mining. In Bitcoin system, the probability of generating blocks is directly proportional to the miners' workload. In PoS system, the probability of block generation is proportional to the coin age. Therefore, the miners no longer need to invest a lot of computing power to win the competition.

Second, it is more difficult for the adversary to attack the cryptocurrency system. In PoS, the main chain is defined as the chain that consumes the most coin age. Each block's transaction will submit the consumed coin age to this block to increase the probability. In this case, if the adversary wants to initiate an attack on the main chain, he must own a large sum of coins and accumulate enough coin age. The cost of getting a large sum of coins in the PoS system is higher than the cost of mastering most of the computing power in the PoW system. Besides, once the attack is implemented, not only the system will be destroyed, but also the wealth the attacker owns will damage. This may reduce the attacker's motives from the beginning. And once the block is generated, the coin age will be immediately cleared, which also guarantees that the attacker cannot continue the attack [13].

However, the PoS consensus mechanism is not perfect as well.

The first is the distribution of the initial currency. Currently, the cryptocurrency systems using PoS have two methods to supply the initial currency. One is to use PoW for the early stage of mining and then use PoS for system maintenance. The other is initial public offerings, but lack of trust. The currency is concentrated in the hands of developers and a few people, unlike everyone in the PoW mechanism has the opportunity to get coins.

Second, PoS encourages the behavior of hoarding. The coin-stake transaction in PoS generates blocks and benefits by destroying the coin age, but the coin age of other common transactions packaged into the block is also reset to zero. This coin age does not bring stakeholders the benefit. It just disappears in vain for them.

The third is since the coin age will also accumulate when the node is offline, the node may prefer not to go online until the coin age has accumulated to a certain extent [14]. Lack of enough online nodes will make it easy to launch network attacks. What is more, due to the lack of online nodes, the speed of data synchronization and transaction response will be affected.

The next problem is costless simulation. This suggests that in the absence of PoW, PoS is a proof of a virtual resource. There is nothing that prevents users from doing it over and over, perhaps in parallel in multiple times. In PoW, all the parties must commit to the execution of consensus and advance that execution. This is not the case in PoS, because it is "nearly" costless to execute PoS protocol. In principle, there is virtually nothing at stake and one would be capable of advancing multiple different executions of the protocol so that it can find the one that is more favorable. That could be lead to the so-called "nothing-at-stake" attack. Let us bring back Figure 3.2 for more illustration. If one is a validator, then he can simply put his money in both the blue chain and green chain without any fear of repercussion at all. No matter what happens, he will always win and have nothing to lose, despite how malicious his actions may be.

The last is the "long-range" attack. In long-range attacks, there is a victim node that tries to distinguish between two alternative histories without access to recent information. If a node is constantly online, it is easy to know about what happens in the network. But if the node joins the network after a big hiatus or it is a new node, then the bootstrapping problem may arise. How does it synchronize with the blockchain without any recent information?

After the appearance of PPC's version of PoS, researchers have modified the shortcomings of it and then invented some derivative PoS-based protocols, such as PoSV [15] and DPoS.

PoSV is an improvement on the issue that the coin age in PoS is a linear function of time, aiming at eliminating the hoarding phenomenon of stakeholders. PoSV means PoS velocity that is currently used by Reddcoin. PoSV changes the linear function of the coin age and time in PoS to an exponential decay function, that is, the growth rate of the coin age gradually decreases with time and tends to be zero. In this way, the coin age of the new coin grows faster than the old until it reaches the upper bound, which moderates the stakeholders' hoarding phenomenon to some extent.

## 3.1.4   Delegated proof-of-stake

In order to further speed up the transaction and solve the security problem that the offline node in the PoS can also accumulate the coin age, Daniel Larimer proposed DPoS in April 2014 [16], which is currently the consensus mechanism for BitShares and Crypti platform. In DPoS, the system introduces two roles called witness and delegate, both of which have multiple members. The candidates of these two roles are selected by the stakeholders with an approval voting process according to the amount of their stakes. Stakeholders with more than 51% stakes are able to vote for the $N$ witnesses and delegates. The witnesses themselves are irrelevant to the transaction accounts they participate in. They only participate in the block generation and obtain revenue from transaction fees. As the joint signers of the stakeholder's account, delegates are responsible for adjusting the parameters such as the process of generating the block of the witness and the transaction fees. The adjustment is performed under the supervision of the stakeholders. Compared with the node feature of PoS that each node has equal rights to generate a block, nodes of DPoS are divided into delegates and witnesses, which have different rights, respectively. As shown in Figure 3.4, the delegates are responsible for voting and the witnesses just need to be their follower nodes. That is the critical difference between PoS and DPoS consensus.

DPoS mechanism is similar to the decision of the board of directors in the real world. Stakeholders vote for a delegate. The system calculates a certain number of delegates with the most votes based on the stakes of stakeholders, and the delegate takes turns to generate the block in the prescribed order. After voting by all stakeholders, the trust in the system has been concentrated by a small number of participants, and the node does not have to wait for confirmation of a considerable number of untrusted nodes after the transaction is initiated, but only the delegate needs to verify the transaction. This voting mechanism concentrates the power of all users in the hands of a few people but greatly shortens the confirmation time of transactions. Compared with the PoW-based system, the block generation time is shorter, and the throughput has been greatly improved. Taking BitShares as an example, its peak throughput can be thousands of transactions per second. The confirmation time is reduced to the seconds, which brings cryptocurrency technology to a new level.

But similar to the reality, once the power is concentrated in the hands of a few people, we have to be wary whether this group of people will harm justice for their own interests. For example, in BitShares system, if 101 delegates are elected and generate blocks, the 101st delegate will get 1/101 of the transaction fee, but the 102nd delegate has nothing to gain. The steep decline in earnings may prompt the 102nd delegate to make himself among the top 101 by some means, such as sharing

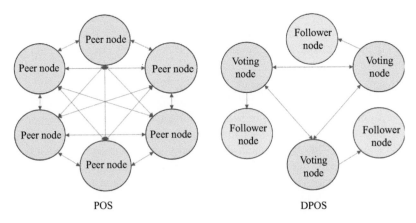

*Figure 3.4   Node differences between PoS and DPoS*

part of the transaction fee with the stakeholders. In addition, ordinary users have to worry about whether the delegate will harm the interests of them to cater to the major stakeholders and earn transaction fee.

In another version of DPoS protocol, the node has to pay a price to become a delegate, such as paying a deposit to a security account. If the node does something evil, the deposit will be confiscated [17]. Conversely, if the delegate maintains the system well, he will share the block transaction fee with other delegates, so that the reward will positively encourage the delegate to work harder to maintain system security. Since the block is signed by the delegates, in turn, if a delegate is offline and misses signing the block, he will face the risk of being replaced by other candidate delegates. Therefore, the delegate must guarantee sufficient online time for the profit. This version of DPoS protocol is also known as deposit-based PoS.

## 3.1.5    *Practical Byzantine fault tolerance*

The aforementioned consensuses all belong to the permissiveness consensuses, which means that the number of distributed nodes involved cannot be predicted. When multiple participants of a distributed system intend to modify the state of the system through additional blocks, they cannot simply determine it via the mechanism that most people make decisions. These update operations can only be optimized by PoW or PoS. For those scenarios in which the participants are relatively fixed, the nodes of the distributed system have been determined in advance. Therefore, the majority rule can be selected. PBFT [18] is a permissive protocol that participants determine and agree on the majority rule. It was proposed by Miguel Castro and Barbara Liskov in 1999. Before introducing that let us take a look at the original BFT mechanism.

Nodes with Byzantine failures are called Byzantine nodes, while other nodes are non-Byzantine ones. The BFT system satisfies the following conditions for each request: all non-Byzantine nodes use the same input information to produce the same result; if the input information is correct, then all non-Byzantine nodes must receive this information and calculate the corresponding result.

The assumptions commonly used by the Byzantine system include the following:

1.  The behavior of the Byzantine nodes can be arbitrary, and the Byzantine nodes can collude.
2.  Errors between nodes are irrelevant.
3.  Nodes are connected through an asynchronous network, and the messages in the network may be lost, out of order or delayed, but most protocols assume that the message can be delivered to the destination in a limited time.
4.  The message transmitted between the servers can be sniffed by the third party, but the third party cannot falsify the content of it or verify the integrity of it.

The original BFT system lacks practicality due to the need to demonstrate its theoretical feasibility. Also, additional clock synchronization mechanism is required, and the complexity of the algorithm increases exponentially as nodes increase.

Compared to the traditional BFT algorithm, PBFT reduces the time complexity from exponential to polynomial, which not only greatly improves efficiency but also makes it the first widely used Byzantine consensus algorithm. It can resist a certain number of Byzantine nodes in the system. In a PBFT-based blockchain system, the system that tolerates $f$ Byzantine fault nodes needs at least $3f + 1$ participating nodes and then reaches a consensus in polynomial time. From the practical perspective, PBFT is now the default consensus algorithm of a famous blockchain project, Hyperledger, hosted by the Linux Foundation.

The PBFT consensus divides nodes into two types: primary nodes, which are responsible for sorting the client's requests, and the rest are backup nodes, which execute the requests in the order provided by the primary node. The algorithm specifies three basic protocols: agreement, checkpoint, and view change. The agreement is to ensure that requests from clients are executed in a fixed order on each server. It contains five stages: a request, a pre-prepare, a prepare, a commit and a reply, as Figure 3.5 shows. Usually, a consensus process will be performed in the same view. However, when the primary node fails, the view-changing protocol replaces the primary node with the backup node in sequence and ensures that the request that has been executed by the normal node is not tampered with. During the consensus process, the node records the log at any time. If the log is not cleaned up in time, the system resources will be occupied by useless information, which will affect the overall performance. At the same time, the states of different nodes may be inconsistent because the asynchronous nature of the system cannot guarantee that each node performs the same request. Therefore, the checkpoint protocol is executed periodically to handle the log and correct node status.

The PBFT consensus process in the blockchain system is summarized as follows:

1. A primary node is first elected from the nodes of entire system and is responsible for generating the new block.
2. Each node broadcasts the new transaction to the entire system. Then the primary node sorts the transactions to be placed in the new block from the network into a list and broadcasts the list to the entire system.

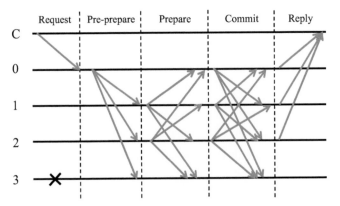

*Figure 3.5   Five stages in the process of PBFT consensus*

3.  After each node receives the transaction list, the transaction is executed simulatively according to the sequence. After all transactions are executed, a hash digest of the new block is calculated on the basis of the transaction results and broadcasted to the entire system.
4.  If a node receives $2f$ ($f$ is the number of malicious nodes that can be tolerated) digests from other nodes, and these digests are the same as themselves, it broadcasts a commit message to the entire system.
5.  If a node receives $2f + 1$ commit messages, it can formally submit a new block, as well as its locally transacted blockchain and state database.

The PBFT consensus is generally suitable for private blockchain and consortium blockchain scenarios where the source of nodes is relatively reliable. It has many advantages as follows:

* The operations of PBFT-based system can be separated from the existence of the currency. The consensus nodes are composed of the business participants or supervisors; hence, the security and stability are guaranteed by the business-related parties. But the PoW, PoS and DPoS system cannot be separated from the existence of currency. Their systems must have a reward mechanism for the currency, and the security of systems is actually guaranteed by the holders of the system currency. However, when a blockchain system is actually applied in commerce, the value of the assets carried by it may far exceed the value of the currency issued by it and it will be unreliable to let stakeholders guarantee the security and stability of it.
* The delay of the PBFT consensus protocol is about 2–5 s, which basically meets the requirements of commercial real-time processing scenarios.

As for the weaknesses, PBFT is a weakly synchronous protocol, so it relies critically on network timing assumptions and only guarantees liveness when the network behaves as expected.

To improve that Andrew Miller proposed the HoneyBadgerBFT [19], the first practical asynchronous BFT protocol that guarantees liveness without making any timing assumptions, in 2016. The core process of HoneyBadgerBFT consists of "atomic broadcast" and "asynchronous common subset." It uses $N$ binary consensus protocol instances and determines a common subset based on the instance results. For higher efficiency, HoneyBadgerBFT adopts two methods: (1) mitigate single-node bandwidth bottleneck by splitting transactions; (2) improve transaction throughput by selecting random trading blocks in batch transactions and matching threshold encryption. Experiments shows that compared with the traditional PBFT consensus, its efficiency is significantly increased.

### 3.1.6 Other consensus protocols

The four mentioned earlier are the common consensus protocols adopted by the current blockchain systems and all have actual implementations as support. However, the analysis shows that there are some potential flaws in these incipient consensus protocols. In recent years, many researchers have conducted in-depth research on the consensus problem and proposed some new algorithms. Among them, we introduce several representative algorithms with better performance, including the Ripple, Proof-of-Activity (PoA) [20], Algorand [21], Snow White [22], Casper and Ouroboros Genesis consensus [23].

### 3.1.6.1    Ripple

Ripple is an Internet-based open-source payment protocol that enables decentralized currency exchange, payment and clearing functions. In Ripple's network, transactions are initiated by the client (application) and broadcasted to the entire network via tracking nodes or validating nodes. The main function of the tracking node is to distribute transaction information and respond to the client's ledger request. The validating node can add new data to the ledger through the consensus protocol.

Ripple's consensus is achieved between the validating nodes. Each validating node is preconfigured with a list of trusted nodes called UNL (unique node list). The nodes on the list can vote on the transaction. Every few seconds, the Ripple network will perform the following consensus process:

1. Each validating node continuously receives the transactions sent from the network. After validating with the local ledger data, the illegal transactions will be directly discarded, and the legal transactions will be aggregated into a candidate set. The transaction candidate set also includes transactions left over from previous consensus processes that cannot be confirmed.
2. Each validating node sends its own transaction candidate set as a proposal to other validating nodes.
3. After the validating node receives the proposal sent by other nodes, if it is not from the node on the UNL, then the node ignores it; if it is from the node on the UNL, it will compare the transaction in the proposal with the local candidate set. If there exists a same transaction, the transaction will get a vote. In a certain period of time, the transaction will enter the next round when getting more than 50% of the votes. If not, it will be left to the next consensus process to validate.
4. The validating node sends the transaction with more than 50% of the votes as a proposal to other nodes and raises the threshold of the required number of votes to 60% then repeats steps 3 and 4 until the threshold reaches 80%.
5. The validating node officially writes the transaction confirmed by more than 80% UNL nodes into the local ledger, which is called the Last Closed Ledger, i.e., the last (latest) status of the ledger.

In Ripple's consensus algorithm, the identity of nodes participating in voting has been known in advance. Therefore, it is more efficient than many anonymous consensus algorithms such as PoW, with a few seconds to confirm the transaction. Of course, Ripple is only suitable for the permissioned chain. The BFT capability of it is $(n-1)/5$, which can tolerate the Byzantine faults of 20% nodes in the entire network without affecting the correct consensus.

### 3.1.6.2    Proof-of-activity

The PoA, proposed by Bentov *et al.*, combines the characteristics of PoW and PoS. PoW could lead to the centralization of computing power, while PoS/DPoS tends to form an oligarchy of stake due to the scale effect of stakes. The centralization of computing power or stakes poses a potential threat to the safety and stability of the blockchain systems.

The miners in the PoW system are pursuing the maximization of their own interests. For higher economic benefits, the security of the cryptocurrency network may be jeopardized, and the stakeholders are suitable to help one to accomplish this task. Based on this assumption, the basic idea of the PoA's ability to prevent excessive centralization of computing power and stakes is to allow participants in the transaction to participate more in the generation of blocks to counterbalance the dominant miners.

The specific method of PoA is as follows. The miner generates a new block header that satisfies the difficulty, and the header includes the hash value of its predecessor and the information of $N$ traders involved in the possible new block. After mining the block header, the miners broadcast the (possible) new block header. The relevant stakeholders and the participants of the $N$ transactions use their private keys to sign the transaction, and the last-signed trader packs the block into blocks then broadcasts it and participates in the competition of recording the ledger as traditional Bitcoin does. Through this process, miners and trading participants share the revenue of ledger. The signature of these $N$ participants is the PoA. The advantage is that the miners who dominate the computing power are not able to monopolize the ledger-recording ability without the cooperation of the traders (as it cannot be signed by their private key).

The PoA consensus combines the common features of PoW and PoS, which can avoid the centralization trend in the process of blockchain evolution (including the centralization of computing power and stakes). The biggest significance of the PoA consensus is to prevent non-interested attacks. The so-called non-interested person refers to an attacker who has strong computing power but only holds a few stakes. Even if the digital assets collapse, the loss of non-interested person is not too much. Therefore, non-interested person will use any means of attack without regarding the consequences. The PoS part of the PoA algorithm makes it very rare for non-interested person to build a block, so an effective attack cannot be performed. In the PoA algorithm, the lucky stakeholder relies on his capital to make a profit, which will encourage stakeholders to hold stakes for a long time and help preserve the value of digital assets and reduce fluctuations. The PoW part of the PoA consensus controls the speed of the new block header through the difficulty of the Hash algorithm and stabilizes the network to avoid the fork. However, the previous advantages are obtained at a price. The PoW part brings electricity consumption, and the PoS part causes the new block header to be discarded with a large probability, which also forms a waste of computing power.

### 3.1.6.3   Casper

Casper is a security-deposit-based PoS protocol prepared by Ethereum, the blockchain-based distributed computing platform and operating system, from 2014. To address the nothing-at-stake attack of PoS, Casper has implemented a process; in this way, they can pass away all malicious elements. This is how PoS works under Casper: the validators take some parts of their Ethers (also known as tokens issued by Ethereum) as stakes. After that they begin to validate the blocks, i.e., when they discover a block that can be regarded to be added to the chain, they will validate it by placing a bet on it. If the block is appended, then the validators will get a reward proportional to their stakes. However, if a validator performs maliciously and tries to perform a "nothing at stake," he will immediately be dressed down, and all of his stakes will be slashed.

Casper is specially designed to run in a trustless setting and also can be more Byzantine Fault Tolerant. Anyone who performs maliciously will be immediately punished with his stakes being slashed off. This is the most unique feature it differs from other PoS protocols. Moreover, Casper has more critical incentives to ensure network security, including punishing miners who perform offline, involuntarily or not. This indicates that validators have to be careful about node uptime. Carelessness or laziness will result in the loss of their stakes. This property alleviates censorship of transactions and the entire availability.

Apart from that a validator's signature is only economically meaningful if the validator currently has a deposit. Therefore, when clients receive and authenticate the state of the consensus, their authentication chain stops in the list of currently bonded validators. In PoW consensus, on the other hand, the authentication chain ends in the genesis block, and it means that if you know the genesis block, you can authenticate the consensus. A client who has no idea about the list of currently bonded validators must authenticate this list out-of-band. This restriction solves the long-range-attack problem by requiring that everyone authenticates the consensus against current information.

### 3.1.6.4    Snow White

Snow White is a PoS derivative consensus protocol adopting the ideas of a simpler protocol dubbed Sleepy [24]. Sleepy aims to achieve the guarantees on chain growth and chain quality, as well as consistency with 51% of honest nodes online. It is designed for deployment in a permissive context and relies on the assumption on the stake assigned by some trusted sources, which makes Sleepy very desirable for blockchains where the set of stakeholders is known in advance. The challenges of choosing a suitable mining function and source of entropy are addressed in the work, and proof is given that no committee member can manipulate the protocol to get profit.

Regarding to Snow White, it is an extension of Sleepy and is designed to provide similar blockchain-derived guarantees in a permissionless setting. The problem, however, is much more difficult: it is nontrivial to choose suitable committee members for the block lottery, and ensure no coalition of the committee members to get profit. The solving protocol is simple: in each step, a committee mines as in Sleepy, with a shared source of entropy $h_0$. With enough bits of entropy in $h_0$ and an appropriately selected committee weighted on stake, it is possible to prove the desired result of chain quality, growth and consistency. Choosing both the committee and $h_0$ such that no adversary gain substantial advantage by deviating from the protocol is the key to the construction and concrete parameters of the protocol.

### 3.1.6.5 Algorand

The Algorand consensus, found by the 2012 ACM Turing Award winner Silvio Micali, is a new consensus based on PoS and cryptology. The name "Algorand" is synthesized by two words: algorithm and random, meaning that it is a public ledger protocol based on a random algorithm. According to its analysis, Algorand has the characteristics of short agreement time, strong anti-attack ability, low computing power and better economy.

Algorand employs a similar concept of "Write-Ahead Logging" in the traditional database. In Algorand, the consensus toward a new block is reached through a Byzantine agreement called BA*. Generally speaking, the execution of BA* consists of two phases: (1) synchronously determine the highest priority block; (2) reach consensus on two options: either to agree on a proposed block or to agree on an empty block. Each phase has several steps. The process for the first phase is shown in Figure 3.6. Algorand can reach consensus within roughly 1 min.

Algorand divides the participants into two roles: leaders and verifiers. Both roles are uncertain and based on the previous block. That is, before each block is generated, a batch of potential leaders are generated first. These leaders know and can prove to the entire system that they are the producers of a candidate block. Each potential leader generates a candidate block and attaches its one-time signature and signature public key to the entire system for verification. At last, the verifiers vote for the determination of whether the block generated by the leader will be adopted or not. Once the verifiers have reached a consensus on a new block, more than half of the verifiers will sign the block with their own private key, and the block will be broadcasted in the Algorand network.

To ensure the unpredictability of potential leaders and verifiers, Algorand modifies the structure of the traditional block by adding a field called "block

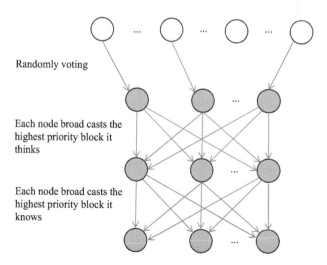

*Figure 3.6    The first phase of BA\**

quality." The field is also a hash value that equals to the block quality of the previous block plus the one-time signature of the current block leader and a sequence number of the block in current round (when a new block is empty, it is the common hash value of the block quality of the previous block and the height of the current empty block). Since the field can only be determined after the previous block is authenticated by the legal verifiers' votes and the formation of the block header, there is little time left for the attacker to control the candidate leader. Even if the attacker controls the leader in advance, since the block has been distributed to the entire system, and all verifiers have also verified the validity of the block, the attacker cannot modify the existing transaction. In addition, Algorand determines the generation of the block by not only considering "one-person-one-vote" but also the generation of blocks based on stakes.

Micali has made a detailed theoretical analysis for Algorand in the agreement time, the probabilities of block forks and the tolerance of system partitions. The problem of Algorand is that the algorithm is relatively complex to implement. However, recently a new blockchain system called ArcBlock startups to adopt Algorand in production. ArcBlock uses Algorand and its variant to pick where the smart contract will execute from, as well as for the high-performance blockchain that powers its native tokens.

### 3.1.6.6    Ouroboros Genesis

Ouroboros Genesis is a PoS-based consensus protocol that provides security against fully adaptive corruption in the semi-synchronous setting for the first time. It is the third and the latest version of Ouroboros consensus, the first provable secure and robust PoS algorithm proposed by academia and adopted by industry in 2017. Compared with the former versions, the biggest improvement of Ouroboros Genesis is to solve the problem of long-range attack aroused by the ordinary PoS consensus.

Before introducing this new consensus, let us review the situation of long-range attack. A new party is trying to find "what is the right history" but does not have any information about the protocol. There are honest parties providing one blockchain and an "adversary" providing another. The only information the new party has is the genesis block and it is faced with this decision of choosing the correct blockchain. In the PoW world, what can be proved is that the main chain (maintained by honest parties) is going to have the most blocks, meaning the adversary chain will be substantially shorter and this will enable the new party to connect to the correct blockchain. This is a powerful idea but relies on the assumption that the majority is made up by honest parties who follow the protocol, not adversaries.

However, what Ouroboros has done is to show that the problem of an adversary reusing an opportunity to issue a block in multiple paths of a fork can be overcome. There are three important quantities when studying the execution of it. Every path in the execution will have these three quantities:

*Gap:* the difference in length between a certain path in the execution and the leading path.

*Reserve:* the number of adversarial indices appearing after the label of the last honest vertex of the path.

*Reach:* subtract gap from reserve to see what the reach of that path is.

Then look at whole execution. There are other two concepts:

*Max reach:* maximum reach across all times.

*Margin:* what is the second best disjoint reach.

The margin needs to always be below zero. That would be a setting that the adversary will not be able to fool an honest party that tries to connect in this protocol execution. So the max reach and margin are the two fundamental quantities that are interesting when analyzing protocol executions. The researcher team can show that the adversary will win if and only if the margin is at least 0. What is interesting now is that these two quantities together define a random walk. Even though it is more complex than the random walk analyzed in Bitcoin, it still has good features that can be used to prove security.

Then going back to the long-range attack question, when you are dealing with two chains, which have forked at certain point, and you need to choose the correct blockchain. If the fork is somewhat recent, either by short-range attack or a disagreement between nodes that was produced naturally because of network conditions, then the longest chain rule will apply. But if the fork is bigger than $k$ blocks, then the following plenitude rule will apply, i.e., if the majority of parties follow the protocol, then at any sufficiently long time segment, the corresponding chain will be more dense (especially after a fork). They are able to prove that adversarial blockchains shortly after the divergence point will exhibit a less dense block distribution. This rule determines what is the right blockchain to connect to. Go to the moment chain diverges, and shortly after, isolate a certain region of blocks. Within the certain time range, look at which of the two chains is more dense. The party is going to follow the chain that is more dense within that time range. This rule is still quite simple to implement, meaning it is quite easy to program and it works to enhance the longest chain rule.

## 3.2 Consensus comparison

Through the aforementioned introduction to blockchain consensus protocols, we can find that different consensus protocols have their own advantages and disadvantages. In view of the different characteristics of the consensus mechanism, it can be evaluated from the following aspects:

- Security. Whether it is able to prevent double spend attack, selfish mining attack or tolerate other failures.
- Scalability. The ability to support the expansion of network nodes. Scalability is one of the key factors to be considered in the design of a blockchain. It is roughly composed of two parts: to increase the numbers of system nodes and verification confirmations, and to increase the communication load and operation load, which is generally measured by throughput.

- Performance. The delay from the creation of a transaction to the final record in the node storage system. In other words, it is the number of responses per second that the system can handle. For example, the Bitcoin system has up to seven transactions per second, which is far from the performance of the existing centralized trading system.
- Energy. It means that the energy consumed by each node for reaching the consistency of the transaction under the guidance of the consensus, including CPU, memory and battery.

There is a brief comparison about the characteristics of these consensus protocols, including the total number of nodes, permission restriction, scalability, energy consumption, delay, throughput and their typical representations, as shown in Table 3.2.

Since PBFT requires permission, there is no limit to the number of nodes except PBFT consensus on the participating nodes. Also, PBFT's scalability is relatively low comparing to other consensus protocols. In terms of energy consumption, due to the need for complex hash computing, PoW thus has the largest energy consumption and the energy consumptions of other consensus protocols are relatively lower. Due to the intervals of blocks and the need for multiple confirmations, the throughput of PoW consensus is far less than other consensus protocols.

Each consensus has its own shortcomings. As for the systems based on PoW, the more incentives the nodes with stronger computing power gain, the more centralized the computing power tends to be. PoS and DPoS systems also have similar

*Table 3.2  Blockchain consensus comparisons*

| Consensus | PoW | PoS | DPoS | PoA | Ripple |
|---|---|---|---|---|---|
| Number of nodes | Unlimited | Unlimited | Unlimited | Unlimited | Limited |
| Permission | No | No | No | No | Yes |
| Scalability | High | High | High | High | High |
| Energy consumption | High | Low | Low | Low | Low |
| Delay | High | Low | Low | High | Low |
| Throughput | Low | Low | High | Low | High |
| Example | Bitcoin | PPCoin | BitShares | Decred | Ripple |

| Consensus | Casper | Snow White | Algorand | Ouroboros Genesis | PBFT |
|---|---|---|---|---|---|
| Number of nodes | Unlimited | Unlimited | Unlimited | Unlimited | Limited |
| Permission | No | No | No | No | Yes |
| Scalability | High | High | High | High | Low |
| Energy consumption | Low | Low | Low | Low | Low |
| Delay | Low | Low | Low | Low | Low |
| Throughput | High | High | High | High | High |
| Example | Ethereum | None | ArcBlock | Cardano | Hyperledger |

problems with the centralization of stakes. New consensus protocols like Algorand can theoretically avoid the earlier situations, but taking time to verify the practical effects of them. Although the blockchain system based on PBFT does not have the problems of computing power and stake centralization, its scalability is limited and the delay and throughput will decrease significantly as the number of nodes increases.

## 3.3   Incentives and consensus

The use of the incentive mechanism is mainly to reward participants of the blockchain systems to promote more distributed nodes to participate in system calculations. Due to the need of permission in the consortium Blockchain and the private Blockchain, the participants record their own data with purpose based on their own specific applications. During this, there is endogenous positivity, so the blockchain system does not need to provide additional incentive mechanism. Hence, the incentive mechanism is mainly aimed at blockchain-based crypto-currency systems. Incentives include issuance and distribution mechanisms.

In Bitcoin, the system generates a block approximately every 10 min and the value of each block is determined by the block number. The producers in the first 210,000 blocks can earn 50 Bitcoins, and then for every 210,000 blocks generated later in the blockchain, the producer's income of each block is halved on this basis. The total number of Bitcoins is 21 million, which will be completely released in the next 100 years in the form of an exponential half-decrement. All participants compete openly and fairly to obtain these Bitcoins with their own computing power. As for now, the player can earn 12.5 Bitcoins for each block generated. In addition to gaining revenue through generating blocks, participants also receive Bitcoin as a transaction fee from a certain proportion of transactions based on the transaction volume and the number of bytes generated by the transaction. After all Bitcoins are issued, participants will earn revenue mainly from these transaction fees. From the perspective of incentives, the issuance mechanism of various alt-coins is similar to that of Bitcoin, except that the total issuing amount of currency, the rate of currency generation and transaction fees are slightly different.

Such incentive mechanism contributed to the emergence of "Mining Rig" and "Mining Pool." In the aforementioned PoW mechanism (as well as PoS and DPoS), the process of finding the lucky number *Nonce* that meets the required block is called mining. The node that implements the mining work is called a miner. In order to ensure the issuance mechanism of the cryptocurrency and prevent the block from being generated too fast due to the continuous increase of system capability, the cryptocurrency systems adopt dynamic difficulty adjustment mechanisms, i.e., the difficulty is increased or decreased according to the rate of block generation at intervals to ensure a smooth block-generating rate. *Nonce* is currently only able to be solved violently, and with the increasing quantity of participating nodes and computing power, mining is becoming more and more difficult.

Participants use mining rigs to increase profits. Due to the fact that mining rigs mostly use custom chips, they are optimized for hash algorithms and their hash calculation speed is several orders of magnitude higher than that of general-purpose computers. In addition, for most miners, their computing power is very limited, if they compete independently, they will work for a long time. However, the mining can be carried out in parallel, so more and more miners decide to mine together to form a mining pool, and the mining pools share the revenue according to their respective computing power. These pools can simultaneously mine one or more kinds of cryptocurrency systems. Miners, mining pools and their corresponding distribution mechanisms are all generated under the incentive mechanism of blockchain cryptocurrencies. They are not part of the blockchain incentives, but a division model of labor developed spontaneously under the blockchain crypto-currency ecosystem.

In fact, the consensus algorithm and the incentive mechanism of blockchain are tightly connected and indivisible. The consensus algorithm stipulates the behavior norm and sequence of actions that miners must obey in order to maintain the security, consistency and activity of the blockchain ledger; the incentive mechanism stipulates the economic rights and interests issued in the process of consensus to encourage the miners to verify the blockchain data faithfully and efficiently. From the research point of view, if the operation of blockchain system is modeled as a large-group game process of miners and mining pools, then the consensus algorithm will decide the structure and shape of the game tree, and the incentive mechanism will determine their profit of each leaf node in the game tree. Toward the end, not only the consensus and incentive mechanism have the necessity of independent optimization, but it is more important to optimize the consensus–incentive mechanism jointly to realize the "adaptation" of them, which is also the key issue to restrain the emerging block-withholding attack, selfish mining and other strategic behaviors and ensure the healthy and stable operation of blockchain system. More research work is urgently needed to follow up in the future.

## 3.4    Conclusions and future directions

In recent years, as the blockchain technology has received extensive attention, consensus algorithms have been studied by more and more people. As an important part of the blockchain, the consensus algorithm embodies the performance and functionality of the blockchain system. At present, new consensus mechanisms emerge one after another, presenting the following trends:

*Hybridization of proof methods.* The threat of PoW comes from miners with high computing power, and the security risks of PoS are active major stakeholders. Researchers suggest to combine PoW with PoS, so if someone wants to launch 51% attack, the malicious node needs to master most of the computing power and most of the stakes, which becomes a more difficult condition to achieve. If someone does this, the entire blockchain system will be destroyed due to excessive centralization.

*Diversification of proof methods.* Early PoW and PoS mechanisms have the problems of waste of resources and low initiative of nodes. Researchers have developed Proof-of-Time [25], Proof-of-Store, Proof-of-Existence [26], Proof-of-Contribution, Proof-of-Authority, Proof-of-Flow, Proof-of-Taste, Proof-of-Concept [27], Proof-of-Elapsed Time, Proof-of-Luck, Proof-of-DDoS [28], Proof-of-Burn and other mechanisms for the purpose of reducing the cost of mining competition or improving resource utilization and application scenarios. The new proof methods will continue to emerge. However, when designing consensus algorithms, the key point to consider is to make the mining power sufficiently dispersed, to increase the difficulty of attackers to master most of the competitiveness, and to reduce the possibility of individual nodes or organizations rewriting the blockchain. In this way, we can effectively prevent the double spend attack and ensure the security of the system.

*Increasing needs of centralization consensus.* In public chains, anyone can join and maintain a node and enjoy all the data fairly. But when it comes to internal information of a company or organization, a consortium chain or a private chain is definitely a better choice. Since the nodes in these two chains are provided by consortium members or the enterprise, the credibility is guaranteed. Therefore, when designing the consensus algorithm, the process of intermediate election, verification or the competition of mining power can be eliminated. These algorithms have a certain degree of centralization. If they are used in the public chain, they will be questioned because of their unfairness. However, in the consortium chain that does not require thorough decentralization, such algorithms generally exhibit better performance than public chain algorithms due to the simplified consensus process. As the demand for the consortium or private chains increases, the centralized consensus algorithm will receive more attention and development.

*Designing reasonable incentives.* In the blockchain, incentives are often introduced to deal with technical problems. For example, the IPFS [29] technology for solving the blockchain storage problems is also a combination of incentive mechanisms to encourage users to assist in storing data fragments before they can form a complete project Filecoin. Therefore, if we combine the specific processes of consensus and design more reasonable incentive measures, we will achieve twice the result with half the effort in actual operation and will also have a positive effect on the safety and continuity of the system. In addition, researchers have been arguing whether there is a need for internal tokens in the consortium chain. Some researchers argue that it is necessary to add coins to implement reward and punishment functions in some consortium chains with incomplete trust. Through the continuous exploration of more researchers, we believe that there will be more solutions suitable for the consortium chain incentives in the future.

# References

[1]   Schneider FB. Implementing fault-tolerant services using the state machine approach: a tutorial. ACM Computing Surveys. 1990;22(4):299–319.

[2]   Wan S, Li M, Liu G, *et al.* Recent advances in consensus protocols for blockchain: a survey. Wireless Networks. To appear doi: 101007/s11276-019-02195-0.

[3]   Tanenbaum AS and Steen MV. Distributed Systems: Principles and Paradigms. Tsinghua University Press; 2002.

[4]   Lamport L, Shostak R, and Pease M. The Byzantine Generals Problem; 1982.

[5]   Dwork C and Naor M. Pricing via processing or combatting junk mail. In: Proc. of International Cryptology Conference on Advances in Cryptology; 1993. p. 139–147.

[6]   Back A. Hashcash – a denial of service counter-measure. In: Proc. of USENIX Annual Technical Conference; 2002.

[7]   Nakamoto S. Bitcoin: A Peer-to-Peer Electronic Cash System. Available: https://bitcoinorg/bitcoinpdf. 2008.

[8]   Laszka A, Johnson B, and Grossklags J. When bitcoin mining pools run dry. In: Proc. of International Conference on Financial Cryptography and Data Security; 2015. p. 63–77.

[9]   de Vries A. Bitcoin's growing energy problem. Joule. 2018;2(5): 801–805. Available from: http://www.sciencedirect.com/science/article/pii/S2542435118301776.

[10]  Tromp J. Cuckoo cycle: a memory bound graph-theoretic proof-of-work. In: Proc. of International Conference on Financial Cryptography and Data Security; 2015. p. 49–62.

[11]  King S and Nadal S. PPCoin: Peer-to-Peer Crypto-Currency with Proof-of-Stake; 2012.

[12]  Houy N. It will cost you nothing to 'kill' a proof-of-stake crypto-currency. Social Science Electronic Publishing. 2014;34(2).

[13]  Group B. Proof of Stake versus Proof of Work White Paper. Available: http://bitfurycom/content/5-white-papers-research/posvs-pow-102pdf. 2015.

[14]  Lampson BW. How to build a highly available system using consensus. In: Proc. of International Workshop on Distributed Algorithms; 1996. p. 1–17.

[15]  Wood G. Ethereum: A Secure Decentralised Generalised Transaction Ledger; 2014.

[16]  Blog TB. Thoughts on Delegated Proof of Stake and BitShares. Available: http://www8btccom/thoughts-ondelegated-proof-of-stake-and-bitshares. 2014.

[17]  Larimer DSF and Kasper L. BitShares 2.0: Financial Smart Contract Platform; 2015.

[18]  Fan J, Yi LT, and Shu JW. Research on the technologies of Byzantine system. Journal of Software. 2013;24(6):1346–1360.

[19]  Miller A, Xia Y, Croman K, *et al.* The Honey Badger of BFT Protocols. Available: https://eprint.iacr.org/2016/199. Cryptology ePrint Archive, Report 2016/199. 2016.

[20]  Bentov I, Lee C, Mizrahi A, *et al.* Proof of activity. ACM SIGMETRICS Performance Evaluation Review. 2014;42(3):34–37.

[21]   Micali S. ALGORAND: The Efficient and Democratic Ledger; 2016.

[22]   Daian P, Pass R, and Shi E. Snow White: Provably Secure Proofs of Stake. Available: https://eprint.iacr.org/2016/919. Cryptology ePrint Archive, Report 2016/919. 2016.

[23]   Badertscher C, Gazi P, Kiayias A, *et al.* Ouroboros Genesis: Composable Proof-of-Stake Blockchains With Dynamic Availability. IACR Cryptology ePrint Archive. 2018;2018:378.

[24]   Pass R and Shi E. The Sleepy Model of Consensus. Available: https://eprint. iacr.org/2016/918. Cryptology ePrint Archive, Report 2016/918. 2016.

[25]   CHRONOLOGIC. Chrono Logic Whitepaper. Available: https://chron-ologicnetwork/uploads/ChronologicWhitepaperpdf. 2017.

[26]   Crosby M and Kalyanaraman V. Blockchain technology: Beyond bitcoin. Applied Innovation Review. 2016;2(6-10):71.

[27]   Kim HM and Laskowski M. Towards an ontology-driven blockchain design for supply chain provenance. In: Proc. of Workshop on Information Technology and Systems; 2016.

[28]   Wustrow E and Vandersloot B. DDoSCoin: cryptocurrency with a malicious proof-of-work. In: Proc. of USENIX Conference on Offensive Technologies; 2016. p. 168–177.

[29]   Benet J. IPFS – Content Addressed, Versioned, P2P File System. Eprint Arxiv. 2014.

*Chapter 4*

# Blockchain applications, projects and implementations

*Haojun Huang[1], Geyong Min[2], Wang Miao[2] and Haozhe Wang[2]*

In this chapter, we first present potential blockchain applications in the world and then summarize the ongoing blockchain projects and its implementations, along with comprehensive compares among them.

## 4.1  Blockchain applications

Blockchain has been being used in a variety of network interaction systems, including finical sector, smart contracts, public services, IoT, social networks, reputation systems and security services [1–7]. Generally, these applications can be fell under five categories illustrated in Figure 4.1. The first and second categories are digital currency as well as financial and business services, enabling the user to have more approaches to manage and control their wealth. Examples include financial derivatives, digital wallets, peer-to-peer (P2P) lending, mobile payment and wills. The third category is record-keeping application, which provides the services of decentralized data storage and attestation services; a perfect example is blockchain that can safely store all types of licenses, registration forms, certifications and records, proving their existence and authenticity anytime. The fourth category is blockchain network security service. Finally, there are blockchain government applications, including online voting and decentralized governance, and reputation systems. All these multifold applications are built-in two or more features of blockchain to work. The details of such five categories of blockchain applications are described in the following sections.

### 4.1.1  Original intention: digital currencies

The original purpose of blockchain is designed for digital currency from January 2009 with the emerging of blockchain. A blockchain-based digital currency like

[1]Department of Information Engineering, Huazhong University of Science and Technology, Wuhan, China
[2]Department of Computer Science, University of Exeter, Exeter, UK

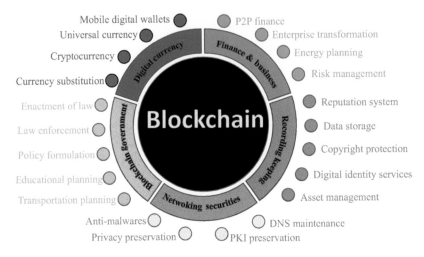

*Figure 4.1    The representative applications of blockchain*

Bitcoin is a kind of currency, which is created, managed, controlled and transferred in the digital world. Compared to the physical currency, digital currency exhibits similar properties but owns unique features for wealth management, e.g., fast and low-cost transactions and high security of ownership guarantee.

Blockchain as the underpins of finance has been considered as the most important form for digital financial system on the Internet. The first blockchain-based digital currency is Bitcoin. Like traditional money, Bitcoin and its imitators can be used as money to purchase the items in the physical world. However, due to the lack of the financial regulation, Bitcoin has not been fully accepted by the physical business and is mainly used in the transactions on Internet, e.g., social networks, online donations and online gaming. As an alternative currency for the traditional currencies, Bitcoin improves the health of the financial system developments. For example, since the birth of the blockchain technologies, the transmission fee of the credit card payment has been reduced from 3% to 1%, which is a good phenomenon for economic development. In addition, compared to the traditional financial system, the money could be received nearly real time without any checking or approving of the third-party institute.

Bitcoin and other blockchain-based currencies have revolutionized the ways that the financial system, the trade and the commerce are running. Indeed, Bitcoin is not just an upgrade service of digital currencies; the underlying technologies, e.g., intelligent contracts and distributed storage and verifications, enable us to do more things that are difficult for the traditional financial system. Actually, being the payment medium is the main application for the blockchain technologies. In blockchain systems, the transaction happens between two parties on the Internet in a decentralized and distributed way and does not involve any third party. In addition, the transactions in blockchain system are encrypted to avoid the tamper, therefore, different from the existing currencies, blockchain-based cryptocurrencies are developed based on a programmable open network, where the transactions are transparent to each node on the Internet. Targeting to become a fully programmable open network, Blockchain 1.0 of cryptocurrency has been evolved into Blockchain 2.0 to embrace more robust functions.

## 4.1.2   Function evolution: financial and business services

Blockchain already brings a significant evolution for financial market and business applications beyond currency, with the emerging smart contracts. It can help traditional organizations build decentralized systems with the higher security, reliability and efficiency. The reputation mechanism generated in this system will facilitate the evolution of the business models and enterprises that highly rely upon the third-party payment and funds trusteeships. It has been employed in the business model equity-based crowdfunding, P2P lending and Internet insurance in Internet finance and also plays an important role in bank and securities service. In traditional securities trading, settlement organizations, banks, securities company and exchanges require to work together. However, due to the characteristics of programmable and automated contracts, blockchain brings the benefits of the cost reduction and the higher transmission efficiency. It avoids the tedious settlement procedures in exchanges.

There have emerged a number of blockchain-based business applications over the past few years, mainly in the form of finance. Blockchain-based systems like Ethereum support the "real-time" mode in transactions. This instant arrive, fast and accurate transaction mode makes the bank service (including cross-border transfer) faster and safer than conventional Smart Worldwide Financial Technology (SWFT) mode. Currently, R3CEV [8] and banks, securities and financial organizations shift their focuses on the blockchain technologies. Three examples of these applications include blockchain marriage, blockchain SolarCoin and Clean Water Coin (CWC).

Blockchain marriage is one of the important attempts based on open repositories, which can promote the marriages to be more transparent, free and fair. Bigamy and cheating in marriages would not be problems with the open file support. With this smart contract mode, the elderly caring, house buying, bear children's situation and other living things will be convenient and improved.

Blockchain SolarCoin is another important business application of blockchain to fulfill the requirements of green energy. Even though the new energy was encouraged to be exploited for many years, there is still a long way to go. Blockchain will accelerate this step. Blockchain SolarCoin is the currency, which has been used in solar energy generation. It was reported that the 98.5 billion SolarCoins have been mined and used as incentives to reward the activities of solar energy generation.

The recent important business application of blockchain is to relieve the water crisis [9]. It was reported that there are around 1 billion people living without clean water even fell ill or died for unsafe water in the world. Water safety and sanitation have been a long-term world problem, especially in the undeveloped area. Blockchain has become a promising solution to this issue. The first initiative of CWC was designed and launched in 2015 for the clean water project. In CWC system, the miners are participating in the water blockchain development and management and will donate 1% of CWC to support clean water system.

### 4.1.3    Digital art: record-keeping services

Record-keeping service is one important application of blockchain, in which all blockchain data stored at each node via cryptography and hashing can provide a paradigm-shifting improvement. Digital art means the intellectual property (IP) in the blockchain. Art relates to the patent that defines a party owns a specific IP. Digital art is used in the process of the digital asset protection and validation. Another concept in digital art is the identity. In blockchain system, a digital identity is linked to a specific user who has a unique wallet address. For realizing the digital asset attestation, blockchain technologies of hashing algorithms and timestamping are used to prevent the malicious modifications or attacks. For record-keeping services, the functions of distributed data storage and blockchain attestation are classified as digital art. Currently, digital art in blockchain system is mainly used to realize the functions of registering IP and providing services of the data storage and attestation.

The characteristics of redundant data backup, decentralization, immutability, high security and privacy protection make blockchain especially appropriate for important network data storage and management, avoiding large-scale data loss or leakage caused by attacks or improper authorization. For example, blockchains can safely store all types of licenses, registration forms, certificates, certifications and records and easily prove their existence and authenticity anytime. A number of audit firms like Deloitte have exploited blockchain to conduct audits in low-cost and efficient real-time manners, while Factom has designed an accurate set verifiable and irrevocable audit notarization processes and methods [10] based on the blockchain. Similar to Bitcoin, arbitrary blockchain data can be abstracted from hash/Merkle tree and stored in the blockchain. In addition, multi-signature in blockchain can flexibly configure network permission of data access, for example, it requires the private key authorization of three out of five persons to permit access rights. Thus, network security can be guaranteed built on the consensus among nodes and asymmetric encryption.

With the development of the cloud computing, various online file sharing and storage services, e.g., Google Drive, Dropbox and Microsoft 365, have appeared to enable users to free their local storage and update and access the files to/from the remote cloud. The storage companies provide small amount of storage space and sell the extra spaces to the users in the terms of a monthly subscription fee. However, the management and operation of the file storage system are not very efficient. As the monthly cost is paid in advance, users always pay more than the cost that they need. For example, a user makes the payment for 200 GB storage, but he actually uses only a small part of 200 GB. The blockchain system is built based on a decentralized storage system, where each user owns a small amount of storage space. This mechanism could be used to create a distributed sharing and storage service with the higher resource utilization and much lower cost. The individual could rent out their local storage to other people to make earning. The files could be encrypted and cannot be accessed except the user who stored them. For file storage, blockchain has been used a secure system to store the personal health information among different hospitals and various forms of files, e.g., documents, multimedia and daily data.

There are two examples of digital identity services in blockchain systems: OneName and BitID. The main objective of these two services is to validate the identity of the users accessing a certain website. The mechanism of the identity service is to leverage the wallet address to confirm the identity of the visitor. This could accelerate the validation process for the website visitors, enhancing the user experiences received, improve the security of the website resources and protect the anonymity of the website visitors. In addition, this process could also promote the commercial activities as the website users leveraging their wallet address to login and could also use cryptocurrency to make the payment on the website.

Blockchain has a broad application in asset management, which can provide the real-time control of tangible and intangible assets. By exploiting the features of blockchain technology, e.g., non-tampering, it could achieve the higher security and reliability in the management of intangible assets, such as IP protection and web domain management. Furthermore, it can design unique identification to form digital intelligent assets, such that the distributed asset authorization and control can be achieved. For example, we can realize flexible supply chain management and product traceability combined with the asset marking and identification technology of IoT.

Another important application of blockchain is copyright protection. The holders of copyright write their works into blockchain and private key will help to generate the digital signature. The public key could be used to verify the correctiveness of the digital signature. Once the verification is successful, it means the work indeed belongs to the holder for the only private key can generate the signature. In addition, it is possible to use the hash code algorithm SHA256 to calculate the digital fingerprint of the work and verify the copyright status through digital fingerprint comparison. Besides, it can cover all kinds of complex verification situations by means of content based on technologies such as distributed retrieval.

## 4.1.4  Security solution: network security

Blockchain has become a promising solution for network security due to its characteristics of traceability, immutability and forgery prevention. It realizes reliable information transmission over unreliable networks. To some extent, blockchain has filled our gaps in security and reliability [11], and we have to default encryption in 2018.

Specifically, it can ensure the network security of edge equipment through blockchain authentication [11,12]; it realizes data sharing without privacy leakage via data encryption authorization on the database ChainSQL; it provides multiple data centers service through blockchain multi-active disaster tolerance database among all participants [13] and it guarantees that the operation records cannot be tampered and avoids potential network attacks caused by vulnerabilities.

Nowadays, blockchain has been used to improve network security in finance, healthcare, Internet and other major companies. The followings, but not limited to, are some typical applications of blockchain with the purpose of emphasis on network security:

- Private information protection: Engineers of the Defense Advanced Research Projects Agency are trying to create a secure and noninvasive blockchain-based messaging service. By applying the blockchain in secure communications, this kind of message service will be available in the near future.
- Upgrade or even replace public key infrastructure (PKI): PKI is a public key cryptography that protects email, message applications, websites and other communications. However, most implementations rely on centralized third-party certification authority to issue, revoke or store key pairs, which may compromise encrypted communication and deceive identities. Publishing keys on blockchain can eliminate the propagation risks of wrong keys.
- Safe domain name system (DNS): DNS is the most important infrastructure in the network, which has been centrally deployed in the world. Once it was attacked, the networks cannot fully work well. Within blockchain-based DNS like Namecoin, the domain name resolution services will be distributively provided in a crowdsourcing manner. The operations on DNS increase, deletion and modification will be reached consensus among all nodes in blockchain. Therefore, DNS can be much safer with blockchain.
- Infrastructure confidence: The emerging projects like Nebulis exploit blockchain platforms, e.g., InterPlanetary File System and Ethereum to provide the registration and parsing services. Key services provide an opportunity for large-scale outages; therefore, blockchain will help the Internet to trust infrastructures.
- Fight against distributed denial of service (DDoS) attacks: Gladius, blockchain start-up, claims that its distributed ledger system can prevent DDoS attacks by "allowing you to connect the protection pool around you for better protection." In it, the dispersed network allows the user making extra bandwidth out on loan, which "is assigned to the node and be shunted to sites under DDoS attacks to ensure that they are at a minimum level." In addition, blockchain can improve the security of IoT devices from data integrity and secure digital identity authentication to prevent DDoS attacks. There is a "CIA three principles: Confidentiality, Integrity and Availability" role for blockchain to improve its resilience, encryption, auditing and transparency.

However, blockchain is not omnipotent for network security. It requires to work together with the other solutions such as firewalls and antivirus software to fight against a variety of network attacks. Essentially, it provides security services from data itself, while the other solutions provide the three-party software to protect data.

## 4.1.5  Blockchain government

Blockchain government, as a part of Blockchain 3.0, is one emerging application in the near future. The idea is to provide government services with the higher efficiency and security and much lower costs, which would remain at least as good as that of traditionally government implementations. A large number of new and different kinds of governance models and services would be built on blockchain. Blockchain governance utilizes the characteristics of record-keeping service of blockchain. Blockchain-based record keeping provides various merits to improve the efficiency and security of governance, e.g., timestamping and high reliability. For the governance, blockchain provides a permanent, non-tampering, reliable and record-keeping repository. This repository could be used to store the files of the society information, criminal records, credits and so on. Due to its high availability, blockchain-based repository could be built as a universal record-keeping system for the society government.

## 4.2  Blockchain projects and implementations

In order to demonstrate the possibility to implement the ideas of blockchain and to determine performance characteristics, a large number of organizations and companies have started to test the performance of the blockchain in various application scenarios, such as bank transfer, land title registration and product origin tracking. The blockchain was originally used in the areas of bank and financial sectors and increasingly entered into other sectors, e.g., logistics, trade, e-commerce, electricity sourcing and pricing, sports betting, IoT, farm-to-table production and government sectors [3,14]. Up to now, the number of the financial companies and institutes that integrated their products with blockchain has reached more than 40. Blockchain helps these companies to save the transmission cost, avoid the potential frauds and improve the business efficiency by getting rid of the constraints of the third parties.

All existing executions originate from the research community and industry. There have emerged a number of blockchain projects and platforms implemented in the world, including Bitcoin, Litecoin [15], Ethereum, Hyperledger Fabric/ Sawtooth, Corda, Ripple [16], BigchainDB [17], Quantstamp [18], Stratis [19], Wanchain [20], Nebulas, Zilliqa [21], Colored Coins [22], Decentralized Accessible Content Chain (DACC), Open Assets [23], Counterparty [24], NXT [25], Open Transactions [26], BitShares, Metaverse [2], Cardano, ArcBlock [27] and EOS [28]. These ongoing and upcoming projects and platforms can be felt under Blockchain 1.0, 2.0 and 3.0, respectively, as illustrated in Table 4.1. The intent of Table 4.1 is to give an understanding of the mainstream projects of blockchain and summarize their objectives and goals. In this section, we introduce these implementations and products from industry.

## 4.2.1  Bitcoin

Bitcoin is the first global blockchain-based distributed platform that was designed to work in P2P networks. The white paper of Bitcoin was published by a person

*Table 4.1  Ongoing blockchain projects in the world*

| Blockchain | Projects | Focus | Goals |
|---|---|---|---|
| Blockchain 1.0 | Bitcoin https://bitcoin.org/ | Cryptocurrency, digital cash | Building decentralized digital currency |
| | Litecoin https://litecoin.org/ | Internet currency | Enabling instant, near-zero cost payments |
| Blockchain 2.0 | Ethereum http://ethereum.org/ | General-purpose Turing-complete cryptocurrency platform | Own blockchain, Ethereum virtual machine |
| | Corda http://www.corda.net/ | Financial agreements between regulated financial institutions | Offering at least five interlocking but distinct services |
| | Hyperledger Fabric https://www.hyperledger.org/ | Smart contracts, building supply chain solutions | Accelerating the adoption of a ledger-based solution for cross-industry chain scenarios |
| | Hyperledger Sawtooth https://www.hyperledger.org/projects/sawtooth | Distributed ledgers and safe smart contracts | Building, deploying and running distributed ledgers |
| | Ripple https: ripple.com/ | Gateway, payment, exchange, remittance network; smart contract system: Codius | Separate blockchain |
| | BigchainDB https://www.bigchaindb.com/ | Blockchain database | Deploying blockchain proof-of-concepts, platforms and applications |
| | Quantstamp https://quantstamp.com/ | Security-aware smart contract, proof-of-audit | Building security-aware blockchain software for smart contract verification |
| | Stratis https://stratisplatform.com/ | Business processes simplification blockchain as a service | Streamline business processes with blockchain |
| | Nebulas https://stratisplatform.com/ | Value of blockchain data | Building an incentive-based, self-evolving and value-based blockchain platform |
| | Zilliqa https://zilliqa.com/ | Fast, secure and decentralized business models | Developing secure and decentralized applications |
| | DACC | Digital content, media industry | Developing blockchain-based content |

*(Continues)*

| Name / URL | Description | Type |
|---|---|---|
| https://dacc.co/ | ... platform and applications | platform and applications |
| Counterparty — https://www.counterparty.co/ | Overlay protocol for currency issuance and exchange Bitcoin | Blockchain overlay |
| Mastercoin — http://www.mastercoin.org/ | Financial derivatives | Bitcoin blockchain overlay |
| NXT — http://www.nxtcommunity.org/ | Altcoin mined with proof-of-stake consensus model | Bitcoin blockchain overlay |
| BitShares — http://bitshares.org/ | Decentralized crypto-equity share exchange | Separate blockchain |
| Open Assets — https://github.com/ | Open Assets colored coin issuance and wallet | Bitcoin blockchain overlay |
| Colored Coins — http://coloredcoins.org/ | Bitcoin asset marking for digital/physical assets | Bitcoin blockchain overlay |
| Blockchain 3.0 — ArcBlock — https://arcblock.io | Cloud computing, self-evolving ecosystem | Removing application barriers |
| Cardano — https://www.Cardano.org/zh/home-3/ | Cryptocurrency | Evolving out of a scientific philosophy and a research-first-driven approach |
| EOS — https://eos.io/ | Enterprise operation system | Delivering value through blockchain |

named Satoshi Nakamoto [29], which may also be a group of people. The first open-source software of Bitcoin was launched in the early 2009. As of this writing, it has been updated to version 5.0.

Essentially, Bitcoin is a kind of cryptocurrency and used as digital cash. Unlink the traditional digital currency, which requires a centralized organization, such as bank or financial institute, Bitcoins are generated, managed and transmitted based on peer-to-peer networks, without any third-party intermediaries. The participants in the P2P networks are responsible for verifying the transaction by cryptography and recording the verified ones in a blockchain, also known as a ledger in Bitcoins. Bitcoins are automatically generated every 10 min and are used as the rewards to the miners, who solved complex mathematical problems in the past 10 min. Based on the investigation conducted by the researchers in the University of Cambridge, approximate 2.9–5.8 million users are using cryptocurrency, most of which are Bitcoins [30]. Up to February 17, 2019, one Bitcoin is equal to \$3,691.58.

The creation of Bitcoin provides a new way for the transaction on the Internet. The full picture of Bitcoin includes several parties, system software developers, Bitcoin miners, merchant processing services, the end users and even the mining machine producers. Following the Bitcoin, there have been similar alternative digital currencies that are designed and launched by exploiting the similar working mechanism as Bitcoin, but with slight modifications in the process of the mining and transactions. Different countries have different altitudes and policies about the legislation of Bitcoin transaction. The opponent of Bitcoin argues that Bitcoin has always been used in the illegal activities, such as criminal, terrorists and drug. In addition, the mechanism of Bitcoin, e.g., mining and transaction, results in the waste of electricity energy and the low asset security. For instance, it was reported that the global Bitcoin mining activity has consumed between 1 and 4 GW of electricity at the end of 2017. An approximation of \$37 million of digital cryptocurrency was stolen from a South Korean exchange in June 2018. In addition, the evidence found by US government shows that Bitcoin was used as the payment for the Russian interference activities of the 2016 US election.

## 4.2.2   Ethereum

Ethereum is a blockchain-based computing platform and featured by integrating smart contract functionality [8,31]. With the aim of providing decentralized cryptocurrency service, a researcher, named Vitalik Buterin, designed and launched Ethereum in 2013. Currently, Ethereum is the largest blockchain platform worldwide of cryptocurrency service [32].

Ethereum leverages an approach of transaction-based state transitions to realize proof-of-transaction (proof-of-work (PoW) and proof-of-stake (PoS)). In 2014, an online crowd sale was held to Ethereum, where the sale participants use Bitcoin to buy Ethereum value taken (Eher). Ethereum platform went online in 2015, after pre-mining around 11.9 million coins, which takes up 13% of all Ethereum supplies. Through using the concept of presale, Ethereum fixes its Eher price to Bitcoin, which provides a healthy environment for Ethereum development.

Ethereum inherits and develops and expands Bitcoin, including the methodologies of creating, storing and trading cryptocurrency, and validating and coping the block data among multiple nodes globally. In 2016, due to the collapse of the most notable Ethereum project, named Decentralized Autonomous Organization (DAO), Ethereum was divided into two sub-blockchain system: the original one is called Ethereum Classic (ETC) and the new blockchain is Ethereum (ETH) [29]. Over 2017, Ethereum currency had raised over 130 times, to over $1,400.

Compared with Bitcoin, Ethereum uses a very different method to realize consensus. The validation period is shortened from every 10 min to every 12 s, significantly accelerating the transaction time. Instead of using stable blocks, Ethereum creates a new protocol named Greedy Heaviest Observed Subtree to compute and reach consensus. In addition, Ethereum proposed a new PoW that consists of a series of hash functions. Although Ethereum is a distributed platform, it is managed by a nonprofit foundation, which is responsible for platform plan, optimization and decision-making. A series of changes have been scheduling to update and enrich the function of Ethereum platform. Therefore, Ethereum is still in development with the aim of supporting the securer, more reliable services for cryptocurrency.

### 4.2.3 Corda

Corda is a distributed blockchain ledge platform, the aim of which is to provide financial services among financial organization with limited trusts. The underlying technology of Corda is mainly based on Bitcoin and the upper level application mainly focuses on banking services. The approach to develop platforms has been derived from the specific needs of banking. It has selected the desirable characteristics of blockchains like Bitcoin and Ethereum while leaving the adverse elements that could make blockchains not appropriate for many bank use cases.

Corda was designed to solve the legal issues in the financial system such as how to deal with the controversial contracts or agreements. Unlike Bitcoin and Ethereum, which distribute all transactions in the network, it does not allow to copy and share all data with all participants, even though it is encrypted. The only sharing information is whatever the members choose is necessary.

Although, inheriting from different blockchain systems, Corda supports different kinds of consensus mechanism, it does not launch any cryptocurrency. The main function of Corda is to enable financial manager or regulator to monitor nodes and realize legitimated access to a certain data, which mean only the party that is legal has the access to the data. In addition, Corda allows the legal parties to confirm the transaction to create block, which is not accessible by unrelated people or party.

Corda is a tailor-made solution for financial institutions, which offers at least five interlocking but distinct services, derived from blockchain but used in a different manner, including validation, consensus, uniqueness, immutability and authentication. These services can be selected and customized to different financial scenarios to solve different business problems.

### 4.2.4    Hyperledger Fabric/Sawtooth

Hyperledger is distributed financial blockchain platform initialized by Linux Foundation in December 2015. The ambition of this platform is to provide an open hub for enterprise-level blockchain projects to be developed and commercialized. Hyperledger has implemented a variety of blockchain projects, mainly, including the full-blown Fabric and Sawtooth.

*Hyperledger Fabric* is a distributed ledge platform that allows smart contracts to be created and implemented. The key feature of Hyperledger Fabric is its modular architecture that allows different functions to be implemented in the pluggable manner. Different from the application that is developed within a modular architecture, Hyperledger Fabric provides a plug-and-play service for function creation, significantly speeding the design period. The smart contracts that present the system logic are stored in the container. Digital asset and IBM are the main contributors to the developments of Hyperledger Fabric.

Different from Bitcoin and Ethereum, it introduced member management service for enterprises. A developer preview of the Hyperledger Fabric has been released in 2016 [33]. There are two kinds of peers running for ledger protocol: validation peers and non-validation peers. Validation peers are responsible for the transaction validation, system consensus and ledger maintenance, while non-validation peers are nodes that are to connect clients to validate transactions.

*Hyperledger Sawtooth* is an enterprise-level distributed ledger platform, which creates, deploys and runs ledgers. The methodology of Hyperledger Sawtooth is to realize distributed ledgers and safely implement smart contract. Hyperledger Sawtooth provides various distributed ledger services such as asset ownership maintenance.

Hyperledger Sawtooth creates an environment that multiple institutes or enterprises could equally make decision for a certain financial issue. Based on different business requirements, it enables the participants to choose suitable transmission policies, access permissions and consensus algorithms. By decoupling the core system from the applications, Hyperledger Sawtooth significantly reduces the complexity of developing blockchain applications. For instance, the application developers are not required to have a lot of knowledge of the core system design. They can choose the business rules according to their application requirements. By decoupling the core system from the application design, Hyperledger Sawtooth brings new features for the application developments, such as parallel execution and access permission.

### 4.2.5    Ripple

Ripple is an online exchange system operated by US-based Ripple Labs Inc., providing services for cryptocurrency, commodities, fiat currency and so on. It was designed based on a distributed open-source Internet protocol. The ambition of the Ripple is to create a distributed platform to providing "secure, instantly and nearly free global financial transactions of any size with no chargebacks."

Ripple inherits a public ledger, named XRP [34]. The consensus algorithms in XRP facilitate the implementation of the financial services in a distributed manner [35].

Although Ripple was created by Ripple, the operation and management of the Ripple system are consisted by the contributors from various organizations, e.g., Massachusetts Institute of Technology, Internet operators, private companies and research institutes. As the main technologies of Ripple coming from XRP, Ripple platform inherently supports the cryptocurrency of XRP. Up to September 2018, XRP is ranked as the third in the market share of cryptocurrency [36].

Research and applications have shown that Ripple system as distributed ledgers has a number of advantages over cryptocurrencies like Bitcoin. In reality, Ripple has been used in many banks and payment networks such as UniCredit, UBS and Santander.

### 4.2.6   BigchainDB

BigchainDB is complementary to decentralized storage, processing and communication building blocks [17]. The white paper and open-source software of BigchainDB were first launched in February 2016 and have been improving continuously ever since. Essentially, it is blockchain database with distinct database and blockchain properties, including the high network throughput, the shorten transaction latency, enhanced query functionality, distributed operation, decentralized control and data immutability.

There are some inherent issues in its initial design. The first one is that given a bounded subset of the nodes, the system could not handle arbitrary faults, which means the system is not Byzantine fault tolerant (BFT) [37]. The second is that only two nodes are charging for processing the data write in the database, which may create the reliability issue for the whole system. And the third one is that only one logical database exists in the system, which means the system could be easily attacked by a malicious user through obtaining the database control.

To overcome the abovementioned issues, BigchainDB 2.0 was designed and launched in May 2018. The updated version is a BFT system that enables the system to be resilient to the node fails. The new system can work well with the failures of up to a third of the nodes in the network. BigchainDB 2.0 provides various use cases for the application developments. The application developers could utilize and customize the services and use cases of BigchainDB 2.0, e.g., transaction proof and database, to meet the requirement of their business requirements.

### 4.2.7   Quantstamp

Quantstamp, short for Quantstamp protocol, is a security-aware blockchain software developed by Quantstamp company for blockchain smart contract verification. It aims to help blockchain developers and projects around the world to perform cost-effective security audits on their contracts. Quantstamp has designed a publicly verifiable record to build the trust among the parties of smart contract. It currently provides simple and quick Oyente and Mythril analyzers, with smart contract while without special configuration, and is also exploring other analyzers to add to the system in the future.

Currently, Quantstamp is working on the Ethereum platform. When the transaction is authorized, users can directly use an open interface to submit their audit requests. The node responsible for permission in Quantstamp receives this request and conducts the audit for the transaction. Once the audit is finished, a publicly readable audit report together with a hash value will be created and stored in blockchain, which can only be viewed and cannot be tampered anymore.

### 4.2.8    Stratis

Stratis is a distributed blockchain platform designed to facilitate the institutes or companies to develop blockchain-based applications. Similar to the cloud computing that developers can design applications without the need to have their own physical machines, the aim of Stratis is to enable developers to design, deploy and evaluate their blockchain-based applications without the need to have their own network infrastructure. This reduces the costs and development complexity compared with an in-house implementation.

Currently, the applications on the Stratis platform are mainly developed in C# language and Microsoft .NET framework. These applications can call the Stratis application programming interfaces (APIs) and framework based on their needs. For application developers, Stratis reduces the hardware and software requirements, simplifies the development processes, shortens the development life cycle and accelerates the capitalization of the blockchain applications.

It offers a solution for the fast creation of individual chains on the basis of their own blockchain. These chains can vary in accordance with the needs of your company and even play a popular function of the blockchain, such as Ethereum or Lisk that can be tested individually or simultaneously.

### 4.2.9    Wanchain

Wanchain is a distributed blockchain platform to provide the communications among different digital currencies. The objective of Wanchain is to establish an online market that different digital currencies can be traded with each other. Similar to the traditional financial organization, e.g., bank, Wanchain plans to provide services for the digital currencies, breaking the barriers among digital currencies and creating a global-level digital trade platform.

Through leveraging Wanchain platform, different blockchain ledgers could communicate and exchange with each other in a distributed and secure manner. The advanced cryptographic algorithms are used to create the protocol for cross-chain communication. The new protocol is capable of generating a distributed ledge that securely stores the data of both interchain and intra-chain transactions. With Wanchain, a blockchain network, no matter it is a public or private chain, could be linked to another blockchain ledgers and asset transfers could be exchanged among two ledgers. For cross-chain trade, Wanchain supports both the smart contracts and the token exchange. The working mechanism of Wanchain is similar to a traditional bank, where an individual or institute could set up an account and receive the financial services from Wanchain bank, such as digital currency exchange, making payments, and transaction settlements.

## 4.2.10 Nebulas

Nebulas is an incentive-based, self-evolving and value-based blockchain platform, with the aim of providing the search service within a blockchain system. It focuses on searches among decentralized applications, smart contracts and user's blockchain asset, through defining rank value, executing self-evolution and building positive feedback for the community ecosystem.

Based on blockchain valuation mechanism, Nebulas proposes future-oriented incentive and consensus systems, and the ability to self-evolve without forking. In order to promote ecosystem development, a developer incentive protocol is designed to promote the application development. The best application will be chosen and rewarded certain amount of coins, incentivizing the developers to design more valuable applications for the community ecosystem. With the aim of building indexes for smart contracts, Nebulas captures the web page data and builds up a mapping relationship between the captured data and the smart contracts to be indexed. In addition, the developers are encouraged and rewarded to assist Nebulas to offer search services, such as uploading the verified smart contracts, analyzing the code semantics, generating the code indexes and realizing the search services for the similar codes and smart contracts. In addition, it involves the activity of smart contract standardization. With a unified standard, the smart contracts are created, managed and implemented in a similar form and description, which could increase the readability, efficiency and compatibility during creation and content search of smart contracts.

## 4.2.11 Zilliqa

Zilliqa is a novel blockchain platform designed to securely scale in an open, permissionless distributed network. It aims to rival traditional centralized payment methods such as VISA and MasterCard. The core feature that makes it scalable is sharding, which divides the network into several smaller component networks capable of processing transactions in parallel. As a result, its transaction rate increases as the mining network expands. As of this writing, it is being developed, starting with a public testnet and the source code for open-source review in December 2017.

Zilliqa leverages PoW to establish identities and perform sharding and reaches a consensus built on Practical Byzantine Fault Tolerance (PBFT) among participants. Furthermore, its unprecedented throughput implies that the processing fee per transaction can be very low. For current popular blockchains, participants ought to compete for the few transactions processed per second. As a result, transactions with low or insufficient fees experience delays in processing. Such issues will be significantly alleviated in Zilliqa as the number of transactions processed per second becomes several hundred more and beyond.

Zilliqa can support a smart contract platform with a formally verifiable language that is sharding-friendly, i.e., it will allow users to compute programs in parallel, harnessing the full computational capacity of the mining network. For instance, it will allow users to build distributed advertising networks and decentralized exchanges, conduct parallel auctions and deploy MapReduce-style trading algorithms, run a shared economy, etc.

### 4.2.12   Decentralized Accessible Content Chain

Decentralized Accessible Content Chain [38], referred to as DACC, has been considered as the first content-based blockchain in digital media industry with unique blockchain infrastructure and full developer tools. It aims to place content creators back to the center of the stage, eliminate the intermediaries that cause unnecessary friction of content creation and also to develop a modular-based decentralized file system plugged in other public chains.

The developed distributed file system is characterized by identity and access management (IAM), public chain and development tools and enables all users and content creators to store and manage their data in a secure manner. The public chain is based on network IAM system, delegated proof of stake (DPoS)/verifiable random function (VRF) consensus and virtual machine. It has revolutionized the digital content and media industry and empowered the content creators in the long run. IAM can guarantee that the authenticated members can visit the content that is open to them, and both user authentication and authorization are under the control of content creators. The incentive mechanisms have been designed to incentivize more and more content creators, governors and users to devote oneself to the development of DACC. In addition, a series of tools have been developed to enable all users and entities to build various content-related applications.

DACC will revolutionize the digital media economy by innovative technology, distributed global community and special token model and reward system, which will finally empower real creators in the digital media industry.

### 4.2.13   Cardano

Cardano has been considered an emerging distributed Blockchain 3.0 platform evolved out of scientific philosophies. Nowadays, it becomes more and more intelligent and is with more functions than existing platforms for introducing multilayer protocols and smart contracts to it.

Cardano has proposed a PoW-based Ouroboros consensus [39] to allow all participants to reach agreements. This consensus eliminates additional resource consumption at individual nodes, enabling its large-scale potential applications. In addition, it develops precise cryptocurrencies characterized by distribution and cryptography to protect user privacy.

Cardano has performed advanced functions with its multilayer protocols and introduced a settlement layer, linking to control layer that runs smart contracts, to execute basic operations. In order to fulfill the ever-growing requirements, a software update will be developed and is available to all users on the web.

### 4.2.14   ArcBlock

ArcBlock is an extensible, scalable and easy-to-use Blockchain 3.0 platform designed to run in the cloud natively or on a single computer. The primary purpose

*Table 4.2  Comparisons among blockchain platforms*

| Blockchain platforms | Permissioned mechanism | Data model | Consensus protocol | Smart contract | Database | Digital currency |
|---|---|---|---|---|---|---|
| Bitcoin | Public | Transaction-based | PoW | – | Level DB | Bitcoin |
| Ethereum | Public | Account-based | PoW/PoS | Solidity/Serpent | Level DB | Ethernet coin |
| Corda | Consortium | Transaction-based | Raft | Java/Kotlin | Relation DB | – |
| Hyperledger Fabric | Consortium | Account-based | PBFT/SBFT | Go/Java | LevelDB/CouchDB | – |
| Hyperledger Sawtooth | Public/Consortium | Account-based | PoET | Python | – | – |
| Ripple | Public | Account-based | RPCA | – | RocksDB/SQLite | XRP |
| BigchainDB | Consortium | Transaction-based | Quorum Voting | Crypto-conditions | Rethink/Mongo DB | – |
| Quantstamp | Public | – | – | Solidity | Level DB | QSP token |
| Stratis | Public | Transaction-based | Raft | C# | Relation DB | STRAT |
| Wanchain | Public | Account-based | PoS | Solidity/Serpent | Level DB | Wancoin |
| Nebulas | Public | Transaction-based | Raft | Java/Kotlin | Relation DB | NAS tokens |
| Zilliqa | Public | Account-based | PoW/PBFT | Scilla | Relation DB | ZIL |
| DACC | Public | Transaction-based | DPoS/VRF | Java/Kotlin | Relation DB | DACC tokens |
| Cardano | Public | Account-based | Ouroboros | Java/Kotlin | Relation DB | ADA |
| ArcBlock | Public | Transaction-based | Algorand | Java/Kotlin | Relation DB | ABT |

is to remove the blockchain application barriers, mainly referring to friendliness to consumers, cost, lock-in platform and lack of features. It not only provides users with the necessary components but also designs advanced business rules for blockchain applications.

ArcBlock introduces a suite of revolutionary technologies like cloud computing to fulfill the requirements of mainstream blockchain applications. Different from its predecessors, ArcBlock is a self-evolving and reusable service, not just acts as a software package or a series of APIs. It serves as a bridge between the existing systems with blockchain networks, enabling automatic business transactions related to the current platforms. Being an incentive-based system, ArcBlock enables miner nodes in the world to share infrastructures and thus provides reusable elements and novel services to all users. It will reward all participants who provide resources or services to the platform.

In addition to cloud computing, ArcBlock introduces Blocklet, which is a clever combination of the latest technologies like serverless computing and microservice framework, into blockchain. It is an advanced application protocol executed on all platforms in different languages and can provide better service performance with its native platform.

Currently, ArcBlock is open to public by introducing the open chain access protocols. Developers can estimate all blockchain protocols without restriction. This protocol enables novel blockchain platforms to be implemented with emerging technologies. In addition, it allows a variety of applications to run on multichain blockchain, greatly increasing the quality of experience (QoE) of users.

Generally, current blockchain platforms are built on several prerequisites, which directly determine their application space [1,40–47]. In order to facilitate understanding of them, we summarize their prerequisites, elaborated in Table 4.2, including permissioned mechanism, data model, consensus protocol, smart contract, database and digital currency. Current blockchain platform technologies are limited in scope and fall short of meeting the requirements of global-scale distribution platforms that enable the programmable economy and society. Notice that each blockchain platform has its inherent advantages and disadvantages, it is hard to say whether a blockchain platform is good or not in reality. Therefore, we should make a trade-off between the deployment cost and the desired performance to develop suitable blockchain platforms for real-world applications.

# References

[1]   Pilkington M. Blockchain technology: Principles and applications; 2016.
[2]   Tapscott D and Tapscott A. Blockchain revolution: How the technology behind Bitcoin is changing money business and the world; 2016.
[3]   Wilkinson S, Boshevski T, Brandoff J, *et al.* Storj a peer-to-peer cloud storage network; 2014.

[4] Lei A, Cruickshank H, Cao Y, *et al.* Blockchain-based dynamic key management for heterogeneous intelligent transportation systems. IEEE Internet of Things Journal. 2017;4(6):1832–1843.

[5] Mougayar W. The business blockchain: Promise, practice, and application of the next Internet technology. John Wiley & Sons; 2016.

[6] Walport M. Distributed ledger technology: Beyond blockchain. UK Government Office for Science; 2016;1. p. 1–88.

[7] Ren Z, Cong K, Aerts T, *et al.* A scale-out blockchain for value transfer with spontaneous sharding. In: 2018 Crypto Valley Conference on Blockchain Technology (CVCBT). IEEE; 2018. p. 1–10.

[8] Cachin C. Blockchains and consensus protocols: Snake oil warning. In: European Dependable Computing Conference; 2017.

[9] Zheng Z, Xie S, Dai HN, *et al.* Blockchain challenges and opportunities: A survey. International Journal of Web and Grid Services. 2018;14 (4):352–375.

[10] Courtois NT. On the longest chain rule and programmed self-destruction of crypto currencies. arXiv preprint arXiv:14050534. 2014.

[11] Bag S, Ruj S, and Sakurai K. Bitcoin block withholding attack: Analysis and mitigation. IEEE Transactions on Information Forensics and Security. 2016;12(8):1967–1978.

[12] Xiong Z, Feng S, Niyato D, *et al.* Optimal pricing-based edge computing resource management in mobile blockchain. In: 2018 IEEE International Conference on Communications (ICC). IEEE; 2018. p. 1–6.

[13] Herbaut N and Negru N. A model for collaborative blockchain-based video delivery relying on advanced network services chains. IEEE Communications Magazine. 2017;55(9):70–76.

[14] Gilad Y, Hemo R, Micali S, *et al.* Algorand: Scaling byzantine agreements for cryptocurrencies. In: Proceedings of the 26th Symposium on Operating Systems Principles; 2017. p. 51–68.

[15] www.coinmarketcap.com. [cited 2017 Nov 12]. Available from: https://coinmarketcap.com/coins/views/all/.

[16] Schwartz D, Youngs N, Britto A, *et al.* The Ripple protocol consensus algorithm. Ripple Labs Inc. White Paper. 2014;5(8).

[17] McConaghy T, Marques R, Miiller A, *et al.* BigchainDB: A scalable blockchain database [White Paper], BigChainDB; 2016.

[18] Quantstamp. The protocol for securing smart contracts [White Paper]; 2017. Available from: https://quantstamp.com/.

[19] Stratis. [White Paper]; 2018. Available from: https://stratisplatform.com/.

[20] Wanchain. [White Paper]; 2017. Available from: https://www.wanchain.org/.

[21] Zilliqa. The Zilliqa project: A secure, scalable blockchain platform [White Paper]; 2018. Available from: https://zilliqa.com/.

[22] Colored Coins. [Technical White Paper]; 2018. Available from: http://coloredcoins.org/.

[23] Open Assets. [White Paper]; 2018. Available from: https://github.com/.

[24]    Counterparty. [White Paper]; 2018. Available from: https://www.counter-party.co/.

[25]    Nxt. Whitepaper: Nxt. Wiki; 2018. Available from: https://nxtwiki.org.

[26]    Odom C. Open-Transactions: Secure contracts between untrusted parties [White Paper]; 2016. Available from: https://github.com/Open-Transactions.

[27]    ArcBlock. [White Paper]; 2017. Available from: https://www.arcblock.io/en/.

[28]    EOS: Enterprise Operation System. [White Paper]; 2019. Available from: https://eos.io/.

[29]    Nakamoto S. Bitcoin: A peer-to-peer electronic cash system; 2008.

[30]    Nakamoto S. Re: Bitcoin P2P e-cash paper. The cryptography mailing list; 2008.

[31]    Christidis K and Devetsikiotis M. Blockchains and smart contracts for the Internet of things. IEEE Access. 2016;4:2292–2303.

[32]    Buterin V. Ethereum 2.0 mauve paper; 2016.

[33]    Androulaki E, Barger A, Bortnikov V, *et al.* Hyperledger Fabric: A distributed operating system for permissioned blockchains. In: Proceedings of the thirteenth EuroSys conference; 2018. p. 1–15.

[34]    Poon J and Dryja T. The Bitcoin lightning network: Scalable off-chain instant payments; 2016.

[35]    Wang W, Hoang DT, Hu P, *et al.* A survey on consensus mechanisms and mining strategy management in blockchain networks. IEEE Access. 2019;7:22328–22370.

[36]    Cachin C and Vukolic M. Blockchain consensus protocols in the wild. arXiv preprint arXiv:1707.01873. 2017.

[37]    Tschorsch F and Scheuermann B. Bitcoin and beyond: A technical survey on decentralized digital currencies. IEEE Communications Surveys and Tutorials. 2016;18(3):2084–2123.

[38]    Decentralized Accessible Content Chain (DACC). [White Paper]; 2018. Available from: https://dacc.co/.

[39]    David BM, Gazi P, Kiayias A, *et al.* Ouroboros Praos: An adaptively-secure, semi-synchronous proof-of-stake protocol. IACR Cryptology ePrint Archive. 2017;2017:573.

[40]    Sawtooth documentation; [cited 2018 Dec 12]. Available from: https://goo.gl/izmMYn/.

[41]    Antshares. Antshares: Digital assets for everyone [White Paper]; 2016. Available from: https://www.antshares.org.

[42]    Suankaewmanee K, Hoang DT, Niyato D, *et al.* Performance analysis and application of mobile blockchain. In: 2018 International Conference on Computing, Networking and Communications (ICNC). IEEE; 2018. p. 642–646.

[43]    BitGo. The challenges of block chain indexing; 2015. Available from: https://blog-archive.bitgo.com/the-challenges-of-blockchain-indexing/.

[44]    Back A, Corallo M, Dashjr L, *et al.* Enabling blockchain innovations with pegged sidechains. 2014;72. http://www.opensciencereview.com/papers/123/enablingblockchain-innovations-with-pegged-sidechains.

[45]   Zhang Y and Wen J. The IoT electric business model: Using blockchain technology for the Internet of things. Peer-to-Peer Networking and Applications. 2017;10(4):983–994.

[46]   Sidhu J. Syscoin: A peer-to-peer electronic cash system with blockchain-based services for e-business. In: 2017 26th International Conference on Computer Communication and Networks (ICCCN). IEEE; 2017. p. 1–6.

[47]   Bruce J. The mini-blockchain scheme rev 3. Online, July. 2014.

*Chapter 5*

# Blockchain for Internet of Things

*Xu Wang[1], Xuan Zha[2], Guangsheng Yu[1], Wei Ni[3] and Ren Ping Liu[1]*

Internet of Things (IoT) technology is digitizing the physical world by connecting enormous and heterogeneous devices and unleashing great economic benefit. However, data privacy, security and trust issues in current solutions are seriously limiting the adoption of IoT applications. Blockchain, a decentralized and tamper-resistant ledger, maintains consistent and immutable blocks of data at different servers and has the potential to tackle the security concerns in IoT applications. Inherent features in IoT, such as the massive IoT devices, heterogeneous IoT networks, limited battery, low computing power and communication bandwidth, make it hard to directly adopt blockchain technology in IoT application. This chapter presents a comprehensive survey on existing blockchain and IoT technologies and emphasizes on the challenges and limitation. Current studies, projects and designs on Blockchain-IoT systems are introduced and compared to illustrate the feasibility of the integration of blockchain and IoT. Blockchain technologies that can potentially address the critical challenges in IoT applications and suit the features of the same are identified with potential adaptations and enhancements elaborated on blockchain data structures, key blockchain technologies and consensus protocols. Future research directions of blockchain are collated for effective adoption in IoT applications.

## 5.1 Introduction

IoT is set to ubiquitously connect a huge number of devices (embedded with sensors and actuators) to the Internet, digitizing the physical world into computer-based data systems [1,2]. It is poised to transform human life and unleash enormous economic benefits by providing fine-grained control and efficiency [3]. A promising development has been foreseen with an expected global economic impact of more than $11 trillion by 2025 [4]. The potential benefits of IoT would come at

[1]Global Big Data Technologies Centre, University of Technology Sydney, Ultimo, Australia
[2]China Academy of Information and Communications Technology (CAICT), Beijing, China
[3]Data 61, CSIRO, Sydney, Australia

a cost of exposure to new threats and attacks. Data integrity is particularly vulnerable in IoT (e.g., to tampering), given the sheer scale and volume of IoT devices, nonhomogeneous network structure, limited device computing power as well as the immense volume of data generated across the networks [5].

Traditional security mechanisms alone, such as cryptographic techniques [6], are not enough to preserve data integrity in this enormous scale, thus seriously restricting the adoption of IoT in the future. Particularly, IoT suffers from the lack of a solid base on security and integrity. The Internet, on which IoT is based, is inherently insecure, where data security was an afterthought in the design as can be evident from continual patches and manual handling [7]. Moreover, IoT has a substantially different architecture from the Internet, extending network connectivity and computing capability to objects with limited computing power, such as sensors and throw-away items, and allowing these devices to generate, exchange and consume data with minimal human interventions [8]. Simply extending computationally demanding and costly Internet security solutions to IoT is neither scalable nor practical [3].

Being a distributed, incorruptible and tamper-resistant ledger database, blockchain has the potential to address the critical security issues of IoT, particularly on data integrity and reliability [9]. Blockchain allows software applications to send and record transactions/events in a trustworthy and distributed (peer-to-peer (P2P)) manner. Blockchain is rapidly gaining popularity and used extensively for applications, including smart contracts [10], distributed storage [11] and digital assets [12]. The potential applications of blockchain in IoT include recording events (such as temperature, moisture or location changes) and creating tamper-resistant ledgers that are readable only to certain parties, e.g., specific participants in a supply chain.

With blockchain technologies, the security requirement of IoT can be fulfilled [13]. The following prominent features of blockchain can contribute to the integrity of IoT applications and so enhance the IoT security:

- *Decentralization:* The P2P network setting of blockchains is inherently suited for IoT networks that are typically distributed, for example, blockchain in vehicular ad hoc network (VANET) [14,15]. Blockchains can record transactions between multiple parties without central coordination. This can provide flexible network configurations and reduce the risks of single-point failures.
- *Integrity:* Blockchains are able to keep transactions permanently in a verifiable way. Specifically, the signatures of the senders in transactions can guarantee the integrity and non-repudiation of the transactions. The hash chain structure of blockchains ensures that any recorded data cannot be updated, even partly. The consensus protocols of blockchains can guarantee valid and consistent records. The protocols can also tolerate failures and attacks, e.g., attackers with less than 1/2 hash power in proof-of-work (PoW), or less than 1/3 of nodes in practical Byzantine fault tolerance (PBFT) consensus protocol [16]. All these are critical to IoT applications, where IoT data can be generated and processed by heterogeneous devices or in heterogeneous network environments.

- *Anonymity:* Blockchains can use changeable public keys as users' identities to preserve anonymity and privacy [17]. This is attractive to many IoT applications and services, especially those that need to keep confidential identities and privacy [18].

Interests in applying blockchain to IoT networks have already emerged in academia and industry, with the goal of providing security [19–25]. In this sense, cloud can provide distributed storage for IoT applications, while blockchain can secure the integrity of the storage and prevent data tampering. Blockchain and cloud can be integrated as blockchain-based distributed cloud [26].

However, existing blockchain technologies can be inefficient for IoT applications, due to the aforementioned massive deployment of IoT devices, non-homogeneous network structure with strong partitioning and subsequently huge sensory data and demands for high capacity in blockchain (i.e., high transaction or block generation speed) [27]. Particularly, physical characteristics of IoT devices and networks, such as limited bandwidth and connectivity, nontrivial network topology and unpredictable link delays, can cause discrepancy or inconsistency between the records maintained in a distributed fashion at different locations. In fact, the record generation speed needs to be restrained by the propagation speed of blocks that are the data units of blockchains. Existing blockchain technologies, which nearly unexceptionally operate at the application layer and neglect these physical aspects of networks and devices, substantially reduce the block generation speed to be far slower than the propagation, thus resulting in inefficient uses of blockchain.

In this chapter, we investigate the key challenges and the benefits of blockchain in IoT applications. The state-of-the-art blockchain technologies in terms of consensus protocols and data structures are analyzed. The limitations of the current blockchain technologies for IoT applications, as well as future potential research directions, are presented.

The rest of this chapter is organized as follows. In Sections 5.2 and 5.3, the preliminaries on IoT and blockchain are presented, respectively. Section 5.4 elaborates on the current applications of blockchain to IoT, including the structure of blockchain-based IoT applications, potential blockchain designs and security issues. In Section 5.5, we compare representative designs of blockchain and discuss their suitability for IoT applications. Future directions of blockchain research for IoT are pointed out in Section 5.6, followed by conclusion in Section 5.7.

## 5.2 Limitations of IoT security

IoT network prevails with its ability to interconnect numerous devices possessing various sensing and computing abilities with little human interventions [28]. Sensing and actuating devices form heterogeneous IoT networks to provide various applications. Typical IoT applications include smart home, smart transport, eHealth and smart grid [29].

A typical IoT architecture consists of *perception, networking, service and interface layers* from bottom to top [30]. The perception layer, also known as the sensor layer in other IoT architectures summarized in [31], consists of sensors and actuators collecting and processing environmental information to perform functions, such as querying temperature, location, motion and acceleration. The perception layer is an indispensable part of a variety of IoT applications [29]. Various types of end devices can be adopted in the perception layer to bridge the physical and digital worlds. Typical end devices include Radio-Frequency IDentification (RFID), wireless sensors and actuators, Near-Field Communications (NFC) and mobile phones. For example, RFID tag is a small microchip attached to an antenna. By attaching RFID tags to objects, the object can be identified, tracked and monitored during logistics, retailing and supply chain. The networking layer is responsible for connecting other smart things, network devices and servers. The service layer creates and manages specific services to meet the IoT application requirements. The interface layer facilitates data use interactions with objects for specific applications [30].

## 5.2.1   Characteristics of IoT

IoT applications have the potential to affect every aspect of the human daily life. They can be classified into the following four domains: transportation and logistics, healthcare, smart environment (including smart home) and personal and social applications [32]. The end devices, communication and networking technologies differ to meet targets and demands of various applications. The following are two main aspects that differ among applications.

- Mobility versus stable topology: The topology of IoT applications can vary with different speed. The typical applications with stable and mobile topologies are smart home and VANETs for transportation application, respectively. Most devices in smart home are stable and consist a stable network topology, while vehicles move rapidly and lead to time-varying topologies. The mobility of the end devices makes the network connectivity unpredictable and entities management challenging [33].
- Low-cost versus high-capacity performance: IoT devices are heterogeneous with different hardware platforms and abilities. One type of IoT devices is sensors with tiny size and limited resources for processing, communication and storage. Such devices are typically low cost and thus can be widely deployed in large scales to measure temperature, pressure, humidity, medical parameters of human bodies, and chemical and biochemical substances [34]. They typically communicate in wireless ad hoc or mesh networks such as ZigBee [35]. Such sensors are often powered by limited battery, making limited energy a major concern. Recently, new communication technologies, e.g., NB-IoT [36], have been proposed to extend the lifetime of sensors, but sensors are still limited in process, communication and storage abilities. Another type of IoT devices can be more expensive and more powerful, such as mobile phones and vehicles. They have large battery and stronger capabilities of computing and storage. Hence, such kind of devices can contribute to higher capacity.

Implemented with heterogeneous end devices and different protocols, IoT networks have some common IoT-specific characteristics as follows:

- Enormous number of nodes and big IoT data: The number of IoT devices will continuously increase. The number of connected devices in IoT is expected to increase up to 20.4 billion by 2020 [37]. IoT faces not only a large number of nodes but also growing demand for capacity, as numerous end devices sense and collect mass data.
- Decentralization: Decentralization and heterogeneity are the two major characteristics of IoT [38]. Decentralization is essential given the large number of IoT nodes, such as in the smart city, because the data to be processed at the same time are considerably huge [39]. IoT devices collect, process and store data in a decentralized manner. Decentralized algorithms in IoT, e.g., clustering algorithms in wireless sensor network and decentralized computing, can contribute to the capacity and scalability of IoT [39].
- Unstable and unpredictable connections: The unstable and unpredictable connections of IoT devices are not only caused by the mobility and the sleep/idle mode of IoT devices but also typical unreliable wireless links to IoT devices [40]. As a result, an IoT network may divide into disconnected partitions and the partitions can vary with time.

## 5.2.2   Security analysis on IoT

Specific characteristics of IoT make data security a severe problem in IoT [32]. First, many IoT devices are deployed in human unfriendly and unattended areas, and it can be impossible to keep an eye on the huge number of devices all the time. This makes devices vulnerable to multidimensional harms [41]. For example, adversaries may physically capture and control these devices to invade IoT networks [42]. Traditional security mechanisms [43], such as the asymmetric encryption, are computationally demanding for IoT devices with limited abilities. Data from sensors can be stored, forwarded and processed by many different intermediate systems, which increases the risk of being tampered and forged. The unreliable and open wireless channels with broadcast nature bring additional risks to data security. The complexity of the IoT system further increases the abovementioned vulnerabilities [44].

The following summarizes the typical attacks on IoT networks from the bottom layer to the top [45].

### 5.2.2.1   Attacks to end devices

Adversaries physically capture and control the nodes via node capture attacks. The secret information stored in the captured nodes, such as keys and certificates, become visible to the adversaries [42]. The adversaries can further utilize the captured information to pretend as legitimate nodes and perform other attacks, such as the false data injection attack [46].

### 5.2.2.2   Attacks to communication channels

Adversaries may eavesdrop on and interfere with transmitting channels, exploiting the broadcast nature of radio. If signals are not encrypted, the adversaries can readily obtain the information. Even if the signals are encrypted, the adversaries are still able to analyze the streams of signals and infer private information, such as the locations of the sources or destinations [47]. The adversaries can also interfere and even jam the wireless channels by sending noisy signals [48].

### 5.2.2.3    Attacks to network protocols

By exploiting the vulnerabilities of network protocols, the adversaries can launch Sybil attack, replay attack, man-in-middle, blackhole, wormhole attacks and so on [49]. For example, a Sybil device impersonates several legitimate identities in IoT systems. Such attacks would compromise the efficiency and accuracy of voting mechanism and multipath routing protocols [49].

### 5.2.2.4    Attacks to sensory data

IoT networks can communicate by using ad hoc protocols, i.e., messages are transmitted hop-by-hop till reaching their destination. This provides the adversaries opportunities to tamper data or inject false data. An adversary, as a forwarder, can tamper and forward the messages to other nodes, known as data tampering [18]. Authentication algorithms are deployed to prevent the data tampering. False data injection attack refers that adversaries send false data across the targeted network with legitimate identities [46]. Once the false data are accepted, IoT applications may return erroneous instructions or provide wrong services, compromising the reliability of IoT applications and networks. For example, the traffic congestion may aggravate if vehicles accept false road assistant messages. False data injection attacks can hardly be prevented by authentication algorithms.

### 5.2.2.5    Denial-of-service (DoS) attack

The denial-of-service (DoS) attack represents a category of attacks, which exhaust resources and congest services of IoT systems [48]. For example, a sleep deprivation attack [50] is to break the programmed sleep routines and keep devices or nodes awake all the time until they are out of battery power supply. IoT devices have limited network and communication resources, and thus the DoS attacks can be catastrophic. Such attacks exhaust the limited energy of sensory nodes, reduce the network connectivity, paralyze the entire network and reduce network lifetime [50].

### 5.2.2.6    Software attacks

Software attacks refer to a series of attacks that utilize backdoors of software to modify software and control operations [51]. Typical software attacks include malicious virus/worm/scripts [51]. Intrusion detect system and other traditional Internet security mechanisms are used to tackle the software attacks [52].

Security is a critical concern to IoT applications. Particularly, the integrity of IoT data and devices, e.g., sensor readings and actuator commands, is the basic guarantee for securing IoT operations. Effective mechanisms need to be designed to protect IoT communications for confidentiality, integrity, authentication and nonrepudiation of information flows [53]. The IoT devices need to be identified to ensure the data integrity from the origin, which conventionally relies on trusted third parties, e.g., identity provider [54]. The authentication and encryption algorithms are used to protect the confidentiality and integrity of IoT data [55]. After the sensory data are sent to the data storage, the data security relies on the data storage service [56].

## 5.3 Existing blockchain technologies

Blockchain provides decentralized data storage service with a tamper-resistant ledger consisting of blocks chained in serial in distributed networks. It can record and secure transactions or transactional events using cryptography [57]. The first blockchain was proposed by Satoshi Nakamoto in 2008 [58] and implemented in 2009 as the enabling technique for the proliferating cryptocurrency—Bitcoin [59].

Blockchain records data in a secure and distributed manner. The basic unit of records in blockchain is the transaction. Each time a new transaction is generated, it is broadcasted to the entire blockchain network. Nodes receiving the transaction can verify the transaction by validating the signature attached to the transaction and mine verified transactions into cryptographically secured blocks. Such nodes are known as block miners (or miners for short). To allow a miner to create a block, a consensus problem needs to be solved in a distributed manner. The miners that manage to solve the consensus problem broadcast their new blocks throughout the network [60].

Upon the receipt of a new block, the miners yet to be able to solve the consensus problem append the block to their own chains of blocks locally maintained at the miners, after all the transactions enclosed in the block are verified and the block is also proven to provide the correct answer to the consensus problem. The new block contains a link to the previous block in the chains, as shown in Figure 5.1, by exploiting cryptographic means. All miners can synchronize their chains on a regular basis, and specific terms are defined to ensure the consistent ledger shared across the distributed network, e.g., Bitcoin blockchain only keeps the longest chain, in the case where there is discrepancy among the chains.

In the following, more detailed descriptions are provided on these key components of blockchain, i.e., the data structure, the consensus protocol, smart contracts and the security analysis on blockchain.

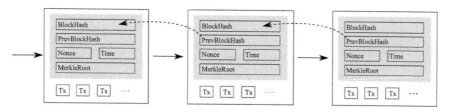

*Figure 5.1   Blockchain data structure*

## 5.3.1   General data structure

As the basic units in blockchain, transactions are the records of events observed by the miners in the network. A cryptographic private key is used to sign a transaction. The resultant signature is attached to, as an integral part of, the transaction, providing a mathematical proof that the transaction comes from the owner of the private key. The public key, corresponding to the private key, is known to miners for verifying the genuineness of the transaction. It can be achieved via using the public key as the source address in the transaction, preloaded the public key at all miners, or attached the public key and the digital certificate of the public key to the signatures for transmission. Powered by cryptography, the transaction binds an event and its initiator without doubt. Transactions were first used in Bitcoin to capture the financial interactions between two financial parties [58]. Transactions have also been used to elaborately assign the ownership rights and realize programmable events [61,62].

An ordered, backward-linked list of blocks is maintained, as a local record of transactions, at every miner of a network [63]. Being the element of the ledger, every block encapsulates a batch of verified transactions. Every block also has a header containing a link to the parent (previous) block (which is the hashed value of the parent block, e.g., in Bitcoin blockchain), and an answer in response to the consensus problem. The block header may contain other fields, such as timestamp, depending on specific demands. Each block is uniquely identified by a hash value, generated using the cryptographic hash algorithm on the header of the block.

The sequence of hash operations, which link each block to its parent block, creates a tamper-resistant chain that can trace back all the way to the first block ever created. In this way, blocks are chained together to act as the ledger at every individual node, as shown in Figure 5.1. Note that the link to the parent block is inside the block header and thereby affects the current block's hash value. To modify one block in an available chain, the following blocks, including the child and grandchild blocks, would all need to be recalculated to meet all relevant consensus problems. However, such recalculation is meant to be prohibitive, e.g., requiring intractable computations in the Bitcoin blockchain. Moreover, the existence of long chains of blocks further secures the intractability of tampering in practice and constructs tamper-resistant ledger. The locally maintained chains of blocks are regularly compared and updated across the network [64]. Only one chain, e.g., the longest chain in the Bitcoin blockchain, is publicly accepted to be the ledger of the entire system, and all the locally maintained chains are updated accordingly.

The block header also includes a field that contains information of all transactions in the current block, e.g., the Merkle root in the Bitcoin blockchain [65]. Typically, a Merkle tree [66] is built with transactions as leaves, to improve storage efficiency in a block. The Merkle tree has the tree structure in which every leaf node is a transaction and every non-leaf node is the hash of its child nodes, as shown in Figure 5.2. The root of the tree is named "Merkle root." By using the Merkle tree, peers in the Blockchain network can confirm whether a transaction has

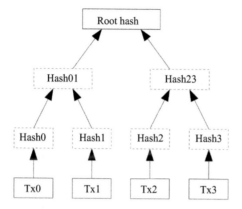

*Figure 5.2    Transactions are hashed in a Merkle tree [58]*

been mined into a block by verifying the hash of the corresponding branches rather than the transactions mined in the block; or in other words, the entire Merkle tree. By this means, the requirement of storage, memory and network capacity can be highly reduced.

Transactions and blocks are spread and verified across the network (in a P2P manner) to form distributed consensus. Take Bitcoin, for example. When a node generates a valid transaction, the node sends an inventory (inv) message containing the hash of the transaction (TXID), instead of actual transaction data, to all of its neighbors. Neighbors who do not have this transaction respond to the sender. Accordingly, the transaction is transmitted to those neighbors. Once the transaction has been successfully verified, it is further spread to their subsequent neighbors. This progress continues until the entire network receives the transaction.

## 5.3.2    Byzantine Generals' Problem and consensus protocol

A fundamental theory that blockchain exploits extensively is Byzantine Generals' Problem [67]. The Byzantine Generals' Problem is an agreement problem first generalized in [68]. The problem describes the case that peers try to reach a consensus, while traitors among the peers may betray the others and prevent them from reaching the consensus. Possible strategies of the betrayers include ignoring messages, providing fake messages, forging messages of others and "two-face" behavior [69], i.e., a node sends conflicting opinions to different nodes. These strategies can lead to Byzantine failures in networks that require consensus [68].

The Byzantine fail mode is the worst failure mode that distributed servers can fail [69]. The failure modes include authentication-detectable Byzantine failures [70] that Byzantine faulty servers forging are detectable with authentication mechanism; performance failures [71] that servers have to deliver correct results but may be early or late; omission failures [72] that service requests are subject to late service responses; crash failures [68] that a server does not respond to any requests; and fail-stop failures [73] that the state of the server exhibiting crash failures can be detected by other correct servers. The double-spending attack, a type of "two-faced" attack [69], also belongs to the Byzantine failure. The attackers of double-spending attacks are betrayed commanders in the Byzantine Generals' Problem [68].

There is a large body of research on replication techniques to tolerate Byzantine failures and implement highly available systems, where, however, most research on replication was focused on techniques that tolerate benign faults [74–76]. Earlier Byzantine agreement protocols [68,77] employed signaling expensive recursive confirmations to gain a whole picture of systems before solving the Byzantine Generals' Problem. The communication overhead of the protocols is so high and typically exponential to the number of peers [78]. Without assumptions about the behavior of faulty processes, techniques that tolerate Byzantine faults, such as BFT in [68], can provide a potential solution to blockchain. A popular technique is state machine replication that is a general method for implementing a fault-tolerant service by replicating servers and coordinating client interactions with server replicas [79].

Consensus protocols, the key of Blockchain to maintain a distributed and consistent ledger without centralized coordination, provide solutions to Byzantine Generals' Problem in blockchain [80]. Consensus protocols define the law of block generations and block selections. Miners in a blockchain network mine blocks by solving the consensus problem, which prevents any of potentially adversarial participants or compromised miners from hijacking the block generation process. The consensus problem can be announced by blockchain service providers, or also be generated in a distributed manner following a globally agreed criterion. For any miner, a consensus problem can be locally developed on the basis of the last publicly accepted block in the blockchain, the block/transaction that the miners trying to mine and the complexity requirement of the problem specified within the last consistent block of accepted blockchain. Moreover, the miners are also able to verify each other's blocks based on their blocks and the predefined criterion.

Consensus protocols in open access networks allow unverified and untrustworthy miners to mine blocks without the requirement of verifying their identities. Such kind of blockchain is known as public blockchain. The typical consensus protocols of public blockchain, i.e., blockchain in open access networks, include PoW adopted by Bitcoin, and proof-of-stake (PoS) adopted by Peercoin [81]. However, independent miners can still produce different blocks at the same time, causing disruptions in the growth of blockchain. These disruptions are known as fork, i.e., the locally maintained chains of blocks become inconsistent between different nodes [82]. Moreover, a large number of miners expend their resources for mining over the same transactions, leading to considerable energy waste and delay.

The other kinds of blockchains are private blockchain or permissioned blockchain, i.e., blockchain in permissioned networks [83], where authenticated participating miners notify each other in a P2P fashion of their observations of transactions. BFT algorithms [68] can be exploited at every miner to synthesize their own observations and those of the others, producing consistent blocks in a distributed manner.

### 5.3.3   Security analysis on blockchain

Blockchain attracts attentions for its highly anti-tampering property in decentralized networks. Specifically, blockchain does not require peers to trust each other. However, blockchain still exhibits vulnerabilities [84]. Typical security threats to blockchain are as follows:

- Double spending: Adversaries attempt to mislead the transaction receivers with conflicting transactions, e.g., spending the same coin in Bitcoin. Possible attack methods include sending conflicting transactions [85] and pre-mining one or more blocks to get conflicting transactions accepted by the blockchain [86].

- Attacks on consensus protocols: Attackers could break the security assumption of consensus protocols by possessing a considerably large chunk partition of the computing power of the entire network. Such attackers can control and reconstruct the chain. An example is the 51% attack in PoW blockchains, e.g., Bitcoin [87]. The attackers, owning more than a half of the hash power, can make blockchain accept illegitimate blocks, by solving the consensus problem (e.g., PoW in Bitcoin) faster than the rest of peers. Currently, it has proved that 33% hash power is sufficient to overpower PoW [88].

- Eclipse attacks: Eclipse attacks refer to the attacks in P2P networks where adversaries monopolize all connections to the legitimate nodes and prevent the legitimate nodes from connecting to any honest peers. Eclipse attack to blockchain first arose in Bitcoin [89,90] through the randomized protocol, which defines that a node in Bitcoin connects to a certain number of selected neighbors to maintain the P2P communications and blockchain-related functions. Ethereum was recently reported to have been exposed to Eclipse attacks as well, through the Kademlia P2P protocol adopted in Ethereum [91].

- Vulnerability of smart contracts [92]: Smart contracts are susceptible due to the openness and the irreversibility of blockchain. Bugs and frauds are transparent to the public, including adversaries. Also, it is challenging to make up bugs in the deployed smart contracts due to the irreversibility of blockchain. An outstanding example is the attack to the decentralized autonomous organization (DAO) in 2016, known as the DAO attack, which resulted in a forked Ethereum blockchain [92].

- Programming fraud: The attackers can exploit frauds in programming codes to extract properties of blockchain, such as the piracy attack reported in 2018 [93].

- Distributed DoS (DDoS) attack [94]: The adversaries exhaust the blockchain resources (such as exhausting the whole network processing capability) by launching a collaborative attack. In 2016, adversaries took underprice EVM instructions to slow down the processing of blocks [95]. The huge number of accounts with low balance produced by adversaries led to a DDoS attack.

- Leakage of private key [96]: The attackers can steal the private key of an account to take over the account. This can be achieved via traditional network attacks [96] or capturing physical nodes [97].

## 5.4    Blockchain for IoT: applications

IoT networks are data centric, where data are uploaded by a large number of end devices. This makes both data and devices the targets of potential attacks on IoT. Sensory data in an IoT system can be personal or sensitive [32], e.g., medical IoT [98] or from national applications, e.g., the IoT-based smart grid [99] and nuclear factory [100]. The integrity and privacy of the data are significant. Blockchain is believed to hold the key to settle security, data integrity and reliability concerns in IoT networks [12]. Provided guaranteed data integrity, blockchain has drawn a lot of attentions for various IoT applications (e.g., supply chain management [101] and smart city [102]), beyond the cryptocurrency.

### 5.4.1    Blockchain platforms for IoT

Launched in 2008, Bitcoin is the first popular blockchain application and introduces blockchain technology to the public [58]. Created for decentralized cryptocurrency application, Bitcoin runs the PoW consensus protocol on a public P2P network where nodes are free to join and leave the network. Bitcoin employs the longest chain block structure where the orphan blocks (i.e., blocks at the same height) are dropped. Bitcoin platform focuses on the cryptocurrency application and is the most widely used cryptocurrency.

Proposed in 2013 and launched from 2015, Ethereum has become the second largest cryptocurrency platform by market capitalization [103]. Ethereum also runs the PoW consensus protocol on a public P2P network and employs the Greedy Heaviest-Observed Sub-Tree (GHOST) block structure to utilize the orphan blocks for security improvement. Due to its outstanding support on the smart contract and popularity in the open-source community, Ethereum has been widely used in blockchain-IoT research. Ethereum supports light nodes for resource-limited devices, which only store headers of blocks and do not participate in block mining.

Started in 2015 and mainly contributed by IBM, Hyperledger Fabric has become the most popular open-source private blockchain platform [104]. Different from Bitcoin and Ethereum, Fabric is designed for enterprise and aims the following requirements: identifiable participants, permissioned networks, high transaction throughput, low latency of transaction confirmation and privacy and confidentiality of transactions. To achieve these, Fabric works on private networks, where nodes need to be authorized before entering the networks. With a limited number of miners running the BFT consensus protocol, Fabric achieves high throughput and low latency for practical applications but can only tolerate a limited number of failed miners. Fabric also supports encryption of transactions and then provides access control for data sharing and auditing.

Powered by the native cryptocurrency EOS, EOSIO is another popular blockchain and smart contract platform designed for the real world [105]. EOS provides role-based security permissions, industry-leading speed and secure application processing. The consensus protocol of the EOSIO consists of the delegated PoS and asynchronous BFT and can conduct millions of transactions per second while eliminating transaction fees.

IOTA targets at providing blockchain solutions for IoT networks [21]. From 2016, IOTA is built based on the technology "Tangle" with no chains, no blocks and no fees. Tangle inherits the anti-tampering distributed ledger of blockchain, using a directed acyclic graph (DAG) structure, instead of chains' structures as in Bitcoin. Transactions are the only storage units in IOTA. Each transaction confirms another two previously published transactions. Transactions are verified in parallel and accepted by Tangle almost instantly, which provides IOTA high capacity in terms of transaction rate. IOTA supports four types of nodes, i.e., full node, headless node (specifically full nodes running in the local console), light wallet and Android wallet [106]. Ability-limited IoT devices, e.g., battery-powered nodes, are restricted to run light wallets in IOTA. Some real-world applications are built on the IOTA platform [107]. CarPass, a secondhand car market project, adopts IOTA to maintain a "twin record" and serve as an immutable version of correct mileage on users' vehicles odometer [108].

InterPlanetary File System (IPFS) is a distributed system for storing and accessing files, websites, applications and data [109]. Running over decentralized networks, IPFS can support a resilient Internet, make censor content hard and speed up the web. IPFS and blockchain technology can be integrated to provide trust services for IoT applications with massive data. For example, the IPFS is used for off-chain data management in addition to the blockchain-based sharing service [110].

## 5.4.2   Blockchain-based industrial IoT projects

Blockchain technology has been widely adopted in industrial IoT-application-specific targets. Back to 2014, IBM and Samsung Electronics proposed a blockchain-based project, i.e., Autonomous Decentralized Peer-to-Peer Telemetry, which advocates device democracy to be the future of IoT [22,23]. Furthermore, a blockchain-based data sharing service for businesses and industries was also been launched by IBM [24,25], where IoT data can be shared through private blockchain ledgers to prevent disputes among business partners.

Most existing blockchain technologies have focused on the application layer and been developed for data integrity, such as supply chains, and trading services, such as sharing economy and power trading.

IBM develops the food trust services based on the Hyperledger Fabric platform and carries out pilots on an international food supply chain with Walmart [111]. All the records along the supply chain, such as audits, agricultural treatments, identification numbers, granted permissions and updates from IoT devices, are logged in the blockchain platform in a real-time and tamper-resistant way. With a farm-to-table approach, their blockchain solution can reduce the time for tracking mango origins from 7 days to seconds while promoting transparency across the food supply chain.

Established in 2017, UCOT integrates blockchain technology and the latest 5G IoT technology to provide trusted industrial supply chain solutions [112]. Physical objects are interpreted to digital identities by UCOT tags which can be QR codes, NFC tags and RFID tags according to specific requirements. The tags interact with

5G IoT devices, and all the activities are recorded in the UCOT blockchain as proof. On top of the blockchain-based supply chain management platform, UCOT supports various advanced services such as anti-counterfeiting, smart agriculture, food traceability, pharmaceuticals tracking, alcohol identification, cold chain logistics and asset tracking.

The project slock.it enables the sharing economy of things, where the IoT layer connects devices to the blockchain for control access [113]. slock.it runs on top of the public Ethereum blockchain and is driven by solidity-based smart contracts. slock.it enables IoT devices of any size to access blockchain data securely, take payments autonomously and interact with human, machines and anything in between. The clients on IoT devices are very light as they are stateless and only store a list of nodes in the network.

Power Ledger is proposed to trade energy, environmental commodities and renewable energy credits in a transparent, secure and efficient way by developing blockchain technology [114]. Power Ledger also enables the trading of asset ownership and then promotes the green energy market. Power Ledger adopts a hybrid public and consortium blockchain structure. The public Ethereum block-chain processes token exchange, while a fee-less Ethereum blockchain handles the high transaction volume of P2P energy trading.

### 5.4.3   Blockchain-based academic IoT designs

The designs of the token system and smart contract in blockchain provide an incentive for autonomous IoT applications. Lin *et al.* introduce blockchain to the IoT knowledge trading market, which ensures knowledge management and trading decentralization, non-tampering, efficient automation and fairness [115]. They develop a proof of trading consensus protocol to reduce the resource consumption of PoW and a noncooperative game-based pricing strategy to improve knowledge quality under the same budget. In EdgeChain [116], a private blockchain and its token system are integrated to link the edge cloud resource pool with each IoT device account and resource usage and hence regulate the IoT device behavior in an undeniable and automated manner.

Blockchain technology can provide trusted, secure and privacy-preserved ser-vices for IoT applications. The services can be adopted to authenticate resource constrained, low-cost IoT devices. In [117], device IDs are generated by the phy-sically unclonable functions and then uploaded to the blockchain by registered manufacturers. IoT devices can be verified by checking whether their IDs are present in the blockchain. The services can also be adopted to for trusted data services. In [118], a blockchain-based infrastructure is developed to support security and privacy-oriented smart contract services for the IoT sharing economy in smart cities. The processing results in smart cities, such as significant event information and semantic digital analytics, are saved in blockchain to facilitate sharing economy services.

As a decentralized system, blockchain can achieve anonymous communication with its pseudonymous addresses design. In [119], electric vehicles can have multiple pseudonymous addresses obtained from a trusted authority, such as government department. The pseudonymous addresses are used for energy trading and hiding the true identities of vehicles. The pseudonymous design has also been adopted to keep the true identities private from the roadside units in the vehicular data sharing [120].

## 5.4.4   The structure of blockchain-based IoT applications

Two different structures can be applied in IoT-blockchain applications depending on the various abilities of IoT devices.

### 5.4.4.1   IoT-involved blockchain

IoT devices would join the blockchain network and be part of the core functions of blockchain [14], such as generating transactions of raw sensory data, verifying transactions and even mining blocks. Three virtual roles, i.e., light node, full node and miner [121], needed to be supported in blockchain-IoT networks. The vehicle ad hoc network demonstrated on the left-hand side of Figure 5.3 is a potential application running on this structure [15]. The miners mine transactions into blocks and store all blocks and have the highest demand for storage and computation. The full nodes store all the blocks, including the block headers and block bodies but do not play block mining. The full nodes require massive storage and a certain level of computation. The IoT end devices run as light nodes in blockchain networks. The IoT devices can generate private keys independently or register with the certificate authority (CA) for access control and audit. The light nodes store the block headers and generate transactions but not mine blocks, they can be supported by the Simplified Payment Verification (SPV) technology [58], as will be introduced later. The light nodes can require less storage and computing power, as compared with

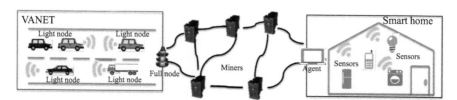

*Figure 5.3   Illustration of the structure of blockchain-based IoT networks, where the VANET on the left-hand side is an example of the IoT-involved blockchain structure, and smart home on the right-hand side of the figure is an example of the blockchain as the service for IoT. IoT data collected by light and full nodes in VANET are sent to miners in the form of transactions, while agents generate and send transactions to miners for sensors in smart home, based on the data collected by sensors. Miners of both structures are computationally capable devices forming P2P networks to generate blocks and implement blockchains; see the middle of the figure*

the full nodes and miners. Wallet [122] is a special type of light nodes, requiring the minimum storage and computing power. Wallet only has the basic function of transactions and has to be served by full nodes to retrieve data mined in blocks. Take the Hyperledger Fabric, for example [104], new clients, e.g., IoT devices, would need to register and enroll with the CA first and then maintain their private keys. Here, private keys possessed by clients (light nodes) are applied to generate signatures of transactions to valid the owners of transactions. The clients only generate and broadcast transactions.

### 5.4.4.2    Blockchain as a service for IoT

Blockchain provides a service layer [104,123–125] to integrate with the typical IoT architecture, such as the four-level architecture introduced in Section 5.2. Typically, this structure consists of three virtual roles, i.e., sensor, agent and miner [123]. The smart home demonstrated on the right-hand side of Figure 5.3 is a typical IoT application running on this structure [126]. IoT sensors collect sensory data and interact with blockchain services through blockchain agents. The sensors do not take part in blockchain functions. The agents can interpret the collected sensory data as transactions and broadcast the transactions into the blockchain network [123]. The agents can also take responsibilities of transaction securities using the private keys of the agents, while the IoT devices do not have the keys and are not involved in the blockchain. Miners, forming a P2P network, implement the core function of the blockchain, i.e., verifying transactions and mining transactions into blocks.

### 5.4.4.3    Blockchain-based IoT-edge computing

Edge computing provides real-time data processing services for IoT applications where distributed edge servers are located closer to IoT devices/applications compared with centralized cloud servers [127]. Edge computing can be an auspicious solution to enabling resource-limited IoT devices to join the heavy block mining process. As suggested in [128], the heavy PoW tasks can be offloaded to the edge computing servers, where the offloaded PoW mining tasks are priced by the provider. The mining tasks can also be offloaded to a group of nearby users [129]. Meanwhile, the content caching, i.e., storing the blocks chained with their hash values, can also be offloaded to edge computing nodes. There is a trade-off between offloading and caching for IoT devices, where the offloading saves computing and storage but consumes energy and time on the communications, while the caching strategy can reduce the communication overhead but increase the computing and storage cost. Such trade-off widely exists in the edge computing and can be formulated as an optimization problem [130].

The payload of light IoT devices can be further reduced by letting the edge computing servers to run all the blockchain services, including the block mining process and the chain data storage. In EdgeChain [116], the heavy PoW mining work is only done by the edge servers, while the resource-constrained IoT devices are only blockchain and smart contract clients. By introducing blockchain to edge computing, the data integrity and security during the task offloading process can be guaranteed [131].

#### 5.4.4.4   Comparison

The IoT-involved blockchain structure achieves security and data integrity by deploying the blockchain directly on end devices. IoT devices running light node can generate and verify messages in the form of transaction with the help of the SPV technology. On the contrary, the data integrity in the case of blockchain as the service relies on the security and trustworthiness of the agents. Due to the fact that the agents act as proxies between the IoT devices and the blockchain network, the agent can carry out the man-in-the-middle attacks, e.g., injection, tampering and forging. In the meantime, the agents increase the risk of single-point failure.

The structure of "blockchain as services" is easy and flexible to deploy. With the assistance of agents, the IoT module maintains its own characteristics to some extent and, therefore, requires limited modifications on the current system to partner with the blockchain. For example, the redundancy of sensory data can be solved by using traditional aggregation algorithms [132] at the agents. The aggregated results can reduce the volume of sensory data and relieve the high requirement of IoT applications on the transaction capacity. In contrast, in an IoT-involved blockchain, the IoT devices have to be reprogrammed to run blockchain applications. The blockchain applications can be resource consuming, e.g., computation and connection, and can only be deployed on specific devices.

The structure of "blockchain as services" scarifies the decentralization of blockchain where the blockchain can be tampered if a limited number of centralized blockchain servers are compromised. The blockchain-based IoT-Edge computing is a more decentralized structure, where IoT devices can join the blockchain with the help of the edge computing servers. The payload of IoT devices could be adjusted according to the required trust level and resource budget of IoT devices.

### 5.4.5   Challenges of applying blockchain in IoT applications

Current blockchains are designed to run in P2P homogeneous networks. However, the characteristics of IoT, for example, limited resource of end devices as compared to high-performance servers or desktop computing devices, prevent directly deploying blockchain for IoT. The application of blockchain on IoT devices faces the following challenges.

*Computation*: The blockchain activity is unaffordable for the light-weight IoT devices. Some advanced cryptography algorithms, e.g., zero-knowledge [133] and attribute-based encryption (ABE) [124], used in the privacy-preserving blockchains are too heavy for IoT devices. A full node in blockchain has to verify and search every block and transaction, which can also be a heavy load for the resource-limited IoT devices [134]. The PoW-like consensus protocols are unable to run on IoT devices. In the case of Bitcoin, the whole network can conduct around 1,020 hashes per second [135]. Modern graphics processing unit can achieve about 107 hashes per second [136]. However, even a powerful IoT device, e.g., Raspberry pi 3 [137], can only achieve about 104 hashes per second [138]. As a result, the IoT devices cannot contribute enough computational resources and afford the PoW tasks.

*Storage*: A massive storage required by blockchain can be prohibitive for IoT devices. There are more than $6 \times 105$ blocks in Bitcoin in 12 years. The size of the whole Bitcoin blockchain is around 270 GB [135]. There are about $6 \times 106$ blocks in Ethereum. The size of the whole Ethereum blockchain is around 400 GB [139]. The storage of all blocks is necessary. Without this massive data, the IoT devices are unable to verify the transactions generated by others. Also, a transaction sender needs historical data, e.g., balance and transaction index, to generate new transactions. As a result, the IoT devices should either trust itself by taking the storage load or trust remote servers that impose extra communication overhead and secured communication between the IoT devices and the trusted servers, although the storage demands can be relieved by running IoT devices as light nodes in blockchain system, which, however, still need to store the block headers. Even with advanced blockchain technology, e.g., SPV technology, the header size can be reduced to about 80 bytes for a Bitcoin block [65] and 500 bytes for an Ethereum block [140]. Moreover, it is expensive to store data on blockchain. For example, the cost per gigabyte data storage in Ethereum is about $2 \times 105$ US dollars [141]. Specifically, a single nonzero 32 bytes data costs 20k gwei/gas and 1 ether is worth roughly 12.90 US dollars [141]. The price is too expensive to be practical in IoT applications. IoT generates big data. The total size of data could be explosive in blockchain-powered IoT because every block would be duplicated $n$ times in an $n$-node blockchain network.

*Communication*: Nodes in blockchain require frequent transmissions and data exchanges. This is because blockchain runs on a P2P network and keeps on exchanging data to maintain consistent records, e.g., for the latest transactions and blocks. Wireless communication technologies, widely used to connect IoT devices, suffer from shadowing, fading and interference, and far unreliable than wired connections [142] in typical blockchain projects, e.g., Bitcoin. The capacity of wireless technologies is far lower than the requirement of blockchain. For example, Bluetooth (IEEE 802.15.1) can provide 720 kbps data rate; ZigBee (IEEE 802.15.4) can provide 250 kbps data rate; Ultra-wideband (UWB, IEEE802.15.3) can provide 110 Mbps data rate; Wi-Fi (802.11 a/b/g) can provide 54 Mbps data rate [35]. NBIoT [36] can provide around 100 kbps signal rate [143].

*Energy*: Some IoT devices are designed to operate for a long time with battery energy supple. For example, an IoT device is designed to consume 0.3 mWh/day and operate at least 5 years using a CR2032 battery with the capacity of 600 mWh [143]. IoT devices adopt energy-saving strategies, e.g., sleep mode [144], and high-efficiency communication technologies, e.g., NB-IoT [143]. However, the computation and communication required by blockchain operations are typically energy hungry. For example, SHA-256 requires around 90 nJ/B [145]. The normalized communication energy cost of Bluetooth is around 140 mJ/Mb; ZigBee is around 300 mJ/Mb; UWB is around 7 mJ/Mb, and Wi-Fi is around 13 mJ/Mb [35]. As a result, the aforementioned energy budget of 0.3 mWh/day can only support about 0.5 MB data (half of a Bitcoin block) processing and transmission using the ZigBee protocol.

*Mobility and partition of IoT*: The wireless network can be divided into an infrastructure mode, in which all packets are forwarded by network infrastructures (base stations), and an ad hoc mode, where the network does not rely on preexisting infrastructures and each node forwards data for other nodes [146]. The mobility of IoT devices can undermine blockchain performance. In the infrastructure-based wireless network, the mobility of devices can lead to the growth of signaling and control messages [147]. In contrast, in wireless ad hoc networks, network partitioning divides the networks into disconnected parts when mobile nodes move with diverse patterns [148].

*Latency and capacity*: High latency of blockchain is used to ensure consistency in the decentralized blockchain networks. The latency that is typically tolerant to blockchain is unacceptable for many IoT applications. For example, the block confirmation time of 10 min in Bitcoin is too long for delay-sensitive IoT applications, such as vehicle networks. As a matter of fact, high latency of blockchain leads to the limited blockchain capacity. The capacity of blockchains, e.g., 1 MB per 10 min of Bitcoin, is far lower than the requirement of IoT applications. The capacity requirement of IoT varies with different applications. For example, in the application of IoT-based smart city [149], the vehicular traces of 700 cars in 24 h is 4.03 GB, around 0.24 MB per hour per car. Meanwhile, the parking lot data from 55 points is 294 KB in around 5 months, i.e., 36 B/day per point. The capacity requirement of IoT applications would continuously proliferate with the increasing number of IoT devices.

## 5.4.6    Potential blockchain designs in IoT applications

### 5.4.6.1    Format of transactions

Different from transactions in Bitcoin, the transactions in IoT applications need to support user-defined data structures [150]. A practical example is the transaction in IoT applications built on Ethereum [103,150,151]. Different from a Bitcoin transaction, an Ethereum transaction has a data field indicating the data to be transferred. The data field has variable length, and a sender can pay a higher transaction fee for a longer data field. Note that the transaction fee should be less than the gas limit per block in Ethereum. In other words, the data field cannot enlarge unlimitedly.

The transaction confirmation delay can be affected by transaction size, especially in the IoT networks with unreliable wireless channels. Small transactions can achieve a high transmission success rate and low transmission delay. The User Datagram Protocol (UDP), as a light-weight protocol, is widely used in IoT [152]. Due to the fact that UDP does not provide error-correction, it is better to keep the transaction size less than the payloads of network protocols, e.g., UDP and IP, to avoid fragmentation and improve the transmission success rate. As a result, smaller transactions are expected to be observed by a large number of miners with higher probabilities to be mined into blocks, than large transactions.

The delay can be mitigated with agents that wirelessly connect IoT devices and connect the miners with wire. The agents equally broadcast the transactions with different sizes to the miners.

### 5.4.6.2    Incentive and token

Transaction fee is important to balance the transaction cost and adjust the block-chain resource consumption. For example, transaction fee is used to measure the complexity of transactions in Ethereum [140]. The transactions consuming more resources incur higher transaction fees. On the other hand, the transaction fee also provides a way to reallocate resources, especially in capacity-limited public blockchains, e.g., Bitcoin with the capacity of 7 tps. In the case of large number of transactions at a moment, transactions can suffer from long confirmation time, and transaction senders can pay more transaction fees to the miners to be given priority (e.g., shorter confirmation time).

The incentive of transaction fee (token) is also attractive and non-negligible in IoT networks. A token system in blockchain can be used as a reliable reputation or trust system [153]. The transaction fee can increase the cost of attacks in comparison with traditional IoT attacks, e.g., the forged message and DoS attack, and hence discouraging the malicious behaviors [140].

IoT devices may not be able to mine blocks to earn tokens for transaction fees due to their limited resources and typically poor (wireless) backbone links. The IoT devices can "sell" its service, e.g., the renewable energy [154], for tokens. As a return, the service users, e.g., the IoT administrator or cluster header, recharge the IoT devices. The IoT devices are expected to actively take part in blockchain and obey benign behavioral patterns, although they are prone to act selfish attack [155] with limited bandwidth, energy and computation resources. With smart contract technologies, the IoT devices can purchase resources, e.g., power or data pack. This can motivate the IoT devices to earn tokens.

### 5.4.6.3    Off-chain payment

The off-chain payment scheme is proposed to handle frequent and small-amount transactions in throughput-limited blockchains and therefore minimizes the cost and reduces the confirmation delay of IoT applications trading on blockchains. The off-chain payment scheme moves the transactions outside of blockchain and saves the result of a batch of transactions in the blockchain. Lightning network is popular off-chain payment solution that implements the hashed time lock contracts with bidirectional payment channels [156]. In the lightning network, transacting parties first need to create a transactional channel with a multi-signature wallet and deposit a certain amount of tokens into the wallet. With the wallet, the transacting parties can perform unlimited transactions that reallocate the tokens in the wallet. When the transactional channel gets closed, the channel algorithm updates the latest balance to the blockchain. The hashed time lock contract mechanism ensures that all transactions are undeniable and prevents the double-spending attack.

### 5.4.6.4    Smart contract

A smart contract is a piece of "cryptoeconomically secured execution of code" that runs on the basis of blockchain [157–159]. Without any assistance of third parties, the smart contract self-executes the corresponding contractual clause once the defined condition is triggered. In addition, it also provides real-time auditing, since all actions are recorded and verified as transactions in a decentralized blockchain ledger. These transactions are trackable and undeniable, hence enhancing the machine-execution security [160]. Smart contract translates various assets, such as IoT devices and digital assets, into virtual identities in blockchain, and enables them to interact with other assets [10]. Smart contract is appealing to replace normal contracts as an efficient and secure method. The code of smart contract is stored in blockchain and identified by a unique address. A smart contract can be called in two ways: one is by validated transactions with a smart contract address in the receiver field; the other way is the internal execution of code [140]. Therefore, all execution records can be traced using the blockchain ledger. The smart contract is executed independently and automatically on every node in the blockchain network. Several blockchain projects, including Ethereum and Bitcoin, have implemented smart contract [161–169]. As IoT expects sensors in unmanned areas running and acting automatically with defined rules in decentralized manner, the smart contract has the potential to improve the efficiency and security of IoT applications. IoT devices can carry out autonomous transactions through smart contracts [13]. With smart contract, blockchain is used to replace the intelligent transportation structure and realize reliable firmware update of IoT devices [170].

### 5.4.7  Security discussions on blockchain-based IoT applications

Although blockchain technology is known to be tolerant to the Byzantine Problem, blockchain has unsolved security issues that would continue to exist in blockchain-based IoT networks.

#### 5.4.7.1  Privacy

Blockchain can suffer from privacy issues, including user's privacy and data confidentiality, due to the fact that transactions are designed to be publicly viewed and verified by all the peers.

1. Users privacy: Although a user can create multiple virtual identities independently in blockchain, the one-to-many mapping between a physical user and virtual identities can be constructed on the basis of a transaction graph [171–173], and the identity of a physical user can be conjectured [174–176].

    A fully anonymous electronic cash should achieve untraceability (or in other words, for each incoming transaction all possible senders are equiprobable) and achieve unlinkability (or in other words, for any two outgoing transactions, it is impossible to prove they are sent to the same person) [177]. Bitcoin is not anonymous but pseudo-anonymous [177,178]. That is achieved by three means, the mapping of a physical user to the virtual identity is maintained by the user only; virtual identities are allowed to be independently generated as many as required; mixing service is provided to mix the funds of a number of virtual identities to confuse and prevent backtracking the original sources of funds [179].

The user's privacy is protected by advanced cryptography technologies in recent blockchains. Hawk [180] attempted to solve the privacy issue of smart contracts in public blockchain, which automatically generates an efficient cryptographic protocol using cryptographic primitives, namely, zero-knowledge proofs [181]. Zero-knowledge proof enables a statement to be verified without any information except the statement itself [182]. Zero-knowledge proof has also been used in Zerocoin [183], Zerocash [184], Provisions [185], etc., to achieve anonymous proof of ownership instead of the public-key-based signatures. Although privacy-preserving, the zero-knowledge-based cryptocurrencies require more resources that highly restrict their applications. For example, a Zerocoin transaction is longer than 45 kB and needs 450 ms to be verified [184]. Generating a Zerocash transaction consumes around 3.2 GB of memory and around 50 s computing time [133]. Another key technology to preserve privacy of users is ring signature [186,187], which is performed by any member of a group of users with its private key and others' public keys. In ring signature, a statement is endorsed by members in a particular group of people. For example, Monero [188] is an untraceable blockchain based on ring signature which breaks the link between sender and transaction. The ring signature does not guarantee the unlinkability of the transaction and receiver, as the transactions do need the address of the receiver to be delivered. CryptoNote [177] achieves the unlinkability with a single address by performing Diffie–Hellman exchanges to get a shared secret between the sender and the receiver. One-time destination key is then gener-ated by the sender and used as the temporary address of the receiver of the transaction. Once the transaction is identified by checking every passing transaction, the real receiver can recover the corresponding one-time key and spend the fund. Note that there is a trade-off between privacy and capacity because the size of a transaction would grow with an increasing size of the group.

2.  Data privacy: The aforementioned untraceability and unlinkability do not interact with or support data confidentiality. IoT-blockchain also needs to keep data confidential. The confidentiality of blockchain can be preserved by con-fidential transaction technologies. For example, Elements project [189] and Monero [190] keep the content of transactions, i.e., the amount to be trans-ferred, only visible to intended participants. Meanwhile, the content can be verified such that no more coins than available ones can be spent in a crypto-graphic means. Confidential transactions utilize several cryptographic technol-ogies, including Borromean ring signatures [191] and Pedersen commitment schemes [191].

Another possible solution for privacy is the ABE [192], where secret keys are generated on the basis of the attributes of peers. By applying ABE, sensory data in transactions can be encrypted and decrypted by the miners and users, using decryption credentials from attribute authorities, if and only if attributes of the miners or users satisfy the access structure of the ciphertext [124]. Fully homomorphic encryption (FHE) [193] that allows computations on the encrypted data provides another solution. Although FHE achieves higher confidentiality as the data is processed without data decryption [19], it is inefficient and thus has not been implemented in practice [20].

### 5.4.7.2 Identity and device management

In IoT applications, the owners should know the identities of their devices and vice versa [44]. However, in current public blockchains, e.g., Bitcoin and Ethereum, peers are defined by their public addresses that can be created independently without prior notification to the others. A query–answer model-based name service is proposed in [194], where virtual identities of IoT devices are verified according to their latest activities. It is considered in [194] that a physical node can be interpreted as multiple virtual nodes in blockchains. In the case of private blockchains, the peers need to be authorized to enter the blockchain network. As a result, the identity management is the fundamental requirement of private blockchains. For example, Hyperledger Fabric provides identity management to implement the enrollment and transaction certificates [104].

### 5.4.7.3 Access control

As a distributed system, blockchain enables IoT devices to formulate their own access control policies and take full control of their own data, achieving device democracy [23]. One technology to implement access control is programmable smart contracts [195]. The smart contracts, implementing access control policies, can be either deployed upon data, subject to the identity of the data controller or specific data; or upon the data controller for multiple data subjects. The other way to implement access control is to use the blockchain as a database to store all access control policies for each pair of resource and requester in the form of transactions [196,197]. If an access request is admitted, the access grant transaction can be recorded in the blockchain and broadcast to the blockchain network. Otherwise, the access request transaction is rejected and a notification is sent to its sender.

## 5.5 Blockchain for IoT: technologies

In this section, we discuss typical technologies of blockchains which can be used in IoT applications. We first present three categories of current blockchain networks and map IoT applications into suitable blockchain categories. Further, the core function of blockchain, namely, the consensus protocol, is analyzed from two key points, followed by represent blockchain projects compared in the suitability in IoT applications.

Based on access controls of the blockchain networks, the state-of-the-art blockchains can be categorized into public blockchain, private blockchain and hybrid blockchain which mixes of the former two.

1. *Public blockchain*: The dominant class of blockchain is public blockchain in which, with no access control, any uncertified, untrustworthy node can read and record transactions and take part in mining blocks and contributing to

blockchain [198]. Designed for open-access public distributed networks, public blockchains can provide strong scalability. However, preserving the consistent records of public blockchain becomes increasingly difficult, as the network scales up and would compromise the block generation rate of public block-chain consequently. This is due to the fact that, without access control, public networks do not have strict control policy on the identification and certification of any participants [83], and therefore the implemented consensus protocols have to scarify the block generation rate for security. Specifically, PoW and proof-of-transfer (PoX) are normally used in public blockchain as consensus protocols, achieving lower block generation rate compared with PBFT algorithm used in private blockchain, which will be analyzed in detail later in this section.

2. *Private blockchain*: Another popular class of blockchain is private blockchain that resides in closed proprietary networks with stringent access control and read/write permission, as well as participant identification and certification [199]. Private blockchains can meet the privacy requirement and has been increasingly drawing attention from financial institutions [200]. The proprie-tary networks, on which private blockchains operate, can be optimized for high speed and low latency [201]. For example, a high speed of up to tens of thousands transactions per second can be achieved in private blockchains [202].

   Private blockchain adopts BFT protocols, i.e., PBFT and its variability, as consensus protocols, which provide higher capacity with restricted access control. The access control provided by private blockchain further protects IoT applications from external adversaries [203]. In general, private blockchain is suitable for IoT applications with small scale of miners, because of the high communication complexity and overhead of BFT protocols. When the network size goes beyond 20, the capacity of private blockchain dramatically slows down [204].

   Apart from various BFT consensus protocols, private blockchain can use other efficient consensus protocols, e.g., Paxos [74] and Raft [205], in response to specific types of failures, e.g., crash failures [68] and fail-stop failures [73].

3. *Hybrid blockchain*: Another class of blockchain is a hybrid blockchain that was proposed to leverage the advantages of public and private blockchains, to be more specific, the block generate rate of private blockchain and the scalability of public blockchain [201].

   For instance, Luu *et al.* [206,207] developed a computationally scalable Byzantine consensus protocol for blockchains, where the capacity of block-chain can scale nearly linearly (i.e., $O(\log nn)$ or $O(\log\log nn)$) with the computation capability. In this design, a permissionless distributed network is uniformly clustered into smaller committees. First, the peers in network need to solve the PoW puzzle to prove their identities and avoid Sybil attack. Then peers are uniformly clustered into committees based on their computational power revealed through the required time to solve the PoW puzzle. Each committee processes a disjoint set of transactions. The intra-committee con-sensus is achieved by using Byzantine consensus protocols, i.e., PBFT. The final consensus among committees, achieved by the Byzantine consensus protocols, is broadcasted across the network. This hybrid design exhibits strong scalability to large-scale networks with, e.g., 1,600 nodes.

Another recent example of hybrid blockchain is ByzCoin [82] that dynamically forms hash power-proportionate consensus groups to collect recently successful block miners. Communication trees can be employed to optimize transaction commitment and verification under normal operation.

More examples of hybrid blockchain include a resilience optimal Byzantine consensus algorithm that Crain *et al.* [208] proposed for consortium blockchain which relies on neither a leader, nor signatures or randomization. The proposed consensus protocol involves reducing multivariate Byzantine consensus to binary Byzantine consensus satisfying a validity property. The property is that if all nonfaulty processes propose the same value, no other value can be decided.

The hybrid blockchain is attractive to IoT applications due to the complexity and heterogeneity of IoT networks. A hierarchical blockchain structure was proposed for the smart home applications, where a private blockchain, maintained by resourceful "miners," runs at every home and public blockchain runs on the "miner" network [126].

The abovementioned three kinds of blockchain are suitable for different applications. The consensus protocol is the core to ensure the function of blockchain. In the blockchain network, nodes broadcast transactions throughout the whole network and reach consensus on the accepted transactions by following the consensus protocol. Consensus protocol addresses two major problems: What is the principle to validate unit data? and What is the structure of unit data in the blockchain ledger?

## 5.5.1 *The principle of unit data validation*

### 5.5.1.1 Proof-of-work

PoW provides a practical means to achieve consensus among the chains of blocks generated in a distributed fashion, meanwhile preventing untrustworthy participants from tampering or corrupting the chains. PoW produces problems that are hard to accomplish but easy to be verified, e.g., using hash functions that are one-way functions easy to compute with a given input but hard to derive the input from the output. Take the Bitcoin blockchain, for example. Every block in Bitcoin takes around 10 min to be mined across the entire network. On the other hand, the answer for PoW can be easily verified with a hash operation. In this way, Bitcoin can implement a one-CPU-one-vote strategy [58] to prevent Sybil attack [209] where a single entity can pretend to be multiple identities in a consensus process.

Bitcoin PoW is set by a global target at the $i$th epoch, denoted by $T_i$. By adjusting the 32-bit "nonce" field, the hash of a valid block header, concatenating all the fields in the header, including version, previous block header hash, Merkle root hash, time, $n$Bits and nonce, needs to be equal to or less than the target [210]. A smaller $T_i$ is a stricter target and it is hard to find a hash outcome equal to or less than a small $T_i$ through adjusting the "nonce" field.

Once a new block is generated, it is sent to the whole network using flooding algorithms [211], i.e., every incoming packet is sent through every outgoing link. When a peer in Bitcoin network receives a new block, it checks whether the "*n*Bits" value matches the target renewal process and calculates the hash of the block header to check whether the hash of the header meets the claimed target in the "*n*Bits" field. The receiver also checks other content of the block for validation [134].

In general, PoW is only used to find the nonce and does not contribute useful services. An exception is that Permacoin [212] uses PoW to provide data pre-servation service. Permacoin requires peers to invest storage to store files, and computational resources to carry out the proof process and provide services.

### 5.5.1.2  Proof-of-transfer

Participating peers can also be validated via other proofs, instead of finding the nonce, i.e., PoW. Another popular proof is PoS [81], which is an energy-saving alternative to PoW. Instead of demanding users to find a nonce, PoS requires the peers to prove the ownership of the amount of currency under the assumption that the peers owning more currencies would be less likely to attack the network's integrity. Originating from [213], an account-balance-based selection has been developed to approve blocks. However, such selection is inherently unfair because a single richest participant is bound to dominate the network.

Proof-of-activity (PoA) [214] incorporates PoW and PoS. First, the miners try to generate empty block headers, i.e., header data that consist of the hash of the previous block, the miner's public address, the index for the block and a nonce, by solving a hash puzzle like PoW. After that the empty block headers are broadcasted to the network. $N$ "lucky" stakeholders are selected to sign the block header. The $N$th stakeholder combines the empty block header, which has been approved by $(N - 1)$ stakeholders, and transactions into a block. The reward is shared among the $N$ stakeholders and the miner. Unlike PoW, the attacks with more than 50% hash power in PoA are unable to dominate the existing block chain or determine the chain extension. However, PoA requires the empty block header to be signed and broadcast $N$ times, hence increasing communication complexity and reducing system capacity.

Many other solutions have also been proposed in coupling with the stake size to decide which one to generate the next block. In particular, BlackCoin [215] uses randomization to predict the next generator, and Peercoin favors coin-age-based selection [81]. Compared to PoW, PoS is more energy efficient. Unfortunately, since the cost of mining blocks in PoS is low, and nearly zero, PoS is vulnerable to attacks, e.g., long-range attack, nothing at stake attack, initial distribution attack, bride attack, coin age accumulation attack and precomputing attack [216]. For example, an attacker having enough stake can attempt to overwrite the blockchain from some existing block. Even adversaries with a minority set of stakes in PoS-based blockchain can produce a valid alternative blockchain starting from the genesis block (or any sufficiently old block), known as the long-range attack. The nodes newly joining the blockchain network are not able to reliably distinguish the actual blockchain and the alternative blockchain. On the contrary, such attacks are prevented by the enormous amount of computing power/time needed to reconstruct the blockchain in PoW.

Other proposed PoX approaches used in public blockchain include proof-of-deposit (PoD) [217], proof-of-burn (PoB) [218] and proof-of-elapsed-time (PoET) [219]. In PoD, the participation in mining requires depositing coins in a time-locked bond account, during which the coins cannot be transferred. Each miner has a voting power corresponding to the amount of the locked coins. A block is valid, as long as it receives 2/3 of the total voting power. The voting process resembles to PBFT and is a round-based consensus protocol. The voting process consists of three steps: propose, pre-vote and pre-commit. After a peer has received more than 2/3 of precommits, it proceeds to extend its chain. PoD can destroy the bonded coins of a participator who signs conflicting transactions, so as to avoid double-spending attack [217]. In PoB, a miner sends coins to an un-spendable address, i.e., burn coin, to mine blocks. The coins, from un-spendable addresses, can be shared between miners who mine blocks as rewards. However, the coin burn is uncontrollable and the total coin can decrease [218]. Contributed by Intel, Sawtooth uses PoET [219] as the consensus protocol. In PoET, every node is given a trusted random time. After the time expires, the corresponding node can generate a block. PoET is based on the Intel trust platform Software Guard Extensions [220].

### 5.5.1.3  Practical Byzantine fault tolerance

BFT [68] is typically used in private blockchain to formulate consensus protocols and guarantees consistency by exploiting the solutions to the Byzantine Generals' Problems—agreement problems, as described in Section 5.3.2. Particularly, the PBFT algorithm [16] has been extensively used to eliminate the Byzantine failures. In 1999, Castro and Liskov proposed the first BFT, state machine replication algorithm, named "practical Byzantine fault tolerance (PBFT)" [16], which yields a communication overhead of $O(n^2)$ in a network of $n$ peers. As a leader-based BFT algorithm, PBFT has one *primary* and $(n - 1)$ *backups* in an $n$-node network, where the backups can be corrupted. The *primary* is responsible for receiving the requests from clients and initializing the algorithm. Inspired by Viewstamped Replication [221] and illustrated in Figure 5.4, PBFT consists of four stages: (a) a client sends a request to invoke a service operation to the primary; (b) the primary multicasts the operation to the backups; in specific, the *primary* (replica 0) assigns the sequence number to the $m$th request from the client and multicasts a *PRE-PREPARE* message with the assignment; (c) replicas execute the request and reply to the client; if a *backup* agrees on the assignment, i.e., correct and validated parameters, it multicasts a *PREPARE* message. When a *backup* receives messages that agree on the assignment from a quorum, i.e., $2f$-validated and consistent *PREPARE* messages from different *backups*, it multicasts a *COMMIT* message. A *backup* executes the request $m$ and sends a reply to the client after receiving $2f$-validated and consistent *COMMIT* messages; and (d) the client waits for $(f + 1)$ replies from different replicas with the same result that is the result of the operation tolerant to up to $f$ failures.

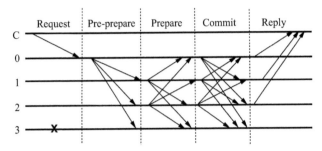

*Figure 5.4    The PBFT operation in the case of no primary faults [16], where C is the client, replica 0 is the primary, replica 1 to replica 3 are backups and replica 3 is faulty*

The PBFT algorithm is resilient. It has been proved that the PBFT algorithm can ensure $n$ peers within a synchronous and reliable network to reach consensus, as long as there are no more than $\frac{n-1}{3}$ betrayed peers [68]. Specifically, the algorithm only requires $n \geq 3f + 1$ replicas to tolerate up to $f$ faulty replicas and guarantee the consistent, fault-free output to the client [222]. This is because $(3f + 1)$ *PREPARE* messages at any backup node, including its own, are sufficient at the second stage for a credible, uncorrupted backup to generate a genuine *COMMIT* message. The third and fourth stages can both guarantee the received consistent replies to outnumber the up to $f$ faulty replies at any backup and the client.

The PBFT algorithm is efficient and is able to process thousands of requests per second with processing latency in sub-milliseconds [223]. However, apart from the $O(n^2)$ overhead, PBFT also necessitates all participating nodes to be adequately identified, certificated and authorized. For these reasons, the PBFT algorithm is suitable for private blockchain in a relatively small and controllable scale.

The PBFT algorithm is susceptive to partitioning in networks. A partition cannot extend its own chain unless the number of trustworthy nodes in the partition, denoted by $n_{pb}$, meets $n_{pb} \geq n - \lfloor (n-1)/3 \rfloor$; where $n$ is the total number of nodes in a network.

This is because PBFT can tolerate at most $\lceil (n-1)/3 \rceil$ faulty replicas out of a total of $n$ replicas [16].

### 5.5.1.4   Variability of PBFT

Miller *et al.* [224] developed an asynchronous BFT protocol, named "HoneyBadgerBFT," which can guarantee availability in the absence of time synchronization. HoneyBadgerBFT reduces the atomic broadcast protocol [225] for an asynchronous common subset (ACS) which provides better efficiency. The ACS primitive allows each node to propose a value and guarantees that every node outputs a common vector containing the input values of at least $(n - 2f)$ correct nodes in a network of $n$ peers with $f$ failures. HoneyBadgerBFT requires $O(n)$ communication cost in a network of $n$ peers. Therefore, HoneyBadgerBFT can support large network applications and achieve more than 1,500 transactions per second in a network of 104 peers.

A recent international umbrella project on blockchain, named Hyperledger, is focused on practical blockchain techniques and implements BFT algorithms in blockchain [226]. Hyperledger is an open source collaborative effort created to advance cross-industry blockchain applications. Hosted by the Linux Foundation, the project is participated by leading organizations in finance, banking, IoT, supply chain, manufacturing and technology. The Hyperledger contains a series of independent blockchain projects, e.g., Fabric [104], Burrow [227], Iroha [228] and Sawtooth [229].

Fabric is the flagship project contributed by digital asset and IBM. Fabric has a modular architecture and supports loading modules dynamically, e.g., consensus protocols and membership services. Fabric uses PBFT as its default consensus protocol. To keep Fabric programmable, smart contracts are specially designed to be hosted by container technologies, named "chaincode." Burrow is an extension of Ethereum and focuses on the permissioned smart contract service. It uses TenderMint [217], a BFT-type middleware for blockchain, as the consensus protocol. Iroha aims to provide encapsulated C++ components for other projects. Iroha also applies PBFT as its consensus protocol.

## 5.5.2    The structure of unit data

The structure specifies how unit data are stored and how to decide the main ledger. It refers to the case that more than one ledger exist at the same time in a distributed network. If the different ledgers are all accepted, the blockchain network gains more capacity but also the risks to double spending. Double-spending attack refers to the fault that a coin is successfully spent more than once [58]. In general case, double-spending attack leads to contradictory records in a distributed system. Blockchain can only ensure that all records are consistent at the end. Before eventually accepted, the records can be temporarily accepted and then dropped. This makes the double-spending attack possible.

### 5.5.2.1    Chained blocks

In a blockchain with chained-data structure, such as Bitcoin, only a single chain can be eventually accepted across the system, and the chain is named the main chain [81]. Each block contains a cryptographic hash of the previous block header, using the SHA-256 hash algorithm, which links the current block to the previous block, as shown in Figure 5.1. This prevents tampering upon the blockchain. It is possible that the chains maintained at different parts of the network are inconsistent, due to a limited view of each part on the rest of the network; or in the other words, network partitioning that can prevail in future IoT networks. To address this, Bitcoin takes a simple rule that has the system to only take the longest of the chains as the main chain and discard the rest [58]. For practical implementation, a peer in blockchain switches to the longer blockchain if it sees one, or retains its own.

A double-spending attack can be undergone, when conflicting transactions/ blocks exist in different partitions. Bitcoin recommends the coin receivers to wait for six block confirmations [58], to prevent double-spending attacks. A double-spending attack also occurs in chained blockchain by leveraging the consensus protocols. Take 51% attack [87] PoW, for example. If a powerful node holds more than 50% of the network computational resource, the powerful attacker is able to generate blocks so fast and hijack the main chain yielding the longest chain rule. As a result, the attacker can dominate the chain of arbitrary length. By 2020, the network hash rate is about 1,020 hash per second [135], and the 51% attack becomes nearly impossible. Moreover, Bitcoin limits the block generation rate to be one block per 10 min, so as to mitigate inconsistency. This has been achieved by adjusting the difficulty of PoW as described earlier in this section.

### 5.5.2.2  Directed acyclic graph

Other solutions for consensus exploit the fact that some abandoned blocks, mined under a consensus protocol but excluded from the main chain because of forks, can be used to improve the capacity. This can be achieved by adjusting the data structure. One of the consensus protocols, named Tangle [230], uses DAG to organize blocks, instead of chain, where DAG is a finite directed graph with no directed cycles. In Tangle, a transaction must approve (point to) two previous transactions. Finally, one of the conflicting records can win the approval competition and be accepted. Unlike the single copy in the chain structure, Tangle does not drop conflicting transactions and keeps them in different branches of DAG. The DAG structure can achieve better capacity.

### 5.5.2.3  Greedy Heaviest-Observed Sub-Tree

Another protocol, named Greedy Heaviest-Observed Sub-Tree (GHOST), arranges blocks in tree structures [231,232]. It takes the path from the genesis block, the first block in the blockchain, to the heaviest sub-tree that has the maximum number of blocks, or in other words, contains the heaviest computation quantity as the publicly accepted main chain. GHOST can speed up generating blocks from around 10 min per block in Bitcoin to 12 s per block in Ethereum [140,233]. As a result, the capacity of blockchain can be improved.

### 5.5.2.4  Mix structure

Bitcoin-NG (next generation) [234] is a public blockchain protocol that puts the task of block generation to computational powerful leaders to accelerate transaction confirmation. Bitcoin-NG decouples Bitcoin's blockchain operations into two phases of leader election and transaction serialization. The leader election is based on the speed of solving computationally demanding puzzles like PoW. The elected leader is recorded in the key blocks. The leader has the responsibility of serializing transactions by generating microblocks. A microblock contains transactions and a header referring to the previous block. The microblock does not contain the nonce and therefore can be generated in a predefined rate that can be much higher than the generation rate of key blocks. The key blocks and microblocks are chained together

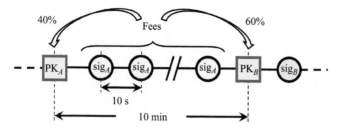

*Figure 5.5*   *The structure of the Bitcoin-NG chain. Microblocks (circles) are signed with the private key matching the public key in the last key block (squares). Fee is distributed 40% to the leader and 60% to the next one [234]*

like Bitcoin, as shown in Figure 5.5. Each block has a header containing the unique reference of its predecessor.

### 5.5.3   *Comparison of blockchain for IoT application*

A comparative summary of existing blockchain techniques for IoT application is provided in Table 5.1 with emphasis on their suitability for IoT networks. All IoT devices can use the blockchain services. Resourceful IoT devices with powerful computational ability, persistent power supply, sufficient storage and high-speed network connections, such as vehicles [14], can be miners or full nodes in blockchains. The IoT devices with less powerful computing capability, e.g., smart TV, can be light nodes in blockchain and obtain blockchain services via full nodes or miners. The IoT devices with limited storage, computing and communication abilities can interact with the blockchain core functions via agents (e.g., the full nodes) [123]. The consensus protocols are the core functions that decide the performance of blockchain-based IoT applications, such as block rates, consistency, scalability, and security. PoW-based consensus protocols are reported to be the most secure in open networks [236]. However, PoW eliminates the potential of block mining at IoT devices due to its heavy computational requirements. PoS-based consensus protocols can significantly reduce the energy consumption, as compared with PoW. PoS provides a chance for IoT devices to take part in block mining. However, the block generation rate of each of PoW-based and PoS-based consensus protocols is limited. PBFT-based consensus protocols for private blockchains can serve IoT systems with high block generation rate but bring constraints on the number of miners that can be involved [78]. Besides the consensus protocols, e.g., PoW, PoS and PBFT, the capacity and scalability also rely on the running environment and configurations, such as network speed and block size. The superscripts "−," "+" and "#" are indicative of different sources of the displayed data.

Table 5.1 *Performance comparison of blockchain in IoT application*

| Name | Type | Consensus protocol | Capacity | Scale | Application | Merits | Demerits |
|---|---|---|---|---|---|---|---|
| Bitcoin [58] | Public | PoW$^+$ Longest chain | 7 tps$^-$ | 10$^{5\#}$ | Cryptocurrency | High partition tolerance Tamper-resistant | Limited capacity High complexity |
| Ethereum [235] | Public | PoW$^+$ | Block time | 10$^{5\#}$ | Cryptocurrency smart contract | Programmable | High complexity |
| IOTA [21] | Public | GHOST PoW$^+$ TANGLE | 12s >800 tps | 10$^3$ | BC platform BC platform IoT | High partition tolerance High capacity No transaction fee partition tolerant | Not programmable |
| Fabric [104] | Private | PBFT | 10$^5$ tps | 20 | Smart contract BC platform | High capacity No fork | Low partition tolerance High communication overhead Limited scalability Authentication center required |
| Burrow [227] | Private | TenderMint | 10$^5$ tps | Tens | Smart contract | Modular architecture Smart contract support | Authentication center required |
| Sawtooth [229] | Public | PoET | N.A. | N.A. | BC platform | Low complexity | Only works with Intel CPU |
| Ppcoin [81] | Public | PoS | 0.1 tps$^\#$ | 10$^{3\#}$ | Cryptocurrency | Low complexity | Risk of attack from the richest |
| Bitcoin-NG [234] | Public | PoW | tens tps$^\#$ | 10$^3$ | Blockchain | Low complexity | Risk of malicious leader |
| SCOIN [206] | Public | SCP | >22 tps | 80 | Cryptocurrency | Committee structure | High complexity |
| Slimcoin [218] | Public | PoB | N.A. | N.A. | Cryptocurrency | Low complexity | Risk of coin loss |

N.A., not available; BC, blockchain.

- The superscript "−" indicates theoretical analysis. For example, Bitcoin has a theoretical upper bound of 7 tps for the transaction rate which is limited by the block generation rate and the block size.
- The superscript "+" indicates experimentally validated results.
- The superscript "#" indicates historical records. For example, Ethereum network has more than 30,000 nodes across the world in June 2017 [237]. In this sense, those results could be underestimated due to the lack of stress-tested.

Among the aforementioned blockchain projects, Ethereum is appropriate for many IoT applications with large numbers of IoT devices and inhomogeneous network structures. As a public blockchain, Ethereum exhibits strong scalability by supporting massive heterogeneous devices. The major drawbacks of Ethereum for IoT applications are high computational complexity and limited capacity. Nevertheless, Ethereum is evolving with efficient PoS consensus protocols in Ethereum Serenity milestone [238], which makes Ethereum more IoT friendly. On the other hand, Fabric is applicative for the IoT networks with immense data. Fabric has embedded blockchain into its client–service model and has achieved high capacity, up to tens of thousands transactions per second. However, Fabric requires a controllable network environment and cannot be as publicly accessible as the Ethereum.

## 5.6    Future research directions

This section presents future directions in optimizing security, scalability and capacity of blockchain for future large-scale high-capacity IoT applications. The design of blockchain for IoT application would also adapt to the specific properties of IoT networks, such as immense scale, inherent partitioning incomplete network connectivity, nontrivial topology, nonzero propagation delay, heterogeneous data and finite device memory.

### 5.6.1    Hierarchical chains

Different blockchains, such as low and secure public blockchains and efficient and centralized blockchains, can be integrated to fulfill different requirements on security, efficiency, capacity, latency and scalability. In [239], a public and immutable data chain, such as Ethereum, stores encrypted data for the tamper-resistant data service. Key chains maintained by service providers of IoT applications keep keys and access policies for the encrypted data in the data chain. The key chains employ the chameleon hash algorithm for chain update by permitted miners. In [240], a group chain keeps lists of miners selected with PoW tasks, while a vice chain, which is maintained by selected miners without heavy PoW work, stores transactions. The vice blockchain runs much faster than the group chain. In this way, the blockchain system capacity and scalability can be significantly improved.

### 5.6.2    Sharding

Sharding blockchain [241] is a novel mechanism to enable transactions to be processed in parallel. By this means, the block generation rate of blockchain can be significantly improved. The early sharding proposals, e.g., [207], only shard transaction processing and maintain a single public blockchain. Ubiquitously deployed IoT networks are expected to generate huge amounts of data across large landscapes. On the other hand, the data of IoT may exhibit strong locality and heterogeneity and can be only useful to local regions. This gives an opportunity of developing sharding blockchains in IoT environments. A primary chain can be designed to capture important but less frequent global events of interest across large IoT networks, while secondary chains can be designed to record frequent local events of interest only to regional networks. The two sets of blockchains can operate at different time scales. The hash values of the secondary chains can be secured in the primary chain in a transactional fashion. Particularly, the primary chain, recording less frequent global events, can be synchronized at significantly lower paces, thereby reducing the capacity requirement for preserving consistency across a large network scale. The two sets of blockchains need to be interconnected to guarantee the integrity of all records, both globally and locally. With an emphasis on implementation, some initial research activities have been reported in [242].

### 5.6.3    Side chain

Apart from the ubiquity of IoT networks, some IoT devices can have the capability of traveling over large distances, such as those installed on air crafts, inter-continental trains and ships [243]. The integrity of the data these IoT devices can generate, such as the erosion of aircraft components, is equally, if not more, important to those generated by static IoT devices. However, the data of nomadic IoT devices can be mined in blocks while the devices are away from home networks or network partitions and embedded in different blockchains. The migration and integration itself is a form of tampering. The migration of the blocks or segments involving the blocks' back to the home networks is important to maintain consistent records of nomadic devices but is challenging due to the tamper-resistant nature of blockchain. The side chain technology [200,244] provides a solution to transferring assets between multiple blockchains. With the side chain technology, the tokens can be transferred among different blockchains in a decentralized way. The asset transfer process is similar to the currency exchange [244]. However, more challenges associated with side chains to be addressed include the proliferation of the chains in home networks and the implantation of the chains into the main chain.

### 5.6.4    IoT-specific consensus

Specifically designed consensus protocols for various requirements would be important to benefit IoT-blockchain applications that are data centric. The consensus protocol can be designed to reach data consensus by validating transaction data instead of the syntax of the transactions only. Note that sensor observations are highly correlated in the space domain, due to high density in the network topology. Furthermore, the nature of the physical phenomenon constitutes the temporal correlation between consecutive observations of a sensor node. Spatial and temporal correlations, along with the collaborative nature of IoT, raise potentials to develop content-oriented consensus protocol [245]. The correctness of sensory data can be cross-validated with sensory data from its neighbors and historical data [246].

### 5.6.5   Simplified payment verification

The task of block mining can be too heavy, and the size of blockchain data can be too large, to be implanted in IoT devices. An SPV technology [58] makes it possible to verify transactions without running block mining task and storing all historical blocks. The blockchain nodes powered by SPV only need a small amount of resources and can be deployed on IoT devices. In SPV, a node only needs to keep the chained block headers and a Merkle branch linking to the transaction to the verified. Although the SPV node cannot validate the transaction by itself, it can check whether the blockchain network has accepted the transaction by comparing the Merkle branch linking to the transaction. For example, the Ethereum SPV nodes have been deployed on smart bicycles [151]. Light node is an SPV implemented in Ethereum [121]. The light nodes need to fetch blockchain data from the nodes owing all the blocks, e.g., the light Ethereum subprotocol server in Ethereum [121].

### 5.6.6   Editable blockchain

The storage of IoT devices can be very limited for the explosively growing size of a blockchain ledger, as a huge number of IoT devices keep recording a large amount of events in the long term. Even in the case of Bitcoin recording financial data, its total size has grown up to 149 gigabytes by December 2017 since the genesis block in 2009 [247]. However, the data of some IoT applications will be meaningless after a constant duration. For example, the record of food is meaningless after the food has been consumed. Hence, such data can be deleted from the blockchain to decrease the blockchain storage. Also fraud actions and records on IoT blockchains raise demand for editable blockchain technology without breaking the trust of the stored data. Editable blockchain enables delete or modify some blocks when satisfying specific conditions. As the "editability" is somewhat contrary to the inherent "immutability" of blockchain, the editable blockchain is required to guarantee secure conditions and records for any edit actions. Currently, editable blockchains have been designed with cryptographic algorithms, such as variations of the chameleon hash function [248].

## 5.7   Conclusion

This chapter surveyed the use of blockchain to resolved the myriad of data security concerns in IoT. The impact of massive IoT devices, limited computing power, low communication bandwidth and error-prone radio links on the performance of blockchain was studied. The state-of-the-art blockchain technologies were analyzed in detail, followed by comparison of the technologies in terms of applicability to the IoT scenarios. Research directions were pointed out to improve capacity, security and scalability of blockchains for future effective integration of blockchain and IoT technologies.

# References

[1]    Gubbi J, Buyya R, Marusic S, *et al*. Internet of Things (IoT): A vision, architectural elements, and future directions. Future Gener Comput Syst. 2013;29(7):
       1645–1660.

[2]    Wang H, Liu RP, Ni W, *et al*. VANET modeling and clustering design under practical traffic, channel and mobility conditions. IEEE Trans Commun. 2015;63(3):870–881.

[3]    Weber RH. Internet of Things – New security and privacy challenges. Comput Law Secur Rev. 2010;26(1):23–30.

[4]    Manyika J. The Internet of Things: Mapping the value beyond the hype. McKinsey Global Institute; 2015.

[5]    Zha X, Ni W, Liu RP, *et al*. Secure data transmission and modelling in vehicular ad hoc networks. In: 2015 Proc. IEEE Globecom Workshops (GC Wkshps'15); 2015. p. 1–6.

[6]    Katagi M and Moriai S. Lightweight cryptography for the internet of things.

[7]    Fabian B and Gunther O. Security challenges of the EPCglobal network. Commun ACM. 2009;52(7):121–125.

[8]    Rose K, Eldridge S, and Chapin L. The Internet of Things: An overview. The Internet Society; 2015. p. 1–50.

[9]    Zheng Z, Xie S, Dai HN, *et al*. Blockchain challenges and opportunities: A survey. Int J Web Grid Serv. Forthcoming.

[10]   Christidis K and Devetsikiotis M. Blockchains and smart contracts for the Internet of Things. IEEE Access. 2016;4:2292–2303.

[11]   Betts B. Blockchain and the promise of cooperative cloud storage; 2017. Available from: http://www.computerweekly.com/feature/Blockchain-and-the-promise-of-cooperative-cloud-storage.

[12]   Dorri A, Kanhere SS, and Jurdak R. Blockchain in Internet of Things: Challenges and solutions; 2016. Available from: http://arxiv.org/abs/1608.05187.

[13]   Kshetri N. Can blockchain strengthen the Internet of Things? IT Prof. 2017;19(4):68–72.

[14]   Sharma PK, Moon SY, and Park JH. Block-VN: A distributed blockchain based vehicular network architecture in smart city. J Inf Process Syst. 2017;13(1):184–195.

[15]   Leiding B, Memarmoshrefi P, and Hogrefe D. Self-managed and blockchain-based vehicular ad-hoc networks. In: 2016 Proc. ACM Int. Joint

Conf. Pervasive Ubiquitous Comput.: Adjunct. New York, NY, USA; 2016. p. 137–140.

[16]    Castro M and Liskov B. Practical Byzantine fault tolerance. In: Proc. 3rd Symp. Operating Syst. Des. Implementation (OSDI'99). New Orleans, LA, USA; 1999.

[17]    Khalilov MCK and Levi A. A survey on anonymity and privacy in Bitcoin-like digital cash systems. IEEE Commun Surv Tutor. 2018;20(3):2543–2585

[18]    Zha X, Zheng K, and Zhang D. Anti-pollution source location privacy preserving scheme in wireless sensor networks. In: Pro. 13th Annu. IEEE Int. Conf. Sensing, Commun., Netw. (SECON'16); 2016. p. 1–8.

[19]    Zyskind G, Nathan O, and Pentland A. Enigma: Decentralized computation platform with guaranteed privacy. arXiv preprint arXiv:150603471. 2015.

[20]    Zyskind G, Nathan O, and Pentland AS. Decentralizing privacy: Using blockchain to protect personal data. In: 2015 Proc. IEEE Secur. and Privacy Workshops (SPW'15). IEEE; 2015. p. 180–184.

[21]    IOTA. IOTA; 2017. Available from: https://www.iotatoken.com.

[22]    Panikkar B, Nair S, Brody P, *et al.* ADEPT: An IoT practitioner perspective. IBM; 2014. Available from: http://static1.squarespace.com/static/55f7374 3e4b051cfcc0b02cf/55f73e5ee4b09b2bff5b2eca/55f73e72e4b09b2bff5b3267/ 1442266738638/IBM-ADEPT-Practitioner-Perspective-Pre-Publication-Draft-7-Jan-2015.pdf?format=original.

[23]    Brody P and Pureswaran V. Device democracy: Saving the future of the internet of things. IBM; 2014. Available from: https://public.dhe.ibm.com/ common/ssi/ecm/gb/en/gbe03620usen/global-business-services-global-busi-ness-services-gb-executive-brief-gbe03620usen-2017pdf.

[24]    IBM Watson. Internet of Things; 2017. Available from: https://www.ibm. com/internet-of-things/.

[25]    O'Connor C. What blockchain means for you, and the Internet of Things; 2017. Available from: https://www.ibm.com/blogs/internet-of-things/wat-son-iot-blockchain/.

[26]    Fedak J. How can blockchain improve cloud computing; 2016. Available from: https://medium.com/iex-ec/how-blockchain-can-improve-cloud-com-puting-1ca24c270f4f.

[27]    Chen M, Mao S, and Liu Y. Big data: A survey. Mobile Networks Appl. 2014;19(2):171–209.

[28]    Pticek M, Podobnik V, and Jezic G. Beyond the Internet of Things: The social networking of machines. Int. J. Distrib. Sens. Netw. 2016;12(6): 8178417.

[29]    Perera C, Zaslavsky A, Christen P, *et al.* Context aware computing for the Internet of Things: A survey. IEEE Commun Surv Tutor. 2014 First quarter; 16(1):414–454.

[30]    Xu LD, He W, and Li S. Internet of Things in industries: A survey. IEEE Trans Ind Inf. 2014;10(4):2233–2243.

[31]  Al-Fuqaha A, Guizani M, Mohammadi M, *et al*. Internet of Things: A survey on enabling technologies, protocols, and applications. IEEE Commun Surv Tutor. 2015 Fourth quarter;17(4):2347–2376.

[32]  Atzori L, Iera A, and Morabito G. The Internet of Things: A survey. Comput Networks. 2010;54(15):2787–2805.

[33]  Zha X, Ni W, Wang X, *et al*. The impact of link duration on the integrity of distributed mobile networks. IEEE Trans Inf Forensics Secur. 2018;13(9): 2240–2255.

[34]  Sethi P and Sarangi SR. Internet of Things: Architectures, protocols, and applications. J Electr Comput Eng. 2017.

[35]  Lee JS, Su YW, and Shen CC. A comparative study of wireless protocols: Bluetooth, UWB, ZigBee, and Wi-Fi. In: Proc. 33rd Annu. Conf. the IEEE Ind. Elect. Soc. (IECON'07); 2007. p. 46–51.

[36]  Ratasuk R, Vejlgaard B, Mangalvedhe N, *et al*. NB-IoT system for M2M communication. In: 2016 Proc. IEEE Wireless Commun. and Netw. Conf. Workshops (WCNCW'16); 2016. p. 1–5.

[37]  Statista. Internet of Things (IoT) connected devices installed base worldwide from 2015 to 2025 (in billions); 2016. Available from: https://www.statista. com/statistics/471264/iot-number-of-connected-devices-worldwide/.

[38]  Vermesan O, Friess P, Guillemin P, *et al*. Internet of things strategic research roadmap. Internet of Things-Global Technol Soc Trends. 2011;1(2011): 9–52.

[39]  Tsai CW, Lai CF, Chiang MC, *et al*. Data mining for Internet of Things: A survey. IEEE Commun Surv Tutor. 2014;16(1):77–97.

[40]  Zha X, Ni W, Zheng K, *et al*. Collaborative authentication in decentralized dense mobile networks with key predistribution. IEEE Trans Inf Forensics Secur. 2017;12(10):2261–2275.

[41]  Gan G, Lu Z, and Jiang J. Internet of Things security analysis. In: 2011 Int. Conf. Internet Technol. and Appl.; 2011. p. 1–4.

[42]  Alsaadi E and Tubaishat A. Internet of things: features, challenges, and vulnerabilities. Int J Adv Comput Sci Inf Technol. 2015;4(1):1–13.

[43]  Liu X, Zhao M, Li S, *et al*. A security framework for the Internet of Things in the future internet architecture. Future Internet. 2017;9(3).

[44]  Roman R, Najera P, and Lopez J. Securing the Internet of Things. Computer. 2011;44(9):51–58.

[45]  Lin J, Yu W, Zhang N, *et al*. A survey on Internet of Things: Architecture, enabling technologies, security and privacy, and applications. IEEE IoT J. 2017;4(5):1125–1142.

[46]  Xu R, Wang R, Guan Z, *et al*. Achieving efficient detection against false data injection attacks in smart grid. IEEE Access. 2017;5:13787–13798.

[47]  Mehta K, Liu D, and Wright M. Protecting location privacy in sensor networks against a global eavesdropper. IEEE Trans Mobile Comput. 2012;11(2):320–336.

[48] Namvar N, Saad W, Bahadori N, *et al.* Jamming in the Internet of Things: A game-theoretic perspective. In: 2016 IEEE Global Commun. Conf. (GLOBECOM); 2016. p. 1–6.

[49] Zhang K, Liang X, Lu R, *et al.* Sybil attacks and their defenses in the Internet of Things. IEEE IoT J. 2014;1(5):372–383.

[50] Mosenia A and Jha NK. A comprehensive study of security of Internet-of-Things. IEEE Trans Emerg Top Comput. 2017;5(4):586–602.

[51] Perry JS. Anatomy of an IoT malware attack; 2017. Available from: https://www.ibm.com/developerworks/library/iot-anatomy-iot-malware-attack/.

[52] Wang X, Zheng K, Niu X, *et al.* Detection of command and control in advanced persistent threat based on independent access. In: Proc. 2016 IEEE Int. Conf. Commun. (ICC'16); 2016. p. 1–6.

[53] Boritz JE. IS practitioners' views on core concepts of information integrity. Int J Account Inf Syst. 2005;6(4):260–279.

[54] Fongen A. Identity management and integrity protection in the Internet of Things. In: Proc. 3rd Int. Conf. Emerg. Secur. Technol. (EST'12); 2012. p. 111–114.

[55] Pohls HC. JSON sensor signatures (JSS): End-to-end integrity protection from constrained device to IoT application. In: Proc. 9th Int. Conf. Innovative Mobile Internet Serv. in Ubiquitous Comput. (IMIS'15); 2015. p. 306–312.

[56] Wang C, Wang Q, Ren K, *et al.* Privacy-preserving public auditing for data storage security in cloud computing. In: Proc. 29th Annu. IEEE Int. Conf. Comput. Commun. (INFOCOM'10); 2010. p. 1–9.

[57] Davidson S, De Filippi P, and Potts J. Economics of blockchain; 2016. Available from: https://papers.ssrn.com/sol3/papers.cfm?abstractid=2744751.

[58] Nakamoto S. Bitcoin: A peer-to-peer electronic cash system; 2008. Available from: https://bitcoin.org/bitcoin.pdf.

[59] Bitcoin; 2017. Available from: https://bitcoin.org/en/.

[60] Miller A, Litton J, Pachulski A, *et al.* Discovering Bitcoin's public topology and influential nodes; 2015. Available from: https://allquantor.at/block-chainbib/pdf/miller2015topology.pdf.

[61] Coindesk. How do Bitcoin transactions work?; 2015. Available from: http://www.coindesk.com/information/how-do-bitcoin-transactions-work/.

[62] Wyman O. Blockchain in capital markets; 2016. Available from: http://www.oliverwyman.com/content/dam/oliver-wyman/global/en/2016/feb/BlockChain-In-Capital-Markets.pdf.

[63] Swan M. Blockchain. O'Reilly Media; 2015.

[64] Tschorsch F and Scheuermann B. Bitcoin and beyond: A technical survey on decentralized digital currencies. IEEE Commun Surv Tutor. 2016 Third quarter;18(3):2084–2123.

[65] Bitcoin Developer Guide; 2017. Available from: https://bitcoin.org/en/developer-guide.

[66] Merkle RC. Protocols for public key cryptosystems. In: Proc. 1st IEEE Symp. Secur. Privacy (SP'80); 1980. p. 122–122.

[67]    Ghosh D. How the Byzantine general sacked the castle: A look into blockchain; 2016. Available from: https://medium.com/@DebrajG/how-the-byzantine-general-sacked-the-castle-a-look-into-blockchain-370fe637502c.

[68]    Lamport L, Shostak R, and Pease M. The Byzantine generals problem. ACM Trans Program Lang Syst. 1982;4(3):382–401.

[69]    Poledna S. Fault-tolerant real-time systems: The problem of replica determinism. vol. 345. Springer Sci. & Business Media; 2007.

[70]    Dolev D and Strong HR. Authenticated algorithms for Byzantine agreement. SIAM J Comput. 1983;12(4):656–666.

[71]    Cristian F, Aghili H, Strong R, *et al.* Atomic broadcast: From simple message diffusion to Byzantine agreement. Inf Comput. 1995;118(1):158–179.

[72]    Perry KJ and Toueg S. Distributed agreement in the presence of processor and communication faults. IEEE Trans Software Eng. 1986;SE-12(3): 477–482.

[73]    Schlichting RD and Schneider FB. Fail-stop processors: an approach to designing fault-tolerant computing systems. ACM Trans Comput Syst. 1983;1(3):222–238.

[74]    Lamport L. The part-time parliament. ACM Trans Comput Syst. 1998; 16(2):133–169.

[75]    Mostefaoui A, Rajsbaum S, and Raynal M. A versatile and modular consensus protocol. IRISA; 2001.

[76]    Charron-Bost B and Schiper A. The heard-of model: Computing in distributed systems with benign faults. Distrib Comput. 2009;22(1):49–71.

[77]    Pease M, Shostak R, and Lamport L. Reaching agreement in the presence of faults. J ACM. 1980;27(2):228–234.

[78]    Fitzi M and Maurer U. Efficient byzantine agreement secure against general adversaries. Distrib Comput. 1998:134–148.

[79]    Marandi PJ, Primi M, and Pedone F. High performance state-machine replication. In: Proc. 41st Int. Conf. Depend. Syst. Netw. (DSN'11). IEEE; 2011. p. 454–465.

[80]    Crosby M, Pattanayak P, Verma S, *et al.* Blockchain technology: Beyond Bitcoin. Appl Innov. 2016;2:6–10.

[81]    King S and Nadal S. Ppcoin: Peer-to-peer crypto-currency with proof-of-stake; 2012. Available from: https://peercoin.net/assets/paper/peercoin-paper.pdf.

[82]    Kogias EK, Jovanovic P, Gailly N, *et al.* Enhancing Bitcoin security and performance with strong consistency via collective signing. In: Proc. 25th USENIX Secur. Symp. (USENIX Secur. 16). USENIX Association; 2016. p. 279–296.

[83]    Buterin V. On public and private blockchains. Ethereum Blog; 2015. Available from: https://blog.ethereum.org/2015/08/07/on-public-and-private-blockchains/.

[84]    Conti M, Lal C, Ruj S, *et al.* A survey on security and privacy issues of Bitcoin. arXiv preprint arXiv:170600916. 2017.

[85] Karame GO, Androulaki E, and Capkun S. Double-spending fast payments in Bitcoin. In: Proc. 19th ACM Conf. Comput. Commun. Secur. (CCS'12). ACM; 2012. p. 906–917.

[86] Finney H. Best practice for fast transaction acceptance-how high is the risk; 2011. Available from: https://bitcointalk.org/index.php?topic=3441.0.

[87] Bastiaan M. Preventing the 51%-attack: A stochastic analysis of two phase proof of work in Bitcoin; 2015. Available from: http://referaat.cs.utwente.nl/conference/22/paper/7473/preventingthe-51-attack-a-stochastic-analysis-of-two-phase-proof-of-work-in-bitcoin.pdf.

[88] Eyal I and Sirer EG. Majority is not enough: Bitcoin mining is vulnerable. In: 2014 Proc. Int. Conf. Financial Cryptography Data Secur. (FC'14). Springer; 2014. p. 436–454.

[89] Heilman E, Kendler A, Zohar A, *et al.* Eclipse attacks on Bitcoin's peer-to-peer network. In: Proc. 24th USENIX Secur. Symp. (USENIX Secur.'15). Washington, DC; 2015. p. 129–144.

[90] Nayak K, Kumar S, Miller A, *et al.* Stubborn mining: Generalizing selfish mining and combining with an eclipse attack. In: 2016 Proc. IEEE Eur. Symp. Secur. Privacy (EuroSP'16); 2016. p. 305–320.

[91] Yuval Marcus EH and Goldberg S. Low-resource eclipse attacks on Ethereum's peer-to-peer network; 2018. p. 15. Available from: https://www.cs.bu.edu/~goldbe/projects/eclipseEth.pdf.

[92] Atzei N, Bartoletti M, and Cimoli T. A survey of attacks on Ethereum smart contracts (SoK). In: Proc. 6th Int. Conf. Principles Secur. Trust; 2017. p. 164–186.

[93] SlowMist Security Team. Billions of tokens theft case cause by ETH ecological defects; 2018. Available from: https://paper.tuisec.win/detail/eb44c15d3627fe2.

[94] Vasek M, Thornton M, and Moore T. Empirical analysis of denial-of-service attacks in the Bitcoin ecosystem. In: 2014 Proc. Int. Conf. Financial Cryptography Data Secur. (FC'14). Springer; 2014. p. 57–71.

[95] Meegan D. Ethereum continues to suffer from DDoS attacks; 2016. Available from: https://www.ethnews.com/ethereum-continues-to-suffer-from-ddos-attacks.

[96] Verbucheln S. How perfect offline wallets can still leak Bitcoin private keys. arXiv preprint arXiv:150100447. 2015.

[97] Smache M, Mrabet NE, Gilquijano JJ, *et al.* Modeling a node capture attack in a secure wireless sensor networks. In: 2016 Proc IEEE 3rd World Forum on Internet of Things (WF-IoT'16); 2016. p. 188–193.

[98] Yang Y, Liu X, and Deng RH. Lightweight break-glass access control system for healthcare Internet-of-Things. IEEE Trans Ind Inf. 2018;14(8):3610–3617.

[99] Chin WL, Li W, and Chen HH. Energy big data security threats in IoT-based smart grid communications. IEEE Commun Mag. 2017;55(10):70–75.

[100]  Langner R. Stuxnet: Dissecting a cyberwarfare weapon. IEEE Secur Privacy. 2011;9(3):49–51.

[101]  Korpela K, Hallikas J, and Dahlberg T. Digital supply chain transformation toward blockchain integration. In: Proc. 50th Hawaii Int. Conf. Syst. Sci.; 2017.

[102]  Biswas K and Muthukkumarasamy V. Securing smart cities using blockchain technology. In: Proc. 18th IEEE Int. Conf. High Performance Comput. Commun.; 14th IEEE Int. Conf. Smart City; 2nd IEEE Int. Conf. Data Sci. Syst. (HPCC/SmartCity/DSS'16); 2016. p. 1392–1393.

[103]  Buterin V. Ethereum: A next-generation smart contract and decentralized application platform; 2014. Available from: https://github.com/ethereum/wiki/wiki/White-Paper.

[104]  Fabric; 2017. Available from: https://github.com/hyperledger/fabric.

[105]  EOS; 2020. Available from: https://eos.io/.

[106]  Wallet Knowledge Base; 2018. Available from: https://iotasupport.com/walletknowledgebase.shtml..

[107]  What Is IOTA?; 2018. Available from: https://themerkle.com/what-is-iota-cryptocurrency/.

[108]  Trust Your Odometer? Blockchain test aims to turn tide on car tampering; 2017. Available from: https://www.coindesk.com/trust-odometer-blockchain-test-aims-turn-tide-car-tampering/.

[109]  IPFS; 2020. Available from: https://ipfs.io/.

[110]  Arachchige PCM, Bertok P, Khalil I, *et al.* A trustworthy privacy preserving framework for machine learning in industrial IoT systems. IEEE Trans Ind Inf. 2020;16(9):6092–6102.

[111]  Kamath R. Food traceability on blockchain: Walmart's pork and mango pilots with IBM. J Br Blockchain Assoc. 2018;1(1):3712.

[112]  UCOT; 2020. Available from: https://www.ucot.world/.

[113]  slock.it; 2020. Available from: https://slock.it/.

[114]  Power Ledger; 2020. Available from: https://www.powerledger.io/.

[115]  Lin X, Li J, Wu J, *et al.* Making knowledge tradable in edge-AI enabled IoT: A consortium blockchain-based efficient and incentive approach. IEEE Trans Ind Inf. 2019;15(12):6367–6378.

[116]  Pan J, Wang J, Hester A, *et al.* EdgeChain: An edge-IoT framework and prototype based on blockchain and smart contracts. IEEE IoT J. 2018;6(3): 4719–4732.

[117]  Guin U, Cui P, and Skjellum A. Ensuring proof-of-authenticity of IoT edge devices using blockchain technology. In: 2018 IEEE International Conference on Internet of Things (iThings) and IEEE Green Computing and Communications (GreenCom) and IEEE Cyber, Physical and Social Computing (CPSCom) and IEEE Smart Data (SmartData); 2018. p. 1042–1049.

[118]  Rahman MA, Rashid MM, Hossain MS, *et al.* Blockchain and IoT-based cognitive edge framework for sharing economy services in a smart city. IEEE Access. 2019;7:18611–18621.

[119]   Kang J, Yu R, Huang X, *et al.* Enabling localized peer-to-peer electricity trading among plug-in hybrid electric vehicles using consortium block-chains. IEEE Trans Ind Inf. 2017;13(6):3154–3164.

[120]   Kang J, Yu R, Huang X, *et al.* Blockchain for secure and efficient data sharing in vehicular edge computing and networks. IEEE IoT J. 2019;6(3): 4660–4670.

[121]   McKinney J. Light client protocol; 2017. Available from: https://github. com/ethereum/wiki/wiki/Light-client-protocol.

[122]   IOTA. Light vs. full node; 2018. Available from: https://iota.readme.io/v1. 2.0/docs/light-vs-full-node.

[123]   Dorri A, Kanhere SS, and Jurdak R. Towards an optimized BlockChain for IoT. In: Proc. 2rd Int. Conf. Internet-of-Things Design Implementation. ACM; 2017. p. 173–178.

[124]   Rahulamathavan Y, Phan RCW, Misra S, *et al.* Privacy-preserving Blockchain based IoT ecosystem using attribute-based encryption. In: 2017 Proc. IEEE Int. Conf. Advanced Netw. Telecommun. Syst. Odisha, India; 2017.

[125]   Sharma PK, Chen M, and Park JH. A software defined fog node based distributed blockchain cloud architecture for IoT. IEEE Access. 2018;6:115–124.

[126]   Dorri A, Kanhere SS, Jurdak R, *et al.* Blockchain for IoT security and privacy: The case study of a smart home. In: 2017 Proc. IEEE Int. Conf. Pervasive Comput. Commun. Workshops (PerCom Workshops); 2017. p. 618–623.

[127]   Shi W, Cao J, Zhang Q, *et al.* Edge computing: Vision and challenges. IEEE IoT J. 2016;3(5):637–646.

[128]   Xiong Z, Zhang Y, Niyato D, *et al.* When mobile blockchain meets edge computing. IEEE Commun Mag. 2018;56(8):33–39.

[129]   Liu M, Yu FR, Teng Y, *et al.* Computation offloading and content caching in wireless blockchain networks with mobile edge computing. IEEE Trans Veh Technol. 2018;67(11):11008–11021.

[130]   Wang F, Xu J, Wang X, *et al.* Joint offloading and computing optimization in wireless powered mobile-edge computing systems. IEEE Trans Wireless Commun. 2018;17(3):1784–1797.

[131]   Xu X, Zhang X, Gao H, *et al.* BeCome: Blockchain-enabled computation offloading for IoT in mobile edge computing. IEEE Trans Ind Inf. 2020; 16(6):4187–4195.

[132]   Al-Doghman F, Chaczko Z, and Jiang J. A review of aggregation algo-rithms for the Internet of Things. In: Proc. 25th Int. Conf. Syst. Eng. (ICSEng'17); 2017. p. 480–487.

[133]   Elements Project; 2017. Available from: https://z.cash/support/zig.html.

[134]   Protocol Rules; 2016. Available from: https://en.bitcoin.it/wiki/Protocol rules.

[135]   Blockchain; 2017. Available from: https://blockchain.info.

[136]    Ethereum Mining Hardware; 2017. Available from: https://www.buy-bitcoinworldwide.com/ethereum/mining-hardware/.

[137]    Raspberry Pi; 2017. Available from: https://www.raspberrypi.org.

[138]    Mining Bitcoin only with raspberry pi; 2016. Available from: https://bitcointalk.org/index.php?topic=1535364.0.

[139]    Etherscan; 2017. Available from: https://etherscan.io.

[140]    Wood G. Ethereum: A secure decentralised generalised transaction ledger. Ethereum Project Yellow Paper; 2014. Available from: https://ethereum.github.io/yellowpaper/paper.pdf.

[141]    Goland YY. Going off chain for storage; 2017. Available from: http://www.goland.org/off chain storage and the_enterprise/.

[142]    Hou IH and Kumar PR. Real-time communication over unreliable wireless links: A theory and its applications. IEEE Wireless Commun. 2012;19(1): 48–59.

[143]    Lauridsen M, Kovacs IZ, Mogensen P, *et al.* Coverage and capacity analysis of LTE-M and NB-IoT in a rural area. In: Proc. 84th IEEE Vehicular Technol. Conf. (VTC-Fall'16); 2016. p. 1–5.

[144]    Liang JM, Chen JJ, Cheng HH, *et al.* An energy-efficient sleep scheduling with QoS consideration in 3GPP LTE-advanced networks for Internet of Things. IEEE J Emerg Sec Top Circuits Syst. 2013;3(1):13–22.

[145]    Westermann B, Gligoroski D, and Knapskog S. Comparison of the power consumption of the 2nd round SHA-3 candidates. In: Gusev M and Mitrevski P, editors. Proc. 2nd Int. Conf. ICT Innovations. Berlin, Heidelberg; 2010. p. 102–113.

[146]    Chen J, Chan SHG, and Liew SC. Mixed-mode WLAN: The integration of ad hoc mode with wireless LAN infrastructure. In: 2003 Proc. IEEE Global Telecommun. Conf. (GLOBECOM'03). vol. 1; 2003. p. 231–235.

[147]    Zorzi M, Gluhak A, Lange S, *et al.* From today's INTRAnet of things to a future INTERnet of things: a wireless- and mobility-related view. IEEE Wireless Commun. 2010;17(6):44–51.

[148]    Wang KH and Li B. Group mobility and partition prediction in wireless ad-hoc networks. In: 2002 Proc. IEEE Int. Conf. Commun. (ICC'02). vol. 2; 2002. p. 1017–1021.

[149]    Rathore MM, Ahmad A, Paul A, *et al.* Urban planning and building smart cities based on the Internet of Things using Big Data analytics. Comput Networks. 2016;101(Supplement C):63–80.

[150]    Huh S, Cho S, and Kim S. Managing IoT devices using blockchain platform. In: Proc. 19th Int. Conf. Advanced Commun. Technol. (ICACT'17); 2017. p. 464–467.

[151]    Jaffe C, Mata C, and Kamvar S. Motivating urban cycling through a blockchain-based financial incentives system. In: 2017 Proc. ACM Int. Joint Conf. Pervasive and Ubiquitous Comput. and 2017 Proc ACM Int. Symp. on Wearable Computers. UbiComp'17. New York, NY, USA: ACM; 2017. p. 81–84.

[152]   Raza S, Trabalza D, and Voigt T. 6LoWPAN compressed DTLS for CoAP. In: Proc. 8th IEEE Int. Conf. Distributed Computing in Sensor Syst. (DCOSS'12); 2012. p. 287–289.

[153]   Chen D, Chang G, Sun D, *et al.* TRM-IoT: A trust management model based on fuzzy reputation for internet of things. Comput Sci Inf Syst. 2011;8(4):1207–1228.

[154]   Mihaylov M, Jurado S, Avellana N, *et al.* NRGcoin: Virtual currency for trading of renewable energy in smart grids. In: Proc. 11th Int. Conf. Eur. Energy Market (EEM14); 2014. p. 1–6.

[155]   He Q, Wu D, and Khosla P. SORI: A secure and objective reputation-based incentive scheme for ad-hoc networks. In: 2004 IEEE Wireless Commun. and Networking Conf. (IEEE Cat. No. 04TH8733). vol. 2; 2004. p. 825–830.

[156]   Poon J and Dryja T. The Bitcoin lightning network: Scalable off-chain instant payments; 2015.

[157]   Raval S. Decentralized applications: Harnessing Bitcoin's blockchain technology. O'Reilly Media, Inc.; 2016.

[158]   Szabo N. Smart contracts: Building blocks for digital markets. EXTROPY. 1996.

[159]   Universa. How smart contracts will kill bureaucracy; 2017. Available from: https://medium.com/universablockchain/how-smart-contracts-will-kill-bureaucracy-c22a48e2e60.

[160]   Dai J and Vasarhelyi MA. Toward blockchain-based accounting and assurance. J Inf Syst. 2017;31(3):5–21.

[161]   Al Khalil F, Ceci M, O'Brien L, *et al.* A solution for the problems of translation and transparency in smart contracts; 2017. Available from: http://www.grctc.com/wp-content/uploads/2017/06/GRCTC-Smart-Contracts-White-Paper-2017.pdf.

[162]   Kaiser I. Yes, Bitcoin can do smart contracts and particl demonstrates how; 2017. Available from: https://bitcoinmagazine.com/articles/yes-bitcoin-can-do-smart-contracts-and-particl-demonstrates-how/.

[163]   Hertig A. How do Ethereum smart contracts work? 2018. Available from: https://www.coindesk.com/information/ethereum-smart-contracts-work/.

[164]   ASOR O. ABOUT $\tau$-CHAIN; 2015. Available from: http://tauchain.org/tauchain.pdf.

[165]   Nxt; 2018. Available from: https://nxtplatform.org/.

[166]   RSK; 2018. Available from: https://www.rsk.co/.

[167]   Lukas K. This is how smart contracts and Ethereum work; 2017. Available from: https://medium.com/startup-grind/gentle-intro-to-blockchain-and-smart-contracts-part-2-30a6c9a40946.

[168]   Blockchain-oracles; 2018. Available from: https://blockchainhub.net/blockchain-oracles.

[169]   Oraclize; 2018. Available from: http://www.oraclize.it.

[170]   Boudguiga A, Bouzerna N, Granboulan L, *et al.* Towards better availability and accountability for IoT updates by means of a blockchain. In: Proc. 2017

IEEE Eur. Symp. Secur. Privacy Workshops (EuroSPW). Paris, France; 2017.

[171]  Reid F and Harrigan M. In: Altshuler Y, Elovici Y, Cremers AB, *et al.*, editors. An Analysis of Anonymity in the Bitcoin System. New York, NY, USA: Springer New York; 2013. p. 197–223.

[172]  Androulaki E, Karame GO, Roeschlin M, *et al.* In: Sadeghi AR, editor. Evaluating User Privacy in Bitcoin. Berlin, Heidelberg: Springer Berlin Heidelberg; 2013. p. 34–51.

[173]  Ron D and Shamir A. In: Sadeghi AR, editor. Quantitative Analysis of the Full Bitcoin Transaction Graph. Berlin, Heidelberg: Springer Berlin Heidelberg; 2013. p. 6–24.

[174]  Ron D and Shamir A. Quantitative analysis of the full Bitcoin transaction graph. In: 2013 Proc. Int. Conf. Financial Cryptography Data Secur. (FC'13). Springer; 2013. p. 6–24.

[175]  Meiklejohn S, Pomarole M, Jordan G, *et al.* A fistful of Bitcoins: characterizing payments among men with no names. In: 2013 Proc. Conf. Internet measurement. ACM; 2013. p. 127–140.

[176]  Biryukov A, Khovratovich D, and Pustogarov I. Deanonymisation of clients in Bitcoin P2P network. In: Proc. 21st ACM Conf. Comput. Commun. Secur. (CCS'14). ACM; 2014. p. 15–29.

[177]  van Saberhagen N. CryptoNote v 2.0; 2013.

[178]  Koshy P, Koshy D, and McDaniel P. In: Christin N and Safavi-Naini R, editors. An Analysis of Anonymity in Bitcoin Using P2P Network Traffic. Berlin, Heidelberg: Springer Berlin Heidelberg; 2014. p. 469–485.

[179]  bitcoinwiki. Mixing service; 2017. Available from: https://en.bitcoin.it/wiki/Mixingservice.

[180]  Kosba A, Miller A, Shi E, *et al.* Hawk: The blockchain model of cryptography and privacy-preserving smart contracts. In: Proc. 37th IEEE Symp. Secur. Privacy (SP'16). IEEE; 2016. p. 839–858.

[181]  Feige U, Fiat A, and Shamir A. Zero-knowledge proofs of identity. J Cryptol. 1988;1(2):77–94.

[182]  Rackoff C and Simon DR. In: Feigenbaum J, editor. Non-Interactive Zero-Knowledge Proof of Knowledge and Chosen Ciphertext Attack. Berlin, Heidelberg: Springer Berlin Heidelberg; 1992. p. 433–444. Available from: https://doi.org/10.1007/3-540-46766-135.

[183]  Miers I, Garman C, Green M, *et al.* Zerocoin: Anonymous distributed ECash from Bitcoin. In: Proc. 34th IEEE Symp. Secur. Privacy (SP'13). IEEE; 2013. p. 397–411.

[184]  Sasson EB, Chiesa A, Garman C, *et al.* Zerocash: Decentralized anonymous payments from Bitcoin. In: Proc. 35th IEEE Symp. Secur. Privacy (SP'14). IEEE; 2014. p. 459–474.

[185]  Dagher GG, Bunz B, Bonneau J, *et al.* Provisions: Privacy-preserving proofs of solvency for Bitcoin exchanges. In: Proc. 22nd ACM Conf. Comput. Commun. Secur. (CCS'15). ACM; 2015. p. 720–731.

[186]    Liu JK, Wei VK, and Wong DS. Linkable spontaneous anonymous group signature for ad hoc groups. In: ACISP. vol. 4. Springer; 2004. p. 325–335.

[187]    Liu JK and Wong DS. Linkable ring signatures: Security models and new schemes. In: 2005 Proc. Int. Conf. Computational Sci. and Its Appl. Springer; 2005. p. 614–623.

[188]    MONERO; 2017. Available from: https://getmonero.org.

[189]    Maxwell G. Confidential Transaction, the Initial Investigation; 2015. Available from: https://elementsproject.org/elements/confidential-transactions/investigation.html.

[190]    Noether S and Mackenzie A. Ring confidential transactions. Ledger. 2016;1:1–18.

[191]    Demirel D and Lancrenon J. How to securely prolong the computational bindingness of pedersen commitments. IACR Cryptol ePrint Arch. 2015; 2015:584.

[192]    Goyal V, Pandey O, Sahai A, *et al.* Attribute-based encryption for fine-grained access control of encrypted data. In: Proc. 13th ACM Conf. Comput. Commun. Secur. CCS'06. New York, NY, USA: ACM; 2006. p. 89–98. Available from: http://doi.acm.org/10.1145/1180405.1180418.

[193]    Gentry C. Fully homomorphic encryption using ideal lattices. In: Proc. of the 41st Annu. ACM Symp. on Theory of Computing. STOC'09. New York, NY, USA: ACM; 2009. p. 169–178. Available from: http://doi. acm.org/10.1145/1536414.1536440.

[194]    Daza V, Pietro RD, Klimek I, *et al.* CONNECT: CONtextual NamE disCovery for blockchain-based services in the IoT. In: 2017 Proc. IEEE Int. Conf. Commun. (ICC'17); 2017. p. 1–6.

[195]    Neisse R, Steri G, and Nai-Fovino I. A Blockchain-based approach for data accountability and provenance tracking. arXiv preprint arXiv:170604507. 2017.

[196]    Ouaddah A, Elkalam AA, and Ouahman AA. Towards a novel privacy preserving access control model based on blockchain technology in IoT. In: Europe and MENA Cooperation Advances in Inf. and Communication Technologies. Springer; 2017. p. 523–533.

[197]    Ouaddah A, Abou Elkalam A, and Ait Ouahman A. FairAccess: A new Blockchain-based access control framework for the Internet of Things. Secur Commun Netw. 2016;9(18):5943–5964.

[198]    Peters GW and Panayi E. In: Understanding modern banking ledgers through blockchain technologies: Future of transaction processing and smart contracts on the internet of money. Cham: Springer International Publishing; 2016. p. 239–278.

[199]    Kravitz DW and Cooper J. Securing user identity and transactions symbiotically: IoT meets blockchain. In: 2017 Proc. Global Internet Things Summit (GIoTS'17); 2017. p. 1–6.

[200]    Pilkington M. Blockchain technology: principles and applications. Research handbook on digital transformations; 2016. p. 225.

[201] Vukolic M. The quest for scalable blockchain fabric: Proof-of-work vs. BFT replication. In: Int. Workshop on Open Problems in Network Secur.; 2015. p. 112–125.

[202] Kotla R, Alvisi L, Dahlin M, *et al.* Zyzzyva: Speculative byzantine fault tolerance. In: Proc. 21st ACM SIGOPS Symp. Operating Syst. Principles (SOSP'07). vol. 41; 2007. p. 45–58.

[203] Sharma PK, Singh S, Jeong YS, *et al.* DistBlockNet: A distributed blockchains-based secure SDN architecture for IoT networks. IEEE Commun Mag. 2017;55(9):78–85.

[204] Guo Y and Mate Jr C. Crysto: A scalable and permission-less blockchain platform; 2017. Available from: https://cdecker.github.io/btcresearch/2017/guocrysto.html.

[205] Ongaro D and Ousterhout J. In search of an understandable consensus algorithm. In: 2014 Proc. USENIX Annu. Tech. Conf. (USENIX ATC 14). Philadelphia, PA; 2014. p. 305–319.

[206] Luu L, Narayanan V, Baweja K, *et al.* SCP: A computationally-scalable byzantine consensus protocol for blockchains. IACR Cryptol ePrint Arch. 2015;2015:1168.

[207] Luu L, Narayanan V, Zheng C, *et al.* A secure sharding protocol for open blockchains. In: Proc. 23rd ACM Conf. Comput. Commun. Secur. (CCS'16). ACM; 2016. p. 17–30.

[208] Crain T, Gramoli V, Larrea M, *et al.* (Leader/Randomization/Signature) free Byzantine Consensus for Consortium Blockchains. arXiv preprint arXiv:170203068. 2017.

[209] Douceur JR. The sybil attack. In: 2002 Proc. Int. Workshop Peer-to-Peer Syst. Springer; 2002. p. 251–260.

[210] Difficulty; 2017. Available from: https://en.bitcoin.it/wiki/Difficulty.

[211] Tanenbaum AS and Wetherall DJ. Computer networks. Pearson; 2011.

[212] Miller A, Juels A, Shi E, *et al.* Permacoin: Repurposing Bitcoin work for data preservation. In: Proc. 35th IEEE Symp. Secur. Privacy (SP'14). IEEE; 2014. p. 475–490.

[213] Szabo N. The idea of smart contracts; 1997. Available from: http://www.fon.hum.uva.nl/rob/Courses/InformationInSpeech/CDROM/Literature/LOTwinterschool2006/szabo.best.vwh.net/idea.html.

[214] Bentov I, Lee C, Mizrahi A, *et al.* Proof of activity: Extending Bitcoin's proof of work via proof of stake. SIGMETRICS Perform Eval Rev. 2014;42(3):34–37.

[215] VasinP. BlackCoin as proof-of-stake protocol v2; 2014. Available from: https://blackcoin.co/blackcoin-pos-protocol-v2-whitepaper.pdf.

[216] Group B. Proof of stake versus proof of work; 2015. Available from: http://bitfury.com/content/5-white-papers-research/pos-vs-pow-1.0.2.pdf.

[217] Kwon J. TenderMint: Consensus without mining; 2014. Available from: https://tendermint.com/static/docs/tendermint.pdf.

[218] Karantias K, Kiayias A, and Zindros D. Proof of burn; 2012. Available from: https://en.bitcoin.it/wiki/Proof_of burn.

[219]  Sawtooth Lake documentation; 2017. Available from: https://intelledger. github.io/introduction.html#proof-of-elapsed-time-poet.

[220]  Intel Software Guard Extensions; 2017. Available from: https://software. intel.com/en-us/sgx.

[221]  Oki BM and Liskov BH. Viewstamped replication: A new primary copy method to support highly-available distributed systems. In: Proc. 7th Annu. ACM Symp. on Principles Distrib. Comput. ACM; 1988. p. 8–17.

[222]  Bracha G and Toueg S. Asynchronous consensus and broadcast protocols. J ACM. 1985;32(4):824–840.

[223]  Guerraoui R, Knezević N, Quéma V, *et al.* The next 700 BFT protocols. In: Proc. 5th Eur. Conf. Comput. Syst. ACM; 2010. p. 363–376.

[224]  Miller A, Xia Y, Croman K, *et al.* The honey badger of BFT protocols. In: Proc. 23rd ACM Conf. Comput. Commun. Secur. (CCS'16). ACM; 2016. p. 31–42.

[225]  Cachin C, Kursawe K, Petzold F, *et al.* Secure and efficient asynchronous broadcast protocols. In: 2001 Proc. Annu. Int. Cryptology Conf. (CRYPTO'01). Springer; 2001. p. 524–541.

[226]  Hyperledger; 2015. Available from: https://www.hyperledger.org.

[227]  Burrow; 2017. Available from: https://github.com/hyperledger/burrow.

[228]  Iroha; 2017. Available from: https://www.hyperledger.org/projects/iroha.

[229]  Sawtooth; 2017. Available from: https://www.hyperledger.org/projects/ sawtooth.

[230]  Popov S. The tangle; 2016. Available from: https://www.iotatoken.com.

[231]  Sompolinsky Y and Zohar A. Accelerating Bitcoin's transaction processing. Fast money grows on trees, not chains. IACR Cryptol ePrint Arch. 2013;2013(881).

[232]  Sompolinsky Y and Zohar A. Secure high-rate transaction processing in Bitcoin. In: 2015 Proc. Int. Conf. Financial Cryptography Data Secur. (FC'15). Springer; 2015. p. 507–527.

[233]  Buterin V. Toward a 12-second block time; 2014. Available from: https:// blog.ethereum.org/2014/07/11/toward-a-12-second-block-time/.

[234]  Eyal I, Gencer AE, Sirer EG, *et al.* Bitcoin-NG: A scalable blockchain protocol. In: Proc. 13th USENIX Symp. on Networked Syst. Design Implementation (NSDI'16); 2016. p. 45–59.

[235]  Ethereum; 2017. Available from: https://www.ethereum.org.

[236]  Kabessa N. PoW vs. PoS; 2017. Available from: https://medium.com/ blockchain-at-columbia/pow-vs-pos-tech-talk-77f9a1bf05d7.

[237]  ethernodes org. Network number 1; 2017. Available from: https://www. ethernodes.org/network/1.

[238]  Ethereum Homestead Documentation–The Homestead Release; 2016. Available from: http://www.ethdocs.org/en/latest/introduction/the-home-stead-release.html.

[239]  Yu G, Zha X, Wang X, *et al.* Enabling attribute revocation for fine-grained access control in blockchain-IoT systems. IEEE Trans Eng Manage. 2020:1–18.

[240]    Lei K, Du M, Huang J, *et al.* Groupchain: Towards a scalable public blockchain in fog computing of IoT services computing. IEEE Trans Serv Comput. 2020;13(2):252–262.

[241]    Yu G, Wang X, Yu K, *et al.* Survey: Sharding in blockchains. IEEE Access. 2020;8:14155–14181.

[242]    Crespo ASP and García LIC. Stampery blockchain timestamping architecture (BTA)-version 6. arXiv preprint arXiv:171104709. 2017.

[243]    Tan L and Wang N. Future internet: The internet of things. In: Proc. 3rd Int. Conf. Advanced Comput. Theory Eng. (ICACTE'10). vol. 5. IEEE; 2010. p. V5–376.

[244]    Back A, Corallo M, Dashjr L, *et al.* Enabling blockchain innovations with pegged sidechains; 2014. Available from: https://blockstream.com/side-chains.pdf.

[245]    Vuran MC, Akan OB, and Akyildiz IF. Spatio-temporal correlation: theory and applications for wireless sensor networks. Comput Networks. 2004;45(3):245–259. In Memory of Olga Casals.

[246]    Romero D, Ioannidis VN, and Giannakis GB. Kernel-based reconstruction of space-time functions on dynamic graphs. IEEE J Sel Top Signal Process. 2017;11(6):856–869.

[247]    Size of the Bitcoin blockchain from 2010 to 2017, by quarter; 2017. Available from: https://www.statista.com/statistics/647523/worldwide-bitcoin-blockchain-size/.

[248]    Ateniese G, Magri B, Venturi D, *et al.* Redactable Blockchain – or – rewriting history in Bitcoin and friends. In: 2017 IEEE Eur. Symp. Secur. Privacy (EuroSP'17); 2017. p. 111–126.

## Chapter 6

# Blockchain in 5G and 6G networks

*Minghao Wang[1], Xuhan Zuo[1] and Tianqing Zhu[2]*

In 2008, Nakamoto [1] presented the Bitcoin, which is a peer-to-peer (P2P) electronic cash system that makes the public begin to pay attention to blockchain technology. Until now, blockchain technology is attracting massive attention and triggering multiple projects in different fields [2]. However, the financial area is still the main application of blockchain technology. The blockchain could be considered as a public ledger in which all transactions are stored in a chain of the block [3]. Every time a new transaction is generated, it is packaged into a new block and attached to the chain. Even for Bitcoin, the public ledger records all transactions since the birth of Bitcoin, and anyone can download, view and even record by themselves.

There are some specific characteristics for blockchain such as decentralization, persistency, anonymity and auditability [4]. Due to these characteristics, blockchain has gained much attention not only in the financial transactions but also in distributed cloud storage, smart property, Internet of Things (IoT), supply chain management, healthcare, ownership and so on [5]. For organization and convenience, the existing and potential activities in the blockchain revolution could be divided into three categories: they are Blockchain 1.0, 2.0 and 3.0, respectively [6].

Blockchain 1.0 was initially used for cryptocurrencies [7]. The primary use of Blockchain 1.0 was for deploying cryptocurrencies in cash-related applications, such as currency transfer, payment systems and remittance. As for Blockchain 2.0, broadly speaking, it includes Bitcoin 2.0, smart contracts, smart property, decentralized applications and decentralized autonomous organizations [6]. The main contribution of Blockchain 2.0 was the idea of using smart contracts [8]. Blockchain 2.0 has broader coverage than Blockchain 1.0, which changed to the digital economy from digital currency. However, Blockchain 3.0 has turned to the digital society. Blockchain 3.0 refers to a vast array of applications that do not involve money, currency, commerce, financial markets or other economic activity [9]. These applications should include many aspects such as art, health, science, identity, education, governance and communication [10].

[1]Centre for Cyber Security and Privacy, School of Computer Science, University of Technology Sydney, Ultimo, Australia
[2]School of Computer Science, China University of Geosciences, Wuhan, China

The blockchain technology could help to make the businesses, governments and logistic systems more reliable, trusty and safety [11]. However, capabilities of the blockchain technology extend far beyond that, which enables existing technology applications to be vastly improved and new applications never previously practical to be deployed [12]. Recently, the combination of blockchain with 5G and 6G networks has attracted more and more attention. By implementing blockchain technology in 5G and 6G networks, some previously existing security and privacy issues can be solved as well.

The new digital business models have changed and eradicated traditional industries with an unprecedented rate [13]. Although digital business models have caused a great impact on traditional industries in 4G networks, it will have a future development in 5G networks, because the 5G network is not only faster than the 4G network but also an overall upgradation of the 4G network. In 5G networks, mobile data traffic will surge. Chaer *et al.* [14] presented three reasons that cause the massive upsurge in mobile data, which are the increase of mobile device usage, content availability and ubiquity in video-streaming service provides and user-created contents being hosted on several social-cloud platforms for consumption by other end users. These reasons drive the development of 5G networks. Moreover, some research found that the blockchain technology could enable completely new technological systems and business models that drive people's research for the combination of blockchain and 5G networks. By combing the blockchain-enabled technology, some original problems that exist in original 5G technologies could be solved as well, such as authentication, access control, verification, spectrum management, network slicing, software-defined network (SDN) and edge computing. Moreover, the applications and services in 5G networks are also improved, such as the smart transport, smart health, smart industry and IoT. These blockchain-enabled technologies, applications and services will be detailed in Section 6.1.

Although one of the goals of 5G networks is to realize the Internet of Everything (IoE), with the development of 5G networks, this goal is far from being realized. However, in 6G networks, the IoE may be realized. Moreover, as 6G networks would be a fully artificial intelligence (AI)-empowered networks, AI would be the most important feature in 6G networks [15]. The applications and services via blockchain in 6G networks do not only include the IoE but also include distributed ledger technology and Edge AI. The blockchain-enabled technologies in 6G networks are also a bit different from those in 5G networks. They are spectrum sharing and blockchain with AI. These technologies, applications and services will be detailed in Section 6.2.

Hence, the key contributions of this survey can be summarized as follows:

1.  The blockchain-enabled technology, application and service via blockchain in 5G and 6G networks are summarized and detailed in this chapter.
2.  The security- and privacy-related issues are discussed in detail. The potential solutions are also mentioned.
3.  The other related issues that exist in blockchain networks are also discussed where the possible solutions are followed.

The remainder of this chapter is structured as follows: Section 6.1 presents the blockchain in 5G networks, which includes blockchain-enabled technology and application and service. Then, in Section 6.2, we describe the usage of blockchain in 6G networks which is structured as the same as Section 6.1. The security and privacy in blockchain are discussed in Section 6.3, which is divided into the security-related, privacy-related and other related issues. Finally, this chapter concludes in Section 6.4. Moreover, some of the references used in this chapter along with further details of several points raised can be found at: security-privacyin5g-6g.github.io.

## 6.1 Blockchain in 5G networks

With the rapid development of the Internet, the arrival of 5G networks has made the Internet enter a new stage. Moreover, the blockchain plays an important role in the 5G network. There are several blockchain-enabled technologies such as authentication, access control and spectrum management, and some services and applications via blockchain in 5G networks such as vehicle and edge computing. These blockchain-enabled technologies, applications and services consist a part of 5G networks. In this part, these technologies, applications and services will be detailed in the following. A summary of the blockchain-enabled technologies, applications and services in 5G networks could be found in Table A.1.

### 6.1.1 *Blockchain-enabled technologies*

#### 6.1.1.1 Authentication

Because of the advent of the 5G era, the new-generation network has become faster and has lower latency and larger capacity than the previous network. However, it is also accompanied by various issues caused by 5G networks. As the entrance and business cornerstone of the wireless network, the authentication will play an essential role in responding to some issues caused by 5G networks such as some security and privacy issues. There are three basic types of authenticating identity. The first type is to verify identity based on known information. The second type is to verify identity based on owned objects. The third type is to verify identity based on unique characteristics [16]. The most basic method in verifying identity authentication is the username and password method. However, as many hackers and malicious attackers exist in the network, only using the username and password method is far from enough. The attacker could easily access personal information such as password via eavesdropping or security vulnerability. So, it is necessary to solve the authentication problem in 5G networks.

Most type of authentication-related problems in the 5G network could be divided into three main aspects. First and also the largest category is authentication problems in the IoT aspect. Second is the authentication problems in handover aspect. The third is the other aspect. Yang *et al.* [17] have mentioned a blockchain-based trusted authentication architecture that could be used in IoT network for ensuring the security of services. Rashid and Pajooh [18] have mentioned a local authentication of the authentication process in the IoT network, which could make devices communicate with other devices and base station via local blockchain implementation without a central authority.

Moreover, Jangirala *et al.* [19] have presented a new efficient, lightweight blockchain-enabled RFID-based authentication protocol called LBRAPS that could be used against various attacks in 5G IoT environment. Zhang *et al.* [20] have presented a blockchain-based robust and universal seamless handover authentication protocol named RUSH that could be used in 5G heterogeneous networks to process the anonymous mutual authentication with a key agreement. Chen *et al.* [21] have presented a blockchain-based authentication scheme in 5G networks which could reduce the authentication frequency when devices move among the access points (APs) and improve the access efficiency. Moreover, Yazdinejad *et al.* [22] have also presented a new authentication method that could remove the unnecessary reauthentication in repeated handover among heterogeneous cells in 5G networks.

### 6.1.1.2   Access control

Massive device networking will become one of the essential features in 5G networks. As we have mentioned earlier, authentication is the entrance and business cornerstone of wireless networks. Access control is also an integral part of the wireless networks, especially in the IoT networks. Access control could be defined as a process that mediates every request to resources and data maintained by a system and determines whether the request should be granted or denied [23]. There are several basic access control approaches have already been used in 5G networks, such as the access control list, the role-based access control and the attribute-based access control [24]. However, these access control methods could not provide a scalable and efficient mechanism to meet the requirements of 5G networks. So, in 5G networks, a new type of control method is required. The blockchain-based access control method could mostly meet requirements.

Most of the blockchain-based access control method is developing a new framework. It is the most direct and effective method. Dukkipati *et al.* [25] have mentioned that most of the methods are not suitable for decentralized and heterogeneous system environment, so they presented a new blockchain-based access control method that could help the user in accessing or controlling their data. Messié *et al.* [26] have presented a new connectivity platform named BALAdIN (Bandwidth Ledger Accounting Networks) that combines the consortium blockchain with access control mechanisms to solving drawbacks of communitarian Wi-Fi and ad hoc networks. Wang *et al.* [27] have presented a blockchain-based framework that could achieve fine-grained access control over data. Dagher *et al.* [28] have also presented a blockchain-based framework that could be deployed in the health-care area that utilizes smart contracts in an Ethereum-based blockchain for heightened access control and obfuscation of data. Xu *et al.* [24] have presented a blockchain-enabled decentralized capability-based access control named BlendCAC that could achieve effective access control processes to devices, services and information. Pinno *et al.* [29] have also mentioned a blockchain-based architecture that is user transparent, user-friendly, fully decentralized, scalable, fault-tolerant and could compatible with a wide range of access control models that could be used in IoT network of 5G networks. Moreover, some other blockchain-based access control frameworks such as BlockTC [30], B-RAN [31] and FairAccess [32] could also be deployed to solve the access control issues in 5G networks.

### 6.1.1.3    Verification

The verification is another key part to ensure the security and privacy in the 5G networks. Different from the traditional verification method, the blockchain-based verification is safer. For example, although some public verification techniques can let the third-party auditor (TPA) verify the data, these techniques are vulnerable to procrastinating auditors who may not verify on-time [33]. Moreover, most of the public verification has the public key infrastructure issues. So, a new way of verification method was needed. Thus, blockchain-based verification was invented to solve the problems of traditional verification methods.

Typically, the blockchain-based verification method is used for two aspects, first is used in the aspect of the financial transaction and the second is used in the data integrity aspect. In the first aspect, Unal *et al.* [34] have mentioned a new method in verification transactions which is based on formal logic and could support formal verification of smart contract policies that could be used in 5G networks. Jiang *et al.* [35] have presented a new distributed and secure data sharing framework named device-to-device blockchain that could verify end users' transactions via a set of APs in 5G networks. Prybila *et al.* [36] have mentioned a blockchain-based runtime verification that could enable a seamless execution monitoring and verification of choreographies.

As for the data integrity aspect, Fisher and Sanchez [37] have presented an invention that could verify the digital content via unique hash encryption and conversion method. Machado and Fröhlich [38] have presented a blockchain-based architecture that could verify the data integrity that is produced by IoT devices even in the realm of cyber-physical systems (CPSs). What is more, Qu *et al.* [39] have presented a framework with layers, intersect and self-organization blockchain structure for device and data verification. Liu *et al.* [40] proposed a blockchain-based framework for data integrity service, which could provide a more reliable data integrity verification for both data owners and data consumers without a TPA. Yue *et al.* [41] presented a Merkle trees method that could effectively improve the performance of data integrity verification via a blockchain-based verification framework.

### 6.1.1.4    Spectrum management

With the development of technologies and the increase of people's demand for the network, the 5G networks become lower latency, higher bandwidth and faster in speed than previous generation networks. More and more services such as remote high-quality video call and big data application need higher bandwidth. Although some of the technologies used in 5G networks have solved some people's demand, some physical constraints such as spectrum limitations still exist. What is more, only considering the human-to-human (H2H) communications in 5G networks is far from enough, machine-to-machine (M2M) communications should also be more considered as massive devices are connected to the Internet. Zhou *et al.* [42] mentioned that compared with the H2H communications, the M2M communication have smaller data size, lower mobility and more infrequent transmissions. However, it is cost-inefficient to build a separate network and allocate a dedicated spectrum for M2M communications [43]. So, spectrum management is a problem that needs to be urgently solved in the field of spectrum area in 5G networks.

Weiss *et al.* [44] mentioned that the blockchain-based spectrum sharing would bring some benefits in decentralization, transparency, immutability, availability and security. Some research mention using the blockchain-based virtual crypto-currency to solve the spectrum sharing problem. For example, Maksymyuk *et al.* [45] presented a new unlicensed spectrum sharing algorithm based on game theory; this algorithm could share the spectrum between operators via using the virtual cryptocurrency. Kotobi and Bilén [46] have presented a virtual currency named "Specoins" that could be used for payment to access spectrum under an auction environment. Moreover, Bayhan *et al.* [47] mentioned a spectrum sensing service named "Spass" that could enhance the spectral efficiency based on the smart contract payment mechanism running on a blockchain.

Different from virtual currency, Zhou *et al.* [43] have also presented a framework that could share the spectrum security. Grissa *et al.* [48] presented a trustworthy spectrum access system named TrustSAS that could enable seamless spectrum sharing between secondary and incumbent users. Moreover, den Hartog *et al.* [49] have also presented a platform that could automate negotiation for spectral resources between AP operators. Sevindik [50] has presented a new technique that could efficiently manage spectrum grants in an unlicensed spectrum environment.

### 6.1.1.5   Network slicing

Network slicing is another primary technology that is used in 5G networks. In order to provide customized services via limited network resources while reducing the expense of 5G networks, the network slicing has been proposed as the main enabler of network service convergence and on-demand customized services [51]. The main idea of network slicing is to operate separate multiple virtual networks on the same physical hardware to support various types of IoT applications [52]. Each network slicing contains a set of virtual network functions related to physical network functions that could enable network services based on the computing and storage capabilities of cloud infrastructure [53]. By deploying network slicing in 5G networks, the network could be divided into some specific services and applications such as smart home, vehicle network and smart factory [54].

The main blockchain-based network slicing method is fastened on the broker application. Nour *et al.* [55] mentioned that the network slice provider needs a brokering mechanism, which allows them to lease resources from different providers securely and privately, to deploy a network slice. Moreover, they have also proposed a blockchain-based broker design to ensure security anonymous transactions in the leasing process for the network slice provider. Backman *et al.* [56] also presented a blockchain slice leasing ledger concept that could utilize 5G network slice broker in a blockchain to reduce service creation time and enable manufacturing equipment autonomously and dynamically acquire the slice needed for more efficient operations. Moreover, Valtanen *et al.* [57] have presented the value of the blockchain network slice brokering use case and the results in the industrial automation application scenario. They show that the blockchain-based network slice brokering has to value beyond expectations.

### 6.1.1.6 Software-defined network

The SDN is an important technology that makes 5G networks unique from previous generations. It could support the dynamic nature of 5G networks while also enhancing its capabilities [58]. In SDNs, the control plane and the data plane are separated from each other to logically centralize the network state and intelligence [59]. The main idea for SDN is to make all the forwarding devices, such as OpenFlow switches, routers and gateways, located on the data plane and let the control plane making the decision. The OpenFlow protocol is the key enabler of SDN and also the first-standard SDN protocol to promote the relaying of information and data packets between the control and forwarding planes [60]. However, with the continuous research of SDN in 5G networks, some limitations of SDN have also been explored, such as the security and scalability. The blockchain-based SDN technology could solve parts of these limitations.

Pourvahab and Ekbatanifard [61] purposed a blockchain-based forensic architecture in SDN, which could solve some security problems such as poor attack detection and slow processing. Yang *et al.* [62] have also mentioned a blockchain technique named BlockCtrl that could improve the security of control plane in SDN. Li *et al.* [63] presented a blockchain-based framework named ChainSDI that could share sensitive data securely. Sharma *et al.* [64] mentioned a framework that combines the SDN and blockchain technology that security could automatically adapt to the threat landscape. Xue *et al.* [65] proposed an SDN data chain based on blockchain that could reduce the cost of network failure recovery and achieve the unified scheduling of business capabilities. Boussard *et al.* [66] have also presented a blockchain-based global trust assessment framework that could store and modify the trust mark of different devices and allocate resources to the different trust level of devices.

### 6.1.1.7 Edge computing

With the popularity of smartphones and wearable devices, edge computing has also attracted people's attention. In some 5G scenarios, sometimes a large set of data streams needs to be handled. However, the removable device only has limited computing resources, which means they cannot handle large data streams well. The edge computing is an excellent method to solve this problem. By using the method, the removable device could offload the computation task to the edge computing nodes, which means it could handle the computing well and reduce self-pressure significantly [67]. In recent years, there are already some types of architectures have been presented, such as cloudlet, edge computing, fog computing, mobile cloud computing, mist computing and mobile edge computing (MEC) [68]. However, it is still a big challenge to deploy the edge computing into 5G network because of its security [69]. In the dynamic edge computing environments, the data computing is vulnerable to different types of malicious attack, such as jamming attacks, sniffer attacks and denial-of-service (DoS) attacks [54]. However, blockchain-based edge computing technology could solve these challenges.

By combining the blockchain and edge computing into one system, it could enable reliable access and control of the network, storage, and computation distributed at the edges, in order to provide a large scale of network servers, data storage, and validity computation near the end in a secure manner [70]. Most of the combination of the blockchain and edge computing is to design a new framework or platform. Zhu [71] proposed a blockchain-based MEC platform named BlockMEC that could distribute computing, control, storage and networking functions to the edge of the network without involving any central controllers. Wu *et al.* [72] have also presented a framework named BlockEdge that first introduces incentive schemes to attract edge nodes to participate in collaborative edge computing tasks. Yang *et al.* [73] mentioned a blockchain-based heterogeneous MEC scheme that could significantly improve the credibility and efficiency of MEC collaboration. Moreover, Zhang and Lee [74] presented a novel blockchain-based signature scheme that could provide a more efficient authentication scheme of authenticating mobile devices.

## 6.1.2   Applications and services via blockchain in 5G networks

### 6.1.2.1   Smart transport

The vehicle network is one of the most important applications in 5G networks. With the development of the vehicle network, the requirements of the vehicle network are getting higher and higher, for example, the data stream. Because the data stream is getting bigger and bigger in the vehicle network, the pressure of traditional centralized management and data storage is followed increasing. The central server could be the bottleneck of the entire system because once the server fails, the whole system would break down [75]. So, making the decentralization, distributed management and storage would be the future technology trends in 5G networks. However, blockchain technology could meet these requirements well. By deploying the blockchain technology into the vehicle network, not only it decentralizes but also significantly improves the security of the vehicle network. Moreover, blockchain technology could also solve some bandwidth issues in-vehicle network [76]. So, the blockchain technology is a promising technology that should be deep researched in the vehicle network.

Most of the researches have proposed a new framework of the combination of vehicle network and blockchain technology. Notably, some of the researches are using blockchain-based SDN technology to solve the problems of the traditional framework. Zhang *et al.* [33] presented a novel blockchain-based distributed software-defined vehicular ad hoc networks framework that could establish a secure architecture to prevent the decline of performance caused by malicious attacks. Gao *et al.* [77] found that with managerial responsibilities shared between the blockchain and the SDN, the pressure of the controller is significantly reduced. It could ensure the effective operation of the vehicle network. Xie *et al.* [78] mentioned scheduling procedures of the blockchain-based framework, which could be used in the vehicle network for detecting the malicious vehicular nodes or messages. Moreover, Wang *et al.* [79] proposed a blockchain-assisted scheme named B-TSCA that could handle the reauthentication problems when vehicles through secure ownership transfer between infrastructures. Liang *et al.* [80] have also proposed a micro-blockchain-based geographical dynamic intrusion detection named MBID that could construct local intrusion detection strategies for vehicles with tamper-resistance.

### 6.1.2.2  Smart health

Health is the cornerstone of people's life. With promising health-care technology, people's lives are guaranteed. So healthcare is also one of the essential applications in 5G networks. People gradually realize the importance of a sound health-care system; for example, more and more people are willing to wear the wearable device. However, due to the rapid increase in the world's population, the traditional health-care system is far from enough for meeting the people's demands. So, more and more countries are vigorously developing smart health systems. In a sophisticated health-care system, you can enjoy an excellent medical system even in a remote area. However, the existing technology is not enough to solve the problems in the current health-care system, for example, privacy issues. Health information is the most private information for everyone. Most people do not want to let others know about his illness. According to these issues, the blockchain technology is proposed for solving these problems.

The combination of blockchain and healthcare in 5G networks could provide a better decentralization, security and privacy [81]. Moreover, it will also reduce the operational costs, simplify the health-care system and improve service efficiency [82]. Most papers used blockchain technology to solve the privacy issues of the health-care system in 5G networks. Lin *et al.* [83] mentioned using a blockchain-based algorithm to allocate communication and computation resources that could optimize the delay of data transmission and computation of the health-care system in 5G networks. Fan *et al.* [84] proposed a blockchain-based data sharing scheme that could be used for solving the private sharing issues in the health-care system. Li *et al.* [63] presented a framework named ChainSDI that could leverage the blockchain technique along with edge computing resources to manage secure data sharing and computing. Yue *et al.* [85] have also mentioned a blockchain-based health-care data gateway that could enable patient to own, control and share their data easily and securely without violating privacy. Liang *et al.* [86] presented an innovative user-centric health data sharing scheme that is based on the decentralized and permission blockchain to protect privacy using channel formation scheme and enhance the identity management. Esposito *et al.* [87] mentioned that blockchain could also be used for protecting the health-care data hosted within the cloud. Witchey [88] proposed a health-care transaction validation system that could compile all the health-care transactions into a chain, in order to provide a comprehensive person's health-care path.

### 6.1.2.3   Smart industry

Except for the vehicle and healthcare, the industry is also an indispensable part of people's lives. Industry 4.0, which also known as the fourth industrial revolution, would introduce the concepts of M2M communication, CPSs and the IoT into the industry [89]. It will be a massive innovation in the industry area. The industry could improve the previous generation industry from different aspects such as the communication between the different industrial components, the monitor and decision process used in industry and efficiently share resources [90]. However, with the development of the industry 4.0, different social challenges and risks are gradually explored, for example, the need for an increased amount of data transmission with improved security, transparency and credibility [91]. Some researchers have begun to deploy blockchain in the industry 4.0 to solve the previous problems.

Sikorski *et al.* [90] have already used blockchain to facilitate M2M interactions and establish an M2M electricity market in the context of the chemical industry. They found by deploying the blockchain; it could show all stakeholders with realistic data produced by process flow sheet models that ensure the authenticity of the data. Jovović *et al.* [91] also presented a blockchain-based data sharing mode that could significantly enhance the security, transparency and credibility of stored data. Wang *et al.* [92] presented a new blockchain-based distributed consensus mechanism named Beh-Raft-Chain that could be used for solving the problem of device collaboration in industry 4.0. Moreover, Mistry *et al.* [93] mentioned that blockchain could revolutionize most of the current and future industrial applications in different sectors by providing fine-grained decentralized access control. Lin *et al.* [94] also presented a blockchain-based system named BSeln for secure mutual authentication, which could be used for enforcing fine-grained access control policies.

### 6.1.2.4   Internet of Things

IoT is a promising application in 5G networks. Although the application of IoT has already deployed in the previous generation of networks, because of the new technologies in 5G networks, the evolution of 5G networks will become the key driving force for the development of the IoT. The new model named 5G IoT is expected to disrupt the global industry [95]. What is more, the recent research found that the combination of blockchain and 5G IoT networks could significantly empower the IoT services and applications [96]. By deploying the blockchain technology, the 5G IoT networks have more potential than before. The blockchain technology could encrypt data at its source and protect it through its life cycle in IoT, and every access to the data is logged on the blockchain which means it is transparent for all users [97]. Moreover, except deploying blockchain in three main applications of 5G networks (vehicle, health and industry) that have been mentioned before, the other blockchain-based IoT applications are also playing an important role in 5G applications, such as unmanned aerial vehicle (UAV) networks, smart grids, smart home and smart city.

Panarello *et al.* [98] have surveyed how blockchain applied in smart cities from main research challenges and future research aspects which include the research of security and privacy, throughput, storage, energy efficiency, incentive and punishment mechanisms, cost and regulation. Dorri *et al.* [99] also mentioned a blockchain-based smart home framework that could significantly improve the security of the core components and functions of the smart home tier. Dai *et al.* [100] have mentioned that the blockchain-based IoT framework named Blockchain of Things would have several benefits such as interoperability across IoT devices, traceability of IoT data, reliability of IoT data and autonomic interactions of IoT systems. Moreover, Samaniego and Deters [101] have mentioned that the blockchain technology could also be used in managing device configuration, storing sensor data and enabling micro-payments. Zhang *et al.* [102] proposed a blockchain-based edge intelligence IoT framework that could achieve flexible and secure edge service management. Dinesh *et al.* [103] have also presented the blockchain-based mmWave communication and MIMO technology that could be used for solving the security and privacy issues in 5G communications process.

## 6.2    Blockchain in 6G networks

The 6G networks would not only be a faster 5G but also fully deployed AI inside. Blockchain-based 5G and 6G networks will have some intersections, but there will also be some differences. In 6G networks, the blockchain-enabled technology should consider the spectrum sharing and blockchain with AI. As for the application and service, it should consider the distributed ledger technology, Edge AI and the IoE. These blockchain-based technologies, applications and services will be detailed in the following. A summary of the blockchain-enabled technologies, applications and services in 6G networks could be found in Table A.2.

### 6.2.1    Blockchain-enabled technologies
#### 6.2.1.1    Spectrum sharing
Although the standards for 6G networks are not fully clear, the general trend is already obvious. Compared with the 5G networks, the 6G networks would increase two orders of magnitude bit rate [104]. Moreover, the available spectrum is becoming less and less. So the spectrum problems are still an essential problem in 6G networks. We need technology that could not only manage the spectrum but also be able to share the spectrum under this technology. The blockchain technology could solve the previous problems. The blockchain could represent the centralized database in spectrum sharing system, which could significantly increase spectral efficiency [105]. Moreover, the blockchain technology in the spectrum

sharing system would allow the users to share the same spectrum in a secure, low cost, smart and efficient spectrum utilization way [106].

Dai *et al.* [107] mentioned that blockchain technology could combine deep reinforcement learning to solve the spectrum sharing problem in 6G networks. Kotobi and Bilen [108] presented a blockchain-based protocol for enabling and securing spectrum sharing, which realizes an auction mechanism based on a first-come-first-served queue to let each primary user advertise their spectrum in a decentralized fashion. This auction method greatly increases the spectrum sharing efficiency. Nguyen *et al.* [54] have also mentioned that the smart contracts technology in the blockchain could alleviate the spectrum-sharing-related cooperation and transparency issues. Mafakheri *et al.* [109] mentioned that blockchain could be deployed in the resource sharing area; for example, spectrum sharing is to support the self-organizing network features for the 6G network.

### 6.2.1.2   Blockchain with AI

For 6G networks, the most convincing technology is that the 6G networks will fully embed AI inside. Back to previous generation network, for example, the 4G networks, there are no AI applications in 4G networks. Although, in 5G networks, there is some limits AI deploying inside, when designing the 5G standard, the application of AI was not considered. So the 5G network does not combine with AI well. As for 6G networks, AI is the top priority. There are already some AI-based technologies for 6G networks have been proposed in a different aspect, such as deploying AI technology in PHY layer aspect and network architecture aspect. However, with the deploying of AI in 6G networks, more and more problems have been found, especially the security and privacy problems. Blockchain technology could handle the previous challenge in AI. By deploying the blockchain in AI, the decision process of the AI methods would be made more understandable and coherent, because all the underlying elements on which the decisions are made could be traced back [110].

Mamoshina *et al.* [111] have mentioned that the blockchain technology could combine with deep learning together to solving data security and transparency. Mcmahan *et al.* [112] mentioned that the blockchain-based AI techniques can offer decentralized learning to facilitate the sharing of knowledge and decision between the different agents, which could be used in a 6G network scenario. A comprehensive survey for the combination of blockchain and AI, which includes the complete review and research challenges, could be found in [113].

## 6.2.2   *Applications and services via blockchain in 6G networks*

### 6.2.2.1   Distributed ledger technology

Distributed ledger technology is one of the most promising technology in 6G networks. The combination of blockchain and distributed ledger technology could be considered as the next generation of distributed sensing services which could ensure the low-latency, reliable connectivity and scalability for the 6G networks [114].

Moreover, by deploying the blockchain-based distributed ledger technology, the security of the 6G network could be improved significantly, especially for the surveillance and governance of the 6G networks. The distributed ledger could remain an immutable and transparent logbook for each event, which means it could be checked and examined at any time by anyone [110]. It also promotes accountability in 6G networks. Ferraro *et al.* [115] have presented a comprehensive survey of the combination of blockchain and distributed ledger technology which could be used in the scenario of smart cities, sharing economy and social compliance for 6G networks. This chapter also presented the advantages and disadvantages of 6G networks that laid the foundation for future research.

### 6.2.2.2　Edge AI

Same as 5G networks, edge computing is promised to become a key part of the upcoming 6G networks. The edge computing technology could provide more bandwidth and reduce latencies [116]. However, different from 5G networks, in 6G networks, edge computing is very likely to be combined with AI because 6G networks will be an AI-empowered network. To enable Edge AI, some new technologies, for example, the new embedded systems technologies that include machine learning, neural network acceleration and reduction, are needed [117]. These new technologies would push the network intelligence to the edge to enable running AI and learning algorithms on edge devices to provide distributed autonomy [114]. However, Porambage *et al.* [118] have mentioned that the combination of edge computing and AI will exist some security-related issues and challenges. The combination of edge computing and AI would not only have some issues about power efficiency but also have some problems in computational complexity, privacy and security problems inside the combination [117]. However, the combination of the blockchain and Edge AI could solve some part of these problems.

Xu *et al.* [119] mentioned, by combining the blockchain with Edge AI, the interests of involved edge servers would be maximized, and the ecosystem would also become bigger. Lin *et al.* [120] presented a knowledge consortium blockchain that could ensure the secure and efficient knowledge management in the Edge AI that could be used for knowledge transfer in 6G networks. Zhang *et al.* [102] proposed a framework which combines the blockchain and Edge AI to achieve the security and flexible edge service management that could also be used in 6G networks. Doku *et al.* [121] mentioned that the data integrity could be ensured by deploying blockchain in Edge AI, and data centralization would also be disrupted because of the combination of the blockchain's trust mechanism and federated learning's ability (Edge AI's technologies). Rahman *et al.* [122] also presented a blockchain-based framework that combines Edge AI to process and extract significant event information, produce semantic digital analytics and finally save results in blockchain and decentralized cloud repositories to facilitate sharing economy services. However, Wang *et al.* [123] mentioned that although the blockchain could solve the security and privacy problems in Edge AI, how to evaluate the contribution of In-Edge AI computation on heterogeneous scenarios and how to distribute the huge computation load of the proof-of-work (PoW) over the edge system is still an open problem.

### 6.2.2.3    Internet of Everything

Compared with 5G networks, future 6G network would not only consist of the IoT but also the IoE. The future 6G IoE networks would not only connect with people and devices but also the computing resources, vehicles, wearables, sensors and even the robotic agents [124]. The propose of IoE is to seamlessly connect people, processes, data and things in an intelligent way [125]. Moreover, Zhang *et al.* [124] mentioned that the tactile IoT would also become an essential component of 6G IoE networks because it demands higher data rates to support touch-related experiences. However, with the developing of the massive devices in 6G IoE networks, the problems of network management and regulatory are gradually emerging. The application of blockchain could solve these problems. By deploying the blockchain into IoE, the data could be stored securely and shared through distributed blockchain (DBC) transactions and protected by consensus protocols and cryptographic security, with no need of entrusting any central party of the ledger maintenance [126]. The blockchain technology could improve the inter-operability, privacy, reliability and scalability of the underlying infrastructure in IoE networks [127].

Cao *et al.* [127] mentioned a blockchain-based reward mechanism that the devices in the IoE networks could share their power or data to get the corresponding reward. It could make the environment of the network more collaborative and trusted. Dai *et al.* [100] also mentioned that blockchain could be used in vehicular-to-anything (V2X) communications to encourage vehicles to trade energy or information with each other. However, there are still many challenges in the combination of blockchain and IoE. Xu *et al.* [128] mentioned in the case of public chains that most of the IoT devices are suffering power-constrained, especially for the devices powered by cellular IoT. They also presented that the lifetime of cellular IoT devices would significantly be reduced when considering the computation of the consensus algorithm. Moreover, because of the decentralization in the blockchain, it will cause an inevitable delay in data transmission. In the V2X environment, a minimal delay may cause an accident. So, these problems urgently need to be solved for the combination of the blockchain with IoE. The blockchain-based IoE network still needs further investigation for its security performance and optimal node deployment [129].

## 6.3    Issues and problems in blockchain networks

Although blockchain is famous for its security, there are still security and privacy issues in the blockchain. Some of the issues are issues of the blockchain itself such as majority attack and fork problem, but some of the issues are caused by the combination of blockchain with other technology, such as quantum communication. In this part, we divided security and privacy issues into three main parts, which are security-related, privacy-related and other related issues. They will be detailed in the following. A summary of issues and solutions in blockchain networks could be found in Table A.3.

## 6.3.1  Security-related issues

As for the security-related part, there are several security issues for the blockchain network. In this part, the main security-related issues, which are majority attacks, fork problem, double-spending, selfish mining attacks and Sybil attacks, will be detailed in the following.

### 6.3.1.1  Majority attack (51% attack)

Because of the decentralization in the blockchain, any transactions in blockchain should be confirmed by most of the people. That ensures the security of the blockchain. However, it will also have its own problem. If one of the users could control 51% of the computing power in the blockchain network, he would able to control the whole blockchain network. Which means, he could modify the transaction data, stop miner mining any available block, stop the block verifying transaction and so on [130]. Although in some applications of blockchain, such as Bitcoin, Litcoin, the majority attack may not be a considerable threat, for consortium-based blockchain networks, several institutions such as private and public have started collaborating [131]. If collusion occurs between these institutions, the majority attack may just be a general threat. Bahack [132] mentioned that some miners who have a relatively large part of computational power could also achieve a similar goal as the majority attack. Kiayias *et al.* [133] presented a majority attack based on the scenario of blockchain-based mining game, which the miner inside could choose to release the mined block or not to hide newly mined blocks probabilistically.

However, there are also some solutions to deal with the majority attacks. Nguyen *et al.* [134] mentioned that the transaction fee could mitigate the majority attack risk and reduce the expected reward because, with the transaction fee, the cost of the attack will increase significantly. The benefit obtained from the majority attack will be far less than the cost of supply. Moreover, Budish [135] also proposed an incentive compatibility condition which could increase the cost of the computation to prevent the majority attack. Zhu *et al.* [136] proposed a controllable blockchain data management model, which could be deployed in a cloud environment to solve the majority attack problems. Dey [131] presented a methodology that used the supervised machine learning algorithm and algorithmic game theory to monitor the users in the blockchain network, in order to stop the majority attack from taking place.

### 6.3.1.2  Fork problems

The fork problem is one of the most important security issues in blockchain, because fork could occur at anytime and anywhere of the blockchain. Hard fork and soft fork are two types of blockchain forks in the blockchain network. The reason why the blockchain fork occurs commonly is that it depends on the software version of each node in blockchain networks. And sometimes the software version for each node is hardly the same. When the new version comes out, the nodes in the blockchain network could be divided into two types. One is the new nodes types that use the latest software version, and another is the old nodes types that use the old software version. So, there will be compatibility issues between the new and the old nodes. The hard fork is a change to the protocol of blockchain to make old nodes unable to be verified if they do not upgrade. However, the soft fork is different. Unlike the hard fork, the new rules defined by the latest software version are compatible with the old version but are stricter than the old version. When a new version is released, the block released by the node that upgraded the new software version can be verified by all nodes. Blocks released by nodes that have not upgraded the new version can only be verified on nodes running the old version of the software. However, there are some security problems that exist in the fork process of the blockchain. Back *et al.* [137] mentioned before some upgrade, the security of the soft-forked features could only achieve simplified payment verification (SPV)-level. Heilman *et al.* [138] mentioned an eclipse attack that could be used by attackers in the fork process to influence the computing resources of the attacked nodes. Although some issues have already been solved, it still needs future discussion for solving other security issues left in fork problem.

### 6.3.1.3    Double-spending problem

The double-spending problem is one of the main important issues in blockchain networks. Although every transaction in the blockchain network would be validated under the consensus mechanism, the double-spending attack could not be avoided [139]. Double-spending attack aims to break the integrity of the blockchain's distributed ledger [134]. It not only aims at attacking the cryptocurrencies such as the double-spending attack in Bitcoin but also aims at the regular blockchain network. In Bitcoin, the purpose of the double-spending attack is to repeatedly spend a few Bitcoins that have already been used [140]. As for in regular blockchain network, the double-spending attack refers to an attacker attempting to record an invalid transaction on the blockchain that is contrary to the transaction on the existing blockchain. The common method is to generate a longer blockchain fork, make the blockchain containing the original transaction discarded by most miners. Karame *et al.* [141] proposed an attack model that could successfully deploy the double-spending attack when knowing the vendor's address. Gervais *et al.* [142] presented two types of double-spending attack that could be used under two scenarios, they are double-spending attack in zero-confirmation transactions and one-confirmation transactions. Rosenfeld [143] presented an analysis of hash-rate-based double-spending, which gives out the protection that can be against double-spending and the way in which this protection can be undermined. Moreover, Karame [144] also mentioned that the initial measures which used to handle fast payments in a blockchain network are not able to stop double-spending. Natoli and Gramoli [145] presented a blockchain anomaly which they experienced when building their private chain that could also leave a potential chance for double-spending attack.

However, there are also some methods that could prevent the double-spending attack in blockchain networks. Karame *et al.* [141] proposed the users inside the network forward all transactions that attempt to double-spend the same coins in the blockchain network. So, when any user received a new transaction, it will check all the transaction history if this transaction using the pending coins or not. Adler *et al.* [146] presented a decentralized oracle named ASTRAEA that could enhance the security of the public blockchain to prevent the double-spending attack.

#### 6.3.1.4 Selfish mining attack

In general, according to the PoW, nodes in the blockchain network can be rewarded on the basis of the computing resources they used for verifying the transaction. The rewards received by nodes are generally proportional to the computing resources used. However, after finishing their work, some nodes would strategically broadcast their blocks to obtain improper benefit. Eyal proposed the selfish mining attack in 2014, which aims to obtain undue rewards or to waste other miner's computing resources. The attacker would hold private blocks and attempt to fork a private chain [147]. Then the selfish miner would start to mine this private chain and try to make this private chain longer than the public chain. As soon as the length of public chain approaches the length of the private chain, the block mined by the attacker would be revealed. That will cause the honest miners to spend many computing resources but cannot get any rewards. Eyal and Sirer [147] also presented a selfish mining state machine that could present selfish mining more clearly. Courtois and Bahack [148] proposed a new concrete and practical block withholding attack which uses the selfish mining attack thought to maximize the advantage gained by selfish miners. Nayak *et al.* [149] mentioned a selfish mining attack method that combines the eclipse attack to achieve the separation of computing power, affect the distribution of mining rewards and reduce the effective computing power in the network to reduce the difficulty of selfish mining attacks. Sapirshtein *et al.* [150] provided an algorithm that could provide the attacker with an optimal policy to let the attacker benefit from selfish mining with lower bounds on the computational power. Saad *et al.* [151] presented a new form of selfish mining attack, which could guarantee high rewards with low cost.

However, there are also some solutions for solving the selfish mining attack. Solat and Potop-Butucaru [152] presented a novel timestamp-free method named ZeroBlock that could prevent the selfish mining attack via exploiting the Poisson nature of the PoW and the current knowledge on the propagation of information in Bitcoin. Grunspan and Pérez-Marco [153] proposed to adjust the difficulty of the mining protocol in order to prevent it from the selfish mining attack. Bai *et al.* [154] presented a novel Markov chain model that could characterize all the state transitions of public and private chains to make the selfish attack easier to detect than before. Ritz and Zugenmaier [155] mentioned using a Monte Carlo simulation to quantify the effect of uncle blocks both to the profitability of selfish mining and the blockchain's security.

#### 6.3.1.5 Sybil attack

Although blockchain systems are effective in preventing some types of attacking such as bad-mouthing attack and whitewashing attack, they are limited in detecting

Sybil attack [156]. Usually, the nodes in the blockchain network could accept several essences because the blockchain network cannot authentically distinguish the physical machines [11]. That will provide a chance for the adversary to create multiple accounts in blockchain networks for deploying the Sybil attacks. Especially when in the absence of a trusted identification authority, the attacker could easily deploy the Sybil attack to severely compromise the initial generation of identities, thereby undermining the chain of vouchers [157]. So, the Sybil attack is also an essential security issue that needs to be mentioned in blockchain networks. There are already some methods that could solve the previous Sybil attack issues. For example, Pass *et al.* [158] proposed to prevent the Sybil attacks according to deploying computational puzzles in the blockchain protocol. Alachkar and Gaastra [159] mentioned that the Sybil attack could be prevented by incorporating blockchain. Moreover, Otte *et al.* [160] proposed a permissionless tamper-proof data structure named "TrustChain" that includes a novel Sybil-resistant algorithm called NetFlow that could protect the blockchain system far from the Sybil attack.

### 6.3.1.6    Distributed denial-of-service (DDoS) attack

The distributed denial-of-service (DDoS) attack is another possible attack that would have a great impact on the security of the blockchain networks. The reason for why blockchain networks are vulnerable to DDoS attacks is because of the framework of the blockchain network. Blockchain is a design based on P2P architecture, and the openness of P2P will lead to DDoS attacks. The nodes in different positions of blockchain networks could jointly launch DoS attacks to hinder the normal operation of the whole system. However, some attack methods need to be used as the basis of DDoS attacks. For example, the attacker needs to obtain a large number of Sybil nodes and uses eclipse attacks to achieve the purpose of controlling the nodes, so that they could get enough nodes for deploying the DDoS attack. Then the attacker could use these nodes to send huge amounts of packages and require service to influence another user's usage. Although there are already some DDoS attacks aims at Bitcoin network, they are all failure because of the specific protocol in the Bitcoin network. Moreover, not all blockchain networks are the same as the Bitcoin network, the robustness of a particular network depends largely on the diversity of the network and the number of nodes and their hash rate. So different websites have different capabilities to resist DDoS attacks.

Golosova and Romanovs [11] mentioned protection in the DDoS's attack which the size of the block is up to 1 MB, the size of each script is up to 10,000 bytes, the check of the signatures is up to 20,000 and the maximums of the multiple signatures are 20 keys. Liu *et al.* [161] proposed to add a transaction fee to prevent DDoS attacks because it can significantly enhance the cost of conducting attacks. Saad *et al.* [162] presented a new method that could optimize the memory pools of blockchain networks to counter the effects of DDoS attacks. Shafi and Basit [163] presented a botnet prevention system for IoT, which uses the benefits of both SDN and DBC to detect the DDoS attacks in blockchain networks. Javaid *et al.* [164] proposed to combine Ethereum with devices together to not only prevent rogue devices from gaining access to the server but also address DDoS attacks by using static resource allocation for devices that could be used in 5G or 6G networks. Moreover, Abou El Houda *et al.* [165] presented a blockchain-based method named Cochain-SC that combines the SDN, blockchain and smart contract to reduce the influence of DDoS attack.

## 6.3.2   Privacy-related issues

Privacy-preserving is the protection of the user's identity information and other sensitive information that the user does not want to disclose. In the blockchain network, it mainly focuses on the user's identity information and transaction information. Therefore, the privacy protection of the blockchain can be divided into transaction privacy leakage and identity privacy leakage. In the following, these two privacy-related issues will be detailed.

### 6.3.2.1   Transaction privacy leakage

The protection for transaction privacy means to make transaction-related data anonymous to unauthorized nodes. For example, in Bitcoin, it refers explicitly to the transaction amount, the public key of the sender of the transaction, the address of the receiver and the purchased content of the transaction. Any unauthorized nodes cannot get any transaction-related information via any methods. In some high privacy-protection-required blockchains, it is also required to split the association between transactions and transactions. So, the unauthorized nodes cannot effectively infer whether two transactions have continuity before and after, whether they belong to the same user or not and other associations. Some applications of blockchain networks have already proposed some solutions for solving the transaction privacy leakage problem. For example, in Monero networks, users can include some chaff coins called "Mixins" to disable the attacker confirm the actual coins spent by the transaction [140]. Kosba *et al.* [166] presented a decentralized smart contract system named Hawk that stops financial transactions to get stored clearly on the blockchain to protect the transaction privacy. However, Miller *et al.* [167] mentioned a heuristic method that could analysis the blockchain network and guess the real input with 80% accuracy. So, the protection for the transaction privacy still needs future research.

### 6.3.2.2   Identity privacy leakage

As for protecting the user identity privacy, it requires the user's identity information, physical address, IP address and the public information such as the user's public key and address on the blockchain, which are not related in the blockchain networks. Any unauthorized node cannot rely on the public data on the blockchain to obtain the user's identity. Moreover, these unauthorized nodes also cannot use some methods such as network monitoring and traffic analysis to trace the user's transactions and identities. There are also several solutions that could prevent the link trade information from identifying users. Nguyen *et al.* [134] mentioned that by using the ring signatures in the blockchain network, the anonymous member in the blockchain network could endorse the message pseudonymous. The ring signatures could protect the participants' privacy well. Ruffing *et al.* [168] proposed a coin mixer method named "CoinShuffle" that would obfuscate the address of coin owners to protect their privacy. Heilman *et al.* [169] proposed an anonymity solution that uses an untrusted third party to issue anonymous vouchers that could ensure the anonymity and fairness of the transaction to protect user anonymity. Yang *et al.* [62] proposed a blockchain-based system that uses the anonymized method to hide the identity information of users to protect the user's privacy in crowd-sensing networks which may be used in 5G or 6G networks.

## 6.3.3 Other related issues

Except for the security-related and privacy-related issues, the other related issues are equally important. In this part, some other related issues that are regulations, scalability and quantum communication will be introduced in the following.

### 6.3.3.1 Regulations problem

The regulation is another issue that exists in the blockchain network. For example, the Bitcoin, because of the decentralization of the system, the central bank has weak control over the economic policy and the amount of the money [130]. It makes the government pay more attention to the blockchain technologies and needs to formulate the new policy to supervise the blockchain network to avoid the risk of blockchain to the market. In the future, the regulation of blockchain will develop in two aspects that are the policy regulations and technical tools, respectively. Not only should the country strengthen the formulation of legal operating rules and necessary policy constraints for blockchain applications in different fields, but companies also need to set up appropriate policy systems according to specific applications [170]. Peters *et al.* [171] provided an overview of the state of regulatory readiness in terms of dealing with transactions in these currencies in various regions of the world. Girasa [172] presented a comparison between the regulation of the virtual currencies and cryptocurrencies, which may lead to future discussion.

### 6.3.3.2 Scalability problem

Poor scalability is a problem that the blockchain needs to solve urgently. Due to the decentralized character of the blockchain, some applications of blockchain networks such as Bitcoin need high computation resource, bandwidth and storage to ensure the integrity of the distributed ledger. Although the transaction process in the blockchain network has a high security level, many limits come with high security. For example, the Bitcoin is a high-level security application of blockchain networks, but it could only process a maximum of seven transactions per second [144]. Moreover, the latency for a confirmed block is 10 min, and a bootstrap time is 4 days [173]. However, the Visa credit system, which plays the same role as the Bitcoin network, could deal up to 56k transactions per second. So, when deploying the blockchain in future 5G and 6G networks, billions of amounts of smart devices and their massive transaction requirements would become a great challenge for the scalability of blockchain networks. The current scalability measures come at odds with the security of the blockchain system [142]. So, the blockchain network still needs future research to balance the security and scalability of it.

Gervais *et al.* [142] have presented a number of countermeasures that could enhance the security of the blockchain network without deteriorating its scalability. Moreover, Croman *et al.* [173] mentioned that in order to enhance the scalability of the blockchain network, multiple abstraction layers in blockchain architecture need to be considered which are network, consensus, storage, view and side layers. Luu *et al.* [174] presented a distributed agreement protocol named ELASTICO that could uniformly partition or parallelize the mining network into smaller committees to increase the scalability of the blockchain network. Moreover, Danezis and Meiklejohn [175] presented a cryptocurrency framework named "RSCoin" that not only guarantees strong transparency and auditability but also adopts sharding technology to improve the scalability of the blockchain network. Eyal *et al.* [176] presented a scalable blockchain protocol named Bitcoin-NG that reduces the influence of the latency to enhance the scalability of blockchain networks.

### 6.3.3.3  Quantum communication problem

The quantum communication is one of the most promising technologies which would be used in 6G networks. Moreover, Gyongyosi and Imre [177] mentioned that quantum computing would be commercialized in the near future. So, we could expect that the quantum communication technology would fully be deployed in future 6G networks. The combination of quantum communication and blockchain technologies would bring some benefits that the normal blockchain technology did not contain, but this combination will also bring some problems. In 6G blockchain networks, deploying the quantum communication technology means that several contemporary public-key primitives need to be replaced with quantum-resistant ones [134]. However, when using quantum algorithms such as Shora in blockchain networks, it is possible to break the RSA encryption [11].

Furthermore, factoring and discrete logarithm-based cryptographic primitives, such as the elliptic curve signature algorithm, also become vulnerable because of deploying large-scale quantum computation [134]. Kiktenko *et al.* [178] proposed a possible solution that utilizes quantum key distribution across an urban fiber network for information theoretically secure authentication that may solve the previous problems. Ikeda [179] presented an in-depth survey of the quantum communication technology to help the readers follow advanced researches on the application of quantum technology to the blockchain industry. However, more problems are waiting to be solved, which means that there is still a long way to study the combination of blockchain networks and quantum communication technology.

## 6.4  Conclusion

Although the blockchain was introduced in 2008 by Nakamoto, it has developed into a hot topic because of its decentralized characteristics. The evolution of the wireless network is moving from 4G to 5G and 6G networks. So the research on the combination of blockchain and 5G and 6G networks should be carried out as soon as possible. In this chapter, we have presented a detailed survey of the blockchain-enabled technologies, applications and services in 5G and 6G networks. Moreover, the challenges and solutions, such as security-related, privacy-related and other related, of deploying blockchain in 5G and 6G networks, are also proposed. We hope that this discussion will stimulate interest and further research on implementing blockchain in future 5G and 6G networks.

## Acknowledgment

This work was supported by an ARC Linkage Project (LP180101150) from the Australian Research Council, Australia.

## Appendix A

*Table A.1   Blockchain-enabled technologies, applications and services in 5G networks*

| Type | Category | Method | Framework/ protocol |
| --- | --- | --- | --- |
| Technologies | Authentication | [18,21,22] | [17,19,20] |
| | Access control | [24,25] | [26–32] |
| | Verification | [34,36,37,41] | [35,38–40] |
| | Spectrum management | [45–47,50] | [43,48,49] |
| | Network slicing | [55–57] | N/A |
| | Software-defined network (SDN) | [62] | [60,61,63–66] |
| | Edge computing | [73,74] | [68,71,72] |
| Application and services | Smart transport | [77,79,80] | [33,78] |
| | Smart health | [83,84,86,87] | [63,85,88] |
| | Industry 4.0 | [90–93] | [94] |
| | IoT | [101,103] | [99,100,102] |

*Table A.2   Blockchain-enabled technologies, applications and services in 6G networks*

| Category | Types | Method | Framework/protocol |
| --- | --- | --- | --- |
| Technologies | Spectrum sharing | [54,107,109] | [108] |
| | Blockchain with AI | [111–113] | [113] |
| Application and services | Distributed ledger technology | [110,115] | [115] |
| | Edge AI | [121] | [102,120,122] |
| | IoE | [127,128] | [100] |

Table A.3  *Issues and solutions in blockchain networks*

| Type | Security and privacy attack | Characteristic | Refs | Solutions |
|---|---|---|---|---|
| Security related | Majority attack | Control 51% computing power to attack | [132,133] | [131,134–136] |
| | Fork problem | Occurs when the software version of nodes in blockchain are different | [138] | The updates of the blockchain version |
| | Double-spending | Aims to break the integrity of the blockchain's distributed ledger | [141–143,145] | [141,143,146] |
| | Selfish mining attack | Aims to let others waste their computing resources | [148–151] | [152–154] |
| | Sybil attacks | Use multiple accounts to attack | [157] | [158–160] |
| | DDoS attacks | Use nodes to send huge amounts of packages and require service | [11] | [11,161–165] |
| Privacy related | Transaction privacy leakage | Make transaction-related data anonymous to unauthorized nodes | [167] | [140,166] |
| | Identity privacy leakage | Make user-related data not related in the blockchain networks | [168] | [62,134,168,169] |
| Other related | Regulations problems | The regulations for blockchain need to be set and clear | [170] | [170,171] |
| | Scalability problems | Because of the high security of blockchain, the scalability of blockchain is poor | [173] | [142,173–176] |
| | Quantum communication problems | It will make some blockchain original encryption method lose efficacy | [11] | [178] |

# References

[1]    Satoshi Nakamoto. Bitcoin: A peer-to-peer electronic cash system. Technical report, Manubot, 2019.

[2]    Michael Nofer, Peter Gomber, Oliver Hinz, and Dirk Schiereck. Blockchain. Business & Information Systems Engineering, 59(3):183–187, 2017.

[3]    Zibin Zheng, Shaoan Xie, Hong-Ning Dai, Xiangping Chen, and Huaimin Wang. Blockchain challenges and opportunities: A survey. International Journal of Web and Grid Services, 14(4):352–375, 2018.

[4]    Quan-Lin Li, Jing-Yu Ma, and Yan-Xia Chang. Blockchain queue theory. In International Conference on Computational Social Networks, pages 25–40. Springer, 2018.

[5]    Karl Wüst and Arthur Gervais. Do you need a blockchain? In 2018 Crypto Valley Conference on Blockchain Technology (CVCBT), pages 45–54. IEEE, 2018.

[6]    Melanie Swan. Blockchain: Blueprint for a new economy. O'Reilly Media, Inc., 2015.

[7]    M.N.Navodana Rodrigo, Srinath Perera, Sepani Senaratne, and Xiaohua Jin. Blockchain for construction supply chains: A literature synthesis. In Proceedings of ICEC-PAQS Conference 2018, 2018.

[8]    Min Xu, Xingtong Chen, and Gang Kou. A systematic review of blockchain. Financial Innovation, 5(1):27, 2019.

[9]    Dmitry Efanov and Pavel Roschin. The all-pervasiveness of the blockchain technology. Procedia Computer Science, 123:116–121, 2018.

[10]    Kyle Burgess and Joe Colangelo. The promise of Bitcoin and the blockchain. Consumers' Research, 2015.

[11]    Julija Golosova and Andrejs Romanovs. The advantages and disadvantages of the blockchain technology. In 2018 IEEE 6th Workshop on Advances in Information, Electronic and Electrical Engineering (AIEEE), pages 1–6. IEEE, 2018.

[12]    Sarah Underwood. Blockchain beyond Bitcoin, 2016.

[13]    Larry Downes and Paul Nunes. Big bang disruption: Strategy in the age of devastating innovation. Penguin, 2014.

[14]    Abdulla Chaer, Khaled Salah, Claudio Lima, Pratha Pratim Ray, and Tarek Sheltami. Blockchain for 5G: Opportunities and challenges. In 2019 IEEE Globecom Workshops (GC Wkshps), pages 1–6. IEEE, 2019.

[15]    Khaled B Letaief, Wei Chen, Yuanming Shi, Jun Zhang, and Ying-Jun Angela Zhang. The roadmap to 6G: AI empowered wireless networks. IEEE Communications Magazine, 57(8):84–90, 2019.

[16]    Ju Xingzhong, Xue Qingshui, Ma Haifeng, Chen Jiageng, and Zhu Haozhi. The research on identity authentication scheme of Internet of things equipment in 5G network environment. In 2019 IEEE 19th International Conference on Communication Technology (ICCT), pages 312–316. IEEE, 2019.

[17]  Hui Yang, Haowei Zheng, Jie Zhang, Yizhen Wu, Young Lee, and Yuefeng Ji. Blockchain-based trusted authentication in cloud radio over fiber network for 5G. In 2017 16th International Conference on Optical Communications and Networks (ICOCN), pages 1–3. IEEE, 2017.

[18]  MA Rashid and Houshyar Honar Pajooh. A security framework for IoT authentication and authorization based on blockchain technology. In 2019 18th IEEE International Conference On Trust, Security And Privacy In Computing And Communications/13th IEEE International Conference On Big Data Science And Engineering (TrustCom/BigDataSE), pages 264–271. IEEE, 2019.

[19]  Srinivas Jangirala, Ashok Kumar Das, and Athanasios V Vasilakos. Designing secure light-weight blockchain-enabled RFID-based authentication protocol for supply chains in 5G mobile edge computing environment. IEEE Transactions on Industrial Informatics, 2019.

[20]  Yinghui Zhang, Robert Deng, Elisa Bertino, and Dong Zheng. Robust and universal seamless handover authentication in 5G HetNets. IEEE Transactions on Dependable and Secure Computing, 2019.

[21]  Zhonglin Chen, Shanzhi Chen, Hui Xu, and Bo Hu. A security authentication scheme of 5G ultra-dense network based on blockchain. IEEE Access, 6:55372–55379, 2018.

[22]  Abbas Yazdinejad, Reza M Parizi, Ali Dehghantanha, and Kim-Kwang Raymond Choo. Blockchain-enabled authentication handover with efficient privacy protection in SDN-based 5G networks. IEEE Transactions on Network Science and Engineering, 2019.

[23]  Pierangela Samarati and Sabrina Capitani de Vimercati. Access control: Policies, models, and mechanisms. In International School on Foundations of Security Analysis and Design, pages 137–196. Springer, 2000.

[24]  Ronghua Xu, Yu Chen, Erik Blasch, and Genshe Chen. BlendCAC: A blockchain-enabled decentralized capability-based access control for IoTs. In 2018 IEEE International Conference on Internet of Things (iThings) and IEEE Green Computing and Communications (GreenCom) and IEEE Cyber, Physical and Social Computing (CPSCom) and IEEE Smart Data (SmartData), pages 1027–1034. IEEE, 2018.

[25]  Chethana Dukkipati, Yunpeng Zhang, and Liang Chieh Cheng. Decentralized, blockchain based access control framework for the heterogeneous Internet of things. In Proceedings of the Third ACM Workshop on Attribute-Based Access Control, pages 61–69, 2018.

[26]  Vincent Messié, Gaël Fromentoux, Xavier Marjou, and Nathalie Labidurie Omnes. BALAdIN for blockchain-based 5G networks. In 2019 22nd Conference on Innovation in Clouds, Internet and Networks and Workshops (ICIN), pages 201–205. IEEE, 2019.

[27]  Shangping Wang, Yinglong Zhang, and Yaling Zhang. A blockchain-based framework for data sharing with fine-grained access control in decentralized storage systems. IEEE Access, 6:38437–38450, 2018.

[28]  Gaby G Dagher, Jordan Mohler, Matea Milojkovic, and Praneeth Babu Marella. Ancile: Privacy-preserving framework for access control and interoperability of electronic health records using blockchain technology. Sustainable Cities and Society, 39:283–297, 2018.

[29]  Otto Julio Ahlert Pinno, Andre Ricardo Abed Gregio, and Luis CE De Bona. ControlChain: Blockchain as a central enabler for access control authorizations in the IoT. In GLOBECOM 2017—2017 IEEE Global Communications Conference, pages 1–6. IEEE, 2017.

[30]  Hui Yang, Yajie Li, Shaoyong Guo, Jian Ding, Young Lee, and Jie Zhang. Distributed blockchain-based trusted control with multi-controller collaboration for software defined data center optical networks in 5G and beyond. In Optical Fiber Communication Conference, pages Th1G–2. Optical Society of America, 2019.

[31]  Xintong Ling, Jiaheng Wang, Taha Bouchoucha, Bernard C Levy, and Zhi Ding. Blockchain radio access network (B-RAN): Towards decentralized secure radio access paradigm. IEEE Access, 7:9714–9723, 2019.

[32]  Aafaf Ouaddah, Anas Abou Elkalam, and Abdellah Ait Ouahman. FairAccess: A new blockchain-based access control framework for the Internet of Things. Security and Communication Networks, 9(18):5943–5964, 2016.

[33]  Dajun Zhang, F Richard Yu, and Ruizhe Yang. Blockchain-based distributed software-defined vehicular networks: A dueling deep q-learning approach. IEEE Transactions on Cognitive Communications and Networking, 5(4): 1086–1100, 2019.

[34]  Devrim Unal, Mohammad Hammoudeh, and Mehmet Sabir Kiraz. Policy specification and verification for blockchain and smart contracts in 5G networks. ICT Express, 6(1):43–47, 2020.

[35]  Li Jiang, Shengli Xie, Sabita Maharjan, and Yan Zhang. Joint transaction relaying and block verification optimization for blockchain empowered D2D communication. IEEE Transactions on Vehicular Technology, 2019.

[36]  Christoph Prybila, Stefan Schulte, Christoph Hochreiner, and Ingo Weber. Runtime verification for business processes utilizing the Bitcoin blockchain. Future Generation Computer Systems, 2017.

[37]  Justin Fisher and Maxwell Henry Sanchez. Authentication and verification of digital data utilizing blockchain technology, 2016. US Patent App. 15/083,238.

[38]  Caciano Machado and Antônio Augusto Medeiros Fröhlich. IoT data integrity verification for cyber-physical systems using blockchain. In 2018 IEEE 21st International Symposium on Real-Time Distributed Computing (ISORC), pages 83–90. IEEE, 2018.

[39]  Chao Qu, Ming Tao, Jie Zhang, Xiaoyu Hong, and Ruifen Yuan. Blockchain based credibility verification method for IoT entities. Security and Communication Networks, 2018, 2018.

[40]  Bin Liu, Xiao Liang Yu, Shiping Chen, Xiwei Xu, and Liming Zhu. Blockchain based data integrity service framework for IoT data. In 2017

IEEE International Conference on Web Services (ICWS), pages 468–475. IEEE, 2017.

[41] Dongdong Yue, Ruixuan Li, Yan Zhang, Wenlong Tian, and Chengyi Peng. Blockchain based data integrity verification in P2P cloud storage. In 2018 IEEE 24th International Conference on Parallel and Distributed Systems (ICPADS), pages 561–568. IEEE, 2018.

[42] Zhenyu Zhou, Jie Gong, Yejun He, and Yan Zhang. Software defined machine-to-machine communication for smart energy management. IEEE Communications Magazine, 55(10):52–60, 2017.

[43] Zhenyu Zhou, Xinyi Chen, Yan Zhang, and Shahid Mumtaz. Blockchain-empowered secure spectrum sharing for 5G heterogeneous networks. IEEE Network, 34(1):24–31, 2020.

[44] Martin BH Weiss, Kevin Werbach, Douglas C Sicker, and Carlos E Caicedo Bastidas. On the application of blockchains to spectrum management. IEEE Transactions on Cognitive Communications and Networking, 5(2):193–205, 2019.

[45] Taras Maksymyuk, Juraj Gazda, Longzhe Han, and Minho Jo. Blockchain-based intelligent network management for 5G and beyond. In 2019 3rd International Conference on Advanced Information and Communications Technologies (AICT), pages 36–39. IEEE, 2019.

[46] Khashayar Kotobi and Sven G Bilén. Blockchain-enabled spectrum access in cognitive radio networks. In 2017 Wireless Telecommunications Symposium (WTS), pages 1–6. IEEE, 2017.

[47] Suzan Bayhan, Anatolij Zubow, and Adam Wolisz. Spass: Spectrum sensing as a service via smart contracts. In 2018 IEEE International Symposium on Dynamic Spectrum Access Networks (DySPAN), pages 1–10. IEEE, 2018.

[48] Mohamed Grissa, Attila A Yavuz, and Bechir Hamdaoui. TrustSAS: A trustworthy spectrum access system for the 3.5 GHz CBRS band. In IEEE INFOCOM 2019-IEEE Conference on Computer Communications, pages 1495–1503. IEEE, 2019.

[49] Frank den Hartog, Faycal Bouhafs, and Qi Shi. Toward secure trading of unlicensed spectrum in cyber-physical systems. In 2019 16th IEEE Annual Consumer Communications & Networking Conference (CCNC), pages 1–4. IEEE, 2019.

[50] Volkan Sevindik. Autonomous 5G smallcell network deployment and optimization in unlicensed spectrum. In 2019 IEEE 2nd 5G World Forum (5GWF), pages 446–451. IEEE, 2019.

[51] Haijun Zhang, Na Liu, Xiaoli Chu, Keping Long, Abdol-Hamid Aghvami, and Victor CM Leung. Network slicing based 5G and future mobile networks: Mobility, resource management, and challenges. IEEE communications magazine, 55(8):138–145, 2017.

[52] Ibrahim Afolabi, Tarik Taleb, Konstantinos Samdanis, Adlen Ksentini, and Hannu Flinck. Network slicing and softwarization: A survey on principles, enabling technologies, and solutions. IEEE Communications Surveys & Tutorials, 20(3):2429–2453, 2018.

[53]    Shunliang Zhang. An overview of network slicing for 5G. IEEE Wireless Communications, 26(3):111–117, 2019.

[54]    Dinh C Nguyen, Pubudu N Pathirana, Ming Ding, and Aruna Seneviratne. Blockchain for 5G and beyond networks: A state of the art survey. arXiv preprint arXiv:1912.05062, 2019.

[55]    Boubakr Nour, Adlen Ksentini, Nicolas Herbaut, Pantelis A Frangoudis, and Hassine Moungla. A blockchain-based network slice broker for 5G services. IEEE Networking Letters, 1(3):99–102, 2019.

[56]    Jere Backman, Seppo Yrjölä, Kristiina Valtanen, and Olli Mämmelä. Blockchain network slice broker in 5G: Slice leasing in factory of the future use case. In 2017 Internet of Things Business Models, Users, and Networks, pages 1–8. IEEE, 2017.

[57]    Kristiina Valtanen, Jere Backman, and Seppo Yrjölä. Creating value through blockchain powered resource configurations: Analysis of 5G network slice brokering case. In 2018 IEEE Wireless Communications and Networking Conference Workshops (WCNCW), pages 185– 190. IEEE, 2018.

[58]    Sahil Garg, Kuljeet Kaur, Georges Kaddoum, Syed Hassan Ahmed, and Dushantha Nalin K Jayakody. SDN-based secure and privacy-preserving scheme for vehicular networks: A 5G perspective. IEEE Transactions on Vehicular Technology, 68(9):8421–8434, 2019.

[59]    Rajat Chaudhary, Gagangeet Singh Aujla, Sahil Garg, Neeraj Kumar, and Joel JPC Rodrigues. SDN-enabled multi-attribute-based secure communication for smart grid in IIoT environment. IEEE Transactions on Industrial Informatics, 14(6):2629–2640, 2018.

[60]    Open Networking Foundation. Software-defined networking: The new norm for networks. ONF White Paper, volume 2, pages 2–6, 2012.

[61]    Mehran Pourvahab and Gholamhossein Ekbatanifard. An efficient forensics architecture in software-defined networking-IoT using blockchain technology. IEEE Access, 7:99573–99588, 2019.

[62]    Mengmeng Yang, Tianqing Zhu, Kaitai Liang, Wanlei Zhou, and Robert H Deng. A blockchain-based location privacy-preserving crowdsensing system. Future Generation Computer Systems, 94:408–418, 2019.

[63]    Peilong Li, Chen Xu, Hao Jin, *et al.* ChainSDI: A software-defined infrastructure for regulation-compliant home-based healthcare services secured by blockchains. IEEE Systems Journal, 2019.

[64]    Pradip Kumar Sharma, Saurabh Singh, Young-Sik Jeong, and Jong Hyuk Park. DistBlockNet: A distributed blockchains-based secure SDN architecture for IoT networks. IEEE Communications Magazine, 55(9):78–85, 2017.

[65]    Chenyu Xue, Ning Xu, and Yin Bo. Research on key technologies of software-defined network based on blockchain. In 2019 IEEE International Conference on Service-Oriented System Engineering (SOSE), pages 239–2394. IEEE, 2019.

[66]    Mathieu Boussard, Serge Papillon, Pierre Peloso, Matteo Signorini, and Erez Waisbard. Steward: SDN and blockchain-based trust evaluation for

automated risk management on IoT devices. In IEEE INFOCOM 2019-IEEE Conference on Computer Communications Workshops (INFOCOM WKSHPS), pages 841–846. IEEE, 2019.

[67] Zehui Xiong, Yang Zhang, Dusit Niyato, Ping Wang, and Zhu Han. When mobile blockchain meets edge computing. IEEE Communications Magazine, 56(8):33–39, 2018.

[68] Pavel Mach and Zdenek Becvar. Mobile edge computing: A survey on architecture and computation offloading. IEEE Communications Surveys & Tutorials, 19(3):1628–1656, 2017.

[69] Jiale Zhang, Bing Chen, Yanchao Zhao, Xiang Cheng, and Feng Hu. Data security and privacy-preserving in edge computing paradigm: Survey and open issues. IEEE Access, 6:18209–18237, 2018.

[70] Ruizhe Yang, F Richard Yu, Pengbo Si, Zhaoxin Yang, and Yanhua Zhang. Integrated blockchain and edge computing systems: A survey, some research issues and challenges. IEEE Communications Surveys & Tutorials, 21(2): 1508–1532, 2019.

[71] Yujin Zhu. A survey on mobile edge platform with blockchain. In 2019 IEEE 3rd Information Technology, Networking, Electronic and Automation Control Conference (ITNEC), pages 879–883. IEEE, 2019.

[72] Bo Wu, Ke Xu, Qi Li, Shoushou Ren, Zhuotao Liu, and Zhichao Zhang. Toward blockchain-powered trusted collaborative services for edge-centric networks. IEEE Network, 34(2):30–36, 2020.

[73] Hui Yang, Yongshen Liang, Jiaqi Yuan, Qiuyan Yao, Ao Yu, and Jie Zhang. Distributed blockchain-based trusted multi-domain collaboration for mobile edge computing in 5G and beyond. IEEE Transactions on Industrial Informatics, 2020.

[74] Shijie Zhang and Jong-Hyouk Lee. A group signature and authentication scheme for blockchain-based mobile edge computing. IEEE Internet of Things Journal, 2019.

[75] Tigang Jiang, Hua Fang, and Honggang Wang. Blockchain-based Internet of vehicles: Distributed network architecture and performance analysis. IEEE Internet of Things Journal, 6(3):4640–4649, 2018.

[76] Sandi Rahmadika, Kyeongmo Lee, and Kyung-Hyune Rhee. Blockchain-enabled 5G autonomous vehicular networks. In 2019 International Conference on Sustainable Engineering and Creative Computing (ICSECC), pages 275–280. IEEE, 2019.

[77] Jianbin Gao, Kwame Opuni-Boachie Obour Agyekum, Emmanuel Boateng Sifah, *et al.* A blockchain-SDN-enabled Internet of vehicles environment for fog computing and 5G networks. IEEE Internet of Things Journal, 2019.

[78] Lixia Xie, Ying Ding, Hongyu Yang, and Xinmu Wang. Blockchain-based secure and trustworthy Internet of things in SDN-enabled 5G-VANETs. IEEE Access, 7:56656–56666, 2019.

[79] Chen Wang, Jian Shen, Jin-Feng Lai, and Jianwei Liu. B-TSCA: Blockchain assisted trustworthiness scalable computation for V2I authentication in VANETs. IEEE Transactions on Emerging Topics in Computing, 2020.

[80]    Haoran Liang, Jun Wu, Shahid Mumtaz, Jianhua Li, Xi Lin, and Miaowen Wen. MBID: Micro-blockchain-based geographical dynamic intrusion detection for V2X. IEEE Communications Magazine, 57(10):77–83, 2019.

[81]    Abdul Ahad, Mohammad Tahir, and Kok-Lim Alvin Yau. 5G-based smart healthcare network: Architecture, taxonomy, challenges and future research directions. IEEE Access, 7:100747–100762, 2019.

[82]    Hendrik L Cech, Marcel Großmann, and Udo R Krieger. A fog computing architecture to share sensor data by means of blockchain functionality. In 2019 IEEE International Conference on Fog Computing (ICFC), pages 31–40. IEEE, 2019.

[83]    Di Lin, Su Hu, Yuan Gao, and Yu Tang. Optimizing MEC networks for healthcare applications in 5G communications with the authenticity of users' priorities. IEEE Access, 7:88592–88600, 2019.

[84]    Kai Fan, Yanhui Ren, Yue Wang, Hui Li, and Yingtang Yang. Blockchain-based efficient privacy preserving and data sharing scheme of content-centric network in 5G. IET Communications, 12(5):527–532, 2017.

[85]    Xiao Yue, Huiju Wang, Dawei Jin, Mingqiang Li, and Wei Jiang. Healthcare data gateways: Found healthcare intelligence on blockchain with novel privacy risk control. Journal of Medical Systems, 40(10):218, 2016.

[86]    Xueping Liang, Juan Zhao, Sachin Shetty, Jihong Liu, and Danyi Li. Integrating blockchain for data sharing and collaboration in mobile health-care applications. In 2017 IEEE 28th Annual International Symposium on Personal, Indoor, and Mobile Radio Communications (PIMRC), pages 1–5. IEEE, 2017.

[87]    Christian Esposito, Alfredo De Santis, Genny Tortora, Henry Chang, and Kim-Kwang Raymond Choo. Blockchain: A panacea for healthcare cloud-based data security and privacy? IEEE Cloud Computing, 5(1):31–37, 2018.

[88]    Nicholas J Witchey. Healthcare transaction validation via blockchain, systems and methods, 2019. US Patent 10,340,038.

[89]    Martin J Kleinelanghorst, Li Zhou, Janusz J Sikorski, *et al.* J-park simulator: Roadmap to smart eco-industrial parks. In ICC, pages 107–1, 2017.

[90]    Janusz J Sikorski, Joy Haughton, and Markus Kraft. Blockchain technology in the chemical industry: Machine-to-machine electricity market. Applied Energy, 195:234–246, 2017.

[91]    Ivan Jovović, Siniša Husnjak, Ivan Forenbacher, and Sven Maček. Innovative application of 5G and blockchain technology in industry 4.0. EAI Endorsed Transactions on Industrial Networks and Intelligent Systems, 6(18), 2019.

[92]    Li-e Wang, Yan Bai, Quan Jiang, Victor CM Leung, Wei Cai, and Xianxian Li. Beh-Raft-Chain: A behavior-based fast blockchain protocol for complex networks. IEEE Transactions on Network Science and Engineering, 2020.

[93]    Ishan Mistry, Sudeep Tanwar, Sudhanshu Tyagi, and Neeraj Kumar. Blockchain for 5G-enabled IoT for industrial automation: A systematic review, solutions, and challenges. Mechanical Systems and Signal Processing, 135:106382, 2020.

[94]  Chao Lin, Debiao He, Xinyi Huang, Kim-Kwang Raymond Choo, and Athanasios V Vasilakos. BSeIn: A blockchain-based secure mutual authentication with fine-grained access control system for industry 4.0. Journal of Network and Computer Applications, 116:42–52, 2018.

[95]  Waleed Ejaz, Alagan Anpalagan, Muhammad Ali Imran, *et al*. Internet of things (IoT) in 5G wireless communications. IEEE Access, 4:10310–10314, 2016.

[96]  Dinh C Nguyen, Pubudu N Pathirana, Ming Ding, and Aruna Seneviratne. Integration of blockchain and cloud of things: Architecture, applications and challenges. arXiv preprint arXiv:1908.09058, 2019.

[97]  Joern Ploennigs, John Cohn, and Andy Stanford-Clark. The future of IoT. IEEE Internet of Things Magazine, 1(1):28–33, 2018.

[98]  Alfonso Panarello, Nachiket Tapas, Giovanni Merlino, Francesco Longo, and Antonio Puliafito. Blockchain and IoT integration: A systematic survey. Sensors, 18(8):2575, 2018.

[99]  Ali Dorri, Salil S Kanhere, Raja Jurdak, and Praveen Gauravaram. Blockchain for IoT security and privacy: The case study of a smart home. In 2017 IEEE International Conference on Pervasive Computing and Communications Workshops (PerCom Workshops), pages 618–623. IEEE, 2017.

[100]  Hong-Ning Dai, Zibin Zheng, and Yan Zhang. Blockchain for Internet of things: A survey. IEEE Internet of Things Journal, 6(5):8076–8094, 2019.

[101]  Mayra Samaniego and Ralph Deters. Blockchain as a service for IoT. In 2016 IEEE International Conference on Internet of Things (iThings) and IEEE Green Computing and Communications (GreenCom) and IEEE Cyber, Physical and Social Computing (CPSCom) and IEEE Smart Data (SmartData), pages 433–436. IEEE, 2016.

[102]  Ke Zhang, Yongxu Zhu, Sabita Maharjan, and Yan Zhang. Edge intelligence and blockchain empowered 5G beyond for the industrial Internet of things. IEEE Network, 33(5):12–19, 2019.

[103]  Besiahgari Dinesh, B Kavya, Dudekula Sivakumar, and Mohammed Riyaz Ahmed. Conforming test of blockchain for 5G enabled IoT. In 2019 3rd International Conference on Trends in Electronics and Informatics (ICOEI), pages 1153–1157. IEEE, 2019.

[104]  Jean Sebanstien-Bedo Orange, Ana Garcia Armada, Barry Evans, Alex Galis, and Holger Karl. White paper for research beyond 5G. Accessed, 23:2016, 2015.

[105]  Tongyi Huang, Wu Yang, Jun Wu, Jin Ma, Xiaofei Zhang, and Daoyin Zhang. A survey on green 6G network: Architecture and technologies. IEEE Access, 7:175758–175768, 2019.

[106]  Samar Elmeadawy and Raed M Shubair. 6G wireless communications: Future technologies and research challenges. In 2019 International Conference on Electrical and Computing Technologies and Applications (ICECTA), pages 1–5. IEEE, 2019.

[107]   Yueyue Dai, Du Xu, Sabita Maharjan, Zhuang Chen, Qian He, and Yan Zhang. Blockchain and deep reinforcement learning empowered intelligent 5G beyond. IEEE Network, 33(3):10–17, 2019.

[108]   Khashayar Kotobi and Sven G Bilen. Secure blockchains for dynamic spectrum access: A decentralized database in moving cognitive radio networks enhances security and user access. IEEE Vehicular Technology Magazine, 13(1):32–39, 2018.

[109]   Babak Mafakheri, Tejas Subramanya, Leonardo Goratti, and Roberto Riggio. Blockchain-based infrastructure sharing in 5G small cell networks. In 2018 14th International Conference on Network and Service Management (CNSM), pages 313–317. IEEE, 2018.

[110]   Tharaka Hewa, Gürkan Gür, Anshuman Kalla, Mika Ylianttila, An Bracken, and Madhusanka Liyanage. The role of blockchain in 6G: Challenges, opportunities and research directions. In 2020 2nd 6G Wireless Summit (6G SUMMIT), pages 1–5. IEEE, 2020.

[111]   Polina Mamoshina, Lucy Ojomoko, Yury Yanovich, *et al.* Converging blockchain and next-generation artificial intelligence technologies to decentralize and accelerate biomedical research and healthcare. Oncotarget, 9(5):5665, 2018.

[112]   H Brendan McMahan, Eider Moore, Daniel Ramage, *et al.* Communication-efficient learning of deep networks from decentralized data. arXiv preprint arXiv:1602.05629, 2016.

[113]   Khaled Salah, Muhammad Habib ur Rehman, Nishara Nizamuddin, and Ala Al-Fuqaha. Blockchain for AI: Review and open research challenges. IEEE Access, 7:10127–10149, 2019.

[114]   Walid Saad, Mehdi Bennis, and Mingzhe Chen. A vision of 6G wireless systems: Applications, trends, technologies, and open research problems. IEEE Network, 2019.

[115]   Pietro Ferraro, Christopher King, and Robert Shorten. Distributed ledger technology for smart cities, the sharing economy, and social compliance. IEEE Access, 6:62728–62746, 2018.

[116]   Chao Li, Yushu Xue, Jing Wang, Weigong Zhang, and Tao Li. Edge-oriented computing paradigms: A survey on architecture design and system management. ACM Computing Surveys (CSUR), 51(2):1–34, 2018.

[117]   Yen-Lin Lee, Pei-Kuei Tsung, and Max Wu. Technology trend of Edge AI. In 2018 International Symposium on VLSI Design, Automation and Test (VLSI-DAT), pages 1–2. IEEE, 2018.

[118]   Pawani Porambage, Tanesh Kumar, Madhusanka Liyanage, *et al.* Sec-EdgeAI: AI for edge security vs security for Edge AI. 1st 6G Wireless Summit. Levi, Finland; 2019.

[119]   Jinliang Xu, Shangguang Wang, Bharat K Bhargava, and Fangchun Yang. A blockchain-enabled trustless crowd-intelligence ecosystem on mobile edge computing. IEEE Transactions on Industrial Informatics, 15(6):3538–3547, 2019.

[120] Xi Lin, Jianhua Li, Jun Wu, Haoran Liang, and Wu Yang. Making knowledge tradable in edge-AI enabled IoT: A consortium blockchain-based efficient and incentive approach. IEEE Transactions on Industrial Informatics, 15(12):6367–6378, 2019.

[121] Ronald Doku, Danda B Rawat, and Chunmei Liu. Towards federated learning approach to determine data relevance in big data. In 2019 IEEE 20th International Conference on Information Reuse and Integration for Data Science (IRI), pages 184–192. IEEE, 2019.

[122] Md Abdur Rahman, Md Mamunur Rashid, M Shamim Hossain, Elham Hassanain, Mohammed F Alhamid, and Mohsen Guizani. Blockchain and IoT-based cognitive edge framework for sharing economy services in a smart city. IEEE Access, 7:18611–18621, 2019.

[123] Xiaofei Wang, Yiwen Han, Chenyang Wang, Qiyang Zhao, Xu Chen, and Min Chen. In-Edge AI: Intelligentizing mobile edge computing, caching and communication by federated learning. IEEE Network, 33(5):156–165, 2019.

[124] Zhengquan Zhang, Yue Xiao, Zheng Ma, *et al.* 6G wireless networks: Vision, requirements, architecture, and key technologies. IEEE Vehicular Technology Magazine, 14(3):28–41, 2019.

[125] Madhusanka Liyanage, An Braeken, Pardeep Kumar, and Mika Ylianttila. IoT Security: Advances in Authentication. John Wiley & Sons, 2020.

[126] Guan Gui, Miao Liu, Fengxiao Tang, Nei Kato, and Fumiyuki Adachi. 6G: Opening new horizons for integration of comfort, security and intelligence. IEEE Wireless Communications, 2020.

[127] Bin Cao, Yixin Li, Lei Zhang, *et al.* When Internet of things meets block-chain: Challenges in distributed consensus. IEEE Network, 33(6):133–139, 2019.

[128] Hao Xu, Paulo Valente Klainea, Oluwakayode Oniretia, Bin Caob, Muhammad Imrana, and Lei Zhang. Blockchain-enabled resource management and sharing for 6G communications. arXiv preprint arXiv:2003. 13083, 2020.

[129] Yao Sun, Lei Zhang, Gang Feng, Bowen Yang, Bin Cao, and Muhammad Ali Imran. Blockchain-enabled wireless Internet of things: Performance analysis and optimal communication node deployment. IEEE Internet of Things Journal, 6(3):5791–5802, 2019.

[130] Iuon-Chang Lin and Tzu-Chun Liao. A survey of blockchain security issues and challenges. IJ Network Security, 19(5):653–659, 2017.

[131] Somdip Dey. Securing majority-attack in blockchain using machine learning and algorithmic game theory: A proof of work. In 2018 10th Computer Science and Electronic Engineering (CEEC), pages 7–10. IEEE, 2018.

[132] Lear Bahack. Theoretical Bitcoin attacks with less than half of the computational power (draft). arXiv preprint arXiv:1312.7013, 2013.

[133] Aggelos Kiayias, Elias Koutsoupias, Maria Kyropoulou, and Yiannis Tselekounis. Blockchain mining games. In Proceedings of the 2016 ACM Conference on Economics and Computation, pages 365–382, 2016.

[134]  Tri Nguyen, Ngoc Tran, Lauri Loven, Juha Partala, M-Tahar Kechadi, and Susanna Pirttikangas. Privacy-aware blockchain innovation for 6G: Challenges and opportunities. In 2020 2nd 6G Wireless Summit (6G SUMMIT), pages 1–5. IEEE, 2020.

[135]  Eric Budish. The economic limits of Bitcoin and the blockchain. Technical report, National Bureau of Economic Research, 2018.

[136]  Liehuang Zhu, Yulu Wu, Keke Gai, and Kim-Kwang Raymond Choo. Controllable and trustworthy blockchain-based cloud data management. Future Generation Computer Systems, 91:527–535, 2019.

[137]  Adam Back, Matt Corallo, Luke Dashjr, *et al.* Enabling blockchain innovations with pegged sidechains. http://www. opensciencereview. com/papers/123/enablingblockchain-innovations-with-pegged-sidechains, 72, 2014.

[138]  Ethan Heilman, Alison Kendler, Aviv Zohar, and Sharon Goldberg. Eclipse attacks on Bitcoin's peer-to-peer network. In 24th USENIX Security Symposium (USENIX Security 15), pages 129–144, 2015.

[139]  Ghassan O Karame, Elli Androulaki, Marc Roeschlin, Arthur Gervais, and Srdjan Capkun. Misbehavior in Bitcoin: A study of double-spending and accountability. ACM Transactions on Information and System Security (TISSEC), 18(1):1–32, 2015.

[140]  Xiaoqi Li, Peng Jiang, Ting Chen, Xiapu Luo, and Qiaoyan Wen. A survey on the security of blockchain systems. Future Generation Computer Systems, 107:841–853, 2020.

[141]  Ghassan O Karame, Elli Androulaki, and Srdjan Capkun. Double-spending fast payments in Bitcoin. In Proceedings of the 2012 ACM Conference on Computer and Communications Security, pages 906–917, 2012.

[142]  Arthur Gervais, Hubert Ritzdorf, Ghassan O Karame, and Srdjan Capkun. Tampering with the delivery of blocks and transactions in Bitcoin. In Proceedings of the 22nd ACM SIGSAC Conference on Computer and Communications Security, pages 692–705, 2015.

[143]  Meni Rosenfeld. Analysis of hashrate-based double spending. arXiv preprint arXiv:1402.2009, 2014.

[144]  Ghassan Karame. On the security and scalability of Bitcoin's blockchain. In Proceedings of the 2016 ACM SIGSAC Conference on Computer and Communications Security, pages 1861–1862, 2016.

[145]  Christopher Natoli and Vincent Gramoli. The blockchain anomaly. In 2016 IEEE 15th International Symposium on Network Computing and Applications (NCA), pages 310–317. IEEE, 2016.

[146]  John Adler, Ryan Berryhill, Andreas Veneris, Zissis Poulos, Neil Veira, and Anastasia Kastania. Astraea: A decentralized blockchain oracle. In 2018 IEEE International Conference on Internet of Things (iThings) and IEEE Green Computing and Communications (GreenCom) and IEEE Cyber, Physical and Social Computing (CPSCom) and IEEE Smart Data (SmartData), pages 1145–1152. IEEE, 2018.

[147] Ittay Eyal and Emin Gün Sirer. Majority is not enough: Bitcoin mining is vulnerable. In International conference on financial cryptography and data security, pages 436–454. Springer, 2014.

[148] Nicolas T Courtois and Lear Bahack. On subversive miner strategies and block withholding attack in Bitcoin digital currency. arXiv preprint arXiv:1402.1718, 2014.

[149] Kartik Nayak, Srijan Kumar, Andrew Miller, and Elaine Shi. Stubborn mining: Generalizing selfish mining and combining with an eclipse attack. In 2016 IEEE European Symposium on Security and Privacy (EuroS&P), pages 305–320. IEEE, 2016.

[150] Ayelet Sapirshtein, Yonatan Sompolinsky, and Aviv Zohar. Optimal selfish mining strategies in Bitcoin. In International Conference on Financial Cryptography and Data Security, pages 515–532. Springer, 2016.

[151] Muhammad Saad, Laurent Njilla, Charles Kamhoua, and Aziz Mohaisen. Countering selfish mining in blockchains. In 2019 International Conference on Computing, Networking and Communications (ICNC), pages 360–364. IEEE, 2019.

[152] Siamak Solat and Maria Potop-Butucaru. Brief announcement: Zeroblock: Timestamp-free prevention of block-withholding attack in Bitcoin. In International Symposium on Stabilization, Safety, and Security of Distributed Systems, pages 356–360. Springer, 2017.

[153] Cyril Grunspan and Ricardo Pérez-Marco. On profitability of selfish mining. arXiv preprint arXiv:1805.08281, 2018.

[154] Qianlan Bai, Xinyan Zhou, Xing Wang, Yuedong Xu, Xin Wang, and Qingsheng Kong. A deep dive into blockchain selfish mining. In ICC 2019—2019 IEEE International Conference on Communications (ICC), pages 1–6. IEEE, 2019.

[155] Fabian Ritz and Alf Zugenmaier. The impact of uncle rewards on selfish mining in Ethereum. In 2018 IEEE European Symposium on Security and Privacy Workshops (EuroS&PW), pages 50–57. IEEE, 2018.

[156] Yuanfeng Cai and Dan Zhu. Fraud detections for online businesses: A perspective from blockchain technology. Financial Innovation, 2(1):20, 2016.

[157] John R Douceur. The Sybil attack. In International Workshop on Peer-to-Peer Systems, pages 251–260. Springer, 2002.

[158] Rafael Pass, Lior Seeman, and Abhi Shelat. Analysis of the blockchain protocol in asynchronous networks. In Annual International Conference on the Theory and Applications of Cryptographic Techniques, pages 643–673. Springer, 2017.

[159] Kotaiba Alachkar and Dirk Gaastra. Blockchain-based Sybil attack mitigation: A case study of the I2P network, 2018.

[160] Pim Otte, Martijn de Vos, and Johan Pouwelse. TrustChain: A Sybil-resistant scalable blockchain. Future Generation Computer Systems, 107:770–780, 2020.

[161] Ziyao Liu, Nguyen Cong Luong, Wenbo Wang, *et al.* A survey on blockchain: A game theoretical perspective. IEEE Access, 7:47615–47643, 2019.

[162] Muhammad Saad, Laurent Njilla, Charles Kamhoua, Joongheon Kim, DaeHun Nyang, and Aziz Mohaisen. Mempool optimization for defending against DDoS attacks in PoW-based blockchain systems. In 2019 IEEE International Conference on Blockchain and Cryptocurrency (ICBC), pages 285–292. IEEE, 2019.

[163] Qaisar Shafi and Abdul Basit. DDoS botnet prevention using blockchain in software defined Internet of things. In 2019 16th International Bhurban Conference on Applied Sciences and Technology (IBCAST), pages 624–628. IEEE, 2019.

[164] Uzair Javaid, Ang Kiang Siang, Muhammad Naveed Aman, and Biplab Sikdar. Mitigating lot device based DDoS attacks using blockchain. In Proceedings of the 1st Workshop on Cryptocurrencies and Blockchains for Distributed Systems, pages 71–76, 2018.

[165] Zakaria Abou El Houda, Abdelhakim Senhaji Hafid, and Lyes Khoukhi. Cochain-SC: An intra- and inter-domain DDoS mitigation scheme based on blockchain using SDN and smart contract. IEEE Access, 7:98893–98907, 2019.

[166] Ahmed Kosba, Andrew Miller, Elaine Shi, Zikai Wen, and Charalampos Papamanthou. Hawk: The blockchain model of cryptography and privacy-preserving smart contracts. In 2016 IEEE Symposium on Security and Privacy (SP), pages 839–858. IEEE, 2016.

[167] Andrew Miller, Malte Möser, Kevin Lee, and Arvind Narayanan. An empirical analysis of linkability in the Monero blockchain. arXiv preprint arXiv:1704.04299, 2017.

[168] Tim Ruffing, Pedro Moreno-Sanchez, and Aniket Kate. Coinshuffle: Practical decentralized coin mixing for Bitcoin. In European Symposium on Research in Computer Security, pages 345–364. Springer, 2014.

[169] Ethan Heilman, Foteini Baldimtsi, and Sharon Goldberg. Blindly signed contracts: Anonymous on-blockchain and off-blockchain Bitcoin transactions. In International Conference on Financial Cryptography and Data Security, pages 43–60. Springer, 2016.

[170] Xuan Han, Yong Yuan, and Fei-Yue Wang. Security problems on blockchain: The state of the art and future trends. Acta Automatica Sinica, 1:206–225, 2019.

[171] Gareth Peters, Efstathios Panayi, and Ariane Chapelle. Trends in cryptocurrencies and blockchain technologies: A monetary theory and regulation perspective. Journal of Financial Perspectives, 3(3), 2015.

[172] Rosario Girasa. Regulation of cryptocurrencies and blockchain technologies: National and international perspectives. Springer, 2018.

[173] Kyle Croman, Christian Decker, Ittay Eyal, *et al.* On scaling decentralized blockchains. In International Conference on Financial Cryptography and Data Security, pages 106–125. Springer, 2016.

[174] Loi Luu, Viswesh Narayanan, Chaodong Zheng, Kunal Baweja, Seth Gilbert, and Prateek Saxena. A secure sharding protocol for open blockchains. In Proceedings of the 2016 ACM SIGSAC Conference on Computer and Communications Security, pages 17–30, 2016.

[175] George Danezis and Sarah Meiklejohn. Centrally banked cryptocurrencies. arXiv preprint arXiv:1505. 06895, 2015.

[176] Ittay Eyal, Adem Efe Gencer, Emin Gün Sirer, and Robbert Van Renesse. Bitcoin-NG: A scalable blockchain protocol. In 13th USENIX Symposium on Networked Systems Design and Implementation (NSDI 16), pages 45–59, 2016.

[177] Laszlo Gyongyosi and Sandor Imre. A survey on quantum computing technology. Computer Science Review, 31:51–71, 2019.

[178] Evgeniy O Kiktenko, Nikolay O Pozhar, Maxim N Anufriev, *et al.* Quantum-secured blockchain. Quantum Science and Technology, 3(3):035004, 2018.

[179] Kazuki Ikeda. Security and privacy of blockchain and quantum computation. In Advances in Computers, volume 111, pages 199–228. Elsevier, 2018.

*Chapter 7*

# EdgeChain to provide security in organization-based multi-agent systems

*Diego Valdeolmillos[1], Roberto Casado-Vara[1] and Juan M. Corchado[1]*

Organization-based multi-agent systems (MASs) are open distributed systems, to which other distributed intelligent systems can be connected. The scalability of virtual organizations (VOs) is an advantage in the development of smart distributed systems, but at the same time it can create security issues as the newly incorporated systems may be malicious. To ensure the security of the system, this work proposes the use of a main blockchain with additional blockchains created by new VOs, which support the main system. Another advantage of agent organizations is that they can be created according to the needs of the system and their function may change whenever required. This chapter introduces the concept of EdgeChain, and a case study is conducted with bank transactions to evaluate the proposal. On certain days of the month, banks have an increase in transactions due to the payment of bills, payroll income, etc. The proposed model is based on virtual agent organizations and will be used to create EdgeChains that optimize on-demand bank transactions. EdgeChains will be created with certain specifications as required (e.g. more processing capacity). In this work, we present a new method based on VOs of agents and blockchain technology, designed to improve the processes according to demand.

## 7.1 Introduction

One of the most discussed topics in the financial services industry today is blockchain technology. Currently, the financial services sector offers the strongest use cases for blockchain technology, although applications of it are growing rapidly in other industries such as transport and agriculture and professions such as accounting, audit and the law. Banks are beginning to use blockchain technology in their daily transactions with customers. But, on certain days of the month, banks have an

[1]IoT Digital Innovation Hub, Bisite Research Group, Edificio Multiusos I+D+i, University of Salamanca, Salamanca, Spain

increase in transactions due to the payment of bills, payroll income, etc. This leads to a collapse in the bank's activities, which can lead to considerable delays in transactions. It may even be possible to assume that a customer will not be able to pay his or her bills on time. Therefore, in this chapter, the authors present an adaptive solution to this problem. Since banks are using blockchain technology to secure their transactions, the problem of blockchain network saturation is a major concern for banks. The authors propose using side chains to optimize the bank's activities on demand. As side chains are blockchains, the security of transactions is not affected. However, sometimes it may be necessary to create a large number of side chains to optimize the proper processes, while other times, it will be necessary to delete these created side chains, so that they cannot collapse the system. Thus, the authors believe that a MAS, which is proven to be capable of coordinating and solving complex problems, must coordinate the creation and destruction of side chains.

In the model proposed in this chapter, we use a MAS and VOs to coordinate the creation and destruction of side chains. These side chains will optimize the daily processes of the bank based on blockchain. The MAS has access to the daily operations of the bank, and when the MAS detects that one of the operations is going to have a large peak of activity, it will create a custom side chain to solve the saturation problem that is being created. For example, suppose that at the beginning of the month the bank's customers have to pay their bills. The bank has a big peak of activity in the task: bill payment. In this case, the MAS creates a customized side chain so that you can optimize bill payment. In order to successfully addressing the realization of the global architecture, three main layers have been proposed around which to develop new methodologies and utilities that have a broad impact on the way a bank's services are understood. The three concentric layers of this architecture are as follows:

- In the external layer, there are components that are in charge of communicating and providing the necessary information for the system computation; these are the edge nodes formed by devices with autonomous processing capacity.
- The middle layer is a secure transaction layer based on blockchain. This layer is structured around the analysis of cutting-edge technologies such as side chain for the optimization of the bank's processes.
- Finally, the central layer is the environment for creating the custom side chain. In this environment, the processes optimized by the side chains will be executed. Once the processes are completed, the MAS coordinates the destruction of these side chains.

The main contribution can be summarized as follows:

1.  A system is proposed that can optimize the day-to-day operation of a bank's operations. This system will use custom side chains for each operation you want to optimize. In this way, the operation does not collapse the daily operation of the bank.

2. A MAS is used to coordinate the daily operation of the bank. If the MAS detects a peak of activity in any of the operations, it will create a custom side chain. In the same way, if the MAS detects that there is a load drop in that activity, it erases the side chain that was created to optimize that activity.

## 7.2  Virtual organization of agents

Agents are entities that interact with the environment and also with other agents, when several agents are able to collaborate to solve a problem; then we have a MAS. The software systems have to be open, allowing the incorporation of new components that work in conjunction with the existing ones.

Ideally, MASs have a decentralized design, where agents can be heterogeneous and can be located at different nodes providing the necessary infrastructure and protocols to enable communications and negotiation between them.

A VO provides a framework for the activity and interaction of agents through the definition of roles, behaviour expectations and authority relationships [1] and provides a separation between the form and the function [2,3].

An agent as an entity can operate within a partnership, in a closed or open environment by cooperating with other agents.

The VOs are formed by entities that may be constituted by members or agents, which have responsibilities, a set of sub-tasks to carry out, included within the objectives of the organization, being structured to follow communication patterns and trying to reach the global objectives of the organization in compliance with rules and restrictions [4]. According to the current situation, any implementation as a virtual open multi-agent organization requires a runtime environment with the following support [5]:

- In VOs, agents may need explicit representation of the organization. It is therefore necessary to create adaptation mechanisms to create organizational structures responsible for coordination, taking into account the heterogeneity of agents and services [6].
- Mechanisms must exist to allow efficient coordination among organizations, as well as control mechanisms that apply organizational constraints.
- The VO must use a standard language understood by the agents to obtain a description and information about the organization itself.
- The agent management system must know the agents that exist inside the existing organizations, in addition to providing the services offered and their description allowing interaction with external agents.
- The VO and their agents should be able to be monitored to support validation and verification processes, providing a mechanism for understanding the environment without requiring entities to notify changes.

The environment determines what is around the scheme [7]: resources, applications, objections, assumptions, restrictions and stakeholders (suppliers, customers and beneficiaries).

The functionality of an organization is determined by its overall objectives which describe the reason for its existence, the strategy to be followed, the functional requirements for the organization and how it interacts with other entities. The objectives can be classified as follows:

- Functional for each organizational unit or group
- Operational, describing the tasks to be completed by the agents

### 7.2.1    Service facilitator

A service facilitator provides the necessary support so that autonomous entities (agents and organizations) can register the description of services as entries in a directory, being its function to act as an identifier manager of entities with services and how to interact with them, helping to locate the necessary services to satisfy their objectives.

The interaction between two entities is modelled as a service, offering capabilities to achieve an objective, verifying conditions for the subsequent exchange of incoming and/or outgoing messages ('one or more'), which once executed has an impact on the environment. In addition, there may be additional parameters, such as security protocols, deadlines or quality of service.

### 7.2.2    Organization management system

Organization management system is the main provider of the services required for the functioning of an organization, responsible for the specification and management of structural components (roles, units and rules) and their execution components.

Structural components are classified into the following:

- Roles that represent the status of the organization include a number of functionalities, limitations, rules that have to be met and the consequences of their actions.
- A unit represents groups of agents and admits recursion, allowing a topological structure of the system.
- The rules indicate the prohibitions and permissions of the roles with respect to the services, their composition or the results.

Organizations are structured in groups of agents and are related by common objectives, having an internal structure that imposes limitations between agents.

## 7.3    Blockchain

The financial crisis of 2008 showed that the centralized financial system had great weaknesses. One year later, an algorithm, Bitcoin [8], based on cryptographic proof capable of changing the financial system and its transactions was born; the associated blockchain technology is capable of validating transactions or ledgers, so that there is no longer a central entity to act as a trusted intermediary, with all the participants being responsible for providing trust and security to transactions.

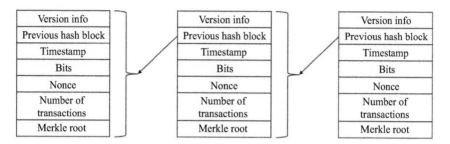

Figure 7.1   General Bitcoin structure

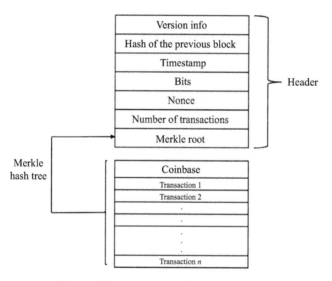

Figure 7.2   Structure of a Bitcoin block

Blockchain is a distributed ledger that solves the consensus problem of the Byzantine generals in which the participants have to agree on a fact before a set of possible malicious attackers who want to modify it [9]; for this, the participating nodes have a complete copy of the chain of blocks.

Figure 7.1 presents a blockchain structure of Bitcoin, where a block (see Figure 7.2) contains information about the transactions and the previous block and is sealed over time to prevent its modification [8]. The trust of the system will depend on the types of blockchain and the members of them; in public ones, the trust is based on their immutability and on consensus algorithms based on cryptographic proofs that the nodes have to solve or on the democratization of the distributed system.

To generate new blocks and verify that the transactions are correct, some nodes in the P2P network compete with each other [10], and they can use their computational capacity to be the first to solve a cryptographic test or to have more chances to generate new blocks by accumulating coins or tokens, or receiving more votes, the node that generates a new block broadcasts it to the rest of the nodes in the network or receives a reward.

Bitcoin [8] uses proof-of-work as a consensus algorithm for block validation. The mining nodes keep a local list of pending transactions, which are used to generate a candidate block to join the blockchain; each miner must solve a cryptographic proof, difficult to solve, but easy to be verified by the rest of the blockchain nodes [11]. It is a random process with low probability, and brute force is used to solve it, which requires CPU or GPU resources and leads to high power consumption [12].

Due to Moore's law [13], in which the computing capacity grows exponentially every 2 years, and the boom of GPU mining and later integrated circuits for specific mining applications, it is necessary to increase the difficulty of the working test, for example, in the Bitcoin protocol, which is directly proportional to the computing power that has the Bitcoin network, so it is defined in the algorithm that the difficulty to solve a block has to last about 10 min, as it is adjusted every 2,016 blocks (2 weeks) [14].

The first miner to solve the puzzle by confirming the transactions of his candidate block will get a reward, the new currencies generated along with the transaction fees. Once the working test is solved, the new block is diffused to the rest of the blockchain nodes, which will verify that the working test is correct, the puzzle has been solved with the estimated difficulty, and the coins defined in the algorithm have been generated exactly. If any of the conditions are not met, the rest of the nodes will reject the block.

With the high-energy consumption necessary to find a consensus in Bitcoin using proof-of-work, the proof-of-stakes arises, which requires showing an ownership of a certain number of assets, assuming that the participants will act in their own interest in fear of losing the money.

Any participant in blockchain can become a validator of the new blocks by sending a special transaction that locks its assets in a deposit, and all the validators of the blockchain will reach a consensus to agree and create new blocks.

There are two variants of this type of consensus [15], the first based on chain, the algorithm selects a validator pseudorandomly over a period of time and assigns it the right to create a new block to join the longest existing blockchain. The second variant is based on Byzantine fault tolerance, in which validators are randomly assigned the right to propose blocks, and the other validators send a vote to agree whether or not to join the chain.

## 7.3.1 Side chain

As an alternative to improve the scalability and even isolate information with different features and interests, multiple blockchains can be used.

A side chain is another blockchain that works together with the main one, allowing atomic transfers of assets between them (see Figure 7.3); for it, a special address is used where those assets are blocked in the main blockchain requesting the use of them in the side chain or creating new ones [16].

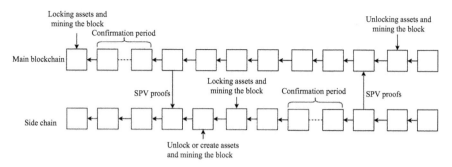

*Figure 7.3   Exchange of assets between blockchain and side chain*

The great advantage of using side chain over a blockchain is the scalability and flexibility, allowing this new blockchain to adapt to the needs [17], thus increasing its functionality such as managing insurance and registrations in the real world through smart contract, creating payment channels and managing different types of assets, whether real or virtual [18].

Another advantage is the high transaction capacity and fast processing of transactions, thus improving performance, allowing micropayments without having to wait for a new block to be created in the main blockchain.

Other possibilities in the use of side chains are the creation of experimental development environments allowing tests without altering the main chain and without changes in the code used by the participating nodes, facilitating the implementation of new functionalities and even testing the main chain.

## 7.4   Edge blockchain

In this chapter, we propose a hybrid model based on side chains and MAS. As there are several nodes for processing transactions and including them in blockchain, each node will contain an agent that will work in conjunction in an environment, and in the case of finding a large number of transactions greater than the blockchain is enabled to process, it will negotiate with the rest of the nodes to deploy one or several side chains if required.

This model is proposed with the main objective of optimizing the services of a business. In this chapter, we will use the services and operations of a bank as a case study. At certain times of the month, bank operations have high workload peaks. For these circumstances, the model we propose will create side chains on demand to optimize that process. The proposed system is described later.

The proposed architecture in Figure 7.4 has four VOs that monitor and control the performance of side chains to optimize the performance of bank services. It also has side chain environment support where custom side chains are created and destroyed to optimize bank services. The VOs have the following characteristics: (1) bank services monitoring agents: in this module, there are the agents that monitor the activities of the

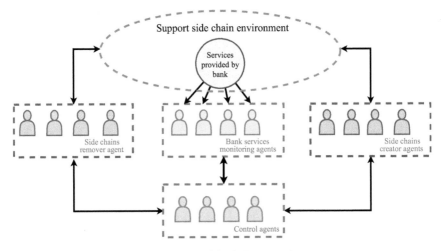

*Figure 7.4   Edge blockchain architecture*

services provided by bank. These agents detect the work peaks and send the order to create side chains to optimize those processes. In addition, the agents of this module provide the features that the custom side chains must have for each of the operations. Finally, if the agents detect that a process no longer has a high workload, they send the command to delete the side chain. (2) Control agents: the agents of this module control the operation of all the agents involved in the monitoring and controlling of the side chains. These agents receive the orders from the bank services monitoring agents and have to control the operation of the other agents. In case it is necessary to optimize a service, the control agents send the necessary information to create the customized side chain to the side chains creator agents. Otherwise, when the control agents receive information from the bank services monitoring agents, the process no longer needs to be optimized. The control agents send the information to the side chains to remove agents that will search for the target side chain and delete it so that it does not overload the banking services environment. (3) Side chains creator agents: these agents have to create side chains that will optimize the banking services. These agents receive the information from the control agents with the characteristics that these side chains must have in order to optimize the service for which they are being created. In this way, side chains are created in a personalized way and can offer a better return on banking services. For example, side chain could be created with more processing speed, with more storage capacity, etc. This way, the side chains creator agents only have to create the new custom side chains on demand from the control agents. (4) Side chains remover agents: these agents are ordered to delete the side chains when they are no longer needed. In this way, the support side chains are maintained with the necessary side chains and thus the service is not collapsed. This is important, as the processing capacity used in the side chain environment support is controlled and no extra resources are used.

Finally, the support side chain environment is the place where side chains are created and allocated resources so that they can manage the services that MAS

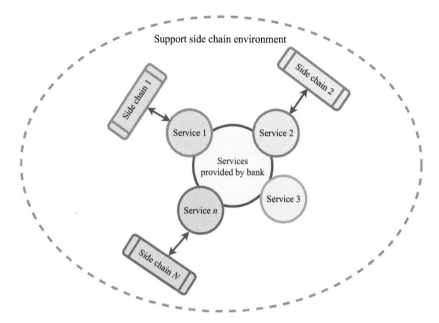

*Figure 7.5    Support side chain environment*

assigns to them. The side chains creator agents assign resources to the side chains when they are created on demand from the control agents. These resources are customized depending on the function the side chain has to do. They can range from less time between block mining (i.e. speed up the time to save the data in the side chain), greater storage capacity in the blocks, etc. Thus, the side chains that are created are customized to optimize the banking service on demand of the control agents.

In Figure 7.5, the support side chain environment is shown. The figure presents services provided by banks, and some of these services are being optimized by side chains, while other services (as they do not have a high workload) do not need to use side chains for efficient performance. Notice that it is not necessary for all services that are supported by side chains, as the use of these side chains is designed to assist services at specific times of high workloads. The rest of the time it would be a great use of resources to keep all these side chains alive. Therefore, the agent control system has to monitor and control the life cycle of the side chains on demand from the bank services monitoring agents.

## 7.5    Case study: bank services optimization

Suppose that for this case study, a bank on the first day of every month has to manage the payment of bills from its users to the government. This bank has blockchain technology implemented in its operations. Each block has a storage capacity of 1 MB, and the blockchain is mining the blocks every 10 min.

### 7.5.1    Scenario: speed-up services

In this scenario, it is assumed that in the morning of the last day allowed for the payment of invoices, all bank branches in the selected city will receive a large influx of users to pay their invoices. This is going to mean the collapse of the bank's infrastructure. In addition, it is important that the bank manages these bill payments as it is the last day, and your customers may not pay these bills and therefore have to face an administrative penalty. In this scenario, the important thing is the speed of the blockchain to mine the blocks, moving to the second place of the storage capacity of the blockchain.

In this way, the bank services monitoring agents detect this sudden high workload and send this information to the control agents. With the information that there is a great workload, the control agents send the information of how the transactions are being made (many transactions in a short time) to the side chains creator agents. These agents will then create a side chain with a reduced mining time (e.g. 5 min) and associate the side chain with the service that needs to be optimized. In this way, the blocks are mined every 5 min instead of every 10 min, and the information is immediately available in the blockchain so that the bank can begin the process with the local government to pay the bank's users' bills.

Figure 7.6 shows different mining times that can be chosen by the control agents to optimize the on-demand services of the bank services monitoring agents.

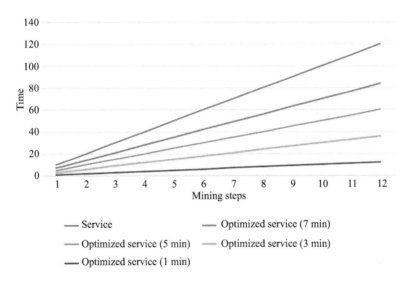

*Figure 7.6*    *Speed-up services via edge blockchain. The x-axis is the mining steps and the y-axis is the time in minutes. The optimized services 7 min (solid orange line), the optimized services 5 min (solid grey line), the optimized services 3 min (solid yellow line), the optimized services 1 min (solid dark blue line) and the regular bank services (solid blue line)*

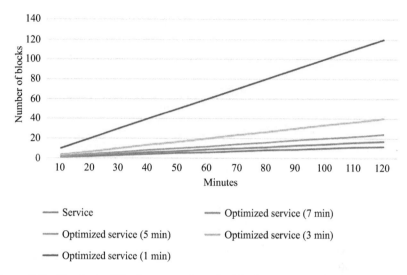

*Figure 7.7  Number of blocks inserted in the blockchain via edge blockchain. The y-axis is the number of blocks inserted in the blockchain and the x-axis is the time in minutes. The optimized services 7 min (solid orange line), the optimized services 5 min (solid grey line), the optimized services 3 min (solid yellow line), the optimized services 1 min (solid dark blue line) and the regular bank services (solid blue line)*

In this case, you can see how the proposed new model accelerates information processing (i.e. reduces the time between block mining). In this way, the bank has the transactions that its users make faster and can begin to manage the payment to the credit institutions of its customers.

Figure 7.7 shows the number of blocks that have been inserted in the block-chain in the different cases, in which the agents build different side chains to optimize the services. The control agents create custom side chains for each case depending on the workload.

## 7.6  Conclusion

In this chapter, we propose a new MAS to optimize the services of a bank. The MAS monitors and controls the bank's services by optimizing its services with the creation of customized side chains on demand from the control agents. These side chains optimize the services they are associated with and when there is no longer a high workload, the control agents remove them. In future work, a demand forecasting system will be implemented to improve the performance of the edge blockchain model proposed in this chapter.

## Acknowledgements

This work was supported by the Spanish Ministry of Economy and Competitiveness (MINECO) and FEDER funds. The project name is 'SURF, Intelligent System for integrated and sustainable management of urban fleets' with an ID TIN2015-65515-C4-3-R.

## References

[1]    Gasser L and Ishida T. A Dynamic Organizational Architecture for Adaptive Problem Solving, vol. 91. AAAI; 1991. p. 185–190.

[2]    Zato C, Villarrubia G, Sánchez A, *et al.* PANGEA – Platform for Automatic Construction of Organizations of Intelligent Agents. In: Distributed Computing and Artificial Intelligence. Springer; 2012. p. 229–239.

[3]    Borrajo ML and Corchado JM. An Agent-Based Virtual Organization for Risk Control in Large Enterprises. In: Uden L, Hadzima B, and Ting IH, editors. Knowledge Management in Organizations. Cham: Springer International Publishing; 2018. p. 277–287.

[4]    Pattison HE, Corkill DD, and Lesser VR. Instantiating Descriptions of Organizational Structures. In: Distributed Artificial Intelligence, vol. I. Elsevier; 1987. p. 59–96.

[5]    Rodriguez S, Julián V, Bajo J, *et al.* Agent-based virtual organization architecture. Engineering Applications of Artificial Intelligence. 2011;24(5):895–910.

[6]    Rodríguez S, Palomino CG, Chamoso P, *et al.* How to Create an Adaptive Learning Environment by Means of Virtual Organizations. In: Uden L, Liberona D, and Ristvej J, editors. Learning Technology for Education Challenges. Cham: Springer International Publishing; 2018. p. 199–212.

[7]    Rodrguez S. Modelo Adaptativo para organizaciones virtuales de agentes. PhD on Computers and Automation, Universidad de Salamanca; 2010.

[8]    Nakamoto S. Bitcoin: A Peer-To-Peer Electronic Cash System; 2008.

[9]    Lamport L, Shostak R, and Pease M. The Byzantine generals problem. ACM Transactions on Programming Languages and Systems (TOPLAS). 1982;4 (3):382–401.

[10]   Casado-Vara R, Prieto J, and Corchado JM. How Blockchain Could Improve Fraud Detection in Power Distribution Grid. In: Graña M, López-Guede JM, Etxaniz O, *et al.*, editors. International Joint Conference SOCO'18-CISIS'18-ICEUTE'18. Cham: Springer International Publishing; 2019. p. 67–76.

[11]   Casado-Vara R, González-Briones A, Prieto J, *et al.* Smart Contract for Monitoring and Control of Logistics Activities: Pharmaceutical Utilities Case Study. In: Graña M, López-Guede JM, Etxaniz O, *et al.*, editors. International Joint Conference SOCO'18-CISIS'18-ICEUTE'18. Cham: Springer International Publishing; 2019. p. 509–517.

[12] Bitcoin Wiki. Proof of Work; 2010 [updated 2016 Jan 20; cited 2018 Aug 12]. Available from: https://en.bitcoin.it/wiki/Proof_of_work.

[13] Mack CA. Fifty years of Moore's law. IEEE Transactions on Semiconductor Manufacturing. 2011;24(2):202–207.

[14] Bitcoin Wiki. Block; 2010 [updated 2018 Mar 16; cited 2018 Aug 12]. Available from: https://en.bitcoin.it/wiki/Block.

[15] Buterin V. Proof of Stake FAQs; 2016. ethereum/wiki Wiki.

[16] Back A, Corallo M, Dashjr L, *et al.* Enabling Blockchain Innovations With Pegged Sidechains; 2014. Available from: http://www.opensciencereview.com/papers/123/enablingblockchain-innovations-with-pegged-sidechains.

[17] Casado-Vara R and Corchado JM. Blockchain for Democratic Voting: How Blockchain Could Cast of Voter Fraud; 2018.

[18] Blockstream. Technologies; 2018 [cited 2018 Aug 17]. Available from: https://blockstream.com/technology/.

*Chapter 8*

# Blockchain-driven privacy-preserving machine learning

*Youyang Qu[1], Longxiang Gao[1] and Yong Xiang[1]*

Blockchain has been and will continue experiencing fast booming with the rising of digital currencies like Bitcoin [1]. As an underlying technology, blockchain provides various advantageous features, such as decentralization, data authentication, trust management, etc. [2]. New paradigms and associated mechanisms are emerging, which brings further vigour to this underexplored field [3].

Despite the benefits provided by blockchain, several key issues are hindering it from further popularization, among which privacy issue is the primary one [4]. Individuals have increasing concerns regarding their sensitive information such as identity [5] and location [5,6] while most blockchain systems store the data in a transparent way, which is a double-edged sword [5]. In addition, the privacy of identity cannot be fully guaranteed by anonymity [6].

Nowadays, machine learning is the dominant technology in a data processing scenario. In addition to improving the learning performances, more and more machine learning techniques focus on privacy-preserving machine learning to make them more feasible and practical. Two leading models are federated learning (FL) and generative adversarial networks [7,8]. In the following sections, the benefits of integrating these two models into blockchain will be discussed in detail from the aspect of privacy protection upgradation.

## 8.1 GAN-DP and blockchain

An increasing volume of data is shared for research or commercial purposes in this big data era. The sensitive information in the shared data attracts continuous attacks from adversaries, which raises great privacy concerns. However, most existing privacy-preserving solutions either sacrifice privacy performances for data utility or overprotect the data resulting in low quality of service [9]. In addition, the poisoning attack emerges and becomes one of the dominant attacks in data sharing field [10]. In the following subsections, a novel model entitled generative

[1]Deakin Blockchain Innovation Lab (DBIL), School of Information Technology, Deakin University, Geelong, Australia

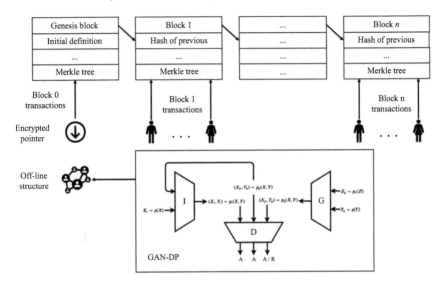

*Figure 8.1    A generalized blockchain-enabled GAN-DP paradigm*

adversarial nets (GAN)-enabled differential privacy (DP) (GAN-DP) is introduced, which provides whole life cycle privacy protection to both data sharing and data propagation. DP provides strict privacy protection in data publishing scenarios [11,12]. First, there is a GAN-enhanced DP to achieve privacy-preserving data sharing. By adding one more perceptron in GAN, a specifically designed game model is designed to derive the Nash equilibrium, namely the optimized trade-off. In addition, an underlying blockchain system is devised to provide decentralized privacy protection when the shared data propagates across networks. The structure is shown in Figure 8.1.

## 8.1.1    Wasserstein generative adversarial net

Wasserstein GAN (WGAN) is an extended version of classic GAN [13]. Instead of simply using Kullback–Leibler divergence (KL-divergence), WGAN adopts an optimal distribution measurement to improve the stability of the learning results [14,15].

To achieve the best performance of KL-divergence, pre-modelling the density is a necessity. Nevertheless, it is not practical in real-world scenarios to predefine the density, especially dealing with low-dimension distributions. This means the two distributions are highly possible not to share an intersection. In this case, KL-divergence cannot function properly. That is also the rationale behind the adoption of the Wasserstein-1 distance.

## 8.1.2    Generator and discriminator

Randomized mechanisms of DP generate random noise, which follows a specific distribution complying with DP requirements. In this model, the generator of

WGAN generates the noise, which is then injected into the raw data. The discriminator tries to distinguish the raw data with the newly generated synthetic data. The dynamic game between these two perceptrons brings mutually improvement of themselves.

The distribution of generator is trained over raw data and a prior of injected noise. Then, the mapping to data space is the generated data. It represents the function consisting of multilayer perceptron with the distribution. The discriminator outputs a probability of if the data is the original one or a synthetic one. It is trained to maximize the distinguish probability while the generator is trained to minimize the probability at the same time. The confrontation between these two perceptrons can be modelled as a two-player zero sum game (min–max problem).

### 8.1.3 GAN-DP with a DP identifier

The classic WGAN generates a randomized synthetic data to mimic the raw data with its best efforts. To further extend the synthetic data complying with DP requirements, it is necessary to add one more perceptron, which is named DP identifier. In this triple WGAN model, two games are played at the same time to derive the Nash equilibrium, which is also known as the optimal solution.

GAN-DP compels differentially private features to be mapped to an associated identifier as an input of the generator. One more parameter is initialized to decide to what extent the generator depends on the input features. Instead of simply focusing on training the distribution, GAN-DP enables the training of differentially private synthetic data built upon the input features.

In this paradigm, two games are played at the same time. Apart from the confrontation between the discriminator and the generator, the other confrontation is modelled between the discriminator and the DP identifier. To achieve a balance between the identifier and the discriminator, NE is defined to denote the Nash equilibrium of both games. If there exists a sufficiently trained generator, which is able to acquire the true distribution, then a cluster of randomized noise data has an identical loss in comparison with the raw data.

As the mainstream privacy-preserving mechanism, DP has strong theoretical foundations with strict proof. This enables a significant improvement of the privacy-preserving model design and deployment. Similar to the most popular randomized mechanisms of DP (Laplace mechanism, Gaussian mechanism, etc.), GAN-DP complies with DP. The model is formulated as follows:

$$\Pr[\mathrm{GAN}(D) \in \Omega] = \exp(\epsilon) \times \Pr\left[\mathrm{GAN}\left(D'\right) \in \Omega\right] \tag{8.1}$$

In the previous equation, $\Omega$ denotes the probability space, which is taken over the randomness of DP determined by GAN-DP. As usual, $\epsilon$ is used as the index to measure the privacy protection level. Theoretically, the value of $\epsilon$ is inside $[0, +\infty]$ while $[0, +3]$ is the practical range for most scenarios. The level of privacy protection improves with the decrease of $\epsilon$'s value, and vice versa.

To compare the data utility, the root-mean-square error (RMSE) is adopted due to its universality and generality. Privacy protection and data utility have a negative correlation, which requires a careful design to achieve an optimized trade-off. RMSE is usually calculated with $\mathrm{RMSE} = \sqrt{\left(\sum |\hat{y} - y|^2\right)}$.

## 8.1.4    Decentralized privacy

In this section, a specially designed blockchain is deployed to resist the data modification, namely the poisoning attack. Blockchain could be regarded as an increasing list of records, which is represented by blocks. In each of the blocks, there are timestamps, a cryptographic hash of the previous block, and the transaction data. In this case, the transaction data is the differentially private data that has been published for research or commercial purposes.

For better clarity, we leverage standard cryptographic building blocks in the proposed model. We use $(G_en, E_en, D_en)$ to denote generator, encryption, and decryption, respectively. A digital signature scheme is represented by $(G_s, S_s, V_s)$, which corresponds to the generator, signature, and verification, respectively. In total, there are three key components in this system: users, services, and nodes. As users are normally anonymous while accessing the services, this system can maintain service profiles and verify identities. The blockchain allows two types of access: $A_{access}$ and $A_{data}$. $A_{access}$ denotes access control management, and $A_{access}$ is for data storage and retrieval. The distributed hash table (DHT) is under the maintenance of nodes. This network of nodes is possibly disconnected from the network to achieve approved operations. The differentially private data is randomly distributed across the network and backup for convenient access. To establish blocks in the blockchain systems, we orderly define composite identity, memory of blockchain, policy, and auxiliary functions, which are necessary protocols to achieve decentralized privacy protection.

In the traditional public blockchain, the blockchain node identity is simply anonymous without further privacy protection. By using a public key, every user can generate an unlimited number of pseudo-identities if necessary. To avoid this issue in the proposed model, we devise a novel composite identity. This composite identity can be regarded as the personalization of identities. When it is shared with different parties, the owner has full access to it while the other parties have limited access according to specific requirements or attributes.

The blockchain is like an account book containing a list of data transactions with timestamps. The first two outputs in a transaction encode the 256-bit memory address pointer along with some auxiliary metadata. The other outputs are leveraged to build the serialized document. This setting allows insertion, deletion, and update operation. We define the policy $P_u$ as a series of permissions that a user can gain from a specific service. For instance, if the user needs to read, update, and delete a dataset, then $P_u$={read, update, and delete}. Any data could be safely stored as service will not break the protocols and label the data incorrectly. In addition, the service can easily observe the anomaly of users as all changes are visible.

As $A_{access}$ is used to conduct access control management, it can change the permissions of users granted by the service. This is accomplished by sending the policy. If the service wants to revoke all the access permissions, the policy will be empty. If it is the first time to send an $A_{access}$ with a new composite identity, the $A_{access}$ will be recorded as a user signing up to a service.

Analogously, $A_{data}$ will manage the data manipulation operations such as read, write, update, or delete. With the assistance of the *Verify()* function, only the service or the permitted users can access the differentially private data. In this protocol, we access the DHT like a normal hash table. In real-world scenarios, these instructions bring about some off-chain network messages which are being sent to the DHT.

## 8.1.5    Further discussion

In this model, only the services have full control over the sensitive data. An adversary can hardly pretend to be a user or corrupt the whole network as the blockchain is fully decentralized. In addition, digital signatures are required for transactions. Therefore, we hold that adversaries are not able to fabricate digital signatures or take control of the majority of the network (over 50%). Furthermore, an adversary cannot tamper the data because it is stored off-chain rather on the public ledger. There are only pointers' information encrypted with the hash function inside the public ledger.

Even if we consider the case that an adversary controls one or some of the nodes in the DHT network, the adversary cannot learn anything about the differentially private data. The rationale behind this is that the data is encrypted with keys that no other nodes have access to. The worst case is that the adversary gains the authority and compromises a few local copies of the data; the system can still recover it as there are abundant replications distributed across the whole network.

Last but not the least, the composite identity mechanism ensures that there is only a tiny probability that the differentially private data is poisoned because this requires the acquisition of both signing key and encryption–decryption key. If the adversaries happen to steal one of the keys, the sensitive data is still safe. In practice, we can also personalize the composite identity so that the comptonization is restricted for the adversaries. A good instance would be different keys for a certain volume of records.

## 8.2    Federated learning and blockchain

The fast proliferation of Internet of Things devices accelerates the development of FL, which addresses several issues, for example privacy protection, latency, and network traffic congestion [16–19]. However, the performances of FL cannot be fully guaranteed because of some existing flaws [20]. Most of the current researches fail to consider an optimized trade-off as well as poisoning attack resistance [21]. Motivated by this, a novel paradigm entitled blockchain-enabled FL is devised to mitigate the flaws [22,23]. Beyond the FL, this new paradigm allows a selected aggregator in each iteration to replace a fixed central server while the model parameters are verified by the users. In addition, blockchain-enabled FL can further provide incentive mechanism to motivate the participation rate while providing poisoning attack proof features with a proof-of-work (PoW) consensus algorithm or its variants [24].

## 8.2.1   Existing issues

FL is primarily designed to provide several advanced features, such as reducing communication overhead, privacy-preserving machine learning, addressing statistical datasets, and non-homogeneity [25]. Most of current researches focus more on local model updating strategy or global model aggregation model [26]. However, the discussion on its real-world deployment is barely discussed from aspects of robustness or other flaws. To popularize the FL paradigm, three key challenges are identified in existing FL systems as follows.

- *Centralized aggregation*: In classic FL systems, a trusted central server is required to conduct aggregation. This potentially results in man-in-the-middle attacks, single-point failure, and so on. Moreover, if there are a huge number of devices joining in the learning network, the limited communication resources (bandwidth) may fail to handle all the requests in real time.
- *Lack of incentive mechanism*: The high-performance devices or devices with high-quality data are not incentivized to participate in the learning process. This leads to delayed convergence with unsatisfying learning results.
- *Low robustness*: Poisoning attacks, as primary attacks in data manipulation domain, are continuously launched in this scenario, which is hard to defend in this distributed FL scenario. It may potentially mislead the learning direction, which causes severe learning deviation.

## 8.2.2   How blockchain benefits FL

The advantageous features of blockchain make joint efforts to address the three identified drawbacks of existing FL systems.

The first drawback of existing FL systems is centralized processing. It leads to possible single-point failure, man-in-the-middle attack, etc. In addition, the volume of involved edge devices is so massive that the network overload becomes increasingly serious due to limited bandwidth and scalability. One of the greatest advantages of blockchain is decentralization (fully or partially) depending on if it is a public, private, or consortium blockchain. The decentralization of FL can avoid potential single-point failure, man-in-the-middle attack, etc. by enabling a device to be the aggregator (central server) in a specific round. The temporary aggregator is selected by a specific consensus algorithm such as PoW or proof-of-stake (PoS). The predefined rules make sure that the selected device has enough computation and storage resources as well as high-quality data. Therefore, PoW is a better choice compared with other consensus algorithms in this particular scenario. In addition, blockchain has the potential to resist Byzantine issues that are primary in existing FL systems. The advanced consensus algorithms and high scalability make sure that eligible updates of the end devices are recorded and used to generate the global updates. In each of the round, only a part of the end devices is chosen based on their performances. The rest of end devices can compete for the next round by upgrading their equipment or improving the data quality. Either way contributes to the fast convergence of current FL system with the impact of Byzantine issues.

The second drawback is the lack of incentive mechanism. An emerging trend is that edge devices with high performances are not sufficiently incentivized to participant and contribute in an FL system. The reason is intuitive that high-performance devices may only gain marginal benefits by working with low-performance devices. But this situation could be significantly solved by the incentive mechanism provided by the blockchain systems. As an underlying structure, blockchain is able to provide rewards to users or miners in it. The rewards could be token, which is the most popular form, data that is an asset in FL scenarios, or even more. High availability also motivates the devices to participate. As it is not compulsory for the end devices to be online on the time, the blockchain provides sufficient flexibility to them such that the high-performance devices still have priority to be chosen after returning from other tasks.

The third drawback is low robustness. Leading attacks such as poisoning attacks and Byzantine attacks mislead the training process and significantly impact the accuracy of the output, disable the convergence of the maintained model, or even lead to denial of services. Security is an advanced built-in feature of blockchain, especially its high resistance to several leading attacks, such as background-knowledge attacks, collusion attacks, distributed denial-of-service (DDoS) attacks, poisoning attacks, Byzantine attacks, and inference attacks. This is guaranteed by the authentication, traceability, persistence, anonymity, and high scalability of the blockchain. As the data cannot be falsified ensured by authentication and traceability, poisoning attacks and inference are difficult to launch. High scalability and verification mechanisms help eliminate DDoS attacks and Byzantine attacks. Moreover, anonymity can defeat background knowledge attacks and collusion attacks to some extent.

## 8.2.3   Blockchain-enabled federated learning

It is intuitive why blockchain and FL can mutually promote each other. FL is distributed and blockchain is decentralized. In addition, both of them focus on privacy and security performances. As mentioned earlier, three key limitations prevent FL from further application and development while blockchain happens to be capable of tackling these issues. The novel paradigm, namely blockchain-enabled FL, is experiencing fast booming. This paradigm has new policies, mechanisms, and architectures to correspondingly solve the aforementioned three challenges.

The blockchain-enabled FL allows cross verification of model updates, especially local model updates, to guarantee the authenticity of the uploaded data. The protocols of the specially designed decentralized ledger have been discussed briefly in Section 8.1. In this paradigm, the block is still consisted of a body and a header.

The header section remains the same while the body section in this case stores the model updates rather than transaction data in the classic scenario. As PoW is deployed as the consensus algorithm, the nonce value is still required in the header along with hash values, generation rate, etc. Other consensus algorithms also work well in this scenario, such as PoS and proof of federated learning (PoFL). For the purpose of storing the model updates of all participating devices, the size of block depends on the header size, model updates size, and the number of devices. Therefore, it is important to limit the number of devices participating in while maintaining the quality of participated devices.

Each of the miners maintains a candidate block which contains the local model update parameters from an associated machine or other miners. The block generation process only stops when the block size or the waiting time is reached. To improve the efficiency, a threshold of waiting time is predefined to filter the resource-constrained devices.

The PoW consensus should be reached in the following phase. The miners keep trying nonce values until a certain condition is met, for example, smaller than a target value. A miner is regarded as the winner for being the first to find the nonce value, and the block is regarded as the candidate block. The generation rate of block can be controlled by changing the difficulty index of the nonce-finding problem.

Moving on, the candidate block is broadcast to the rest of the miners so that all locally maintained ledgers are synchronized. To release the synchronization, any miner who receives the candidate block drops current processing operation by force. However, there is a potential for forking when some miners accidently append wrong blocks to their local ledger. Forking has significant negative impact on the convergence of global model and could be regarded as a type of poisoning attack in this scenario. It may further mislead the subsequent block generation or learning processes.

The forking frequency increases with the increase of blockchain generation rate and broadcasting delay. The operation of forking mitigation results in additional delay. In addition to the previous operations, an incentive mechanism is designed to motivate the devices. The incentive mechanism contains two components: data rewards and mining rewards. First, the component 'data rewards' is given to the miners determined by the data size and data quality contributed to the training task. The second component is positively correlated with the hash rate of the devices associated with the miner. The two rewards will incentivize the devices with high performance, high-quality data, or both.

One potential issue of the incentive mechanism is that malicious adversaries may falsify the actual data size. To prevent this from happening, the local updates will be cross-validated before storing in the blocks. The simplified verification mechanism is to compare the computing time consumption with its sample size. A proper range is defined to distinguish the eligible data from the falsified ones, which follows the proof of elapsed time under Intel's SGX technology.

A generalized blockchain-based FL instance is shown in Figure 8.2. Different from the traditional FL systems, this structure allows fully decentralized FL such

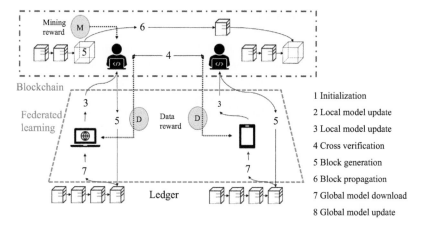

*Figure 8.2 A generalized blockchain-based FL paradigm*

that each device can lead the aggregation process in a specific round of learning. In addition, all the local updates are verified before being processed. In this way, the performance of FL can be further improved.

- Phase 1: The initialization parameters are randomly selected from a predefined value pool of the local and global weights.
- Phase 2: The participants calculate the local model parameters with locally stored data.
- Phase 3: The miners are randomly selected by and associated with devices. After the processing part, the end devices upload the local model parameters with corresponding computing time to associated miners.
- Phase 4: The miners broadcast the local model updates obtained from their associated end devices. At the same time, the miners verify the received local model updates from their associated devices or the other miners in the order of their arrival. The truthfulness of the local model updates is validated if the local computation time is proportional to the data sample size. The verified local model updates are recorded in the miner's candidate block, until the block size or the maximum waiting time is reached.
- Phase 5: Each miner involves in the PoW consensus until finding the nonce or receiving a candidate block from another miner.
- Phase 6: The miner first finding the nonce broadcasts the candidate block to other miners. To prevent forking, an acknowledgement (ACK) signal is transmitted when no miner detects a forking event. All the miners wait until receiving ACK signals of the others. If not, it rolls back and iterates from phase 2 again.
- Phase 7: In this phase, the aggregator computes the global model parameters by aggregating local model parameters saved in the candidate block.
- Phase 8: The end devices obtain global model parameters in the candidate block from its associated miner and continue to the next iteration.

## 8.3    Conclusion remarks

With the integration of blockchain with current leading privacy-preserving machine learning mechanism, the performances of FL and GAN-DP can be further improved, especially the robustness against poisoning attacks. In addition, the deployment of blockchain as the underlying architecture enables decentralization while providing incentive mechanisms. Furthermore, the efficiency can be guaranteed, and the storage resources can be saved with an off-chain structure. Future directions in this field may include the optimization using game theory and reversible blockchain using chameleon hash.

## References

[1]    Eyal, Ittay, Adem Efe Gencer, Emin Gün Sirer, and Robbert Van Renesse. "Bitcoin-NG: A scalable blockchain protocol." In *13th USENIX Symposium on Networked Systems Design and Implementation (NSDI)* 16, pp. 45–59. 2016.

[2]    Crosby, Michael, Pradan Pattanayak, Sanjeev Verma, and Vignesh Kalyanaraman. "Blockchain technology: Beyond Bitcoin." *Applied Innovation* 2, no. 6–10 (2016): 71.

[3]    Dai, Hong-Ning, Zibin Zheng, and Yan Zhang. "Blockchain for Internet of Things: A survey." *IEEE Internet of Things Journal* 6, no. 5 (2019): 8076–8094.

[4]    Zyskind, Guy and Oz Nathan. "Decentralizing privacy: Using blockchain to protect personal data." In *2015 IEEE Security and Privacy Workshops*, pp. 180–184. IEEE, 2015.

[5]    Qu, Youyang, Shui Yu, Longxiang Gao, Wanlei Zhou, and Sancheng Peng. "A hybrid privacy protection scheme in cyber-physical social networks." *IEEE Transactions on Computational Social Systems* 5, no. 3 (2018): 773–784.

[6]    Youyang, Qu, Zhang Jingwen, Li Ruidong, Zhang Xiaoning, Zhai Xuemeng, and Yu Shui. "Generative adversarial networks enhanced location privacy in 5G networks." In *SCIENCE CHINA Information Sciences*, 2020.

[7]    Zhang, Rui, Rui Xue, and Ling Liu. "Security and privacy on blockchain." *ACM Computing Surveys (CSUR)* 52, no. 3 (2019): 1–34.

[8]    Lecuyer, Mathias, Vaggelis Atlidakis, Roxana Geambasu, Daniel Hsu, and Suman Jana. "Certified robustness to adversarial examples with differential privacy." In *2019 IEEE Symposium on Security and Privacy (SP)*, pp. 656–672. IEEE, 2019.

[9]    Konečný, Jakub, H. Brendan McMahan, Felix X. Yu, Peter Richtárik, Ananda Theertha Suresh, and Dave Bacon. "Federated learning: Strategies for improving communication efficiency." *arXiv preprint arXiv*:1610.05492 (2016).

[10]   Goodfellow, Ian, Jean Pouget-Abadie, Mehdi Mirza, *et al.* "Generative adversarial nets." In *Advances in Neural Information Processing Systems*, pp. 2672–2680. 2014.

[11]   Qu, Youyang, Shui Yu, Wanlei Zhou, Sancheng Peng, Guojun Wang, and Ke Xiao. "Privacy of things: Emerging challenges and opportunities in wireless Internet of Things." *IEEE Wireless Communications* 25, no. 6 (2018): 91–97.

[12]   Jagielski, Matthew, Alina Oprea, Battista Biggio, Chang Liu, Cristina Nita-Rotaru, and Bo Li. "Manipulating machine learning: Poisoning attacks and countermeasures for regression learning." In *2018 IEEE Symposium on Security and Privacy (SP)*, pp. 19–35. IEEE, 2018.

[13]   Dwork, Cynthia. "Differential privacy: A survey of results." In *International Conference on Theory and Applications of Models of Computation*, pp. 1–19. Springer, Berlin, Heidelberg, 2008.

[14]   Dwork, Cynthia and Aaron Roth. "The algorithmic foundations of differential privacy." *Foundations and Trends in Theoretical Computer Science* 9, no. 3–4 (2014): 211–407.

[15]   Gulrajani, Ishaan, Faruk Ahmed, Martin Arjovsky, Vincent Dumoulin, and Aaron C. Courville. "Improved training of Wasserstein GANs." In *Advances in Neural Information Processing Systems*, pp. 5767–5777, 2017.

[16]   Pérez-Cruz, Fernando. "Kullback–Leibler divergence estimation of continuous distributions." In *2008 IEEE International Symposium on Information Theory*, pp. 1666–1670. IEEE, 2008.

[17]   Karacan, Levent, Aykut Erdem, and Erkut Erdem. "Image matting with KL-divergence based sparse sampling." In *Proceedings of the IEEE International Conference on Computer Vision*, pp. 424–432. 2015.

[18]   Weng, Jiasi, Jian Weng, Jilian Zhang, Ming Li, Yue Zhang, and Weiqi Luo. "DeepChain: Auditable and privacy-preserving deep learning with blockchain-based incentive." *IEEE Transactions on Dependable and Secure Computing* (2019).

[19]   Shen, Meng, Xiangyun Tang, Liehuang Zhu, Xiaojiang Du, and Mohsen Guizani. "Privacy-preserving support vector machine training over blockchain-based encrypted IoT data in smart cities." *IEEE Internet of Things Journal* 6, no. 5 (2019): 7702–7712.

[20]   Gu, Bruce Shujun, Longxiang Gao, Xiaodong Wang, Youyang Qu, Jiong Jin, and Shui Yu. "Privacy on the edge: Customizable privacy-preserving context sharing in hierarchical edge computing." *IEEE Transactions on Network Science and Engineering* (2019).

[21]   Qu, Youyang, Shui Yu, Wanlei Zhou, and Yonghong Tian. "GAN-driven personalized spatial-temporal private data sharing in cyber-physical social systems." *IEEE Transactions on Network Science and Engineering* (2020).

[22]   Nguyen, Thuy TT and Grenville Armitage. "A survey of techniques for internet traffic classification using machine learning." *IEEE Communications Surveys & Tutorials* 10, no. 4 (2008): 56–76.

[23]   Bagdasaryan, Eugene, Andreas Veit, Yiqing Hua, Deborah Estrin, and Vitaly Shmatikov. "How to backdoor federated learning." In *International Conference on Artificial Intelligence and Statistics*, pp. 2938–2948. 2020.

[24]   Kim, Hyesung, Jihong Park, Mehdi Bennis, and Seong-Lyun Kim. "Blockchained on-device federated learning." *IEEE Communications Letters* 24, no. 6 (2019): 1279–1283.

[25]   Qu, Youyang, Longxiang Gao, Tom H. Luan, *et al.* "Decentralized privacy using blockchain-enabled federated learning in fog computing." *IEEE Internet of Things Journal* (2020).

[26]   Lu, Yunlong, Xiaohong Huang, Yueyue Dai, Sabita Maharjan, and Yan Zhang. "Blockchain and federated learning for privacy-preserved data sharing in industrial IoT." *IEEE Transactions on Industrial Informatics* 16, no. 6 (2019): 4177–4186.

*Chapter 9*

# Performance evaluation of differential privacy mechanisms in blockchain-based smart metering

*Muneeb Ul Hassan[1], Mubashir Husain Rehmani[2] and Jinjun Chen[1]*

The concept of differential privacy emerged as a strong notion to protect database privacy in an untrusted environment. Later on, researchers proposed several variants of differential privacy in order to preserve privacy in certain other scenarios, such as real-time cyber-physical systems. Since then, differential privacy has rigorously been applied to certain other domains, which has the need of privacy preservation. One such domain is decentralized blockchain-based smart metering, in which smart meters act as blockchain nodes sent their real-time data to grid utility databases for real-time reporting. This data is further used to carry out statistical tasks, such as load forecasting and demand response calculation. However, in case any intruder gets access to this data, it can leak privacy of smart meter users. In this context, differential privacy can be used to protect privacy of this data. In this chapter, we carry out comparison of four variants of differential privacy (Laplace, Gaussian, Uniform, and Geometric) in blockchain-based smart metering scenario. We test these variants on smart metering data and carry out their performance evaluation by varying different parameters. Experimental outcomes show at low privacy budget ($\varepsilon$) and at low reading sensitivity value ($\delta$), these privacy-preserving mechanisms provide high privacy by adding a large amount of noise. However, among these four privacy-preserving parameters, the Geometric parameters are more suitable for protecting high peak values, whereas the Laplace mechanism is more suitable for protecting low peak values at ($\varepsilon=0.01$).

## 9.1 Introduction

Vide an insightful privacy definition which can be used to perturb raw data records by adding an adequate amount of noise drawn from respective distribution [1].

[1]Faculty of Science, Engineering and Technology, Swinburne University of Technology, Hawthorn, Australia
[2]Department of Computer Science, Cork Institute of Technology, Cork, Ireland

Informally, the notion of differential privacy guarantees that addition, modification, deletion, or variation of a single record within a data set will not have any significant effect on the output query results [2]. Initially, differential privacy notion was proposed to protect privacy of statistical databases; however, later experiments showed that it can effectively be applied to other real-life scenarios as well, such as real-time reporting and machine learning. Afterwards, researches are being carried out to apply differential privacy in major domains that require privacy protection, including smart grid, cloud computing, industries, and other similar cyber-physical systems [3,4].

Conventional smart grid networks did not use any specific security of privacy strategies and just used to rely on security and privacy provided by communication protocols; however, with the passage of time, it was found out that data of smart grid can be used to carry out major privacy and security breaches [5,6]. Since then, plenty of researches are being carried out to enhance smart grid technology by improving its security and privacy. For example, the uses of homomorphic cryptosystem and trusted remote entity have been proposed by researchers to overcome these eavesdropping issues [7,8]. One such way that effectively enhances the security and trust of smart grid network is the integration of blockchain in smart grid domain [9,10]. Blockchain network ensures that all the communication and storage being carried out via blockchain network is secure and adversaries will not be able eavesdrop into the privacy of blockchain users. This is done by using advanced secure technologies, such as cryptographic hashing, tamper-proof record storing, and strong distributed consensus [11].

Despite this secure nature, it has been highlighted that blockchain-based smart grid network is still vulnerable to certain privacy threats because of its decentralized nature [12]. For example, an adversary can compromise a specific smart meter after analysing the available data on decentralized blockchain ledger. Similarly, the stored data on-grid utility database can be analysed to infer into private information of consumer usage patterns. In order to mitigate such issue, certain researches have been carried out that are involved in the integration of certain privacy preservation approaches in blockchain scenarios, such as zero-knowledge proofs and anonymization [12,13]. These works are viable to a certain extent, but they cannot directly be applied to real-time smart metering networks because the majority of them either work over stored data or only work over private data provenance. One such mechanism that can effectively protect privacy of smart grid users in a decentralized blockchain scenario is differential privacy [14]. Differential privacy can protect this information because of its dynamic nature, especially pointwise perturbation mechanism of differential privacy can protect real-time data without running extensive computationally complex algorithms [15].

In this chapter, we work over the integration of differential privacy protection mechanism in decentralized blockchain-based smart metering scenario. To examine it further, we evaluate four variants of differential privacy (Laplace, Gaussian, Uniform, and Geometric) on real-time smart metering data. In order to check their efficiency and effectiveness, we use mean absolute error (MAE) as evaluation parameter. Experimental results demonstrate that each mechanism has its own pros and cons depending upon the privacy budget, sensitivity value, and the data applied over it. For instance, all mechanisms provide high level of privacy when the privacy parameters ($\varepsilon$ and $\delta$) have low values (e.g. $\varepsilon = 0.01$ and $\delta = 0.01$). However, when these values increase, the privacy of the metre reading value reduces gradually and at $\varepsilon = 1$ and $\delta = 1$, the privacy reaches to a minimum level, although data utility is maximum at this stage. Similarly, among these four privacy notions, the Geometric and Laplace perform better at lower privacy budgets by adding a sharp amount of noise. Specifically, when there are high peak values in metering data (e.g. high usage), then the Geometric mechanism preserves privacy in the most proficient manner, and when the smart metering data has low peaks (e.g. less occupancy/usage), the Laplace mechanism outperforms other mechanisms.

### 9.1.1 Key contributions

The key contributions of this chapter are as follows:

- We integrate differential privacy in blockchain-based smart metering scenario.
- We carry out in-depth performance evaluation of differential privacy mechanisms in decentralized blockchain scenarios at different privacy budget ($\varepsilon$) values.
- From experimental results, we analyse the effectiveness of variants of differential privacy along with the reported MAE rate. We conclude that the Geometric noise addition mechanism outperforms other mechanisms in high peak values; however, for low peak values, the Laplace mechanism outperforms other mechanisms.

### 9.1.2 Related work

Since the advent of modern smart grid, researches are being carried out to make it autonomous, secure, and user-friendly. In order to do so, plenty of works targeted privacy preservation or integration of blockchain in smart grid scenario. For example, the first work that highlighted the use of differential privacy in smart metering scenario was carried out by [16]. The presented work in the article used gamma-distribution-based differential privacy protection to preserve smart metering data and also used encryption-based cryptography to enhance security during transmission. Authors also worked over the phenomenon of multi-slot privacy in which they effectively use the dynamic nature of differential privacy to protect this real-time data. Another similar work was carried out by [17]. The authors for the first time discussed the terminology of pointwise differential privacy protection for real-time smart data. Authors evaluated the use of the Laplace noise and worked over signal smoothing to reduce the risk for privacy leakage in the case of any adversarial attack. Similarly, a work that targets the integration of differential privacy in renewable energy resources has been discussed by authors in [18]. The work discussed the protection of energy being generated from their resources by adding the dynamic Laplace noise depicted in Table 9.1. The work also introduced the concept of peak protection in renewable energy resources reporting to ensure that privacy of smart meter users remains unviolated despite any adversarial attack on grid database.

*Table 9.1 Comparative view of works carried out in smart metering from the perspective of differential privacy (DP) and blockchain*

| Name of strategy | Ref. no. | Major contribution | Parameters enhanced | Considered DP | Considered blockchain | Simulator used |
|---|---|---|---|---|---|---|
| DREAM | [16] | Introduced the concept of DP in smart metering | • Appliance privacy protection | ✓ | ✗ | Electricity trace simulator |
| DP for real smart metering data | [17] | Efficient DP mechanism to balance utility privacy | • Aggregated data protection via smoothing | ✓ | ✗ | N/A |
| DP for RER-based smart metering | [18] | Protected usage and generation privacy of RER-based smart homes | • Peak-load protection<br>• RER generation protection | ✓ | ✗ | Python |
| GridMonitoring | [19] | Monitoring smart grid values via blockchain | • Enhanced provenance and transparency<br>• Enhanced trust | ✗ | ✓ | N/A |
| Lightweight blockchain-based AMI | [20] | AMI network is protected and secured via blockchain | Enhanced received signal strength | ✗ | ✓ | MATLAB® |
| Blockchain-based secure smart grid | [21] | Key-less secure signature scheme for decentralized smart grid | Developed automated access-control manager | ✗ | ✓ | GoEth |
| DP variants in decentralized smart metering | This work | Performance evaluation of DP variants in blockchain-based smart metering | • Comparison of DP variants at different privacy parameters<br>• MAE comparison | ✓ | ✓ | Python |

Similarly, from the perspective of blockchain-based smart grid, a work that discusses the integration of blockchain in grid monitoring scenario was carried out by [19]. Authors in this work used blockchain to ensure transparency and to enhance trust in the network by providing information publicly available to users via decentralized distributed ledger. Furthermore, authors provide a platform to users via which they can monitor their usage without depending upon any third party. One more work that discusses the integration of blockchain in advanced metering infrastructure (AMI) to enhance its security and transparency is carried out by [20]. The major motto of the work is to protect smart meters from various cyberattacks specifically targeting data tampering, and man-in-the-middle attacks. Authors did this by proposing a lightweight blockchain-based solution for decentralized AMI network. Similarly, authors in [21] proposed a keyless blockchain-based signature scheme for smart grid network via which they enhance security of traditional smart grid.

Authors also discussed the aspect of trusted third-party breaches and failures and suggested that the use of blockchain-based secure platform is a viable solution to overcome these issues. Furthermore, authors claimed that the proposed strategy turns blockchain network into an automated manager to carry out access-control operation on smart grid. Another significant contribution carried out by authors is the enhancement of storage cost over the decentralized blockchain network, which is one of the major issues blockchain is facing nowadays.

After analysing all these works, we can say that to the best of our knowledge, no work that discusses the integration of differential privacy in blockchain-based smart metering network has been carried out in the literature. In this chapter, we not only discuss the integration of differential privacy in decentralized smart metering but also evaluate four major mechanisms of differential privacy in this network to check their effectiveness.

The remainder of this chapter is organized as follows: Section 9.2 discusses preliminaries of our work, including differential privacy, blockchain, and real-time smart metering. Section 9.3 provides a detailed discussion about system model, differentially private reporting algorithms, along with design goals and adversary model. Furthermore, Section 9.4 provides performance evaluation of variants of differential privacy in blockchain-based smart metering scenario. Finally, Section 9.5 presents conclusion and future directions.

## 9.2   Preliminaries of our work

In this section, we discuss the preliminaries involved in our evaluation, ranging from differential privacy mechanisms to blockchain and smart grid.

### 9.2.1   Differential privacy mechanisms

Differential privacy can be termed a notion to protect privacy in an adversarial environment [22]. Formally, differential privacy can be defined as a randomize response that ensures that query evaluation of two neighbouring data sets varying by just one element will produce similar output results that will introduce randomness in the results [23]. The equation is as follows:

$$P_r\left[F_{(db_1)} \in R\right] \leq \exp(\varepsilon) \times P_r\left[F_{(db_2)} \in R\right] + \delta \tag{9.1}$$

In above-mentioned equation, $\varepsilon$ is the privacy budget that controls the amount of noise being added, $\delta$ is the sensitivity value that is usually determined on the basis of data set, and $R$ is the query output range for query function $F$. Similarly, the formula of sensitivity calculation for two adjacent data sets $(db_1)$ and $(db_2)$ can be defined as follows [3,24]:

$$\Delta F_s = \max_{db_1,db_2} \|F(db_1) - F(db_2)\| \tag{9.2}$$

Apart from the formal definitions, researchers worked over proposing various variants of differential privacy to support different privacy needs. These variants can be classified into distribution protection mechanisms and data perturbation mechanisms. In this section, we discuss four major data perturbation mechanisms named Laplace, Gaussian, Uniform, and Geometric mechanisms of differential privacy. A detailed discussion about notions and variants of differential privacy can be found in [25].

### 9.2.1.1    Laplace mechanism

Laplace mechanism is considered to be the pioneering mechanism which was used by C. Dwork at the time of proposal of this notion of differential privacy perturbation. Afterwards, this notion has been used widely to protect privacy at different application scenarios [26]. Taking insights from sensitivity equation (9.2), we can demonstrate the Laplace noise by considering $S_c = \Delta F_s/\varepsilon$ as follows [27]:

$$Lap(S_c) = \exp\frac{|x - \mu|}{S_c} \tag{9.3}$$

Since the standard deviation of the given function is calculated using an exponential distribution which is symmetric with respect to parameter $\sqrt{2}b$, then the probability density function (pdf) of traditional Laplace noise at mean value $(\mu)$ is defined as follows:

$$pdf(x) = \frac{\exp\frac{|x-\mu|}{b}}{2b} \tag{9.4}$$

The noise is then computed via pdf and then added to the query/pointwise reading result in order to protect privacy.

### 9.2.1.2    Gaussian mechanism

Gaussian mechanism also known as bell curve distribution has also been widely used as a traditional notion of differential privacy. The bell shape of the Gaussian probability distribution provided fine-grained noise that can be added to query evaluation in order to integrate randomness in the output results [3]. The standard formula for the Gaussian mechanism is as follows:

$$pdf(x) = \frac{1}{\sqrt{2\pi b^2}} e^{-\frac{(x-\mu)^2}{2b^2}} \tag{9.5}$$

In the above-mentioned equation, $b$ or the standard deviation is used as a scale to choose the appropriate amount of noise, which is controlled by the privacy budget value $\varepsilon$.

### 9.2.1.3   Uniform mechanism

The concept of using the Uniform distribution as a notion of differential privacy has been proposed by plenty of researchers because of its strong privacy along with low computational complexity. For example, Kalantari *et al.* analysed privacy-utility trade-offs via uniform differential privacy and integrated this concept with hamming distortion in [28]. Similarly, Geng and Viswanath discussed it under the umbrella of optimal noise-adding mechanisms in their article [29].

Formally, the Uniform distribution noise is a discrete noise addition mechanism which works over sensitivity value $(0, \delta)$, instead of just being dependent upon $\varepsilon$. Noise in this mechanism is computed using the Uniform probability distribution as follows:

$$pdf(x) = \begin{cases} \frac{\delta}{\Delta} & \text{if } \forall \ \frac{\delta}{2\Delta} \le k \le \frac{\delta}{2\Delta} - 2 \\ 0 & \text{Otherwise} \end{cases} \tag{9.6}$$

### 9.2.1.4   Geometric mechanism

Geometric differential privacy mechanism was also proposed by researchers under the umbrella of oblivious notions of differential privacy. This notion is pretty diverse and plenty of sub-mechanisms/variants have been proposed that constitute of various ways to draw differentially private noise from the Geometric distribution. For example, authors in [30] discussed it as a discrete version of traditional Laplace mechanism and state that it generates optimal utility value for all types of Bayesian information counting queries. Similarly, Ghosh *et al.* proposed the notion of the Geometric and truncated Geometric differential privacy noise addition to perturb query results [31]. Formally, the Geometric mechanism of differential privacy can be defined as follows:

$$pdf(X - x) = \frac{1 - \alpha}{1 + \alpha} \alpha^{|x|}, \forall x \in \mathbb{Z} \tag{9.7}$$

## 9.2.2   *Real-time smart metering and privacy issues*

Smart meter is a device that serves as a bridge between grid utility and smart homes as it links grid utility with smart home via strong communication medium. Together, all smart meters within a range constitute a network named advanced metering infrastructure (AMI) [32]. In order to carry out various statistical processes such as net metering, demand response calculation, load forecasting, and load scheduling, these smart meters send their actual real-time fine-grained metre reading to grid utility. These values are then stored in their databases which can be accessed for query evaluation after getting approval from authorities. It is definitely a good model to carry out statistical analysis; however, one of the major drawbacks of this model is that it leaks privacy of smart meter users [33]. For example, the reported fine-grained data from smart meters can further be fed to various non-intrusive load monitoring algorithms that can even provide information about usage of any specific appliance at a specific time by visualizing load curves [34].

This information can also lead to carry out various criminal/burglar activities at the time of unoccupancy of house. Therefore, it is important to protect this information via some privacy-preserving mechanisms.

### 9.2.3    Blockchain network

Blockchain came into limelight after successful functioning of decentralized crypto-currency called Bitcoin by Satoshi Nakamoto [35]. Formally, blockchain is categorized into two major types from perspective of permission named permissioned blockchain and permissionless blockchain. Furthermore, from the perspective of availability and controlling authorities, it is categorized into three major types called public, private, and consortium. A detailed discussion about these types and their pros and cons is available in [11]. In this chapter, we use public permissionless blockchain in which every smart meter node can join after filling a detailed form to ensure its legitimacy. Since it is a public blockchain, every blockchain node can participate in the consensus part and can earn extra reward by mining the block. Since smart meters have less computational power, they can only take part in consensus if the provided consensus mechanism is not dependent upon computation power. In order to fulfil this require-ment, we use proof-of-stake (PoS) instead of traditional computationally expensive proof-of-work consensus mechanism. In our PoS mechanism, every smart meter acting as a blockchain node can take part in the mining process after depositing a specific number of tokens in the network. This eradicates the need for having high mining power. Similarly, in this way, smart meters can also incentivize themselves a bit more if they are interested to contribute to the network. The incentive can be in the form of mining reward that a mining node will get if it gets selected as a winning miner.

## 9.3    Functioning and system model

In this section, we present system model, design goals, adversary model, and algorithmic foundation of integration of differential privacy in blockchain-based smart metering scenario.

### 9.3.1    System model

Our application scenario consists of two important entities, i.e. smart homes (deployed with smart meters) and grid utility. Our scenario works over the model of a public blockchain, which means that all the participating nodes can take part in

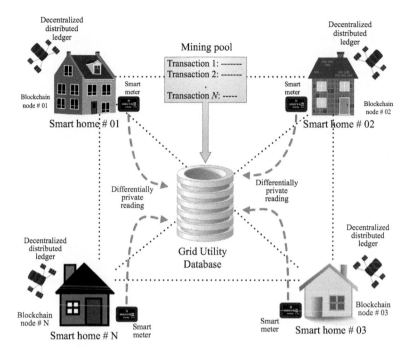

*Figure 9.1    An illustrative demonstrating of our proposed system model for*
*differentially private blockchain-based smart metering*

the mining process. The most important entity in these nodes is smart home that
contains smart meters which are reporting their real-time energy to grid utilities.
Each smart meter is a blockchain node which can take part in the mining process
after adding some tokens as a stake in the network. A detailed system model is
given in Figure 9.1.

From Figure 9.1, it can be seen that each smart home is connected to every
other smart homes via decentralized blockchain network; similarly, these smart
homes are also connected to the grid utility via the same network. However, an
additional feature which distinguishes this specific connection from other is that
these smart homes regularly report their real-time values to grid database utility
after the specified time interval (e.g. 10 min). Grid utility collects these values from
all smart homes and puts these values along with some other transaction values in a
public mining pool. The values at mining pool can be viewed publicly by all mining
nodes in order to facilitate them in mining the block.

On the other hand, all miner nodes (smart homes) participate in the mining
process by putting some stakes in the network. In PoS mining, a miner is chosen in
accordance with the sake it has invested in the network. For example, a node which
has invested 50% stakes as compared to all other nodes has approximately 50%
chances of being selected as the miner. Contrary to this, if the proportion of stakes
of some node is even less than 1%, then its chances of winning the mining election

are fairly low. Coming back to the mining process, these miner nodes submit their stakes and wait for the mining process to select miners on the basis of stake probability. The mechanism selects a miner node according to the mentioned process, and the selected miner then moves further towards the next process.

Once the miner gets finalized, it selects all the available transactions from the mining pool, computes their hash, and forms a block-like structure. After the formation of block, this miner disseminates the block to all other blockchain nodes via broadcasting mechanism in order to get verification votes. All receiving nodes compute hash at their end and verify the content of block. Once the verification stage gets completed, the block is then added to the blockchain network and is disseminated as a mined block. In this way, each blockchain node will have a copy of updated decentralized ledger that can be backtracked at any time to ensure transparency and enhance trust in the network.

This complete process involves dealing with real-time reported energy values, therefore protecting the privacy of these readings before disseminating in mining pool, or for verification is pretty important in order to overcome any catastrophe. Therefore, in our proposed model, we protect these readings via adding differentially private noise before transmitting them to grid utility for evaluation. A graphical representation of noise addition via smart homes is provided in Figure 9.1.

## 9.3.2    Design goals

Previous works in privacy protection in real-time smart metering do not incorporate the advantageous nature of blockchain and differential privacy at the same time. Some previous works evaluated the use of differential privacy in smart metering, while some works discussed the integration of blockchain with smart metering. However, no combined literature that integrates all three technologies of smart metering, blockchain, and differential privacy has been discussed by researchers. The design goals of our proposed scenario are as follows:

- Integrating public blockchain network in a smart metering network using the concept of decentralized distributed ledger.
- Enhancing security of smart metering network by providing a model to carry out distributed consensus in the network.
- Maintaining trust and transparency in the network by updating the decentralized ledger after the addition of every new block.
- Ensuring privacy of real-time smart metering data in runtime by adding dynamic differentially private noise in the data.
- Enhancing MAE of the network by carrying out comparison between differential privacy mechanisms.

## 9.3.3    Adversary model

Adversaries in our scenario can be any type of intruders that could be interested to get information regarding real-time usage of smart meter electricity. This could be done in order to get more precise information regarding availability of occupants of smart homes so that they can carry out malicious/burglar activities. Moreover, some adversaries do also require fine-grained data to find out types of appliances being used in smart homes, or to know about appliances which are expected to get damaged in the near future, etc. This is done by certain marketing companies and they use this fine-grained data to carry out targeted advertising [18]. Similarly, man-in-the-middle attack can also be carried out via which the information being transmitted from smart meter to grid utility can be misused after analysing [36]. Furthermore, data linking attack can also be carried out over the stored data in smart grid database, in which the data can be exploited and linked with certain other databases to get to know more information regarding any specific person [37].

In order to overcome these attacks and adversarial behaviours, we first integrate blockchain that ensures security and trust in the network via its cryptographic mechanisms. Furthermore, we work over the integration of variants of differential privacy that enhances privacy of the complete network.

---

**Algorithm 1** Algorithm for selection of differential privacy noise variants

---

1: main()
2:
3:
4:         $^{\varepsilon\delta}MSwitch_{Func}{\leftarrow}R{\leftarrow}{\leftarrow}$Epsilon Value from UserReading
5:         Sensitivity Value from User←Actual Meter Reading from Smart
6:         Meter($_{Func}$Select Noise Function from User) do
7:             Case *Lap*:
8:                 Call *LaplaceNoiseMechanism(ε,$M_R$)*
9:                 Break;
10:            Case *Gaus*:
11:                Call *GaussianNoiseMechanism(ε,$M_R$)*
12:                Break;
13:            Case *Unif*:
14:                Call *UniformNoiseMechanism(ε,δ,$M_R$)*
15:                Break;
16:            Case *Geo*:
17:                Call *GeoNoiseMechanism(ε,$M_R$)*
18:                Break;
19: End Switch
20: end main()

---

## 9.3.4    Algorithmic foundation

Traditional smart meters directly transmit their real-time energy values to smart grid utility without using any type of privacy protection mechanism. However, our proposed model uses the advantages of dynamic differential privacy protection to protect this sensitive data. In order to demonstrate the complete technical functioning of our model, we develop a detailed algorithm containing conditions for all differential privacy variants. The detailed pseudocode is given in Algorithm 2. Similarly, the algorithm for the selection of specific noise addition mechanism is given in Algorithm 1. The algorithm is divided into five major parts, in which the first four parts contain an addition of nose via any variant of differential privacy, while the fifth part comprises computation of absolute error value. First, the input values such as instantaneous metre reading ($M_R$), number of smart meters for that specific slot ($N$), privacy budget ($\varepsilon$), sensitivity ($\delta$), database sensitivity ($\Delta$), and noise function ($F$) are fed to the algorithm to initiate the process. Afterwards, the condition for specific variant of differential privacy is checked. In case the user calls for the Laplace noise addition mechanism, then the first part (1) Laplace privacy mechanism is called for execution. In this part, first of all, the Laplace privacy budget ($\varepsilon_L$) is taken from user. After that, database sensitivity value is computed using (9.2). After computation and collection of these values, the noise is generated using the Laplace noise probability distribution function given in (9.4). The values of $\varepsilon_L$ and $M_R$ are fed to the function to determine the noise scale. After successful computation of noise, this value is added to the metre reading value via $P_V = M_R + noise$. Next, the absolute error function is called to get the value of error, which is then stored to calculate the MAE. After this process, the protected value $P_V$ is transmitted to grid utility to carry out statistical processes.

---

**Algorithm 2** Differential privacy variants in decentralized smart metering

---

Input: $N$, $F$, $M_R$, $\varepsilon$, put$\delta$
Output: $P_V$, $A_E$
(1) Laplace Differential Privacy Mechanism

---

1: if LaplaceNoiseMechanism() then
2:    for (each **j** in **N**) do
3:        $\varepsilon_L \leftarrow$ Laplace Privacy Budget
4:        Database Sensitivity
5:        Generate Laplace Noise via
           $noise = Lap(F,\varepsilon_L,M_R)\,j$
6:            Calculate $P_V = M_R + noise\,j\,j$
           $j$
7:        Call *AEfunction*($P_V,M_R$)
8:        return $P_V, A_E\,j\,j$
9:        end for $j\,j$
10: end if
(2) Gaussian Differential Privacy Mechanism

---

11: if GaussianNoiseMechanism() then
12:　for (each **j** in **N**) do
13:　　　$\varepsilon_G$ 3Gaussian Privacy Budget
14:　　　4 ←Database Sensitivity
15:　　　Generate Gaussian Noise via
　　　　　$noise = Gaussian(F,\varepsilon_G,M_R)$
　　　　　　　$j$
16:　　　　　　Calculate $P_V = M_R + noise\ j\ j$
　　　　　　　$j$
17:　　　Call *AEfunction*$(P_V,M_R)$
18:　　　return $P_V,A_E\ j\ j$
19:　end for $j\ j$
20: end if
(3) Uniform Differential Privacy Mechanism

---

21: if UniformNoiseMechanism() then
22:　for (each **j** in **N**) do
23:　　　$\varepsilon_U$ ←3
24:　　　4 4Database Sensitivity
25:　　　$5_U$ ←5:5 4 Reading Sensitivity Value
26:　　　Generate Uniform Noise via
　　　　　$noise = Uniform(F,\varepsilon_U,\delta_U,M_R)$
　　　　　　　$j$
27:　　　　　　Calculate $P_V = M_R + noise\ j\ j$
　　　　　　　$j$
28:　　　Call *AEfunction*$(P_V,M_R)$
29:　　　return $P_V,A_E\ j\ j$
30:　end for $j\ j$
31: end if
(4) Geometric Differential Privacy Mechanism

---

32: if GeometricNoiseMechanism() then
33:　for (each **j** in **N**) do
34:　　　$\varepsilon_{geo}$ ←eooch ach Privacy Budget
35:　　　metDatabase Sensitivity
36:　　　$P_R$ ←6: metDatabase Sensitivityi$\varepsilon_{geo}$ and $\delta$
37:　　　Generate Geometric Noise via
　　　　　$noise = Geometric(F,P_R)$
　　　　　　　$j$
38:　　　　　　Calculate $P_V = M_R + noise\ j\ j$
　　　　　　　$j$
39:　　　Call *AEfunction*$(P_V,M_R)$
40:　　　return $P_V,A_E\ j\ j$
41:　end for $j\ j$
42: end if

(5) Absolute Error Calculation Function

---

43: Function $AE_{function()}$ do
44:        $M_R \leftarrow$ Meter Reading
45:        $P_V \leftarrow$ Protected Value
        $j$
46:        $A_E = |P_V - M_R|^j \leftarrow$ For Positive Value
47: End Function$^j$

---

Similarly, if the function of the Gaussian noise addition is selected, then the second part (2) of the algorithm is used to compute the Gaussian noise via normal distribution. In this part, the value of the Gaussian privacy budget $\varepsilon_G$ is used to compute noise in a way that it protected the final reading. The noise in this mechanism is computed using the pdf in (9.5). Moving further to the third part, the functionality of the Uniform noise addition mechanism is different from the Gaussian or Laplace mechanism, because in this mechanism, the privacy budget $\varepsilon_U$ is set to be zero, and it does not play any critical role in computation of noisy value. Contrary to this, the Uniform sensitivity value of metre reading ($\delta_U$) is used to generate random noise value via the Uniform distribution, the equation of which has been provided in (9.6). The remainder of the steps for the Uniform noise addition mechanism are the same as that of previous two parts.

Similarly, if the user calls for addition of noise via the Geometric differential privacy mechanism, then the fourth (4) part of the algorithm executes. In this part, the probability of success is computed for the Geometric mechanism by taking into account the value of $\varepsilon$ geo and $\Delta$. After successful computation of success probability (PR), this value is fed to the Geometric noise additions function, which then computes the Geometric noise according to the provided density function. Finally, the fifth part of algorithm calculates absolute error value by subtracting metre reading from the protected noise value. This function of error calculation is called for every individual perturbed value in order to keep a record error in the transmitted readings. Afterwards, these values are accumulated to calculate MAE, which is demonstrated in the next section.

## 9.4    Performance evaluation

In our blockchain-based smart metering scenario, protected real-time data is transmitted from smart meters instead of original real-time data. In order to protect privacy leakage from original data, we use four different variants of differential privacy discussed in the previous section. The noise produced by each variant has different effects on privacy level depending upon the privacy budget ($\varepsilon$) and reading sensitivity ($\delta$). In this section, we first discuss simulation environment and afterwards provide a detailed performance evaluation on the basis of real-time reporting and MAE.

## 9.4.1 Simulation parameters

In order to implement differential privacy variants in our blockchain-based smart metering scenario, we first of all used grid energy data from [38] and modified it accordingly to carry out and experiment for 24-h usage. We carried out performance evaluation of differential privacy variants on above-mentioned real-time smart metering data in which readings are being sent to grid utility after every 10 min. So, for daily usage profile, we carried out an evaluation on 144 data samples collectively for each smart home. To carry out experimental evaluation, we use NumPy v1.14 and pandas v1.0.3 libraries in Python 3.0. In order to implement differential privacy variants, we use respective distribution of NumPy v1.1.4 library and modify the input parameters according to the requirement of each variant given in Section 9.2.1. Furthermore, we generate the graphs at different $\varepsilon$ values for three mechanisms, and for the Uniform differential privacy, we carry out evaluation at different $\delta$ values. In this way, six graphs showing the original and protected readings for each noise-adding variant are generated. Similarly, to take an account of noise and to compare efficiency of each noise addition variant, we pick the best performing $\varepsilon$ value for each variant and compare their MAE values.

## 9.4.2 Private real-time data reporting

Reporting real-time smart meter data can leak users' privacy and can cause serious threats to occupants of smart homes; therefore, we use differential privacy to protect this information. In order to do so, we implement four variants and analysed their output in the form of given graphs. In Figure 9.2, the graph for $\varepsilon = 0.01$ can be seen for the Laplace, Gaussian, and Geometric noise addition mechanisms. Similarly, the graph for $\delta = 0.01$ for the Uniform noise addition mechanism is also plotted in the same figure for comparison purpose. The graph depicts values transmitted in 24 h by using different variants as compared to the actual metre reading. Starting from the first quarter of the graph, ranging from 12.00 a.m. to 6.00 a.m., the usage is pretty low because of night, and only a few peaks can be seen. However, the behaviour of all noise addition mechanisms can be observed clearly. If one closely analyses the graph, it can easily be seen that the Laplace mechanism provided a more diversified amount of noise as compared to any other noise addition mechanisms in this quarter. After Laplace, some variations for the Gaussian mechanism can also be seen for some low peaks such as 4.30 a.m., and after that, at some high peak values the Geometric mechanism shows variance as compared to the other three.

Moving further to second quarter of the graph from 6.00 a.m. to 12.00 p.m., similar trend can be observed that whenever there is a low value of original metre reading, then the Laplace noise addition mechanism provides maximum variance followed by the Gaussian mechanism, which usually provides negative variance as compared to the trend. And whenever there is high peak value, such as 10.30 a.m. when the original usage is around 1,200 Wh, then the Geometric mechanism adds a considerable amount of noise to protect privacy of real-time smart metering data. After that, in the third quarter (which is the most highly utilized quarter), the Geometric noise addition mechanism outperforms other variants due to its usual

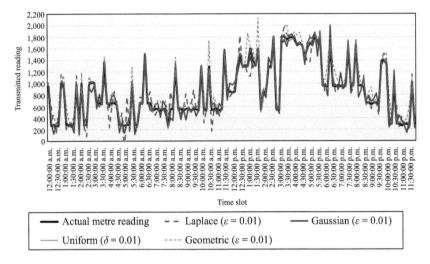

*Figure 9.2    Performance evaluation of differential privacy mechanisms at various privacy parameters*

reputation of protecting reading at higher peaks. As can be seen that around 1.00 p. m., the value of load usage is pretty high around 1,600 Wh, at this stage, the Geometric mechanism provides the highest peak value by providing maximum fluctuation. This trend continues and the Geometric mechanism keeps on dominating other mechanisms because the usage values are pretty high. After Geometric, the second most dominant noise addition mechanism here is the Laplace mechanism which protects the peak values by either adding negative noise or by adding minor positive noise depending upon the noise calculation.

However, the result of the remaining two mechanisms can partially be seen at this stage. In the fourth quarter of the graph from 6.00 p.m. to 12.00 a.m., the load utilization again reduces, and in this quarter, the trend similar to quarter number 2 can be seen, in which the Laplace mechanism dominates due to its low peak values and after that the Gaussian mechanism came into light due to its negative random noise is adding to those low peak values. The variation due to the Geometric mechanism can also be seen in some places, although it is not as dominant as that of the Laplace and Gaussian mechanisms. Throughout the graph, the Uniform noise addition mechanism does not come into limelight because its noise span is pretty low as compared to other three mechanisms. If one zooms the graph, the variations can surely be seen due to the Uniform mechanism, although it gets suppressed due to high variations by other three variants.

A similar trend can be seen for remaining output graphs as well. For example, in Figure 9.3, the graph for $\varepsilon = 0.01$ for the Laplace, Gaussian, and Geometric mechanisms can be seen, whereas $\delta = 0.01$ for the Uniform noise addition mechanism. As the value of privacy budget is increased, which means less privacy protection and more utility, it can be observed that at majority of places, very minimal

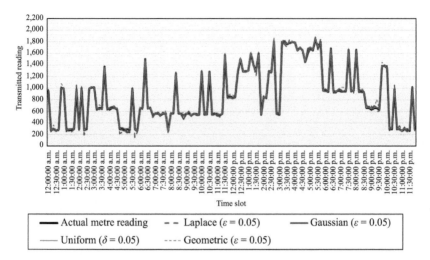

*Figure 9.3    Performance evaluation of differential privacy mechanisms at various privacy parameters*

noise has been added to protect users' privacy. Some low peaks can be seen for the Laplace mechanism in the graph at the time of less usage; however, the majority of added noise values remain unnoticed because of not producing much variation. Moving further to other graphs presented in Figures 9.4–9.6, the variation reduces, and very minimal noise addition can be observed. Finally, in Figure 9.7, when the value of $\varepsilon$ and $\delta$ is increased to '1', the added noise almost reaches 0, which means minimum privacy and maximum utility. At this privacy budget, mostly the actual metre is reported as it is to the grid utility with very minimal and negligible variation because of noise. Therefore, it can be concluded that lower values of privacy parameters provide high privacy protection, and increasing these values results in gradual decrease in privacy protection to a limit that utility becomes maximum with very minimal privacy protection as demonstrated in the graphical figures.

Keeping in view all the graphs and discussion, it can be said that in high peak values, the Geometric mechanism provides healthy variation to protect privacy, and for low peak values, Laplace mechanism followed by the Gaussian mechanism provides considerable variation to protect users' privacy.

### 9.4.3    Mean absolute error

In order to provide statistical analysis regarding differential privacy noise addition variants, we use the parameter of MAE. Formally, MAE can be termed the difference between the noisy value and original reading. The equation for MAE is given as follows:

$$MAE = \sum_{n=1}^{N_R} |P_V - M_R| \tag{9.8}$$

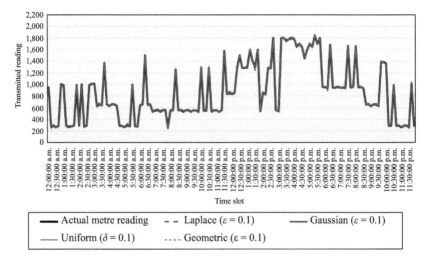

*Figure 9.4    Performance evaluation of differential privacy mechanisms at various privacy parameters*

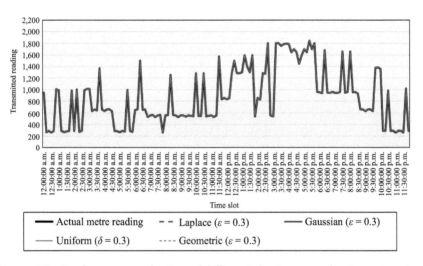

*Figure 9.5    Performance evaluation of differential privacy mechanisms at various privacy parameters*

In the previous equation, $N_R$ is the total number of noisy readings sent in the day. In our mechanism, we accumulate energy usage of every 10 min and then transmit the values to grid utility after the addition of noise. Therefore, $N_R = 144$, although this value can vary according to the data set. Similarly, $P_v$ is the protected noisy value, and $M_R$ is the actual metre reading which demonstrates the actual usage

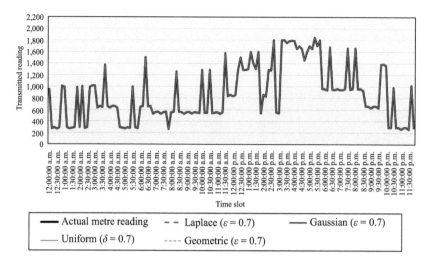

*Figure 9.6   Performance evaluation of differential privacy mechanisms at various privacy parameters*

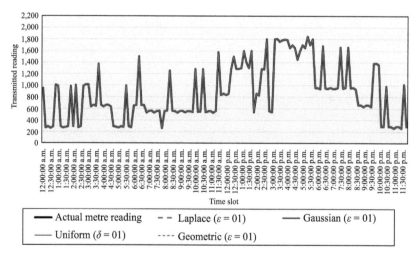

*Figure 9.7   Performance evaluation of differential privacy mechanisms at various privacy parameters*

within 10 min by smart meter user. A graphical illustration of MAE values is given in Figure 9.8.

In Figure 9.8, we show graphical illustration at $\varepsilon$, $\delta=0.01$ and 0.05, because these two privacy parameter values add an adequate amount of noise to protect

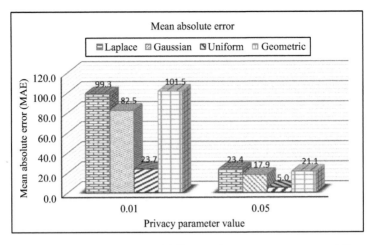

*Figure 9.8    Mean absolute error of differential privacy variants at different
privacy parameters*

privacy. After further increment of $\varepsilon$ or $\delta$, this value of MAE decreases and eventually reduces to approximately 0 at $\varepsilon$, $\delta = 1$. Furthermore, the average metre reading value for 144 readings in daily load is 872 Wh per reading, which means that approximately 872 Wh is being used every 10 min.

It can be seen from the graph that the Geometric noise addition mechanism provides MAE value of 101.5 at $\varepsilon = 0.01$, followed by the Laplace and Gaussian mechanisms which provide MAE of 99.3 and 82.5, respectively. Similarly, at $\varepsilon = 0.05$, the MAE value 23.4 provided by the Laplace is maximum, which is followed by the Geometric and Gaussian noise addition mechanisms as 21.1 and 17.9, respectively. From Figure 9.8, it can be concluded that both the Geometric and Laplace mechanisms provide similar MAE; however, from the previous section, it can be seen that the Laplace provides efficient variation in the case of small metre reading and Geometric provides variation in the case of large used values.

### 9.4.4    Summary and lessons learnt

After careful visualization of real-time smart metering graphs and MAE graph, it can be concluded that both the Laplace and Geometric mechanisms outperform other noise addition variants by providing more variation as compared to the other two. However, if the data usage values are large, then the Geometric noise addition is more suitable because it provides more variation in the case of large values by showing high positive peaks. Contrary to this, the Laplace mechanism usually provides negative peaks in the case of low values to protect user privacy. Furthermore, from the perspective of $\varepsilon$ and $\delta$, the lower these values, the higher the privacy; therefore, in order to protect at least an adequate amount of privacy, $\varepsilon$, $\delta = 0.01$ are the most suitable privacy parameters. Furthermore, MAE evaluation values of the Geometric and Laplace mechanisms are quite similar, which also show that both of the mechanisms are efficient to protect smart metering privacy. If there is a smart home in which on average less energy is used, then the Laplace mechanism (at $\varepsilon = 0.01$) outperforms other privacy-preserving mechanisms, and in case there is a smart home which regularly uses a high amount of energy throughout the day, then the Geometric noise addition mechanism (with $\varepsilon = 0.01$) proves to be the most feasible one to be used.

## 9.5 Conclusion and future directions

Differential privacy appeared as a strong privacy-preserving notion after it is invented by C. Dwork in 2006. Since then, plenty of variants of differential privacy have been proposed by researchers that have been applied over certain real-time application, and real-time smart metering is one of them. Similarly, the security and transparency of smart metering has also been enhanced by the usage of decentralized blockchain technology. In this chapter, we first work over the integration of differential privacy and blockchain in real-time smart metering scenario. Afterwards, we carried out performance evaluation of four variants of differential privacy in the proposed blockchain-based smart metering scenario. The performance evaluation section of this chapter demonstrates that each privacy-preserving mechanism adds differently depending upon the selected privacy parameters and the input data. However, in the case of high peak values the Geometric mechanism surpasses other noise addition variants, although, in case of low peak values in metre reading, the Laplace mechanism performs better at $\varepsilon = 0.01$. As a part of future work, we are working over the integration of differential privacy and blockchain in other cyber-physical systems scenarios.

## References

[1] Wang T, Zheng Z, Rehmani MH, *et al.* Privacy preservation in big data from the communication perspective—A survey. IEEE Communications Surveys & Tutorials. 2018;21(1):753–778.
[2] Dwork C. Differential privacy: A survey of results. In: International Conference on Theory and Applications of Models of Computation. Springer; 2008. p. 1–19.
[3] Hassan MU, Rehmani MH, and Chen J. Differential privacy techniques for cyber physical systems: A survey. IEEE Communications Surveys & Tutorials. 2020;22(1):746–789.
[4] Liu K, Chen J, Yang Y, *et al.* A throughput maximization strategy for scheduling transaction-intensive workflows on SwinDeW-G. Concurrency and Computation: Practice and Experience. 2008;20(15):1807–1820.
[5] Komninos N, Philippou E, and Pitsillides A. Survey in smart grid and smart home security: Issues, challenges and countermeasures. IEEE Communications Surveys & Tutorials. 2014;16(4):1933–1954.

[6]    Puthal D, Nepal S, Ranjan R, *et al.* A dynamic key length based approach for real-time security verification of big sensing data stream. In: International Conference on Web Information Systems Engineering. Springer; 2015. p. 93–108.

[7]    Kumar P, Lin Y, Bai G, *et al.* Smart grid metering networks: A survey on security, privacy and open research issues. IEEE Communications Surveys & Tutorials. 2019;21(3):2886–2927.

[8]    Wang M, Ramamohanarao K, and Chen J. Trust-based robust scheduling and runtime adaptation of scientific workflow. Concurrency and Computation: Practice and Experience. 2009;21(16):1982–1998.

[9]    Gai K, Wu Y, Zhu L, *et al.* Permissioned blockchain and edge computing empowered privacy-preserving smart grid networks. IEEE Internet of Things Journal. 2019;6(5):7992–8004.

[10]   Puthal D, Nepal S, Ranjan R, *et al.* DLSeF: A dynamic key-length-based efficient real-time security verification model for big data stream. ACM Transactions on Embedded Computing Systems (TECS). 2016;16(2):1–24.

[11]   Belotti M, Božić N, Pujolle G, *et al.* A Vademecum on blockchain technologies: When, which, and how. IEEE Communications Surveys & Tutorials. 2019;21(4):3796–3838.

[12]   Hassan MU, Rehmani MH, and Chen J. Privacy preservation in blockchain based IoT systems: Integration issues, prospects, challenges, and future research directions. Future Generation Computer Systems. 2019;97:512–529.

[13]   Wanchun D, Chao L, Xuyun Z, *et al.* A QoS-aware service evaluation method for co-selecting a shared service. In: IEEE International Conference on Web Services; 2011. p. 145–152.

[14]   Hassan MU, Rehmani MH, and Chen J. Differential privacy in blockchain technology: A futuristic approach. Journal of Parallel and Distributed Computing. 2020;145:50–74.

[15]   Eibl G and Engel D. Differential privacy for real smart metering data. Computer Science-Research and Development. 2017;32(1–2):173–182.

[16]   Acs G and Castelluccia C. I have a dream! (differentially private smart metering). In: International Workshop on Information Hiding. Springer; 2011. p. 118–132.

[17]   Eibl G and Engel D. Differential privacy for real smart metering data. Computer Science-Research and Development. 2017;32(1–2):173–182.

[18]   Hassan MU, Rehmani MH, Kotagiri R, *et al.* Differential privacy for renewable energy resources based smart metering. Journal of Parallel and Distributed Computing. 2019;131:69–80.

[19]   Cai X, Wang P, Du L, Cui Z, Zhang W, and Chen J. Multi-objective three-dimensional DV-hop localization algorithm with NSGA-II. IEEE Sensors Journal. 2019;19(21):10003–10015.

[20]   Feng J, Yang LT, Zhang R, Qiang W, and Chen J. Privacy preserving high-order bi-Lanczos in cloud-fog computing for industrial applications, IEEE Transactions on Industrial Informatics. 2020. DOI: 10.1109/TII.2020.2998086.

[21]   Zhang H, Wang J, and Ding Y. Blockchain-based decentralized and secure keyless signature scheme for smart grid. Energy. 2019;180:955–967.

[22] Cao Y, Yoshikawa M, Xiao Y, *et al.* Quantifying differential privacy in continuous data release under temporal correlations. IEEE Transactions on Knowledge and Data Engineering. 2018;31(7):1281–1295.

[23] Huang W, Zhou S, Liao Y, *et al.* An efficient differential privacy logistic classification mechanism. IEEE Internet of Things Journal. 2019;6(6):10620–10626.

[24] Inan A, Gursoy ME, and Saygin Y. Sensitivity analysis for non-interactive differential privacy: Bounds and efficient algorithms. IEEE Transactions on Dependable and Secure Computing. 2017.

[25] Desfontaines D and Pejó B. SoK: Differential privacies. Proceedings on Privacy Enhancing Technologies. 2020;2020(2):288–313.

[26] Hassan MU, Rehmani MH, and Chen J. DEAL: Differentially private auction for blockchain based microgrids energy trading. IEEE Transactions on Services Computing. 2020;13(2):263–275.

[27] Wang P, Xue F, Li H, Cui Z, Xie L, and Chen J. A multi-objective DV-hop localization algorithm based on NSGA-II in Internet of Things. Mathematics. 2019;7(2), Article Number: 184.

[28] Kalantari K, Sankar L, and Sarwate AD. Robust privacy-utility tradeoffs under differential privacy and Hamming distortion. IEEE Transactions on Information Forensics and Security. 2018;13(11):2816–2830.

[29] Geng Q and Viswanath P. Optimal noise adding mechanisms for approximate differential privacy. IEEE Transactions on Information Theory. 2015;62(2):952–969.

[30] Brenner H and Nissim K. Impossibility of differentially private universally optimal mechanisms. In: IEEE 51st Annual Symposium on Foundations of Computer Science; 2010. p. 71–80.

[31] Ghosh A, Roughgarden T, and Sundararajan M. Universally utility-maximizing privacy mechanisms. SIAM Journal on Computing. 2012;41 (6):1673–1693.

[32] Mustapa M, Niamat MY, Nath APD, *et al.* Hardware-oriented authentication for advanced metering infrastructure. IEEE Transactions on Smart Grid. 2016;9(2):1261–1270.

[33] Zhang Z, Cao W, Qin Z, *et al.* When privacy meets economics: Enabling differentially-private battery-supported meter reporting in smart grid. In: 2017 IEEE/ACM 25th International Symposium on Quality of Service (IWQoS). IEEE; 2017. p. 1–9.

[34] Cao H, Liu S, Wu L, *et al.* Achieving differential privacy against non-intrusive load monitoring in smart grid: A fog computing approach. Concurrency and Computation: Practice and Experience. 2019;31(22): e4528.

[35] Wang Y, Wang P, Zhang J, *et al.* A novel bat algorithm with multiple strategies coupling for numerical optimization. Mathematics. 2019;7(2):Article Number: 135.

[36]  Qi L, Dou W, and Chen J. Weighted principal component analysis-based service selection method for multimedia services in cloud, Computing. 2016;98(1–2):195–214.

[37]  Danezis G. Statistical disclosure attacks. In: IFIP International Information Security Conference. Springer; 2003. p. 421–426.

[38]  Muratori M. Impact of uncoordinated plug-in electric vehicle charging on residential power demand. Nature Energy. 2018;3(3):193–201.

*Chapter 10*

# Scaling-out blockchains with sharding: an extensive survey

*Guangsheng Yu[1], Xu Wang[1], Kan Yu[2], Wei Ni[3], J. Andrew Zhang[1] and Ren Ping Liu[1]*

The blockchain technology, featured with its decentralized tamper-resistance based on a peer-to-peer (P2P) network, has been widely applied in financial applications and even further been extended to industrial applications. However, the weak scalability of traditional blockchain technology severely affects the wide adoption due to the well-known trilemma of decentralization-security-scalability in block-chains. In regards to this issue, a number of solutions have been proposed, targeting to boost the scalability while preserving the decentralization and security. They range from modifying the on-chain data structure and consensus algorithms to adding the off-chain technologies. Therein, one of the most practical methods to achieve horizontal scalability along with the increasing network size is sharding, by partitioning network into multiple shards so that the overhead of duplicating communication, storage, and computation in each full node can be avoided.

This chapter presents a survey focusing on sharding in blockchains in a systematic and comprehensive way. We provide detailed comparison and evaluation of major sharding mechanisms, along with our insights analyzing the features and restrictions of the existing solutions. The remaining challenges and future research directions are also reviewed.

## 10.1 Introduction

Working as distributed, incorruptible, and tamper-resistant ledgers, blockchain technology has shown its great potential to tackle critical security and trust challenges in various applications, e.g., cryptocurrency, Internet-of-Things, and edge computing [1–3]. Running over a P2P network, blockchain processes application requests in the form of blockchain transactions [4]. The transactions are mined into

[1]The Global Big Data Technologies Centre, University of Technology Sydney, Ultimo, Australia
[2]The Department of Computer Science and Information Technology, La Trobe University, Melbourne, Australia
[3]Data61, CSIRO, Sydney, Australia

blocks by blockchain miners following consensus protocols, e.g., proof-of-work (PoW) for permissionless blockchains and the Practical Byzantine Fault Tolerance (PBFT) for permissioned blockchains [5], and the blocks are chained with their hash values [1].

The throughput of a blockchain system, defined as the number of processed transactions per second of the blockchain, is far from practical requirements and has become a crucial limitation stopping blockchain from being widely adopted [6]. For example, Bitcoin can only handle up to approximately ten transactions per second with its maximum block size of 1 MB and average 10 min block period [7], which severely hinders the use of blockchains in the high-frequency trading. To handle a great number of transactions, blockchain has been considered as a secure base-layer (or a settlement center for cryptocurrencies) where transactions are processed off-chain and then settled in the blockchain. For example, Lightning network and Raiden network (referring to the state-channel technology) support off-chain payments and broadcast a summary of a batch of off-chain payments to the blockchain [8,9]. Plasma (referring to the side chain technology) builds various applications on the top of Ethereum [10]. These methods, known as the Layer-2 scaling, minimize the interaction with the blockchain to reduce the latency from the users' perspective but do not improve the throughput of blockchains [11].

In contrast, the Layer-1 scaling is designed for improving the throughput of blockchains from the systematic perspective. A blockchain system can be optimized in the following ways to handle a growing amount of work:

- reducing the communication and computation overhead;
- adding resources to a single node, i.e., vertical scaling; and
- adding more nodes to the blockchain, i.e., horizontal scaling [12].

*Reducing overhead:* New blockchain consensus protocols have been developed for high blockchain throughput by reducing the overhead. For example, every PoW winner (i.e., a miner) is eligible for several blocks rather than a single block in Bitcoin-NG [13] and its variations [14,15]. The traditional PBFT consensus protocol has been developed and optimized to reduce the communication overhead and achieve high throughput in large-scale networks [16–19]. However, $O(n)$ ($n$ is the number of participating miners) is the lower bound that this type of technologies can reduce the overhead at most, as every participating miners have to exchange and store messages during every consensus round regardless of the route of transactions.

*Vertical scaling:* Bitcoin tried to improve throughput by vertical scaling methods. For example, increasing the number of allowed transactions in a single block and/or reducing the block period can improve the throughput of Bitcoin but consume more resources, e.g., storage, computation, and bandwidth, of Bitcoin nodes [20–23]. Beyond this, the Greedy Heaviest Observed Subtree (GHOST) [24] is implemented by Ethereum to organize blocks in a tree instead of a chain of blocks and obtain a higher throughput [4]. The GHOST is subsequently extended to the directed acyclic graph (DAG). The DAG is adopted to organize transactions where every transaction contains hash values pointing to existing transactions [25–30].

The DAG structure allows transactions to be confirmed in parallel and thus improves the network utilization ratio given the resources of a node, which improves the throughput of the entire distributed system. However, the vertical scaling methods cannot infinitely improve the throughput, as a blockchain system is designed to run in a decentralized and homogeneous network where the security is closely dependent on the consensus across the entire network. The larger scale the network is, the more bandwidth is needed to achieve the network synchronization, while the bandwidth is the resource that cannot be indefinitely added [20]. This leads to the vertical scaling being compromised to the throughput of resources-limited nodes.

*Horizontal scaling:* Sharding technology, dividing a whole blockchain into multiple shards and allowing participating nodes to process and store transactions of a few shards (i.e., only parts of the blockchain), holds the key to horizontal scaling, also known as the scale-out technology. By taking advantage of the sharding technology that allows partial transactions processing and storage on a single node, the whole blockchain can achieve a linearly increasing throughput with the growing number of nodes. This is important for the adoption of blockchains providing high quantity and quality of services to the public in large-scale networks with infinite growth, which has attracted the interest of researches regarding the improvement of the blockchain scalability.

A number of studies have proposed new sharding mechanisms. Surveys of blockchain scalability which used to only focus on **Reducing overhead** and **Vertical scaling** have been gradually taking the sharding technology into account. However, none of them was able to focus on sharding and systematically introduce the challenges of sharding, features and restrictions of the existing solutions, and the future trends.

## 10.1.1  Our contributions

We provide a more systematic introduction of sharding mechanisms in this chapter than existing surveys and papers. The key contributions are highlighted as follows:

1.  Our work, for the first time, provides an introduction of state-of-the-art sharding mechanisms ranged from Byzantine-faulty-tolerance (BFT)-based to Nakamoto-based sharding mechanisms, while the latter has never been systematized in any of the existing surveys at the time of writing.
2.  We gain our own insights analyzing the features and restrictions into the existing solutions to the intra-consensus-safety, atomicity of cross-shard transactions, and general challenges and improvements proposed by the considered sharding mechanisms. Based on the insights of the features and restrictions of each existing sharding solution, a comprehensive comparison is proposed.
3.  Finally, we point out the current remaining challenges of sharding mechanisms, followed by suggestions for the future trend of designing reliable sharding mechanisms.

## 10.1.2    Related work

The relationship between the existing studies and our work is discussed. Note that all the considered previous studies highlight the trend of scalability in the future of blockchains and intend to accommodate the existing solutions to scale blockchain systems. These solutions include but not limited to upgrading Bitcoin (increasing block size or conducting Segregated Witness), scalable consensus algorithms, state channels, and multiple side chains' structure.

Previous surveys, including [31–38], discuss the aforementioned solutions but involve no information about the sharding which has been realized to be the most practical solution so far for a *scale-out* blockchain system. Thus, there have been several recent studies presenting their own sharding mechanisms, as well as surveys that manage to summarize them and propose new benchmarks [4,39–52]. However, all of these studies compare the sharding with other kinds of solutions by either presenting a vague introduction of only one or two sharding mechanisms, or lacking the insights for evaluation, except [39,43,50–52] putting more efforts on introducing sharding. Authors in [39] make the use of the scale cube architecture, highlighting that the horizontal scalability should only be improved by partitioning the data and consensus. However, it only provides a vague introduction of Ethereum 2.0, and the same problem exists in [43] where the consensus layer is decoupled from the ledger topology layer (which is inappropriate due to the importance of intra-consensus in a sharding system). Authors in [50] present an analytic model in a game-theoretical way that is designed to benchmark the existing sharding mechanisms and aims for design guidance for future solutions. However, *sharding can be thought as the "multiple committees" upon the traditional BFT-based consensus*, as stated in [47,50], which has been outdated as [53] proposes a Nakamoto-based sharding mechanism (Monoxide). A unified comparison between such Nakamoto-based sharding mechanisms and the BFT-based sharding mechanisms is also absent in [51] and the most closely related survey [52] (where the BFT-based sharding mechanisms are focused, as well as the corresponding randomness generators) (Table 10.1).

This chapter as a survey is an extension of [54]. To the best of our knowledge, our work outweighs all the existing surveys in a more systematic way, in regards to the key concept of various sharding mechanisms, and a comprehensive comparison for practitioners based on our insights.

## 10.1.3    Paper outline

The rest of this chapter is organized as follows: Section 10.2 briefly presents an overview of sharding technology and introduces the survey methodology. Section 10.3 presents an introduction of the considered sharding mechanisms, upon which the comparison and discussion are presented in Section 10.4. Section 10.5 concludes the survey.

Table 10.1   Comparison between surveys related to the discussion of sharding
mechanisms

| Number of sharding mechanisms being introduced in the studies | Studies | Insights |
|---|---|---|
| 0 | [31–38] | × |
| 1 | [4,39–44] | × |
| 2 | [45–49] | × |
| 3 | [50] | × |
| 4 | [51] | × |
| 5 | [52] | × |
| 6 | This work extended from [54] | √ |

## 10.2   Sharding review and survey methodology

### 10.2.1   Overview of the sharding technology

Sharding is first proposed by [55] and commonly used in distributed databases and cloud infrastructure. Based on the pioneering proposals [56,57] integrating sharding with permissioned and permissionless blockchain, respectively, the sharding technology is thought to be able to partition the network into different groups (shards), so that the compulsory duplication of three resources (i.e., the communication, data storage, and computation overhead) can be avoided for each participating node, while these overheads must be incurred by all full nodes in traditional non-sharded blockchains. This partition is essential because the restriction incurred by the three resources owned by a single node may make the system unable to take full advantage of a scalable consensus algorithm. Sharding is so far one of the most practical solutions to achieve a *scale-out* system where the processing, storage, and computing can be conducted in parallel, as illustrated in Figure 10.1. As such, the capacity and throughput being linearly proportional to the number of participating nodes or the number of shards become possible, while preserving decentralization and security. However, sharding poses new challenges to blockchains, i.e., the *intra-consensus-safety*, *cross-shard-atomicity*, and the *general improvements* regarding the storage, latency, etc., where the detail is our concentration and is described starting from Section 10.3.

There have been a few studies working on these challenges regarding the sharding in permissionless blockchains [53,57–61], prior to which [56] proposes a sharded permissioned blockchain that will not be discussed in this survey due to its forfeit of permissionless decentralization. Rather, the sharding in permissionless blockchains is focused.

### 10.2.2   Survey methodology

This survey focuses on sharding in permissionless blockchains (as permissioned blockchains do not take full advantage of the sharding technology due to the

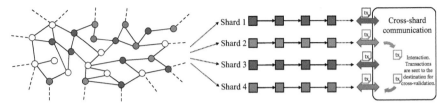

*Figure 10.1    The sharding technology partitions the network into different groups, while each of the groups maintains its own ledger and processes and stores a disjoint set of transactions. By implementing a secure cross-shard communication protocol, such disjoint transaction sets that could not have been interacted become securely verifiable and interactively executable in parallel. Note that nodes in some sharding mechanisms (e.g., Monoxide) can choose to participate in the processing of multiple shards and maintain their ledgers, as illustrated by the multicolored circles, while the unicolored circles denote the nodes only participating in a single shard to which they are assigned in terms of the color*

smaller network size and its forfeit of permissionless decentralization) and is based on the published research papers and other research references of Monoxide [53], Elastico [57], OmniLedger [58], RapidChain [59], Chainspace [60], and Ethereum 2.0 [61]. Our methodology can be characterized as follows:

1.   We clarify the demand for high scalability in Section 10.1, based on the well-known trilemma of decentralization-security-scalability in blockchains. We discuss the potential solutions ranged from the Layer-1 scaling (on-chain scaling) to Layer-2 scaling (off-chain scaling), with the former being focused in order to address the throughput issue. Upon this, we elaborate on the importance of the scale-out technology of Layer-1 scaling, i.e., sharding, which is thought to be orthogonal to any other scalable technologies, and so far the most practical solution to achieve horizontal scalability in large-scale block-chain networks.

2.   We summarize six of the most well-known and typical sharding mechanisms in large-scale permissionless blockchains, i.e., Monoxide, Elastico, OmniLedger, RapidChain, Chainspace, and Ethereum 2.0, which are characterized in *intra-consensus-safety*, *cross-shard-atomicity*, and *general improvements*, respectively, presented in Sections 10.3.1, 10.3.2, and 10.3.3.

3.   Based on the previous description of the considered sharding mechanisms, we provide our own insights in regards to each of the features, (1) what issues in a sharding system the features have addressed; and (2) the restrictions of these features. Besides, we provide a comparison based on the insights, among the considered sharding mechanisms. Finally, the result is characterized in Tables 10.2 and 10.3.

Table 10.2 *A comparison regarding the protocols (ranged from the settings of intra-consensus to the design of cross-shard atomicity, as well as the corresponding overhead) among the discussed sharding mechanisms in this paper is elaborated*

| Network model | | Monoxide | Elastico | OmniLedger | RapidChain | | Ethereum 2.0 | Chainspace |
|---|---|---|---|---|---|---|---|---|
| | | Partial-sync | Partial-sync | Partial-sync | **Intra** Sync **Total** Partial-sync | | Partial-sync | Partial-sync |
| Security model | Threat model | Attackers behave arbitrarily, uncoordinated majority | Attackers behave arbitrarily, slowly adaptive | Attackers behave arbitrarily, slowly adaptive | Attackers behave arbitrarily, slowly adaptive | | Attackers behave arbitrarily, uncoordinated majority | Attackers behave arbitrarily, uncoordinated majority |
| FT | Intra | 50% | 33% | 33% | 50% | | 33% | 33% |
| | Total | 50% | 25% | 25% | 33% | | 33% | 25% |
| Intra-consensus protocol | | PoW-based Chu-ko-nu mining | PBFT | ByzCoinX | 50% BFT | | BFT-based PoS | MOD-SMART implementation of PBFT |
| Randomness ($\mathcal{R}$) | Existence | No | Yes. $\mathcal{R}_i+1$ is generated by the final committee at the end of epoch $i$ | Yes. $\mathcal{R}_i+1$ is generated by using RandHound+VRF in the beginning of epoch $i+1$ | Yes. $\mathcal{R}_i+1$ is generated by the reference committee at the end of epoch $i$ | | Yes. Each $\mathcal{R}$ is generated by using RANDAO +VDF on the beacon chain | Unknown |
| | Use | N/A | 1. The seed of PoW puzzle for the next epoch; 2. Select the intra-leader | 1. Select the intra-leader and the subgroup; 2. epoch reconfiguration; 3. trust-but-verify validation | 1. The seed of PoW puzzle for the next epoch; 2. select the intra-leader; 3. bootstrapping; 4. epoch reconfiguration | | 1. Select the proposer/attesters; 2. select the validators for checkpointing from the global pool | Unknown |
| Members | Allocation | One-off allocation based on the identity (address) of nodes | Allocation based on the least-significant bits of the result of PoW puzzles Unsafe | Allocation based on $\mathcal{R}$ | Allocation based on the result of PoW puzzles | | Allocation based on $\mathcal{R}$ | One-off allocation based on objects |
| | Safe epoch re-configuration | N/A | | Yes, swapping-out bounded by 2/3 at a given time | Yes, swapping-out a constant number of node | | Yes | N/A |

(Continues)

# Table 10.2 (Continued)

| Network model | Monoxide | Elastico | OmniLedger | RapidChain | | Ethereum 2.0 | Chainspace |
|---|---|---|---|---|---|---|---|
| | Partial-sync | Partial-sync | Partial-sync | Intra Total Sync | Partial-sync | Partial-sync | Partial-sync |
| Additional global blockchain | Mixed targets: no; identical targets: yes | Yes, a global ledger | Yes, identity blockchain | Yes, reference blockchain | | Yes, the mainnet and beacon chain | No |
| Transaction structure | Account | UTXO | UTXO | UTXO | | Account | Object-driven, contract-sharded |
| Cross-shard Tx — Support | Yes | No | Yes | Yes | | Yes | Yes |
| Cross-shard Tx — Method | Async, lock-free | N/A | Sync, lock/unlock | Sync, lock/unlock | | Sync, lock/unlock | Sync, lock/unlock |
| Complexity — Communication | Mixed PoW targets: $O(m+n\log_2 n)$ identical PoW targets: $O(m+n)$ | $O(m^2+n)$ | $O(\log_2 m+n)$ | $O(m^2+m\log_2 n)$ | | $O(m^2+n)$ | $O(m^2+n)$ |
| Complexity — Storage | $\Omega(|C|)\sim O(|C|+n|Ch|)$ | $O(n|C|)$ | $O(|C|)$ | $O(|C|+|Cr|)$ | | $\Omega(|C|+n|H|+|Cg|)\sim O(n|C|+|Cg|)$ | $O(|C|+|Cnk|)$ |
| Features and restrictions | Insights 10.1, 10.9, and 10.15 | Insights 10.2, 10.3, and 10.15 | Insights 10.4, 10.5, 10.10, 10.11, 10.14, and 10.16 | Insights 10.6 and 10.12 | | Insights 10.7, 10.8, 10.13, and 10.15 | Insights 10.2, 10.11, and 10.17 |

Table 10.3 *A comparison among the discussed sharding mechanisms in this paper is elaborated*

| | | Monoxide | Elastico | OmniLedger | RapidChain | Ethereum 2.0 | Chainspace |
|---|---|---|---|---|---|---|---|
| Shards' settings | Number of shards ($n$) | $2^{10}$–$2^{18}$ | $<10^2$ | $<2^6$ | $<2^8$ | $<2^9$ | $<10^2$ |
| | Shard size ($m$) | $10^2$–$10^4$ | $<10^2$ | 22–210 | $(2^2-1)$–$2^8$ | $<10^2$ | $<10^2$ |
| Epoch length | | N/A | ~10 min | $\geq$ 1 day | $\leq$ 1 day | 1 week | Exists, details not provided |
| Latency | Transaction confirmation | 23 s | <900 s | ~100 s | 70 s | 6–8 s [62] | 2 s |
| | Epoch reconfiguration | N/A | N/A | 1,000 s | 200–350 s | Unknown | Unknown |
| Upper bound | Improving factor (N) | $n/2$ | $n$ | $1\sim n/2$ | $n/2$ | $n/3$ | $1\sim n/2$ |
| | Throughput | 1.23–2.56 Mtps | 48 ktps | 28.8 ktps | 128 ktps | 134 ktps | <400 tps |
| | Cost | 30–80USD/ hour | 30–35USD/ hour | 0.2–0.3USD/ hour | 0.2–0.3USD/ hour | 0.4–0.45USD/ hour | N/A |

The results of throughput and cost are shown in [54]. The latency is also obtained and shown (N/A, not available).

4.  We discuss the remaining challenges by pointing out the pros and cons of most recently proposed sharding mechanisms (which are outlined in this survey due to the limited space available), e.g., SSChain [63], Thinkey [64], and VAPOR [65]. Finally, we also point out the future research directions.

## 10.3    Description

As a Layer-1 solution to the scalability issue of blockchain systems, and the most practical solution to push blockchain systems to *scale-out* in terms of communication bandwidth, disk storage, and computation (i.e., full-sharded), there are two significant issues each sharding mechanism needs to resolve.

*Intra-consensus-safety*: How to secure the consensus algorithm inside a shard away from both the Nakamoto-based and BFT-based 1% attack [61] in a scalable way, while the latter can also be corresponding to a secure randomness generation process, as discussed in Section 10.3.1; note that 1% attack is an attack strategy in sharded networks where attackers can dominate a single shard more easily than dominating the whole network.

*Cross-shard-atomicity*: How to support the cross-verification, and guarantee the *Atomicity* [66,67] of cross-shard transactions for both unconditional transactions (simple payment) and conditional contract-oriented transactions in an efficient way (inefficient if the latency and overhead for achieving atomic-safe cross-shard transactions are higher than $O(n)$; $n$ denotes the number of shards being partitioned or the number of participating nodes), as discussed in Section 10.3.2.

*General improvements*: Based on the *intra-consensus-safety* and *cross-shard atomicity*, we focus on the improving factor $N$ regarding the multiple of optimized global throughput for each considered sharding mechanism, while $N$ is subject to the linear order $O(n)$. On the other hand, the additional latency and overhead originated from the proposed solutions also reveal the new problems that sharding brings to us. In regard to this, some general improvements are discussed in Section 10.3.3.

### 10.3.1    Intra-consensus protocol

Sharding significantly increases the throughput in $O(n)$, but sacrificing security in intra-consensus protocols, i.e., the per-zone security or 1% attack [53,61]. Concretely, it is categorized into the Nakamoto-based 1% attack and BFT-based 1% attack.

The total amount of mining power among the network, i.e., $\mathbb{P}$, guarantees the low probability for a single entity to dominate over 50% mining power. By purposely dividing the network into $n$ partitions (shards), we can greatly increase the throughput in $O(n)$, where rational miners tend to ideally distribute their mining power in multiple shards (at most $n$ shards) in order for the maximum rewards. However, this also decreases the security of PoW in each shard in $O(1/n)$. Such a system can be more prone to double-spend attack by a malicious miner that only needs to own the mining power $P > \mathbb{P}/n \times 50\%$ due to the smaller shard size compared to the entire network size. This issue deteriorates as $n$ increases in order for a larger throughput, which becomes the most serious barrier to PoW being implemented for the intra-consensus protocol of a sharding mechanism.

On the other hand, BFT-based consensus algorithms are considered instead of PoW in order to solve the security challenge, as discussed earlier. However, such designs introduce another kind of vulnerabilities other than that of the PoW-based one, as discussed in the following.

- It is of importance to carefully design a scheme to generate an unpredictable and unbiasable randomness without any third parties in permissionless blockchains. The randomness can be used to (1) allocate validators (an alias for nodes participating in the intra-consensus process in the context of BFT-based systems) into different shards at the beginning phase and every reconfiguration phase; (2) select the leader of each shard; and (3) decide which shards a cross-shard transaction should broadcast to, etc. Without such a strictly chosen randomness, malicious validators may be able to bias the allocation and control the elections at will, such as collusion within a shard (with a small number of validators due to the weak scalability of traditional BFT-based consensus algorithms [68], e.g., PBFT [5]).

- Then it ends up encountering the dilemma of BFT-based 1% attack that the weak scalability of BFT-based consensus algorithm restricts the shard size, i.e., the number of members in a shard, while too small a size can potentially decrease the security of the intra-consensus with a strict fault tolerance (FT), as described by the following cumulative binomial distribution:

$$s(k, m, p) = P[X \le c] = \sum_{k=0}^{c} (m/k)p^k (1 - p)^{m-k}, \tag{10.1}$$

$$f(k, m, p) = 1 - s(k, m, p), \tag{10.2}$$

where $X$ is the random variable that represents the number of times a malicious miner is picked [13,57,58,69]; $m$ denotes the shard size; $c$ denotes the number of malicious members within a shard; and $p$ denotes the total FT among the entire network. It is strongly suggested that $s(k, m, p)$ should be greater than 99% [69], while only $m \ge 144$ can satisfy, of which the traditional BFT-based consensus algorithm cannot be capable.[*] In order to resolve this, highly scalable BFT-based consensus algorithms with large shard size require more attractions.

In this section, we compare and discuss the intra-consensus protocols of the considered sharding mechanisms, i.e., Monoxide, Elastico, Chainspace, OmniLedger, RapidChain, and Ethereum 2.0. Note that the Shasper used in

---

[*]A few sharding mechanisms are incurring a total 25% FT based on the 33% FT in each shard, e.g., Elastico, OmniLedger, and Chainspace. This can be a BFT-based 1% attack, by dispersing validators into as many shards as possible to maximize the possibility to control some shards. Elastico and Chainspace suffer from this security issue, while OmniLedger implements a scalable BFT-based consensus algorithm to address this issue.

Ethereum 2.0 features its novel and engineering-oriented design that combines the two major issues (*intra-consensus-safety* and *cross-shard-atomicity*) and kills two birds with one store. Elastico and Chainspace use PBFT for intra-consensus that are not discussed in detail in this section, while the randomness generator of Chainspace is not discussed as the detail is not provided in [60].

Also note that a threat model where the attackers can refuse to participate or collude others (behave arbitrarily) takes effect in all discussed sharding mechanisms in this survey. Also, Elastico [57], OmniLedger [58], and RapidChain [59] assume the slowly adaptive attackers (who can only succeed to attack in a long time), while Monoxide [53], Ethereum 2.0 [61], and Chainspace [60] assume a model of uncoordinated majority where all participators are game-theoretically rational, i.e., egoism (with an upper bounded fraction that can coordinate the majority). Therein, Chainspace [60] also introduces an audit scheme to prevent attacks from dishonest shards.

### 10.3.1.1   Nakamoto-based—Monoxide—Chu-ko-nu mining

Monoxide is the first sharding mechanism that eliminates the need for generating randomness and implements Nakamoto consensus algorithm for its intra-consensus. It introduces a one-off bootstrapping in the beginning, to allocate each node (including miners and non-miners) into different shards based on their identity addresses. By using the proposed Chu-ko-nu mining, Monoxide can achieve a large-scale network with a huge number of shards and a flexible shard size. It involves a Merkle Patricia tree (MPT) [70] root consisting of all proposed blocks among multiple shards; thus, the $P/n$ can be multiplied by a factor $k$ ($k$ denotes the number of shards a particular miner manages to mine on). Consequently, dispersing mining power can be reaggregated to solve the 1% attack.

Chu-ko-nu mining is inspired by the merged mining first proposed in [71] and discussed in [72]. Merged mining shares the mining power among a parent chain and multiple auxiliary chains based on the same kind of PoW algorithms being run. As such, those auxiliary chains with relatively smaller mining power can be protected by the total mining power of the parent chain. Likewise, Monoxide shares a similar idea but conducting the mining process across multiple parallel shards without any hierarchy. By involving an MPT root consisting of all proposed blocks among the shards that a specific miner cares about, the effective mining power can be amplified by a factor of $k$. Defined in [53], the effective mining power differs from the physical mining power, in the sense that the physical mining power is calculated in hashrate (the number of hash values that a miner can probe the nonce per second) which directly corresponds to the total mining power $P$, and the hardware performance (e.g., CPU or GPU), while the effective mining power is indirectly obtained by observing the block period and difficulty. They are expected to be equaled in a non-sharded system, while with Chu-ko-nu mining, the normal block can be replaced by a batch-chaining-block (containing the information of the involved shards, e.g., (1) the identity of each shard; (2) from/to which shard the proposed block is received/sent; and (3) the MPT proof of the proposed new block of the local shard associated with the given MPT root, etc.), so that a one-off physical mining can be done to meet the different (or identical) difficulties associated with its shard. Thus, the similar block periods among the shards contribute to an effective mining power of $Pk/n \simeq P$ as $k \to n$, hence addressing the 1% attack.

To be specific, the PoW expression for a miner conducting Chu-ko-nu mining is described as

$$\mathcal{H}(\eta \| \mathcal{H}(x \| MPT_M)) \leq \gamma, \tag{10.3}$$

where $\gamma$ denotes the PoW target corresponding to a certain difficulty; $\mathcal{H}$ denotes the hash function; $\eta$ denotes the nonce that fulfills (10.3); $x$ denotes the header content, including the aforementioned information of the involved shards and the other fields defined in the normal PoW, as well as the inbound and outbound relay transactions in regards to the cross-shard communication (discussed in Section 10.3.2.1); $MPT_M$ denotes the MPT root consisting of all proposed blocks of each involved shard, i.e., $[\mathcal{B}_0, \mathcal{B}_1, \ldots, \mathcal{B}_{n-1}]$ if $k = n$, where each proposed block excludes its $\eta$ and contains its identity and the list of relay transactions.

Thus, the miner can subsequently send the finalized block to its corresponding shard with a satisfied $\eta$, as well as a proof,

$$[MPT_M, \eta, \mathcal{B}_i, \pi_i], \tag{10.4}$$

where $\pi_i$ denotes the MPT proof of $\mathcal{B}_i$ in the given MPT with a root of $MPT_M$. Any node can verify $\mathcal{B}_i$ with $\pi_i$, and malicious miners have to revert the history in all involved shards, i.e., from 0 to $n-1$ in this case, to double-spend the transactions because of $MPT_M$ being already updated with the change of leaves. Thus, the effective mining power is amplified by a factor of $n$.

Note that, Chu-ko-nu mining can handle both the mixed and identical PoW targets of shards in one batch.

- In the case of mixed PoW targets, a miner is allowed to finalize blocks and send them to any shards $i$ to $j$ whose PoW targets have been fulfilled by the current given $\eta$, with the rest of shards whose targets have yet to be satisfied. After that the mining process resumes, while $MPT_M$ is updated because of the just finalized blocks from shards $i$ to $j$.
- In the case of identical PoW targets, a miner can also finalize blocks and send them to all shards regardless of whether the given $\eta$ fulfills the PoW targets or not (assume the PoW targets are asymptotically equal,[†] and there must be some shards accepting its block and some rejecting). In addition to this, a global subnet maintaining and broadcasting headers from all shards where all miners must participate can significantly reduce the communication overhead, by eliminating the need of $\pi_i$.

Having known these two modes, it is observed that accepting/rejecting a block of a single shard is independent of the decisions from other shards, i.e.,

---

[†]Rational miners tend to mine on as many shards as possible so that the PoW difficulties will be self-adapted to be identical.

asynchronization. Such a feature greatly promotes the throughput of Monoxide in a secure way and also allows the *cross-shard-atomicity* in Monoxide, i.e., Relay transactions, as discussed in Section 10.3.2.1.

However, in order to meet the requirement of $Pk/n \simeq P$, Monoxide needs most of miners to conduct Chu-ko-nu mining across as many shards as possible, i.e., $k = n$ in the best case. However, this implies the fact that if miners only mine on $k$ out of $n$ shards, i.e., $Pk/n$, where $k \ll n$, the factor expected to amplify the effective mining power will be too small to secure the mining process, hence reducing the attack cost. On the other hand, rational miners tend to mine on all $n$ shards to reap the maximum profit, which may also result in the power centralization due to the huge cost of bandwidth, disk storage, and computing processors that only the professional mining facilities can afford.

**Insight 10.1** *The amplification to the effective mining power relies on an incentive scheme that should encourage miners to mine across k→n shards in Chu-ko-nu mining. This also poses the issue of power centralization and additional overhead to Monoxide.*

### 10.3.1.2    BFT-based Elastico
Using BFT-based algorithms for the intra-consensus is an alternative to bypass the vulnerability of Nakamoto-based algorithm (Insight 10.1). Thus, including but not limited to Elastico, OmniLedger, RapidChain, Chainspace, and Ethereum 2.0 choose to implement BFT-based algorithm. Therein, Elastico uniformly (re) allocates potential validators in terms of the different least-significant bits of the unpredictable PoW solutions at the beginning of each epoch, followed by running PBFT for the intra-consensus. The randomness used during the mining is generated by a proposed distributed commit-and-xor scheme.

*Consensus algorithm—PBFT's restrictions in sharding*
Due to the weak scalability of PBFT, Elastico incurs an unacceptable failure probability of 8% with $f(k, m, p) = f(6, 16, 0.25)$ based on the result of [68], while it still incurs 2.76% with $f(k, m, p) = f(34, 100, 0.25)$ even extending to a larger scale network of $m = 100$ (which can be the bottleneck [58]) by running powerful servers in cloud. This security issue has been hindering Elastico to be practically used, which is greatly resolved and improved by OmniLedger and RapidChain.

**Insight 10.2** *The traditional non-scalable PBFT incurs unacceptably high failure probability with total FT of only 25%, unless increasing the size of the consensus group, which leads to a chicken-and-egg problem due to huge communication overhead.*

*Generating randomness—distributed commit-and-xor scheme*
The distributed commit-and-xor scheme is implemented for the randomness generation in Elastico. It can be categorized into the commit-and-then-reveal scheme [73], with an exception that the final result (randomness) varies depending on the different combinations of seeds $\lambda_i$ every validator chooses. Concretely, the

randomness generation is conducted by a global subset, i.e., the final committee, and it follows the procedures shown as next.

1. Each member of the final committee chooses a random seed $\lambda_i$ in secret and broadcasts $Hash(\lambda_i)$ to any other members in the final committee. After that members in the final committee agree on a single set of hash values $\mathbb{S}$ [74], with the numbers of $Hash(\lambda_i)$ ranging from $[2m/3, 3m/2]$ ($m$ denotes the size of the final committee).[‡]

2. Only if $\mathbb{S}$ collects at least $2m/3$ signatures, every validator in the final committee reveals their own seed $\lambda_i$ to the public. By collecting and verifying all $2m/3$ (or $m/2+1$) pairs of $(\lambda_i, Hash(\lambda_i))$, the final randomness can be finalized by taking an XOR operation among them. Note that in the case of $3m/2$ pairs are received, the chosen $\lambda_i$ values need to be attached with the PoW solution in order to verify if the randomness is matched. This is because the combination of the seeds chosen by a validator can vary ($m/2+1$ out of $3m/2$).

This design, however, is not perfectly unbiased. It is exponentially biased and bounded by the size of $\lambda_i$, i.e., $|\lambda_i|$, and $m$. In order to prevent the attacks from biasing the randomness by deliberately choosing a specific set of $m/2+1$ values of $\lambda_i$ in his favor, $|\lambda_i|$ should be large enough as $m$ also increases. This incurs large communication overhead, in addition to the overhead of the extra verification during PoW process. In the case of only $2m/3$ values of $(\lambda_i, Hash(\lambda_i))$ being received, the lack of verifiable secret sharing (VSS) [75–79] forces all senders of these $2m/3$ values to be online all the time with no network outage or delay.

**Insight 10.3** *The distributed commit-and-xor scheme of Elastico has weak availability and robustness, and it is not a perfectly unbiased randomness generator unless paying more for the communication overhead.*

### 10.3.1.3 BFT-based Chainspace

Chainspace uses an optimal implementation of PBFT, MOD-SMART [80], which accounts for the intra-part of the S-BAC protocol proposed by Chainspace. However, MOD-SMART does not scale PBFT to address the issue of 1% attack. It decouples the communication and consensus primitives, while it only reduces the overhead of the latter with an unchanged overhead of $O(n^2)$ by replacing the process with the Validated and Provable Consensus. In addition, the high failure probability of the intra-consensus in Elastico also takes effects in Chainspace, which restricts the use of Chainspace in a large-scale network. Note that the stages of propose and view change take as input the elected leader, while the detail of randomness generator is not provided in [60].

---

[‡]In fact, Elastico takes the discrepancies into account, where there can be $3m/2$ messages received by a validator, while there are only $m$ validators in the shard due to the network delay. In this case, other validators can choose only $(3m/2)\times(1/3)+1 = m/2+1$ values of $Hash(\lambda_i)$ to generate their own randomness. In contrast, validators receiving only $2m/3$ values need to choose all $2m/3$ values of $Hash(\lambda_i)$ to generate their own randomness.

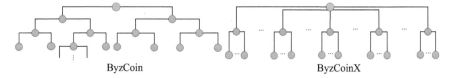

*Figure 10.2    (Left) ByzCoin implements a tree with a fixed branching factor and an increasing depth. (Right) ByzCoinX implements a shadow tree with a fixed depth and an increasing branching factor*

#### 10.3.1.4    BFT-based OmniLedger

OmniLedger combines RandHound [81] and Algorand-based verifiable random function (VRF) [82] to produce an unpredictable and unbiasable randomness under a 25% FT for reallocation and leader-election of each shard and subgroup. Also, a new scalable BFT-based consensus algorithm, ByzCoinX, is proposed by optimizing ByzCoin [69], which resolves the dilemma of BFT-based 1% attack in sharding, by increasing the shard size to hundreds and up to a thousand.

*Consensus algorithm—ByzCoinX*
Initially, ByzCoin [69] was the first scalable consensus protocol that combines PoW and BFT algorithms in a tree-based structure, by means of scalable collective signing (CoSi) [83,84].

ByzCoinX[§] optimizes ByzCoin in terms of the better latency and more robust FT for a shard with hundreds of validators. Concretely, ByzCoinX implements a shallow tree with a fixed depth-3 and an increasing branching factor; see Figure 10.2. Based on the shard size, each group leader is responsible for a group forming a subtree with a fixed number of group members. Note that unlike ByzCoin implementing PoW to elect the group leader within a shifting window, ByzCoinX elects each group leader by the randomness generated at the beginning of the current epoch, followed by evenly allocating the rest of the validators into each group (thus the validators account for the leaves of each subtree). Also, the group leaders maintain their roles until a view change phase occurs, which eliminates the shifting window, as well as the difference of keyblocks and microblocks, as defined in ByzCoin. The leaders of each subtree aggregate at least 2/3 signatures from its children (leaves), followed by the signature regarding each group being sent to the root (protocol leader). The decision can be finalized whenever the root receives at least 2/3 signatures from its children (group leaders).

By using such a new tree-based structure, ByzCoinX can outperform ByzCoin by a better latency for a shard with hundreds of validators due to the shorter path from leaves to the root with a fixed depth, and a robust FT due to the increasing branching factor. When the number of validators goes above a threshold, the latency of ByzCoin outperforms that of ByzCoinX due to the increasing branching factor. On the other hand, ByzCoinX can achieve a failure probability around 1.5%

---
[§]https://github.com/dedis/cothority/tree/master/byzcoinx

with $f(k,m,p) = f(48, 144, 0.25)$, and even 1% with $f(342, 1, 024, 0.3)$ at the cost of latency, as shown in Fig. 10 of [58].

**Insight 10.4** *ByzCoinX improves the scalability with a lower failure probability for the intra-consensus of OmniLedger, by sacrificing the transaction latency in large-scale networks.*

## Generating randomness—combination of RandHound and VRF

In order to address the issue of Insight 10.3, OmniLedger implements a scalable bias-resistant-distributed randomness generator, RandHound [81], combined with a VRF-based leader election algorithm proposed by Algorand [82].

RandHound takes advantage of the following technologies to achieve an unbiasable and unpredictable randomness generator:

- Publicly VSS (PVSS) [77] that allows participating validators to be offline during the reveal phase (as opposed to the traditional commit-and-then-reveal scheme used in Elastico), by broadcasting the secret shares of the original $\lambda_i$ in advanced;
- Schnorr signature [85] that is the foundation of CoSi [83,84] used in ByzCoinX and the threshold signatures [86–90],

so that the communication complexity can be reduced to $O(cm^2)$ from $O(m^3)$ ($m$ denotes the total number of participating validators; $c$ denotes the size of subgroup).

Several subgroups are created by dividing the entire group of the participating validators, with $c$ validators conducting PVSS within their subgroups, respectively. Thus, a client (the leader randomly elected by the VRF) can receive the secret shares based on his choice from the corresponding subgroups in a global run of CoSi. Consequently, the client can construct collective randomness by recovering the received secret shards. Meanwhile, a proof to verify the produced randomness is also recorded for third-party verifications.

OmniLedger implements a VRF-based election in order to randomly choose such a leader as the client among these participating validators. To be specific,

$$\mathcal{R}_{\mathcal{E},view,i}, \pi_{\mathcal{E},view,i} = VRF(config_{\mathcal{E}} \| view, sk_i), \tag{10.5}$$

where $config_{\mathcal{E}}$ denotes the settings predefined by a third party; $sk_i$ denotes the private key of a validator-$i$; $view$ denotes a view number related to a timeout $\Delta$; $\mathcal{R}_{\mathcal{E},view,i}$ and $\pi_{\mathcal{E},view,i}$ denote the final randomness and its proof with specific epoch $\mathcal{E}$ and view for validator-$i$. By default, the validator with the smallest $\mathcal{R}_{\mathcal{E},view,i}$ is selected to be the leader, and view increases if this round of RandHound is timeout.

In the case of view $>5$ (proven $<1\%$ by [58]), the RandHound is replaced by a coin-tossing scheme inspired by [91] that only implements a typical PVSS [78] in a poor complexity of order $O(m^3)$. On the other hand, this protocol still relies on third-party settings config E predefined in the genesis block to prevent the attackers from biasing the result by secretly rerunning the protocol.

**Insight 10.5** *The combination of RandHound and VRF suffers from the reliance on a third-party initial randomness predefined in the genesis block. A falling-back to an inefficient scheme occurs in the context of asynchronous networks, which limits the salability that RandHound could have guaranteed.*

### 10.3.1.5 BFT-based RapidChain

RapidChain [59] implements a VSS-based [75] distributed random generation (DRG) protocol to agree on an unbiased randomness. On top of the DRG protocol, RapidChain addresses Insight 10.5 by introducing a deterministic random graph where a certain fraction (50% with high probability [59]) of the number of malicious validators can be guaranteed in the initial set (the reference committee, similar to the final committee in Elastico), which will be discussed in Section 10.3.3.4. Inspired by [92], in addition, RapidChain resolves the dilemma of BFT-based consensus algorithm in sharding, by increasing the FT of the intra-consensus protocol up to 50%.

*Consensus algorithm—50% BFT with pipelining*
RapidChain aims for higher FT (50% BFT) of the intra-consensus protocol to address the dilemma of BFT-based 1% attack for sharding mechanisms with a small shard size. To be specific, RapidChain runs an autonomous prescheduled scheme within a shard to agree on a timeout $\Delta$, based on which the consensus speed can be adjusted by the system to prevent the asynchronization. This ensures a synchronous network in the long-term, in which a nonresponsive synchronous (with constant rounds) BFT-based consensus protocol with FT of 50% can be used.

However, re-proposing the pending block by the new leader in the next iteration greatly reduces the throughput by roughly half, while the current leader that is corrupted equivocates the consensus (if based on the original version of [92]). In order to address this issue, the pipelining is used where pending blocks can be re-proposed along with the new block that is considered *safe*; see Figure 10.3, ($H_{i+1}$, $H_{i+2}$) are proposed during iteration $i+2$. Note that, a new proposed block is considered safe so long as it points to a pending block that has been collected $m/2+1$ votes. Also note that a valid vote can be either,

- *temporary vote*: an echo associated with the proposed header, $H_i$ of iteration $i$; or
- *permanent vote*: an accept associated with the proposed header, $H_i$ of iteration $i$ (if and only if there is only one version of header $H_i$ received from the leader, and at least $m/2+1$ echoes of the same $H_i$ received from others, tagging the header as pending otherwise).

As there exist multiple versions of headers associated with a specific iteration, e.g., $[H_{i+1}, H'_{i+1}, H''_{i+1} \ldots]$ of iteration $i+1$, only one version is selected by the leader of iteration $i+2$ to be re-proposed along with $H_{i+2}$. Here, $H_{i+2}$ is considered safe as $H_{i+1}$ has been collected $m/2+1$ echoes serving as a proof in iteration $i+1$. Consequently, ($H_{i+1}$, $H_{i+2}$) are accepted if any nodes have received at least $m/2+1$ echoes associated with both $H_{i+1}$ and $H_{i+2}$.

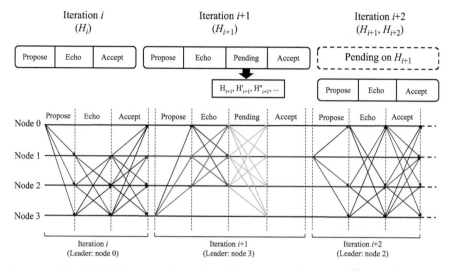

*Figure 10.3* *RapidChain implements a synchronous BFT-based consensus protocol by prescheduling the timeout, based on which the consensus speed can be adjusted by the system, hence achieving FT of 50%. In addition, RapidChain significantly improves the throughput by pipelining the consensus process, i.e., re-proposing the previous pending blocks while agreeing on the current proposed block. The dark red arrows denote that the leader gossips more than one version of $H_{i+1}$, while the yellow arrows denote pending associated with the proposed header of iteration i+1*

Referring to (10.2), the design of 50% BFT achieves a failure probability around 1.5% with $f(k, m, p) = f(17, 32, 0.33)$, and even 1% with $f(51, 100, 0.39)$ at a cost of communication overhead.

**Insight 10.6** *Differing from ByzCoinX in OmniLedger, the 50% BFT of RapidChain solves the BFT-based 1% attack by increasing the FT of intra-consensus protocol, nevertheless, this can only suit small-sized shards (not scalable with communication overhead of $O(n^2)$). In addition, the prescheduled scheme defining the timeout is not conceivably proved synchronous enough to run the pipelining 50% BFT.*

### Generating randomness—VSS-based DRG protocol
The proposed DRG protocol by RapidChain, in fact, only implements a basic VSS-shares scheme, where all participating validators can reconstruct the final randomness $r$ by the share of $r$ (the share equals to $\sum_{l=1}^{m} \rho_{lj}$ calculated by other validators except validator-$j$) received from other validators. Note that $\rho \in F_p$ denoting a finite field of prime order $p$, and $m$ denotes the size of the reference committee. As a result, the DRG protocol encounters a similar issue to that of any

other typical VSS scheme, i.e., non-scalable (even though it suits with the 50% BFT in small-sized shards).

### 10.3.1.6    BFT-based Ethereum 2.0

Ethereum has been running publicly as the first decentralized blockchain platform (blockchain 2.0 [93,94]) that implements a Turing-complete programming language to develop smart contracts for the first time since 2014 [70]. With the gradually rising demands of high throughput, Casper-FFG with sharding (Shasper) is proposed [61] to allow the current Ethereum mainnet (a PoW-based single chain, also referred to Ethereum 1.0) to migrate to the new architecture stably and securely. Note that we mainly focus on Shasper that has been running on testnet at the time of writing (referred to Ethereum 2.0), rather than the still-up-in-the-air Casper-CBC [95], based on which Ethereum plans to end up implementing a PoW-free proof-of-stake (PoS)-based sharded structure. Note that only the intra-consensus protocol and cross-shard transactions of Shasper (referring to Phases 0 and 1, and Phase 4 in [96]) are discussed in this chapter, because the other sub-protocols have not yet been finalized based on the description in [61].

*Consensus algorithm—solving the intra-consensus in a global way*

Shasper also chooses to use the second method (presented in Section 10.3.1), a BFT-based consensus algorithm, to solve the 1% attack issue of intra-consensus. Concretely, the Casper-FFG of Shasper can be regarded as a variation of BFT-based PoS consensus algorithms [82,97] with careful designs for generating randomness, as opposed to the virtual-mining PoS consensus algorithms [98–100]. Note that we assume a scalable BFT algorithm similar to ByzCoin [69] and ByzCoinX of OmniLedger is used in Shasper.

Shasper decouples the member allocation and consensus process, which leads to the fact that the intra-consensus within a shard also involves those validators from other shards being the attesters. The members of attesters group associated with a specific shard can be updated every slot. This also implies that an eligible validator in Shasper should at least store all block headers (headers is called collations in Shasper) of all shards regardless of which shard this validator is allocated at the beginning of every epoch. The procedures are summarized as follows:

1. To become a validator, a node needs to deposit a certain amount of ETH (currently it is set to 32ETH [101,102]) in an official smart contract[¶] on the original PoW-based mainnet. Having known the deposit, the system registers this node as a valid validator on a new individual chain, i.e., the beacon chain, while the beacon chain takes the role of a coordination device of the whole Shasper protocol in regards to managing the global validator pool, randomness generation, incentive, and message exchange.

2. An infrequent shuffling for the global validator pool is executed to reallocate all validators to different shards based on the generated randomness. Such an epoch is currently set to 6.4 min [62,101]. During each epoch, a proposer is

---

[¶]https://github.com/ethereum/eth2.0-specs/blob/dev/specs/core/0 deposit-contract.md

elected on the basis of the randomness from the local validator pool in each shard every 8-s slot [101]. A proposed collation containing transactions of each shard is broadcasted to all attesters assigned to the same shard, followed by a finalized collation being stored in the local ledger if the consensus process succeeds.

3. In addition to the hash value of each block on the PoW-based mainnet required to be stored on the beacon chain, a checkpoint is finalized by 400 validators randomly selected from the global validator pool for each shard every 100 colations [103]. After that these selected validators aggregate all checkpoints and upload them to the beacon chain. By storing the checkpoints as well as the collation headers of all shards, the beacon chain is able to obtain the local state and a group of finalized transactions (and its corresponding receipts) of each shard, referring to the State root and Txgroup root fields in the beacon chain headers, respectively. As a result, the deterministic finality can be achieved rather than a probabilistic one that Ethereum 1.0 used to rely on.

It is worth noting that the members (attesters) participating in the intra-consensus of a shard are, in fact, not limited to the indigenous validators (who have been allocated in a shard at the beginning of the epoch and randomly selected by the generated randomness from the global pool). The group of attesters can be reallocated for each proposed collation in a times slot, which provides the strongest security but incurs huge overhead when, (1) each shard conducts the consensus among continuously updated validators; (2) validators need to store data of more shards; and (3) the 1-slot-period reallocation has to be executed.

**Insight 10.7** *The security level of Ethereum 2.0—Shasper provides more flexible allocation for intra-consensus than that of any other considered sharding mechanisms, nevertheless, by incurring larger overhead.*

*Generating randomness—combination of RANDAO and VDF*
RANDAO [104] is implemented on the basis of the commit-and-then-reveal scheme [73] written in a predefined smart contract running on the beacon chain. To be specific, there are three functions defined in the smart contract, each of which must run in order; see Figure 10.4.

They are described as follows:

1. Commit(): all participating validators select a seed $\lambda$ in secret (e.g., the hash of the parent block), after they have been deposited $32ETH$ in the smart contract. Then each of the validators runs a verifiable delay function (VDF) [105] as a "hash onion" [103,106],

$$VDF(\lambda_I) = Hash(Hash(\ldots Hash(\lambda_i))),$$ (10.6)

where the VDF conducts sufficient times of $Hash()$, e.g., 10,000 times shown in [103] for a sufficiently long period (102 min [101]). As such, some malicious manipulation can be significantly prevented, e.g., deciding not to reveal

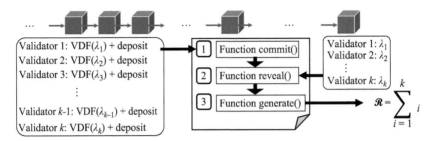

*Figure 10.4    Ethereum 2.0 implements RANDAO and verifiable delay function to generate randomness*

its commitment if $\sum_{i}^{k-1} \lambda_i$ is found biased to $k$th validator. The unbiased randomness is guaranteed by the VDF where only the serial computing can be run regardless of the computation power that is owned by this validator. Also note that each validator can only commit once.

2.  *Reveal()*: validators reveal their own seed $\lambda$ to the smart contract; thus, the contract can verify if the seed matches up with their corresponding commitment by verifying the 10,000 preimages,

$$Hash^{-1}\left(Hash^{-1}\left(\ldots Hash^{-1}\left(VDF\left(\lambda_i\right)\right)\right)\right). \tag{10.7}$$

3.  *Generate()*: the smart contract generates a randomness by adding up all $\lambda_i$. Punishment is applied to those who fail to reveal their own $\lambda$ in time (corresponding to the time overhead of the defined VDF).

However, this design still suffers from three flaws, as shown in the following:

•   A VDF consisting of $n$ times $Hash(\cdot)$ incurs a computation overhead of $O(n)$, which is inefficient. There have been a few advanced VDF schemes proposed by the recent researches [107–109].
•   This design is prone to the censorship attack [110]. Malicious validators can send irrelevant transactions with a high gas fee to fill up a block. Thus, the commit may have to be interrupted as the gas limit of the block is run out.
•   This design is also prone to the grinding attack [111] if the seed $\lambda$ is based on the hash of the parent block, because validators can send arbitrary transactions and try to find out the most biased seed by collecting different sets of transactions.

**Insight 10.8** *Current design of randomness generator in Ethereum 2.0 incurs high computation overhead and is overwhelmingly dependent on the incentive scheme (punishment). It is prone to censorship attack and grinding attack, if the attack cost is acceptable.*

## 10.3.2 Atomicity of cross-shard

It is of importance that a sharding mechanism can support the cross-shard-verification and cross-shard transactions for validators allocated in different shards, according to the result shown in [58,59] (showing that the probability of cross-shard transactions approaches to 100% as the total number of shards increases). Maintaining an individual global root chain may be one of the solutions to verification, but it does not natively support cross-shard transactions without any additional mechanism, e.g., lock/unlock operation in synchronous networks or lock-free operation in asynchronous networks. The demand for a secure protocol of cross-shard transactions gradually outweighs a naive mechanism lacking the support of cross-shard transactions (even it can achieve a high improving factor $N$).

Differing from the traditional database system, the support of cross-shard transactions proposes a challenge to guarantee the *atomicity* of the data that was first defined in [66,67] across multiple shards. Not only a simple payment transaction involving withdraw and deposit operations needs to be atomically protected, but also the demand for the complicated conditional statements attracts more attention to the contract-oriented *atomicity*.

In this section, we compare and discuss the protocols to achieve *cross-shard-atomicity* in the considered sharding mechanisms. We focus on the design of cross-shard transaction, including Monoxide that supports asynchronous lock-free simple payment transactions; OmniLedger, RapidChain, and Ethereum 2.0 that supports simple payment transactions with lock/unlock scheme; and Chainspace that supports cross-shard operations for smart contracts (Elastico is vaguely discussed as it does not support atomic-safe cross-shard transactions).

### 10.3.2.1 Monoxide—relay transactions

In order to bypass the overhead of lock/unlock operation that greatly constrains the throughput and performance in regards to cross-shard transactions, Monoxide proposes *Eventual Atomicity* where a single cross-shard transaction is decoupled into an originated transaction in the local shard, and a relay transaction being put into the outbound transactions set (and hence becoming an inbound transaction when it is received by the destination shard). Rather than the immediate atomicity, *Eventual Atomicity* features its lock-free design and takes advantage of Chu-ko-nu mining across parallel shards in an asynchronous network, in order to maximize the global throughput via simple message exchange.

Concretely, the miners of shard $a$, i.e., an originate shard for a cross-shard transaction $t$, generate a relay transaction $t_r$ in its local outbound transaction set if the withdraw operation passes the verification. Here, the withdraw operation is verified in the form of a local transaction $t_l$, decoupled from $t$, and stored in the local ledger. On the other hand, there are two additional MPT roots regarding (1) the outbound transaction set; (2) the inbound transactions and local non-cross-shard transactions (denoted as $MPT_O$ and $MPT_I$, respectively, and stored in the batch-chaining block defined in Chu-ko-nu mining). By means of $MPT_O$ and $MPT_I$, the miners of shard $b$, i.e., the destination shard for $t$, are able to verify $t_r$ via the attached proof,

$$[ShardID, ShardSize, BlockHeight, i, t_r, \pi_{t_r}] \tag{10.8}$$

where $i$ denotes the index of $t_r$ in the outbound transaction set generated by shard $a$; BlockHeight denotes the height of block $B$ that is stored $t_l$; $\pi_{t_r}$ denotes the MPT proof of $t_r$ in the given MPT with a root of $MPT_O$ stored in the header of $B$. Thus, it can be consequently observed that a cross-shard transaction in Monoxide achieves an improving factor of $N = n/2$ as it is split into the locally executed transactions and relay transactions expected to be outbound.

However, differing from the cross-shard transactions that can be proactively rejected by an acknowledgment from an entity (this is in charge by clients in OmniLedger, as discussed later), the chain forking in Monoxide can cause a reversion of the history and orphan the block containing the $t_l$ that has been executed within a shard. Without any existing of acknowledgment reminding the originated shard the status of $t_r$ in the destination shard, the forking not only invalidates $t_r$ in the destination shard (if $t_r$ has been sent out before the forking occurs) but also invalidates all the subsequent cross-shard transactions relayed to any other shards. This implies the following drawbacks.

*Incompatibility to smart contracts.* There does not exist an upper bound of timeout indicating if Eventual Atomicity of a cross-shard transaction has been finalized, leading to the incompatibility of conditional transactions, e.g., complicated operations in smart contracts.

*Additional latency.* There must be $\lambda$ confirmation blocks delaying the execution of the inbound transaction, i.e., $t_r$, in order to ensure that the corresponding $t_l$ in the originated shard is finalized and unlikely reverted. Also, the absence of acknowledgment and strict upper bound of timeout deteriorates the latency and throughput due to the inevitable message loss, which incurs additional latency.

*Unexpected replay.* To invalidate the inbound transactions $t_r$ and all the subsequent $t_r$s due to the failure and reversion of $t_l$ in the originated shard and prevent the history of all destination shards from being reverted, the history needs to be rebuilt from the genesis block of each shard. This incurs unexpected overhead even if a checkpoint scheme is introduced, e.g., the shard pruning in OmniLedger [58].

**Insight 10.9** *In order to maximize the global throughput, Eventual Atomicity achieves the lock-free asynchronous cross-shard transactions at the cost of incurring Incompatibility to smart contracts, additional latency, and unexpected replay.*

### 10.3.2.2    Elastico—no cross-shard transactions

The elected leader of the traditional PBFT consensus algorithm in each shard finalizes and sends an agreement in regards to local transactions to a global subset, i.e., the final committee, as discussed in Section 10.3.1.2. A final global block is stored in the global ledger and broadcasted to all validators among the network, so that validators can verify the transactions from other shards. However, Elastico does not provide a secure protocol to ensure the atomicity across shards via this global ledger. There will be a fund loss as an unexpected dead-lock occurs if the cross-shard transaction sent to the destination shard gets rejected.

### 10.3.2.3   OmniLedger—Atomix Protocol

To simplify the *cross-shard-atomicity*, OmniLedger proposes a client-driven Atomix Protocol that is UTXO-based, where the communication overhead is shifted outside the shards. This indicates that the clients act as a gateway exchanging messages across multiple shards, by paying an extra cost of overhead.

Concretely, it consists of the following procedures:

1. *Initialize.* A UTXO-based cross-shard-transaction is created and gossiped to all input shards (ISs) by a client, where the inputs of this transaction spend UTXOs in some ISs, while outputs create new UTXOs in some output shards (OSs).
2. *Lock.* The cross-shard-transaction received from the client is stored in the local ledger within the shard after the verification is conducted. Meanwhile, either a *proof-of-acceptance* or a *proof-of-rejection* is created by the shard leaders attached with the corresponding CoSi, in the case that success or failure is returned by the verification, respectively. Therein, a *proof-of-acceptance* contains an MPT proof and the transaction itself.
3. *Unlock.*

(i) *Unlock to commit.* The client issues an *unlock to commit* consisting of the locked cross-shard transaction and the attached *proof-of-acceptance* and gossips it to OSs, as soon as it receives *proof-of-acceptance* from all ISs. After the success of verification, OSs store the cross-shard transaction in the local ledger.

(ii) *Unlock to abort.* The client issues an *unlock to abort* to those ISs issuing a *proof-of-acceptance* to unlock the state, once it receives a *proof-of-rejection* from one IS.

Consequently, a cross-shard transaction containing inputs from one single IS and OS can achieve an improving factor of $N = n/2$, as this transaction is only stored in two shards, i.e., this IS and OS. On the other hand, inputs and outputs of multiple ISs and OSs result in the transaction being stored among the involved shards, i.e., an improving factor of $N = 1$ in the worst case that the entire network is involved.

**Insight 10.10** *Atomix Protocol is, in fact, a band-aid at best. It sacrifices the support of light-weighted clients but requires powerful performance for a client-driven exchange of messages.*

**Insight 10.11** *Atomix Protocol has poorer support for UTXO-based cross-shard transactions as the number of participating shards increases, which is unable to take full advantage of the UTXO format.*

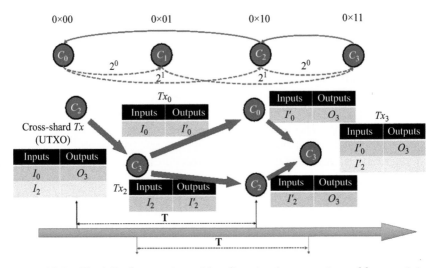

*Figure 10.5*    *(Top) Each committee (shard) maintains a routing table containing*
*$\log_2 n$ other committees. The routing table improves the efficient*
*communication among multiple shards, as described in*
*Section 10.3.3.2. Committee $C_0$ can locate $C_3$ (via $C_2$) responsible*
*for transactions with prefix $0\times11$. (Bottom) To cross-validate a*
*UTXO-based cross-shard transaction, it requires this transaction to*
*be spilt in three-way confirmation*

### 10.3.2.4    RapidChain—three-way confirmation

To verify a UTXO-based cross-shard transaction, there proposes a three-way confirmation in RapidChain to optimize the Atomix Protocol in OmniLedger, as shown
in the bottom part of Figure 10.5. Concretely, $k-1$ sub-transactions ($Tx_0$ and $Tx_2$)
destined for each committee that stores its own $I_i$ of the cross-shard transaction,
with $I_i$ as the inputs and $I'_i$ as the outputs, respectively, and $k$ is the number of inputs
of this cross-shard transaction, are created by the output committee, i.e., $C_3$ as the
$C_{out}$. After passing the verification on each input committees, i.e., $C_2$ and $C_0$ as the
two $C_{in}(s)$ of the original cross-shard transaction, $Tx_0$ and $Tx_2$ are stored in their
own local ledger, respectively. Finally, all $C_{in}(s)$ send the corresponding transactions back to $C_3$ and end up aggregating $Tx_3$ to be finally stored in the local ledger
of $C_3$.

In order to determine the improving factor $N$, we assume that a single committee can only be either a sender committee or a receiver committee (practically a
shard can be both a sender and a receiver) at the same time for simplicity. In the
worst case where a full-sized cross-shard transaction contains only the input from a
single committee, $C_{in}$ has to send this full-sized transaction twice (each corresponds
to invoking the intercommunication once), i.e., first and third handshaking. On the
other hand, the period from $C_{in}$ sending $C_{out}$ the cross-shard transaction to it finishing verifying the sub-transactions received equals to the period from $C_{out}$

finishing verifying the original cross-shard transaction to it finishing verifying the confirmations sent by $C_{in}$, i.e., one block period. It is because the original cross-shard transaction is spilt into

- the sub-transactions that are supposed to be stored in the local ledger of each $C_{in}$ (a full-sized of the original cross-shard transaction with inputs from a single committee or inputs involving all committees);
- the final transaction that is supposed to be stored in the local ledger of $C_{out}$ (another full-sized of the original cross-shard transaction) at the end of the protocol.

Consequently, either of these two kinds of transactions account for the intra-throughput of a committee, hence one block period, as shown by the **T** at the bottom of Figure 10.5. Therefore, an improving factor of $N = n/2$ can be achieved.

**Insight 10.12** *The routing table and three-way confirmation resolve the issue of OmniLedger, by significantly reducing the overhead of communication, even with a large number of participating shards in a single UTXO-based cross-shard transaction. However, by polluting specific routing tables, the eclipse attack* [112] *becomes a concern.*

### 10.3.2.5 Ethereum 2.0—using receipts

Having known the beacon chain, validators can not only address the issue of intra-consensus but also address the issue of *cross-shard-atomicity*, i.e., cross-verifying the normal transactions in each shard the validators care about, and enabling the cross-shard transactions. Note that Shasper so far can only support a simple account-based (as opposed to the UTXO-based) payment transaction, while the design contract-oriented cross-shard transaction has not been finalized and presented.

The cross-shard transactions in Shasper rely on the receipts. Receipts correspond to accepted cross-shard transactions that are used to verify and log the validity of the transactions' operations. Also, the result of these operations can be obtained by the involved validators conducting cross-validation in the destination shards. By means of receipts whose identities are contained in *Txgroup root* field (receipt root), the cross-shard transactions are split into multiple sub-transactions being executed in the originated and destination shards, respectively. This can be regarded as a variation of the synchronous lock/unlock scheme implemented in OmniLedger and RapidChain, while the receipts take the actual role of the lock.

Concretely, a proposed cross-shard transaction, $t$, is split into a group of $t_1$, $t_2$, and $t_3$.

1. The preliminary withdraw operation is executed and stored after $t_1$ is verified in the originated shard (input shard, namely, IS). A receipt corresponding to $t_1$, denoted as $r_1$, is included in *Txgroup root* of the latest collation being proposed by the chosen proposer.

2.  Having waited for a period that $t_1$ has been deterministically finalized by the checkpoints (this period can be shortened to meet different requirements, which is similar to the trust-but-verify transaction validation scheme proposed in OmniLedger; see the first point of Section 10.3.3 and Insight 10.14), a proof-of-receipt is sent to the destination shard (output shard, namely, OS) as the second sub-transaction, i.e., $t_2$.

3.  The OS can mark the $r_1$ as spent, as validators of the OS are able to verify the status of $r_1$ by the corresponding Txgroup root that is stored in the beacon chain, and the received *proof-of-receipt*. Meanwhile, the deposit operation is executed.

4.  The OS sends a proof-of-response as $t_3$ to the original IS, indicating that the whole process of $t$ has been finalized. Validators of the IS can finally confirm this fact by verifying the corresponding receipt of *proof-of-receipt* on the beacon chain.

Consequently, a cross-shard transaction that is account-based in Ethereum 2.0 Shasper can achieve an improving factor of $N = n/3$ due to the preliminary transaction, *proof-of-receipt*, and *proof-of-response*.

**Insight 10.13** *Ethereum 2.0—Shasper introduces account-based cross-shard transactions by implementing the global (stored by all validators) beacon chain to exchange the essential message, i.e., the receipts and proofs. However, Shasper cannot be more than a transitional version due to the disadvantage of possible overhead.*

### 10.3.2.6    Chainspace—the inter-part of S-BAC

S-**BAC** refers to Sharded Byzantine Atomic Commit, whose intra-part makes the use of an optimal PBFT, MOD-SMART, to handle the intra-consensus process; see Section 10.3.1.3. Upon the intra-consensus being finalized within a shard (Chainspace allocates nodes in different shards based on the objects management, as described in Section 10.3.3.6), the elected leader of the shard, the BFT-Initiator, takes responsibility for the atomicity of cross-shard transactions. It is worth noting that Chainspace makes the use of the concept of BFT to ensure such atomicity, which constitutes the inter-part of S-**BAC**.

Concretely, it resembles the Atomix Protocol in OmniLedger, with a crucial optimization where BFT consensus process must be conducted instead of a naive client-driven model. It consists of the following procedures:

1.  *Initialize and intra-consensus.* An object-based cross-shard-transaction $T$ is created by a client and gossip to all shards that manage the input objects, upon which the intra-consensus is conducted in each of these shards with an accept or commit broadcast to other concerned shards. Objects are set to *active* by the matching shards if ending up a commitment of $T$.

2.  *Lock.* All involved objects in $T$ are locked whenever a *commit* is received.

3.  *Unlock.*

(i) *Unlock to commit.* The lock of each involved object in $T$ is released if and only if *commit* is received from all concerned shards, upon which the objects are set to *inactive* and the output objects are created via BFT consensus process in a certain shard.

(ii) *Unlock to abort.* The same locks are released whenever an *abort* is received, upon which the objects are set back to *active* and may be used by other subsequent transactions.

Similar to the problem, the Atomix Protocol of OmniLedger has encountered, i.e., Insight 10.11, the improving factor upon a cross-shard transaction can be ranged from $N = n$ to $N = 1$ with $T$ containing only one input object and no object being output, and $T$ involving all objects around the entire network, respectively.

## 10.3.3  General improvements

In this section, some general key challenges and improvements particularly proposed by the considered sharding mechanisms are listed. Such improvements can be generally implemented to address the new issues the considered sharding solutions pose to the entire system. They include transaction latency, inter-communication protocol, shards ledger pruning, decentralized bootstrapping, securing the epoch reconfiguration, and sharded smart contract.

### 10.3.3.1  Reducing transaction latency

Apart from the throughput, the transaction latency, referring to how long a transaction is deterministically confirmed and finalized, is most likely more sensitive to individual users. It has been shown that the BFT-based 1% attack (refers to Section 10.3.1) can be either resolved by implementing a scalable BFT consensus, e.g., OmniLedger and Ethereum 2.0, or increasing the FT within a single shard, e.g., RapidChain. However, it remains the issue of transaction latency, as described next.

- *The transaction latency deteriorates as a scalable BFT consensus features a large-scale shard size to address the 1% attack,* according to the evaluation shown in [58,69]. Thus, OmniLedger introduces the *trust-but-verify transaction validation* scheme running within each shard to provide the real-time transaction confirmation time, which can also be implemented in any compatible sharding scheme, such as Ethereum 2.0. Concretely, validators of a shard are split into an optimistic group and a core group. The optimistic group is further split into multiple small subgroups (even a subgroup with only one validator is allowed); hence, each subgroup can verify the transactions in a real-time manner. Subsequently, the core group conducts the second verification, where the inconsistent and malicious transactions can be censored. Note that there can be multiple inputs from multiple optimistic subgroups to this second verification in a concurrent manner. Finally, the transactions passing the second verification can be contained in the proposed block and stored in the local ledger.

**Insight 10.14** *The real-time transaction latency is achieved by sacrificing the security, as the further 1% attack can still happen in optimistic groups. Similar to IoTA [25], this real-time transaction latency can only be used in specific scenarios with lower security requirements.*

- *The transaction latency deteriorates as a non-scalable 50% BFT consensus incurs larger communication overhead.* Thus, upon the 50% consensus only agreeing on a digest of the block. RapidChain implements the *information dispersal algorithm* based gossip protocol [113,114] to transmit large payload more efficiently. Concretely, the sender divides the original message into some $n$-equal-sized chunks, followed by applying an $(m, n)$ erasure code scheme to encode the $n$ chunks to $m$ chunks. As a result, each node can reconstruct the original message by receiving valid $n$ chunks from its neighbors with the help of some proofs, e.g., the MPT proofs, hence significantly reduces the latency.

### 10.3.3.2    Intercommunication protocol

Differing from the protocol to achieve the *atomicity-cross-shard*, the inter-communication protocol focuses on the overhead of data transmission among shards. The related schemes discussed in this survey include the following two major types:

- A global root chain acting as a message distributor is implemented, while each validator (or miner in the context of Monoxide) needs to store this chain. Sharding mechanisms using this kind include Ethereum 2.0, Monoxide with identical PoW targets, and Elastico.$^{\parallel}$

**Insight 10.15** *The bottleneck is shifted to the global root chain due to its single-chained structure, as opposed to sharded structure. This can only be a transitional version but not a real solution.*

- The most straightforward way is used by OmniLedger and Chainspace, i.e., full-mesh connection. This requirement tends to hold in those latency-sensitive systems, which incurs a considerable overhead.

In order to bypass the full-mesh connection, RapidChain proposes a novel inter-communication protocol based on a routing table stored by each validator; see the top side of Figure 10.5. It is inspired by Kademlia-based [115] routing protocol, where each validator in a shard maintains a routing table containing all members of its shard as well as $\log_2\log_2 n$ validators of $\log_2 n$ shards which are distance $2^i$ for $0 \le i \le \log_2 n - 1$ away. The intercommunication is conducted by having all validators in the sender shard send messages to all validators on the receiver side. By taking advantage of P2P network, the communication overhead can be significantly reduced.

---

$^{\parallel}$Elastico maintains a final committee where the finalized block is proposed and stored in the global root chain, based on the agreement from each shard. The global chains implemented by OmniLedger and RapidChain, i.e., the identity Blockchain and reference Blockchain, respectively, do not account for this kind as the messages exchanged by these two chains are not related to the actual transactions.

### 10.3.3.3  Shards ledger pruning

The reason most of the existing blockchain system with a single-chained structure [1,70,116–118] tends to store the full version of its chain is that they intend to improve the communication and computation overhead of censorship and audition. Storing a full version of ledger of every shard incurs an unacceptable overhead of disk storage to validators, referring to the calculation in Section 10.4, as validators need to track the history of each shard in order to support the cross-shard transactions, as well as the reallocation (bootstrapping) during each epoch. To solve this, OmniLedger proposes the design of state blocks (SB).

SBs of a shard summarize the state as well as all transactions of its shard associated with each epoch. At the end of each epoch $\mathcal{E}_k$, the selected leader of a shard $i$ constructs an MPT consisting of all the transactions, while the corresponding MPT root is stored in the header of $SB_{i,k}$. As such, the body of $SB_{i,k-1}$ can be pruned if $SB_{i,k}$ passes the verification by other validations in shard $i$ to become the new genesis block of $\mathcal{E}_{k+1}$. The regular blocks are also pruned as soon as $SB_{i,k+1}$ is generated at the end of $\mathcal{E}_{k+1}$, during which it is the clients' responsibility to create and store the transaction proofs to prove the existence of a past transaction to other shards for cross-shard transactions.

The design of SBs is similar to stable checkpoints in PBFT [5], fast-sync mode in Ethereum [116], and stable checkpoints of Node Hash-Chains in Chainspace [60]. According to the evaluation in [60], such kind of pruning incurs an overhead of $O(m + \log T)$ for a partial audit and $O(T)$ for a *full audit*, where $m$ denotes the shard size, and $T$ denotes the number of transactions. The *partial audit* allows any users to obtain a proof to verify the existence of any transactions in any shards; the *full audit* allows a full verification by replaying the entire history of a shard. However, the design of SB raises two issues, (1) the overhead of transaction proofs might become the bottleneck, but it can still be relieved by introducing the Simple Payment Verification [1,116], several multi-hop backpointers [119–121], or proofs of proof-of-work [122,123]; and (2) Insight 10.16.

**Insight 10.16** *The design of State blocks faces the same problem as that of the Atomix Protocol in OmniLedger and light-client protocol in Ethereum 1.0 (if used in Ethereum 2.0), i.e., shirking the most important duty to the client side.*

### 10.3.3.4  Decentralized bootstrapping

For sharding mechanisms involving a randomness generator that is responsible for a PoW-based entry ticket in the BFT-based intra-consensus protocol, it is important to select the initial set with an honest majority, e.g., the final committee in Elastico, and the reference committee in RapidChain.**

---

** OmniLedger eliminates the necessity of an initial global set that is responsible for verifying the PoW result, by using RandHound and VRF. However, an initial global randomness is still needed to derive VRF. Ethereum 2.0 builds the design on top of PoW-based mainnet, where the PoS-based Casper is used instead of PoW.

Thus, RapidChain proposes a decentralized bootstrapping in the form of *sampler-graph election network* [59], with only a hard-coded seed and some network settings. In such an election network, participating validators are uniformly distributed into a few groups, within each of which a PoW-based result is computed by each member based on the randomness generated by the VSS-based DRG protocol (Section 10.3.1.5) and its identification ID. Based on the result, a subgroup can be obtained for each group. Finally, a unique *root group* (it randomly selects the members of the reference committee) can be obtained with 50% honest majority (high probability), when this process is iterated. Consequently, the communication overhead can be improved from $\Omega(n^2)$ to $O(n\sqrt{n})$ with $n$ denoting the total number of participating validators.

## 10.3.3.5  Securing the epoch reconfiguration

For sharding mechanisms running a BFT-based intra-consensus protocol, (new) validators have to be swapped-out and reallocated in other shards every epoch in order to prevent attacks from slowly adaptive adversaries, i.e., attacker can corrupt or distributed denial-of-service (DDoS)-attack validators, but it takes a bounded time for such attacks to take effect. This indicates that the epoch length should be carefully designed to be lower than the bounded time.

Recall that Elastico and Chainspace do not provide such a solution, while Ethereum 2.0 solves the intra-consensus with a global validator pool by frequently updating the member participating in the intra-consensus protocol for each shard. Both of them require validators to track the status of each shard to speed up the reconfiguration phase. OmniLedger implements a random permutation scheme to swap-out the validators, ensuring that the number of validators being swapped is bounded by $k = \log n/m$ at a given time, where $n$ denotes the total number of participating validators; $m$ denotes the number of shards. Here, new validators that require registering their ID on a global identity blockchain are also assigned to random shards. As such, the number of remaining honest validators can be sufficient to reach consensus, while some are swapped-out; thus, the idle phase can last shorter to improve the throughput. However, this scheme incurs a significant delay and scales moderately, which causes 1-day-long epoch that does not suit highly adaptive adversaries (when the bounded time becomes smaller).

In contrast, RapidChain proposes a light-weighted reconfiguration protocol based on the Cuckoo rule [124,125], where only a constant number of validators are allowed to move between committees in each epoch. To be specific, the reference committee ($C_r$) announces a PoW puzzle based on the randomness generated in epoch $i-1$ ($\mathcal{R}_i$) by the DRG protocol, thus validators that wish to participate in epoch $i+1$ (including those that have participated in epoch $i-1$ and epoch $i$) can solve the puzzle and inform $C_r$ by the end of epoch $i$. During epoch $i+1$, $C_r$ defines the active and inactive lists of validators of epoch $i+1$ and swaps-out a constant number of validators from one to another committee based on $\mathcal{R}_{i+1}$ generated in epoch $i$. Finally, $C_r$ agrees on a reference block stored in the local ledger of $C_r$ and broadcasts it to the entire network. This design, compared to that of OmniLedger, incurs less overhead and allows a more frequent epoch reconfiguration to suit more highly adaptive adversaries.

### 10.3.3.6 Sharded smart contract

None of the considered sharding mechanism has achieved the smart-contract-oriented sharded so far except Chainspace that introduces such functionality for the first time. Concretely, Chainspace, inspired by the UTXO model, proposes a new transaction structure based on new atoms *Objects* denoted as *o*. Here, *o* records state in the system with two kinds of unique identifier, i.e., id(*o*) (a cryptographically id that cannot be forged within a polynomial time) and types(*o*) (a pointer to a smart contract *c* that defines types(*o*)). Meanwhile, a contract *c*, referred to a special types of *o*, defines a namespace consisting of types(*c*) (the set of types that the specific *c* has defined) and a checker *v* denoted as *v*(*input*)→{*True, False*}, as shown in (10.10). Such *v* is used to verify procedures proc(*c*), denoted as *p*(*input*)→*output* (defining the operation logic, as shown in (10.9)), by means of a pure function returning a Boolean value.

$$c \cdot p(\textbf{\textit{x}},\textbf{\textit{r}},\textit{parameters}) \rightarrow \textbf{\textit{y}}, returns; \tag{10.9}$$

$$c \cdot v(p,\textbf{\textit{x}},\textbf{\textit{r}},\textit{parameters},\textbf{\textit{y}}, returns, dependencies) \rightarrow \{True, False\}; \tag{10.10}$$

$$[c,p,\textbf{\textit{x}},\textbf{\textit{r}},\textbf{\textit{y}},\textit{parameters}, returns, dependencies] \in Trace \in Tx. \tag{10.11}$$

Note that **x** denotes the input objects that must be active beforehand and be set to inactive when the corresponding new output objects **y** set to active. **r** denotes the reference objects that must also be active, nevertheless, the status of **r** remains unchanged afterward. The *dependencies*, in the form of a list of *Traces* from other contracts other than *c*, is along with all the other items (as shown in (10.11)) so that a single Trace can be obtained to constitute a transaction (*Tx*).

The method to allocate nodes in different shards in Chainspace is by placing the nodes that manage, record, and verify the same set of *o* to a single shard, denoted as $\varphi(o)$. Further, $\Phi(T)$ is defined to denote the concerned nodes of a transaction *T*, where concerned nodes represent the set of nodes managing all **x** or **r** of *T*. To verify a transaction *T*, all $\varphi(o)$ with *o* being involved in *T* as input or reference should ensure the active status. Meanwhile, all $\Phi(T)$ (excluding the *dependencies*) should run the checker *v* of the corresponding contract *c* to validate the *Traces*. As such, a cross-shard consensus algorithm that guarantees the atomicity of smart contracts, i.e., S-**BAC**, is proposed (as discussed in Section 10.3.2.6).

**Insight 10.17** *By modifying the transaction structure and involving the concept of the new atoms and objects, it can safely fragment a smart contract with strong atomicity, but at the cost of considerable overhead and hence low throughput.*

### 10.3.3.7    Replay attacks and defenses against BFT-based cross-shard protocols

As raised by [126] for the first time, the replay attacks and defenses against BFT-based cross-shard protocols have attracted increasing attention (i.e., Monoxide is Nakamoto-based and has a lock-free cross-shard protocol, thus immune to this kind of replay attacks). By utilizing the property of unanimous voting, the replay attacks strategy has the ability to compromise the *cross-shard atomicity* and launch the double-spending attack with a low cost. Specifically, each shard participated in a cross-shard transaction needs to transmit its own decision (i.e., accepting/aborting the transaction) to the other participants, in order to lock/unlock the internal objects and thus guaranteeing the *cross-shard atomicity*. However, an effective replay attack can be easily launched by conducting the following strategy. Here, we consider an attacker and an honest client who is about to sending a cross-shard transaction $T(x_1, x_2) \rightarrow (y_1, y_2, y_3)$ where $x_i$ represents the input objects managed by shard-$i$, and $y_i$ represents the output objects managed by shard-$i$.

1. *Eliciting and invalidating the decision-message sent from shard-1*: The attacker races the client by sending a $T'(x_2, \ldots)$ to shard-2 so that the involved objects will be locked in shard-2.[††] The attacker quickly follows up by submitting $T$ to shard-1 and shard-2. As soon as $T$ reached shard-1, an *accept(T)* is sent out and can be prerecorded by the attacker. In contrast, $T$ will be invalidated in shard-2. An *abort(T)* will be sent out and prerecorded by the attacker due to the locked objects of shard-2.

2. *Compromising the consistency*: At any time, shard-1 is about to sending the decisions, the attacker can race shard-1 by broadcasting and replaying the prerecorded message that always opposes to shard-1. As a result, the input objects of shard-1 is still active, while new output objects have been created in shard-2 and shard-3, i.e., the consistency of the system is compromised. Authors in [126] also point out the reasons making the replay attacks possible. First (①), there lacks a way for the ISs to know the correspondence between a protocol message received (i.e., *accept(T)* or *abort(T)*) and a specific transaction $T$. Second (②), there also lacks a way for the OSs to know the context of a specific transaction as they are, in fact, excluded from the intermediate processing.

To address the limitations, a modified version of Chainspace, Byzcuit [126], is proposed along with two new features. In regards to ①, a sequence number scheme is applied to each transaction to ensure the correspondence, while a dummy object of each OS is added to the input field of a transaction (i.e., forcing the OSs to participate in the intermediate processing) in order to address ②.

**Insight 10.18** *The proposed replay attacks and defenses against BFT-based cross-shard protocols that are significant and worth more attraction. However, the*

---

[††]The destination of $T$ or $T'$ is replaced by a self-driven client in OmniLedger as such a client is considered to be the handler to achieve the *cross-shard atomicity*.

*sequence number scheme still has a synchronization issue, and the dummy object remains poor at the scalability, both of which strive for optimization.*

## 10.4 Discussions

We have elaborated on the designs and protocols of each considered sharding mechanisms, i.e., Monoxide, Elastico, OmniLedger, RapidChain, Ethereum 2.0, and Chainspace, in terms of the intra-consensus, cross-shard atomicity, and *general improvements*, based on which a comprehensive comparison is presented in Tables 10.2 and 10.3.

We conclude that RapidChain and Ethereum 2.0 implement optimizations that reduce restrictions of Elastico and OmniLedger, which leads to RapidChain and Ethereum 2.0 being the most advanced BFT-based sharding mechanisms in terms of throughput and cost. On the other hand, Monoxide pushes the upper bound of throughput to Mega level and opens up a new direction of the Nakamoto-based sharding mechanisms. Chainspace has plenty of room for performance improvement for sharded-smart contract.

Furthermore, we point out the challenges remaining unsolved practically, as well as the future trend being discussed.

### 10.4.1 Future trend for reducing the overhead

Three common pitfalls in existing sharding mechanisms prevent the system from being horizontally scaled to the theoretical upper bound due to the communication and storage overhead.

- *An existing global chain that is needed to be stored by all participating miners/ validators.* Such a global chain tends to be responsible for all global operations, such as generating randomness, cross-validating transactions in different shards, reshuffling operation. However, this simply poses the bottleneck threat (not only the performance bottleneck but also the security bottleneck) back to a single global chain, which is the root issue sharding technologies would have tried to solve. Insight 10.15 and other (most recently proposed) sharding mechanisms hit this pitfall, e.g., SSChain [63] and Thinkey [64]. SSChain simply utilizes a two-layer architecture where a global chain is set to deal with all data migration and reshuffling operations. Thinkey also implements a root chain to achieve the cross-shard transactions and reshuffling operations. **Trend 1: restricting the use of a global chain in any operations, and the bottleneck requiring to be solved if used.**
- *Requiring miners/validators to store ledgers from other shards.* This is necessary in some of the existing sharding mechanisms in order to cross-validating transactions and reshuffling operation. However, it leads to miners/ validators incurring high communication and storage overhead in $O(n)$ ($n$ is the number of shards). Insights 10.1, 10.7, 10.9, 10.10, 10.11, and 10.13 hit this pitfall. **Trend 2: Balancing the storage and communication overhead for**

miners/validators in sending cross-shard transactions and reshuffling, so that the order can be lower than $O(n)$. One of the potential solutions might be the fraud proof that enables light nodes to be as secure as full nodes without needing to store the whole ledger [127], yet it has not been mature at the time of writing.

- Allocating participating nodes to shards based on their business requirements in order to bypass the overhead of cross-shard communication. Business-driven members' allocation for shards has been proposed and discussed in some designs, e.g., Ethereum 2.0 [103]$^{\ddagger\ddagger}$ and VAPOR [65],$^{\S\S}$ in order to reduce (1) the frequency that a participating node gets swapped out; and (2) the ratio of non-cross-shard transactions, for the ease of management and lower overhead. However, this results in a very long epoch reconfiguration for participating nodes and unevenly shard size, which ultimately poses a risk of crowed transactions to a single shard as time passes and the size and throughput increases, thus hitting the bottleneck of intra-consensus. **Trend 3: avoiding simple business-driven members' allocation that risks shards suffering from crowed transactions.**

## 10.4.2    *Future trend for strengthening the security and atomicity*

This trend corresponds to the intra-consensus and atomicity of cross-shard transactions, respectively. We point out the potential direction on more secure intra-consensus and more efficient cross-shard transactions, as shown in the following:

*Intra-consensus:*

- **Trend 4: Scaling the unbiased and unpredictable randomness generator in large-scale networks with as few third-party hardcoded settings as possible.** The unbiased and unpredictable randomness plays an important role in BFT-based intra-consensus design. Improving this kind of algorithms can significantly prevent the validators from being under DDoS attacks. Insights 10.3, 10.5, and 10.8 belong to this aspect.

- **Trend 5: Improving the PoW-based intra-consensus, and generalizing it into other types of Nakamoto-based consensus algorithms.** Chu-ko-nu mining of Monoxide takes advantage of PoW to bypass the vortex of randomness, nevertheless, the security of which is dependent on the storage. As such, the future direction can potentially decouple the security and storage and generalize the concept to other Nakamoto-based consensus algorithms, e.g., PoS.

---

$^{\ddagger\ddagger}$A possible design proposed by Ethereum 2.0 is to merge shards that interact more frequently than others.

$^{\S\S}$Another design proposed by VAPOR is to define a shard as a subset of nodes who care about some transactions. Transactions in VAPOR feature the ownership and record the nodes that have ever held the ownership.

- **Trend 6: Balancing the uses of stochastic and biased members' allocation for shards**. All discussed sharding mechanisms (except Chainspace) use a stochastic allocation. A stochastic allocation is helpful to protect the shards from malicious biased allocations. On the other hand, new notions have been proposed to improve the scalability by taking advantage of a biased allocation. For example, [128] proposes a biased allocation to force the number of members an attacker can own within a single shard to be upper bounded, in order to achieve a total FT of 50%. However, a vulnerability of this mechanism has been revealed that attackers can simply save the redundant resources from a specific shard and has more sufficient resources to control more shards. Thus, a balance of this use still strives for a solution.

*Efficient atomicity:*

- **Trend 7: Enabling efficient conditional cross-shard transactions that enable contract-orient operations.** Only Chainspace and the future phase of Ethereum 2.0 claim to support such conditional cross-shard transactions so far, but at the cost of unacceptable overhead and latency, which requires more focus in the future trend.

## 10.5  Conclusions

This chapter as a survey highlights the importance of sharding for the design of *scale-out* blockchains and systematizes the state-of-the-art sharding mechanisms in regards to the intra-consensus security, atomicity of cross-shard transactions, and general challenges and improvements. We also proposed our insights analyzing the features and restrictions, based on which a comprehensive comparison among the considered sharding mechanisms was obtained.

A list of the key observations and conclusions is as follows:

- For the first time, Monoxide proposes a Nakamoto-based sharding mechanism, but at the cost of storing headers of all shards to guarantee the maximum intra-consensus-safety.
- The traditional PBFT used in Elastico and Chainspace does not guarantee the intra-consensus-safety due to its weak scalability, while the BFT-based sharding mechanisms, i.e., OmniLedger, RapidChain, and Ethereum 2.0, improve the intra-consensus-safety in the sense that scaling the traditional PBFT or increasing the FT of the traditional PBFT.
- The randomness generators of all considered sharding mechanisms in this paper need strict network settings, otherwise the unpredictability and unbiasability in scaled networks will be compromised.
- Monoxide, OmniLedger, RapidChain, and Ethereum 2.0 all propose their own solution to the issue of cross-shard transactions, none of which can support cross-shard smart contracts. Only Chainspace proposes a smart-contract-oriented sharding mechanism, but at the cost of low throughput.

- All considered sharding mechanisms introduce the optimizations to address the new challenges their proposed sharding mechanisms pose to the system, i.e., latency and storage, but further improvements are necessary.

# References

[1]  Nakamoto S. Bitcoin: A peer-to-peer electronic cash system; 2008. Available from: https://bitcoin.org/bitcoin.pdf.

[2]  Novo O. Blockchain Meets IoT: An Architecture for Scalable Access Management in IoT. IEEE Internet of Things Journal. 2018;5(2):11841195.

[3]  Yang R, Yu FR, Si P, *et al.* Integrated Blockchain and Edge Computing Systems: A Survey, Some Research Issues and Challenges. IEEE Communications Surveys Tutorials. 2019 Second quarter;21(2):1508–1532.

[4]  Wang X, Zha X, Ni W, *et al.* Survey on Blockchain for Internet of Things. Computer Communications. 2019;136:10–29. Available from: http://www.sciencedirect.com/science/article/pii/S0140366418306881.

[5]  Castro M, and Liskov B. Practical Byzantine Fault Tolerance. In: OSDI. vol. 99; 1999. p. 173–186.

[6]  Vukolić M. The Quest for Scalable Blockchain Fabric: Proof-of-Work vs. BFT Replication. In: International Workshop on Open Problems in Network Security. Springer; 2015. p. 112–125.

[7]  Tschorsch F and Scheuermann B. Bitcoin and Beyond: A Technical Survey on Decentralized Digital Currencies. IEEE Communications Surveys Tutorials. 2016 Third quarter;18(3):2084–2123.

[8]  Poon J and Dryja T. The Bitcoin lightning network: Scalable off-chain instant payments; 2016.

[9]  Raiden Network; 2015. Available from: https://raiden.network/.

[10]  Poon J and Buterin V. Plasma: Scalable autonomous smart contracts. White paper; 2017. p. 1–47.

[11]  Jourenko M, Kurazumi K, Larangeira M, *et al.* SoK: A Taxonomy for Layer-2 Scalability Related Protocols for Cryptocurrencies. IACR Cryptology ePrint Archive. 2019;2019:352.

[12]  Cattell R. Scalable SQL and NoSQL Data Stores. ACM SIGMOD Record. 2011;39(4):12–27.

[13]  Eyal I, Gencer AE, Sirer EG, *et al.* Bitcoin-NG: A Scalable Blockchain Protocol. In: 13th USENIX Symposium on Networked Systems Design and Implementation (NSDI 16). Santa Clara, CA: USENIX Association; 2016. p. 45–59. Available from: https://www.usenix.org/conference/nsdi16/technical-sessions/presentation/eyal.

[14]  Bentov I, Pass R, and Shi E. Snow White: Provably Secure Proofs of Stake. IACR Cryptology ePrint Archive. 2016;2016:919.

[15]  Kiayias A, Russell A, David B, *et al.* Ouroboros: A Provably Secure Proof-of-Stake Blockchain Protocol. In: Annual International Cryptology Conference. Springer; 2017. p. 357–388.

[16]  Miller A, Xia Y, Croman K, *et al.* The Honey Badger of BFT Protocols. In: Proceedings of the 2016 ACM SIGSAC Conference on Computer and Communications Security. ACM; 2016. p. 31–42.

[17]  Yin M, Malkhi D, Reiter MK, *et al.* HotStuff: BFT Consensus With Linearity and Responsiveness. In: Proceedings of the 2019 ACM Symposium on Principles of Distributed Computing. PODC '19. New York, NY, USA: ACM; 2019. p. 347–356. Available from: http://doi.acm.org/10.1145/3293611.3331591.

[18]  Kotla R, Alvisi L, Dahlin M, *et al.* Zyzzyva: Speculative Byzantine Fault Tolerance. In: ACM SIGOPS Operating Systems Review. vol. 41. ACM; 2007. p. 45–58.

[19]  Gilad Y, Hemo R, Micali S, *et al.* Algorand: Scaling Byzantine Agreements for Cryptocurrencies. In: Proceedings of the 26th Symposium on Operating Systems Principles. ACM; 2017. p. 51–68.

[20]  Croman K, Decker C, Eyal I, *et al.* On Scaling Decentralized Blockchains. In: Clark J, Meiklejohn S, Ryan PYA, *et al.*, editors. Financial Cryptography and Data Security. Berlin, Heidelberg: Springer Berlin Heidelberg; 2016. p. 106–125.

[21]  Garzik J. BIP102: Block size increase to 2MB; 2015. Available from: https://github.com/bitcoin/bips/blob/master/bip-0102.mediawiki.

[22]  Wuille P. BIP103: Block size following technological growth; 2015. Available from: https://github.com/bitcoin/bips/blob/master/bip0103.mediawiki.

[23]  Lombrozo E, Lau J, and Wuille P. BIP141: Segregated witness (consensus layer); 2015.

[24]  Sompolinsky Y and Zohar A. Secure High-Rate Transaction Processing in Bitcoin. In: Böhme R, Okamoto T, editors. Financial Cryptography and Data Security. Berlin, Heidelberg: Springer Berlin Heidelberg; 2015. p. 507–527.

[25]  Popov S. The tangle; 2016. p. 131.

[26]  Churyumov A. Byteball: A decentralized system for storage and transfer of value; 2016. Available from: https://byteball org/Byteball.pdf.

[27]  Baird L. The Swirlds Hashgraph Consensus Algorithm: Fair, Fast, Byzantine Fault Tolerance. In: Swirlds Tech Reports SWIRLDS-TR-2016-01, Tech Rep.; 2016.

[28]  Sompolinsky Y, Lewenberg Y, and Zohar A. SPECTRE: A Fast and Scalable Cryptocurrency Protocol. IACR Cryptology ePrint Archive. 2016;2016:1159.

[29]  Sompolinsky Y and Zohar A. PHANTOM: A Scalable BlockDAG Protocol. IACR Cryptology ePrint Archive. 2018;2018:104.

[30]  Li C, Li P, Zhou D, *et al.* Scaling Nakamoto consensus to thousands of transactions per second. arXiv preprint arXiv:180503870. 2018.

[31]  Kan L, Wei Y, Hafiz Muhammad A, *et al.* A Multiple Blockchains Architecture on Inter-Blockchain Communication. In: 2018 IEEE International Conference on Software Quality, Reliability and Security Companion (QRS-C); 2018. p. 139–145.

[32] Zheng Z, Xie S, Dai HN, *et al.* Blockchain Challenges and Opportunities: A Survey. International Journal of Web and Grid Services. 2018;14(4):352–375.

[33] Sankar LS, Sindhu M, and Sethumadhavan M. Survey of Consensus Protocols on Blockchain Applications. In: 2017 4th International Conference on Advanced Computing and Communication Systems (ICACCS); 2017. p. 1–5.

[34] Gao W, Hatcher WG, and Yu W. A Survey of Blockchain: Techniques, Applications, and Challenges. In: 2018 27th International Conference on Computer Communication and Networks (ICCCN); 2018. p. 1–11.

[35] Wang W, Hoang DT, Hu P, *et al.* A Survey on Consensus Mechanisms and Mining Strategy Management in Blockchain Networks. IEEE Access. 2019;7:22328–22370.

[36] Yang W, Garg S, Raza A, *et al.* Blockchain: Trends and Future. In: Yoshida K and Lee M, editors. Knowledge Management and Acquisition for Intelligent Systems. Cham: Springer International Publishing; 2018. p. 201–210.

[37] Zheng Z, Xie S, Dai H, *et al.* An Overview of Blockchain Technology: Architecture, Consensus, and Future Trends. In: 2017 IEEE International Congress on Big Data (BigData Congress); 2017. p. 557–564.

[38] Goswami S. Scalability Analysis of Blockchains Through Blockchain Simulation. UNLV Theses, Dissertations, Professional Papers, and Capstones; 2017. Available from: https://digitalscholarship.unlv.edu/theses-dissertations/2976.

[39] Bez M, Fornari G, and Vardanega T. The Scalability Challenge of Ethereum: An Initial Quantitative Analysis. In: 2019 IEEE International Conference on Service-Oriented System Engineering (SOSE); 2019. p. 167–176.

[40] Worley C and Skjellum A. Blockchain Tradeoffs and Challenges for Current and Emerging Applications: Generalization, Fragmentation, Sidechains, and Scalability. In: 2018 IEEE International Conference on Internet of Things (iThings) and IEEE Green Computing and Communications (GreenCom) and IEEE Cyber, Physical and Social Computing (CPSCom) and IEEE Smart Data (SmartData); 2018. p. 1582–1587.

[41] Kim S, Kwon Y, and Cho S. A Survey of Scalability Solutions on Blockchain. In: 2018 International Conference on Information and Communication Technology Convergence (ICTC); 2018. p. 1204–1207.

[42] Chauhan A, Malviya OP, Verma M, *et al.* Blockchain and Scalability. In: 2018 IEEE International Conference on Software Quality, Reliability and Security Companion (QRS-C); 2018. p. 122–128.

[43] Yang R, Yu FR, Si P, *et al.* Integrated Blockchain and Edge Computing Systems: A Survey, Some Research Issues and Challenges. IEEE Communications Surveys Tutorials. 2019 Second quarter;21(2):1508–1532.

[44] Casino F, Dasaklis TK, and Patsakis C. A Systematic Literature Review of Blockchain-Based Applications: Current Status, Classification and Open Issues. Telematics and Informatics. 2019;36:55–81. Available from: http://www.sciencedirect.com/science/article/pii/S0736585318306324.

[45]  Mechkaroska D, Dimitrova V, and Popovska-Mitrovikj A. Analysis of the Possibilities for Improvement of BlockChain Technology. In: 2018 26th Telecommunications Forum (TELFOR); 2018. p. 1–4.

[46]  Dinh TTA, Liu R, Zhang M, *et al.* Untangling Blockchain: A Data Processing View of Blockchain Systems. IEEE Transactions on Knowledge and Data Engineering. 2018;30(7):1366–1385.

[47]  Xiao Y, Zhang N, Lou W, *et al.* A Survey of Distributed Consensus Protocols for Blockchain Networks. CoRR. 2019;abs/1904.04098. Available from: http://arxiv.org/abs/1904.04098.

[48]  Wang R, Ye K, and Xu CZ. Performance Benchmarking and Optimization for Blockchain Systems: A Survey. In: Joshi J, Nepal S, Zhang Q, *et al.*, editors. Blockchain – ICBC 2019. Cham: Springer International Publishing; 2019. p. 171–185.

[49]  Sankar LS, Sindhu M, and Sethumadhavan M. Survey of Consensus Protocols on Blockchain Applications. In: 2017 4th International Conference on Advanced Computing and Communication Systems (ICACCS); 2017. p. 1–5.

[50]  Manshaei MH, Jadliwala M, Maiti A, *et al.* A Game-Theoretic Analysis of Shard-Based Permissionless Blockchains. IEEE Access. 2018;6:7810078112.

[51]  Singhal P and Masih S. MetaAnalysis of Methods for Scaling Blockchain Technology for Automotive Uses. CoRR. 2019;abs/1907.02602. Available from: http://arxiv.org/abs/1907.02602.

[52]  Wang G, Shi ZJ, Nixon M, *et al.* SoK: Sharding on Blockchain. In: Proceedings of the 1st ACM Conference on Advances in Financial Technologies. AFT '19. New York, NY, USA: ACM; 2019. p. 41–61. Available from: http://doi.acm.org/10.1145/3318041.3355457.

[53]  Wang J and Wang H. Monoxide: Scale Out Blockchains With Asynchronous Consensus Zones. In: 16th USENIX Symposium on Networked Systems Design and Implementation (NSDI 19). Boston, MA: USENIX Association; 2019. p. 95–112. Available from: https://www.usenix.org/conference/nsdi19/presentation/wang-jiaping.

[54]  Yu G, Wang X, Yu K, *et al.* Survey: Sharding in Blockchains. IEEE Access. 2020;8:14155–14181.

[55]  Corbett JC, Dean J, Epstein M, *et al.* Spanner: Google's Globally Distributed Database. ACM Transactions on Computer Systems. 2013;31(3):8:1–8:22. Available from: http://doi.acm.org/10.1145/2491245.

[56]  Danezis G and Meiklejohn S. Centrally Banked Cryptocurrencies. CoRR. 2015;abs/1505.06895. Available from: http://arxiv.org/abs/1505.06895.

[57]  Luu L, Narayanan V, Zheng C, *et al.* A Secure Sharding Protocol for Open Blockchains. In: Proceedings of the 2016 ACM SIGSAC Conference on Computer and Communications Security. CCS '16. New York, NY, USA: ACM; 2016. p. 17–30. Available from: http://doi.acm.org/10.1145/2976749.2978389.

[58]    Kokoris-Kogias E, Jovanovic P, Gasser L, *et al.* OmniLedger: A Secure, Scale-Out, Decentralized Ledger via Sharding. In: 2018 IEEE Symposium on Security and Privacy (SP); 2018. p. 583–598.

[59]    Zamani M, Movahedi M, and Raykova M. RapidChain: Scaling Blockchain via Full Sharding. In: Proceedings of the 2018 ACM SIGSAC Conference on Computer and Communications Security. CCS '18. New York, NY, USA: ACM; 2018. p. 931–948. Available from: http://doi.acm.org/10.1145/ 3243734.3243853.

[60]    Al-Bassam M, Sonnino A, Bano S, *et al.* Chainspace: A Sharded Smart Contracts Platform. CoRR. 2017;abs/1708.03778. Available from: http:// arxiv.org/abs/1708.03778.

[61]    Buterin V. Ethereum sharding FAQ; 2019. Accessed on 01.08.2019. Available from: https://github.com/ethereum/wiki/wiki/Sharding-FAQ.

[62]    Prestwich J. What to Expect When ETH's Expecting; 2019. Accessed on 01.08.2019. Available from: https://hackernoon.com/what-to-expectwhen-eths-expecting-80cb4951afcd.

[63]    Chen H and Wang Y. SSChain: A Full Sharding Protocol for Public Blockchain Without Data Migration Overhead. Pervasive and Mobile Computing. 2019;59:101055. Available from: http://www.sciencedirect. com/science/article/pii/S1574119218306370.

[64]    Chen S, Dai W, Dai Y, *et al.* Thinkey: A Scalable Blockchain Architecture. CoRR. 2019;abs/1904.04560. Available from: http://arxiv.org/abs/1904.04560.

[65]    Ren Z and Erkin Z. VAPOR: A Value-Centric Blockchain That Is Scale-out, Decentralized, and Flexible by Design. In: Goldberg I and Moore T, editors. Financial Cryptography and Data Security. Cham: Springer International Publishing; 2019. p. 487–507.

[66]    Gray J. The Transaction Concept: Virtues and Limitations. In: VLDB. vol. 81; 1981. p. 144–154.

[67]    Haerder T and Reuter A. Principles of Transaction-Oriented Database Recovery. ACM Computing Surveys (CSUR). 1983;15(4):287–317.

[68]    Dinh TTA, Wang J, Chen G, *et al.* BLOCKBENCH: A Framework for Analyzing Private Blockchains. In: Proceedings of the 2017 ACM International Conference on Management of Data. SIGMOD '17. New York, NY, USA: ACM; 2017. p. 1085–1100. Available from: http://doi.acm.org/ 10.1145/3035918.3064033.

[69]    Kogias EK, Jovanovic P, Gailly N, *et al.* Enhancing Bitcoin Security and Performance with Strong Consistency via Collective Signing. In: 25th USENIX Security Symposium (USENIX Security 16). Austin, TX: USENIX Association; 2016. p. 279–296. Available from: https://www.usenix.org/ conference/usenixsecurity16/technicalsessions/presentation/kogias.

[70]    Wood G. Ethereum: A Secure Decentralised Generalised Transaction Ledger. In: Ethereum Project Yellow Paper. 2014. vol. 151; 2014. p. 1–32.

[71]    Judmayer A, Zamyatin A, Stifter N, *et al.* Merged Mining: Curse or Cure? In: Garcia-Alfaro J, Navarro-Arribas G, Hartenstein H, *et al.*, editors. Data

Privacy Management, Cryptocurrencies and Blockchain Technology. Cham: Springer International Publishing; 2017. p. 316–333.

[72]  BitCoinWIKI. Merged mining specification; 2015. Accessed on 01.08.2019. Available from: https://en.bitcoin.it/wiki/Merged mining specification.

[73]  Naor M. Bit Commitment Using Pseudorandomness. Journal of Cryptology. 1991;4(2):151–158. Available from: https://doi.org/10.1007/BF00196774.

[74]  Pease M, Shostak R, and Lamport L. Reaching Agreement in the Presence of Faults. Journal of the ACM. 1980;27(2):228–234. Available from: http: //doi. acm.org/10.1145/322186.322188.

[75]  Feldman P. A Practical Scheme for Non-Interactive Verifiable Secret Sharing. In: 28th Annual Symposium on Foundations of Computer Science (SFCS 1987); 1987. p. 427–438.

[76]  Pedersen TP. Non-Interactive and Information-Theoretic Secure Verifiable Secret Sharing. In: Feigenbaum J, editor. Advances in Cryptology— CRYPTO '91. Berlin, Heidelberg: Springer Berlin Heidelberg; 1992. p. 129– 140.

[77]  Stadler M. Publicly Verifiable Secret Sharing. In: Maurer U, editor. Advances in Cryptology—EUROCRYPT '96. Berlin, Heidelberg: Springer Berlin Heidelberg; 1996. p. 190–199.

[78]  Schoenmakers B. A Simple Publicly Verifiable Secret Sharing Scheme and Its Application to Electronic Voting. In: Wiener M, editor. Advances in Cryptology—CRYPTO' 99. Berlin, Heidelberg: Springer Berlin Heidelberg; 1999. p. 148–164.

[79]  Rabin T and Ben-Or M. Verifiable Secret Sharing and Multiparty Protocols with Honest Majority. In: Proceedings of the Twenty-first Annual ACM Symposium on Theory of Computing. STOC '89. New York, NY, USA: ACM; 1989. p. 73–85. Available from: http://doi.acm.org/10.1145/73007.73014.

[80]  Sousa J and Bessani A. From Byzantine Consensus to BFT State Machine Replication: A Latency-Optimal Transformation. In: 2012 Ninth European Dependable Computing Conference; 2012. p. 37–48.

[81]  Syta E, Jovanovic P, Kogias EK, *et al.* Scalable Bias-Resistant Distributed Randomness. In: 2017 IEEE Symposium on Security and Privacy (SP); 2017. p. 444–460.

[82]  Gilad Y, Hemo R, Micali S, *et al.* Algorand: Scaling Byzantine Agreements for Cryptocurrencies. In: Proceedings of the 26th Symposium on Operating Systems Principles. SOSP '17. New York, NY, USA: ACM; 2017. p. 51–68. Available from: http://doi.acm.org/10.1145/3132747.3132757.

[83]  Boneh D, Drijvers M, and Neven G. Compact Multi-signatures for Smaller Blockchains. In: Peyrin T, Galbraith S, editors. Advances in Cryptology – ASIACRYPT 2018. Cham: Springer International Publishing; 2018. p. 435–464.

[84]  Syta E, Tamas I, Visher D, *et al.* Keeping Authorities "Honest or Bust" With Decentralized Witness Cosigning. In: 2016 IEEE Symposium on Security and Privacy (SP); 2016. p. 526–545.

[85]  Schnorr CP. Efficient Signature Generation by Smart Cards. Journal of Cryptology. 1991;4(3):161–174. Available from: https://doi.org/10.1007/BF00196725.

[86]  Stathakopoulous C and Cachin C. Threshold Signatures for Blockchain Systems. Swiss Federal Institute of Technology; 2017.

[87]  Desmedt Y and Frankel Y. Threshold Cryptosystems. In: Brassard G, editor. Advances in Cryptology—CRYPTO' 89 Proceedings. New York, NY: Springer New York; 1990. p. 307–315.

[88]  Gennaro R, Jarecki S, Krawczyk H, *et al.* Robust Threshold DSS Signatures. In: Maurer U, editor. Advances in Cryptology—EUROCRYPT '96. Berlin, Heidelberg: Springer Berlin Heidelberg; 1996. p. 354–371.

[89]  Shoup V. Practical Threshold Signatures. In: International Conference on the Theory and Applications of Cryptographic Techniques. Springer; 2000. p. 207–220.

[90]  Boldyreva A. Threshold Signatures, Multisignatures and Blind Signatures Based on the Gap-Diffie-Hellman-Group Signature Scheme. In: Desmedt YG, editor. Public Key Cryptography—PKC 2003. Berlin, Heidelberg: Springer Berlin Heidelberg; 2002. p. 31–46.

[91]  Cachin C, Kursawe K, and Shoup V. Random Oracles in Constantinople: Practical Asynchronous Byzantine Agreement Using Cryptography. Journal of Cryptology. 2005;18(3):219–246. Available from: https://doi.org/10.1007/s00145-005-0318-0.

[92]  Ren L, Nayak K, Abraham I, *et al.* Practical Synchronous Byzantine Consensus. CoRR. 2017;abs/1704.02397. Available from: http://arxiv.org/abs/1704.02397.

[93]  Swan M. Blockchain: Blueprint for a New Economy. Sebastopol, CA: O'Reilly Media; 2015. Available from: http://shop.oreilly.com/product/0636920037040.do.

[94]  Li X, Jiang P, Chen T, *et al.* A Survey on the Security of Blockchain Systems. Future Generation Computer Systems. 2017. Available from: http://www.sciencedirect.com/science/article/pii/S0167739X17318332.

[95]  Zamfir V. Casper-CBC FAQ; 2018. Accessed on 01.08.2019. Available from: https://github.com/ethereum/cbc-casper/wiki/FAQ.

[96]  Ray J. Sharding roadmap; 2019. Accessed on 01.08.2019. Available from: https://github.com/ethereum/wiki/wiki/Sharding-roadmap.

[97]  Kiayias A, Russell A, David B, *et al.* Ouroboros: A Provably Secure Proof-of-Stake Blockchain Protocol. In: The 37th Annu. Int. Cryptology Conf. (CRYPTO '17). Springer; 2017. p. 357–388.

[98]  King S and Nadal S. PPcoin: peer-to-peer crypto-currency with proof-of-stake; 2012. Available from: https://pdfs.semanticscholar.org/0db3/8d32069f3341d34c35085dc009a85ba13c13.pdf.

[99]  Xu C, Wang K, Li P, *et al.* Making Big Data Open in Edges: A Resource Efficient Blockchain-Based Approach. IEEE Transactions on Parallel and Distributed Systems. 2018;30(4):870–882

[100]  Reddcoin; 2018. Available from: https://wiki.reddcoin.com/Main Page.

[101]   Buterin V. Convenience link to Casper+Sharding chain v2.1 spec; 2018. Accessed on 01.08.2019. Available from: https://ethresear.ch/t/conveniencelink-to-casper-sharding-chain-v2-1-spec/2332.

[102]   Park JY. Preparing for Ethereum PoS staking in 2019; 2018. Accessed on 01.08.2019. Available from: https://medium.com/whaley-official/getting-prepared-for-ethereum-pos-staking-in-2019-3a3855e6a018.

[103]   LinkTime. Justin drake-Ethereum, sharding; 2018. Available from: https://www.youtube.com/watch?v=J4rylD6w2S4.

[104]   Randao: Verifiable random number generation; 2017. Available from: https://www.randao.org/whitepaper/Randao v0.85 en.pdf.

[105]   Boneh D, Bonneau J, Bünz B, *et al.* Verifiable Delay Functions. In: Shacham H and Boldyreva A, editors. Advances in Cryptology – CRYPTO 2018. Cham: Springer International Publishing; 2018. p. 757–788.

[106]   Drake J. Minimal VDF randomness beacon; 2018. Accessed on 01.08.2019. Available from: https://ethresear.ch/t/minimal-vdfrandomness-beacon/3566.

[107]   Wesolowski B. Efficient verifiable delay functions; 2018. https://eprint.iacr.org/2018/623. Cryptology ePrint Archive, Report 2018/623.

[108]   Pietrzak K. Simple verifiable delay functions; 2018. https://eprint.iacr.org/2018/627. Cryptology ePrint Archive, Report 2018/627.

[109]   Feo LD, Masson S, Petit C, *et al.* Verifiable delay functions from super-singular isogenies and pairings; 2019. https://eprint.iacr.org/2019/166. Cryptology ePrint Archive, Report 2019/166.

[110]   Buterin V. The problem of censorship; 2015. Accessed on 01.08.2019. Available from: https://blog.ethereum.org/2015/06/06/the-problem-ofcensorship/.

[111]   Chepurnoy A. Interactive proof-of-stake. arXiv preprint arXiv:160100275. 2016.

[112]   Heilman E, Kendler A, Zohar A, *et al.* Eclipse Attacks on Bitcoin's Peer-to-Peer Network. In: 24th USENIX Security Symposium (USENIX Security 15). Washington, DC: USENIX Association; 2015. p. 129–144. Available from: https://www.usenix.org/conference/usenixsecurity15/technicalsessions/presentation/heilman.

[113]   Alon N, Kaplan H, Krivelevich M, *et al.* Scalable Secure Storage When Half the System Is Faulty. In: Montanari U, Rolim JDP, and Welzl E, editors. Automata, Languages and Programming. Berlin, Heidelberg: Springer Berlin Heidelberg; 2000. p. 576–587.

[114]   Alon N, Kaplan H, Krivelevich M, *et al.* Addendum to "Scalable secure storage when half the system is faulty" [Inform. Comput. 174 (2)(2002) 203213]. Information and Computation. 2007;205(7):1114–1116.

[115]   Maymounkov P and Mazières D. Kademlia: A Peer-to-Peer Information System Based on the XOR Metric. In: Revised Papers from the First International Workshop on Peer-to-Peer Systems. IPTPS '01. London, UK, UK: Springer Verlag; 2002. p. 53–65. Available from: http://dl.acm.org/citation.cfm?id=646334.687801.

[116]   Buterin V. Ethereum white paper: a next generation smart contract & decentralized application platform. First version; 2014.

[117]   block one. EOS.IO Technical White Paper v2; 2018. Available from: https://github.com/EOSIO/Documentation/blob/master/TechnicalWhitePaper.md.

[118]   NEO White Paper; 2018. Available from: http://docs.neo.org/en-us/.

[119]   Nikitin K, Kokoris-Kogias E, Jovanovic P, *et al.* CHAINIAC: Proactive Software-Update Transparency via Collectively Signed Skipchains and Verified Builds. In: 26th USENIX Security Symposium (USENIX Security 17). Vancouver, BC: USENIX Association; 2017. p. 1271–1287. Available from: https://www.usenix.org/conference/usenixsecurity17/technicalsessions/presentation/nikitin.

[120]   Back A, Corallo M, Dashjr L, *et al.* Enabling blockchain innovations with pegged sidechains; 2014. p. 72. Available from: http://www open-sciencereview com/papers/123/enablingblockchain-innovations-with-pegged-sidechains.

[121]   Regnath E and Steinhorst S. LeapChain: Efficient Blockchain Verification for Embedded IoT. In: Proceedings of the International Conference on Computer-Aided Design. ICCAD '18. New York, NY, USA: ACM; 2018. p. 74:1–74:8. Available from: http://doi.acm.org/10.1145/3240765.3240820.

[122]   Kiayias A, Miller A, and Zindros D. Non-Interactive Proofs of Proof-of-Work. IACR Cryptology ePrint Archive. 2017;2017(963):1–42.

[123]   Kiayias A, Lamprou N, and Stouka AP. Proofs of Proofs of Work with Sublinear Complexity. In: Clark J, Meiklejohn S, Ryan PYA, *et al.*, editors. Financial Cryptography and Data Security. Berlin, Heidelberg: Springer Berlin Heidelberg; 2016. p. 61–78.

[124]   Awerbuch B and Scheideler C. Towards a Scalable and Robust DHT. Theory of Computing Systems. 2009;45(2):234–260. Available from: https://doi.org/10.1007/s00224-008-9099-9.

[125]   Sen S and Freedman MJ. Commensal Cuckoo: Secure Group Partitioning for Large-scale Services. SIGOPS Operating Systems Review. 2012;46 (1):33–39. Available from: http://doi.acm.org/10.1145/2146382.2146389.

[126]   Sonnino A, Bano S, Al-Bassam M, *et al.* Replay Attacks and Defenses against Cross-shard Consensus in Sharded Distributed Ledgers. CoRR. 2019;abs/1901.11218. Available from: http://arxiv.org/abs/1901.11218.

[127]   Al-Bassam M, Sonnino A, and Buterin V. Fraud Proofs: Maximising Light Client Security and Scaling Blockchains with Dishonest Majorities. CoRR. 2018;abs/1809.09044. Available from: http://arxiv.org/abs/1809.09044.

[128]   Xu Y and Huang Y. An n/2 Byzantine Node Tolerate Blockchain Sharding Approach. In: Proceedings of the 35th Annual ACM Symposium on Applied Computing; 2020 Mar. Available from: http://dx.doi.org/10.1145/3341105.3374069.

*Chapter 11*

# Blockchain for GIS: an overview

*Yong Wang[1], Lizhe Wang[1], Dongfang Zhang[1] and Chengjun Li[1]*

Distributed technology is an important direction in the field of geographic information system (GIS). However, distributed GIS is facing a number of challenges such as decentralization, geospatial data sharing, and privacy and security vulnerabilities. Blockchain technology brings the opportunities in addressing the challenges of GIS. In this chapter, we investigate the integration of blockchain technology with GIS and discuss the opportunities of blockchain GIS. Moreover, our novel architecture of blockchain GIS is proposed, while the potential applications of blockchain GIS are described in detail. Finally, we outline the open research directions in the promising area.

## 11.1 Introduction

Looking back on the history of computing technology development, we can find at least three eras. They are the eras of independent host, client/server computing mode, and distributed computing. The requirement of higher performance, lower cost, and more humanized operation mode is the main driving force of the evolution of computing technology. In line with the development of computing model, geographic information system (GIS) architecture has also evolved from the single-machine architecture GIS to the distributed pattern. Distributed GIS can store large amounts of geospatial data by using more storage nodes and, also, can deal with more users by dispensing requests to different servers [1]. However, due to decentralization, how to guarantee geospatial data traceability and reliability becomes a key technology.

Blockchain has numerous benefits such as decentralization, persistency, anonymity, and auditability. There is a wide spectrum of blockchain applications ranging from cryptocurrency, financial services, risk management, Internet of Things (IoT) to public and social services [2]. At the beginning, blockchain technology was proposed to support cryptocurrencies like Bitcoin. Thus,

[1]School of Computer Science, China University of Geosciences, Wuhan, China

cryptocurrency blockchains and related applications are often labelled as Blockchain 1.0. The introduction of smart contracts to realize decentralized applications (Dapps), decentralized autonomous organizations, smart property, smart tokens, etc. paved the way to automated financial applications based on cryptocurrencies. All these novel applications in the financial area based on smart contracts and digital currencies are labelled Blockchain 2.0. Further, all applications of blockchain technology referable to the wider spectrum of non-cryptocurrency-related distributed ledger are commonly called Blockchain 3.0 applications [3]. Blockchain applications are preferred in many areas for removing intermediaries in order to obtain transparency and security at a low cost. Blockchain applications of GIS belong to applications of blockchain 3.0.

Blockchain is essentially a perfect complement to GIS for the improvement on privacy, security, reliability, and scalability. In this chapter, we investigate a new paradigm of integrating GIS with blockchain and name it as blockchain GIS. In fact, our blockchain GIS has the following characteristics:

- Decentralization: In traditional GIS systems, the centralization manner of geospatial data centre results in extra cost, performance bottleneck, and single-point failure at centralized service providers. Blockchain GIS provides the possibility for processing massive spatial data by decentralization.
- Traceability: Each geospatial data block saved in a blockchain is attached with a historic timestamp consequently assuring the data traceability.
- Reliability: Geospatial data can be ensured by the integrity enforced by cryptographic mechanisms, including asymmetric encryption algorithms, hash functions, and digital signature, all of which are inherent in blockchains.

The main contributions of this chapter are highlighted as follows: (1) the opportunities of integrating blockchain with GIS are discussed. By the way, an architecture of blockchain GIS is proposed based on the discussion by us. (2) We describe application scenarios of blockchain GIS in detail, including reengineering of process involving GIS, geospatial data sharing, and spatial decision-making. (3) Furthermore, we summarize the challenges of efficiency, privacy protection, cross-chain in blockchain GIS.

The rest of the chapter is organized as follows: Section 11.2 presents an overview of distributed GIS and blockchain technology. The junction of blockchain and GIS is discussed in Section 11.3. Section 11.4 describes application scenarios of blockchain GIS. Challenges and issues in this field are discussed in Section 11.5. Finally, Section 11.6 presents our conclusion.

## 11.2    Related technologies

### 11.2.1    Introduction to GIS

As a computer-based tool, GIS is used for storing, collecting, retrieving, transforming, and displaying spatial data. GIS, which offers facilities for data management, data manipulation, data capture, analysis, and presentation, is the combination of cartography, statistical analysis, software, hardware, and data. GIS is usually used as a supporting system for decision-making by offering best possible decisions through non-spatial and spatial data relations, processing, and visualization. With GIS, it is easy to draw maps and visualize spatial distributions. Also, it is possible to not only edit and alter existing data but also measure distances and areas accurately. In the field of health, GIS application is extremely valuable. For example, GIS is used for preparing and viewing diseases maps to easily track diseases and control it over time. Moreover, GIS is employed for mapping populations at risks to make accurate rescuing plans [4].

Over time, geospatial information has evolved from paper maps to desktop GIS, then to web-based GISs, and finally arriving at the current stage of mobile GISs and ubiquitous GIS [5]. Geospatial data are increasing dramatically and lead to overloading in more and more GIS applications. Moreover, supported by global position system, and mobile intelligent terminals, location-based services such as Foursquare, Urbanspoon, and Flickr are developed vigorously. As a result, a large amount of geospatial information is produced at any time.

It is not difficult to find that the distribution of both spatial data and computing models is the main characteristic of GIS. Distributed technology is an important direction of GIS development [6]. The main reasons are listed as follows:

1.  Geographical data have the characteristic of distribution. The production and updating of geospatial data result in huge workload and high costs, which requires the participation of multiple units. These units located in different regions produce their own geospatial databases. In addition, existing geographical data are often stored in different sectors due to different industry functions. The use of distributed management can make full use of the existing resources and save manpower, material, and financial resources.
2.  Reliability and availability are improved. This is the most attractive point of distributed techniques. In traditional centralized GIS database, if database or software fails, the whole system cannot be used. However, when geospatial data are distributed among multiple nodes, even if one node fails, other nodes can continue to work.
3.  Distributed technology can share local autonomous data without centralized control. Each node has the corresponding autonomy to the local database. Meanwhile, the local data can be shared by other nodes.
4.  The data are independent. Distributed database system is not only physically independent but logically independent also. Users can easily access any data without caring about location of data source.

Although distributed technology promotes the development of GIS, however, due to decentralization, how to guarantee geospatial data traceability and reliability is still a key technology [7]. In distributed GIS, it is very important to reach consensus among the untrustworthy nodes in a very short period of time, which is called the consensus of the whole network.

## 11.2.2 *Blockchain technologies*

### 11.2.2.1 History of blockchain development

The development of blockchain has gone through three stages: cryptocurrencies, enterprise application, and value Internet. Details are introduced as follows.

In January 2009, 2 months after the publication of the Bitcoin system paper, the Bitcoin system officially ran and opened the source code to the official birth of the Bitcoin network. In Blockchain 1.0, the use of blockchain technology is mainly concentrated in the field of encrypted digital currency, which is typically represented by Bitcoin system [8].

In order to support applications such as crowdfunding and traceability, Blockchain 2.0 [9] begins to consider user-defined business logic and smart contracts. Thus, blockchain is widely used in various industries. As a result, the trust and cooperation costs in the process of social production and consumption are greatly reduced. Meanwhile, the efficiency of cooperation within and between industries is improved. Ethereum [10] is the typical representative of Blockchain 2.0, which was launched in 2013. In view of the performance problems existing in the Blockchain 1.0, Ethereum has also been improved from the view of consensus algorithm.

Furthermore, blockchains are not limited to cryptocurrencies, which are just a possible implementation of the broader concept of distributed ledger technology. As a matter of fact, distributed ledgers may contain arbitrary information, not necessarily related to money of finance. All applications of blockchain technology referable to the wider spectrum of non-cryptocurrency-related distributed ledger uses are commonly called Blockchain 3.0 applications [11]. The value Internet is a reliable network to realize the collaborative interconnection of various industries, to realize the interconnection of people and all things, and to realize the efficient and intelligent circulation of labour value. The technology is mainly used to solve the problem of consensus cooperation between people, or people and things, and then improve efficiency of trust mechanism.

### 11.2.2.2 Representative system and framework

Bitcoin system, the special system designed for Bitcoin, an encrypted digital currency, is the first typical application of blockchain system. Ethereum is another blockchain system. The main purpose of Ethereum is to expand the Bitcoin blockchain in more fields of applications, so that all developers can use the platform to build a variety of Dapps. Ethereum has improved the mining method of Bitcoin. Thus, the large-scale special mining machine no longer has the advantage, and smart contract is added to the Ethereum platform. Then, developers can build their own Dapps based on the intelligent contract development interface provided by Ethereum virtual machine [12].

Hyperledger [13], an open-source platform of distributed ledger, which is created by the Linux Foundation, was officially launched in December 2015 and consists of a number of subprojects, including platforms and tools. Fabric, a subproject, is a fully functional blockchain system that supports multichannel, mainly

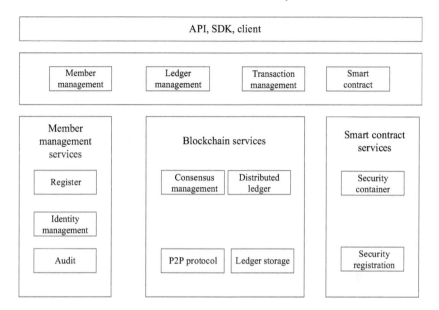

*Figure 11.1 Logical architecture of Fabric*

oriented to enterprise applications [14]. Fabric is an alliance chain system with license management. Traditional blockchain system has no restriction on the addition of nodes, which makes the system very complex. Fabric adopts a node management approach with license authentication. Although the identity of a node is known to the system, the nodes do not trust each other. Here, a consensus algorithm is needed between the nodes to ensure that data can be trusted. The logical architecture of Fabric is shown in Figure 11.1.

Fabric system is mainly used to provide member management, blockchain service, smart contract service, monitoring service, and so on.

## 11.3 Blockchain GIS

### 11.3.1 Opportunities of integrating blockchain with GIS

GIS systems are facing many challenges such as heterogeneity of GIS systems, geospatial data sharing, and privacy and security vulnerabilities in distributed environment. Blockchain technologies can complement GIS systems with the enhanced data sharing capability and improved privacy and security. Moreover, blockchain can also enhance the reliability and scalability of GIS systems. In short, we name such integration of blockchain with GIS as blockchain GIS. Blockchain GIS has the following potential benefits in contrast to incumbent GIS systems.

*Improved security of GIS systems:* On one hand, geospatial data can be secured by blockchains since they are stored as blockchain transactions which are encrypted and digitally signed by cryptographic keys (e.g. elliptic curve digital signature algorithm). Moreover, the integration of GIS systems with blockchain technologies (like smart contracts) can help to improve the security of GIS systems.

*Traceability and reliability of geospatial data:* Blockchain data can be identified and verified anywhere and anytime. Meanwhile, all the historical transactions stored in blockchains are traceable. For example, the work in [15] has developed a blockchain-based product traceability system, which provides suppliers and retailers with traceable services. In this manner, the geospatial data can be inspected and verified. Moreover, the immutability of blockchains also assures the reliability of geospatial data since it is almost impossible to alter or falsify any transactions stored in blockchains.

*Autonomic interactions of GIS systems:* Blockchain technologies can grant nodes of distributed GIS to interact with each other automatically. For example, the work of [16] proposes distributed autonomous corporations (DACs) to automate transactions, in which there are no traditional roles like governments or companies involved with payment. Being implemented by smart contracts, DACs can work automatically without human intervention consequently saving the cost.

## 11.3.2   Architecture of blockchain GIS

We propose the architecture of blockchain GIS as shown in Figure 11.2. In this architecture, the blockchain-composite layer plays as a middleware between GIS and applications. Our design has two merits: (1) offering an abstraction from the lower layers in GIS and (2) providing users with blockchain-based services. In particular, the blockchain-composite layer hides the heterogeneity of lower layers. On the other hand, the blockchain-composite layer offers a number of blockchain-based services, which are essentially application programming interfaces to support various industrial applications. Generally, blockchain GIS applications can be divided into presentation layer, application layer, business layer, and data layer.

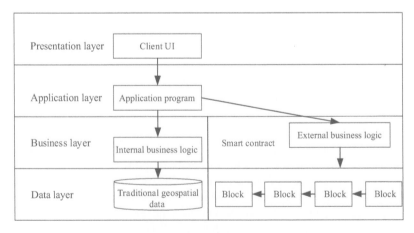

*Figure 11.2   Application architecture of blockchain GIS*

*Presentation layer:* This layer contains what we usually call user interfaces, such as registration interface, transaction interface, and application management interface. This layer is not different from traditional web applications and mobile apps. In fact, users are not aware of the existence of blockchain in this layer.

*Application layer:* The layer where the application logic is located, processes the user input data, determines the specific service according to this data, and then invokes the corresponding service processing interface. If the traditional internal business of the enterprise needs to be dealt with, traditional business interface is invoked. The interface of the blockchain will be called, provided that the blockchain service is required.

*Business layer:* This layer encapsulates all the business logics of GIS application and is the core part of the whole application. The business layer can be divided into two categories: traditional business logic and blockchain business logic. The traditional internal business logic is the same as the traditional application business logic, while the blockchain business logic is realized by the smart contract.

*Data layer:* This data layer is divided into traditional database storage and ledger storage. The logical data and the internal privacy data of the enterprise exist in the traditional database. In addition, the data involving multiple enterprise business logic exist in the blockchain and are shared among enterprises through the blockchain.

## 11.4 Application in GIS

As the first application of blockchain technology, Bitcoin has opened the prelude to the use and promotion of blockchain technology in many fields. From the initial encrypted digital currency to the later financial application, and then to the extensive use in various industries in recent years, blockchain technology is deeply affecting and changing people's cognition and life with its unique value. The application field of blockchain is gradually expanding along with deepening of our understanding on blockchain. At first, we only unilaterally thought that blockchain is fit for virtual currency transactions. However, with the understanding of its chain structure principle and non-tampering characteristics, we are surprised to find that the transactions fit for blockchain are not only limited to currency. In fact, blockchain can be used in a large number of applications in traditional industries.

The essence of blockchain is for conveying trust. That is, where trust requires to be transmitted, blockchain is needed. Financial industry is a branch of blockchain application scenario. The application field of blockchain has been extended to a variety of industries: supply chain, government services, IoT, new energy, and so on. Which fields are suitable for blockchain technology? We think that the suitable scenarios at present have at least three characteristics: first, there are decentralized, multiparty participation and write data requirements; second, the data authenticity requirements are high; and third, there is a requirement for multiple participants who do not want to store each other to establish distributed trust in the initial situation. In fact, many GIS applications have the aforementioned characteristics. It can be seen that blockchain is essentially a perfect complement to GIS with the improved decentralization, privacy, security, reliability, and scalability.

## 11.4.1    Reengineering of process involving GIS

Many companies and organizations are planning to reform their office automation (OA) or enterprise resource planning (ERP) system for better supporting the collaboration with other different departments or among their departments to achieve more business successes. Meanwhile, with the rapid development of various web applications and mobile apps, approval and business processes need to be reengineering. In order to improve efficiency, we even hope to simplify some processes. However, how to ensure security and consistency of data in the process is a very important question, since flowing through different nodes leads to more risks.

The emergence of blockchain technology has further brought a good solution to process reengineering. All parties to the alliance in the blockchain hold the ledger, and in addition, modification and deletion of the data must implement the intelligent contract and consensus established by the parties before it can be dropped into the final data book. Since the ledger data will be stored in the parties to the alliance, the high reliability of the data is ensured.

A supply chain consists of many organizations having different interests. The organizations are often reluctant to share traceability information with each other [17]. Through the process reengineering based on blockchain technology, the security and efficiency of the supply chain can be improved. By adopting a blockchain as data recording standard, it cuts intermediaries and the process can be speeded up as well.

A land registration system is one of the fields where blockchain can be considered as another potential star candidate [18]. The cadastral data should be collected and updated by different organizations, i.e. authorities and possibly private companies, whose databases should be able to communicate with each other. However, in order to maintain data security, cadastral OA and GIS in different organizations are isolated. Based on blockchain network, the cadastral systems of organizations can be connected securely and reengineering of cadastral process can be seen in Figure 11.3. The efficiency of authenticity of applicant identification and submitted materials is greatly improved. No one can tamper with survey cadastral data or forge it. Approval process will be more transparent. Hence, corruption and fraud can be avoided. By utilizing a blockchain-based ledger to store credentials and licensures, sharing and verification of these licensures will become more efficient. Blockchain is a digital decentralized ledger distributed across a network of computers called 'nodes' that keep records of all the transactions, which take place among peers running the same protocol. This ledger runs over the Internet and is cryptographically secure, append-only, immutable, and updateable only via consensus or agreement among the peers.

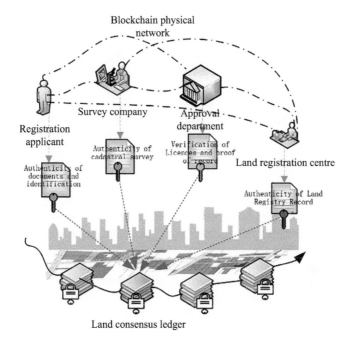

*Figure 11.3   Application scenario of land registration*

## 11.4.2   Application of geospatial data sharing

In recent years, geospatial data have been widely used in many applications to meet the requirement of departments or organizations, such as on traffic, hydrological, administrative zoning, land cadastral, DEM, and so on, for different purpose. If these data can be fully shared, a great deal of repeated collection work can be avoided. Thus, resources of manpower and material can be saved, while the utilization rate of resources can be improved. The COVID-19 pandemic is the biggest global health challenge of the century in the world [19]. Individual geospatial data sharing based on the quick response code tracing technology from Tencent and Alibaba can slow the spreading and reduce the impact by tracing the primary and secondary contacts of confirmed COVID-19. Therefore, with the development of GIS technology and the growth of application requirement, more and more attention will be paid to the sharing and interoperation of data between different GIS.

Distributed GIS is one of the best solutions for massive geospatial data sharing. In order to achieve data interoperability between heterogeneous databases in the construction of distributed GIS, federated database system is proposed to eliminate differences between heterogeneous patterns. However, how to ensure the data security and the consistency of each node in the distributed databases is still the bottleneck.

The sharing service of spatial data mainly includes three levels of content: directory service, data service, and functional service. Considering the limitations

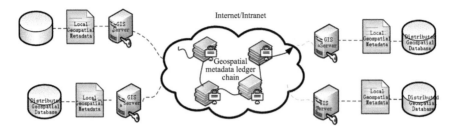

*Figure 11.4    Application scenario of geospatial data sharing*

of blockchain technology, directory service is the first choice of blockchain technology application. Directory service, a standard mode in which spatial metadata system uses metadata technology to provide spatial information service, presents information to users in the form of dynamic classification through the core elements of metadata standard. Users can quickly determine the scope of the required spatial data by browsing the spatial metadata information of the portal and then require the portal to search further within this scope. In blockchain of geospatial data sharing as shown in Figure 11.4, the node of the blockchain mainly plays the service role of integrating the information related to the distributed spatial database of each website into one directory. This service mode not only can greatly facilitate user query but also facilitate the release of network-related information. Blockchain is competent to integrate heterogeneous distributed geospatial data. In addition, directory service needs to be extended. Geospatial metadata ledger also contains data transaction information. Any transaction ever completed is recorded in a geospatial metadata ledger in a verifiable, secure, transparent, and permanent way, with a timestamp and other details. In the blockchain of geospatial data sharing, metadata, and transaction information, geospatial metadata ledger solves the problems of metadata sharing and data transaction supervision. However, due to the limitation of storage capacity of blockchain ledger, as the main body of mass data sharing, blockchain GIS needs to be further addressed to solve large data store for one ledger.

## 11.4.3    Spatial decision-making

Spatial decision-making stresses the need for collaboration and knowledge sharing between users and experts in order to bring a collaborative decision to fruition [20]. GIS based on planning support tools, which offer interactive map visualization and analytical capabilities, has the potential to mediate collaborative spatial planning processes [21]. Environmental pollution is a complex problem requiring many kinds of expertise to fully understand, as pollutants disperse not only locally but also regionally or even globally. GIS plays a very important role for improving remote collaborative analysis experience on consequences of comprehensive evaluation.

The concept of web-based GIS has been proposed as an effective tool for collaborative/group spatial decision-making. Web can be used as an information infrastructure for delivering spatial data and GIS functionalities to the general public [22]. The integration of web-based GIS and multicriteria decision analysis (MCDA) techniques can provide appropriate multicriteria spatial decision support systems (MSDSS) for direct involvement of people in a collaborative spatial planning process. Over the last decade or so, significant research efforts have been made to use web-based GIS and MCDA tools for collaborative spatial decision-making.

However, these efforts as the web-based participatory decision-making tools lack a knowledge sharing mechanism or framework that allows for automatic interpretation as well as exchange and sharing of GIS-MCDA knowledge elements between decision makers. In these tools, exchange of decision knowledge relies on decision makers' common sense to manually interpret the meanings of each other's knowledge and use the right ones.

Agents can be used to carry out some set of knowledge sharing operations on behalf of a decision maker, with some degrees of independence or autonomy, and, in doing so, they employ some knowledge or representation of user's goals and desires [23]. The decision makers' agents can interoperate and exchange decision knowledge with intended and unambiguous meanings, as shown in Figure 11.5. However, it is very important to ensure that agents perform the principal–agent relationship according to the rules and the knowledge base is not tampered.

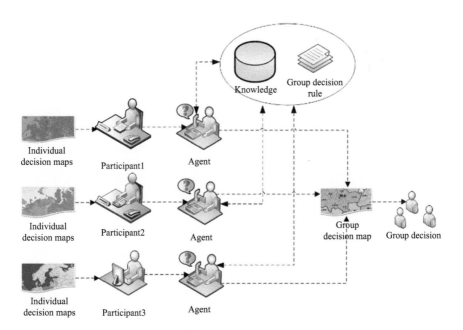

*Figure 11.5   Spatial decision-making by traditional GIS*

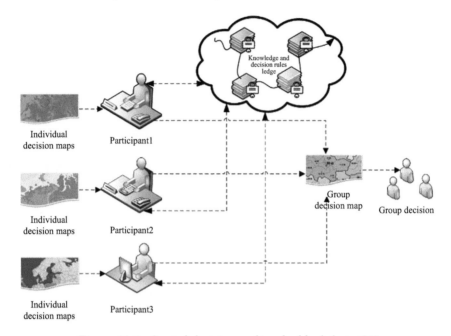

*Figure 11.6   Spatial decision-making by blockchain GIS*

The essence of blockchain is agent framework. The revolution of agent is driven by the change of blockchain technology. Blockchain-based MSDSS (BC-MSDSS) enhance the collaborative/participatory spatial decision-making by providing security knowledge and automatic contract. In BC-MSDSS, there are no more agents and knowledge bases, but knowledge ledgers, as shown in Figure 11.6.

An extension of the current blockchain ledgers that store consensual knowledge and decision rulers can ensure authenticity, automation, and traceability of decision-making. Smart contracts in blockchain, the replacement of agents, are executed automatically once the contract has been deployed on the blockchain.

Evaluation results confirm the effectiveness of comprehensive sharing among user, data, physical, and interaction spaces for improving remote collaborative analysis experience [24]. As different public bodies survey accident data, a collaborative environment is necessary. Moreover, a web-based solution is ideal for permitting multi-user access and data insertion [25].

## 11.5   Challenges and future trends

### 11.5.1   Efficiency

Low throughput was a serious problem for Bitcoin systems, which greatly limits their availability. Later, a large number of blockchain projects were realized aiming at improving performance, either by increasing block size or by increasing block frequency [26]. In the framework of Bitcoin, adjusting such parameters can improve throughput to some extent. However, the upper limit of throughput is hundreds of transactions per second. It is difficult to make an essential break-through. As the representative of the alliance chain, the throughput of Hyperledger Fabric is only a few hundred to thousands of transactions per second, which cannot meet the needs of the current financial system for throughput (tens of thousands of transactions per second). The root cause of low throughput lies in the consensus process. In a completely decentralized environment, in order to be recognized by most nodes, multiple interactions are often required. Meanwhile, each interaction is accompanied by network delay. Consequently, the throughput of blockchain sys-tem is difficult to be improved.

Asynchronous consensus is a kind of approach in which there is no need to reach a consensus immediately after the block is out of the block. In asynchronous consensus, each node follows a certain rule and tries its best to get out of the block. The mainstream approach is to synchronize all the nodes with each block and then continue the next block after the consensus is passed. If the rules are reasonable, the individual nodes can still reach one after a while. The famous asynchronous graph algorithm is one of representatives of asynchronous consensus [27].

Random consensus is another method. When participating in consensus among all nodes in the whole network is showing low efficiency, the direct idea to improve the performance is to replace the consensus among all nodes with the consensus among some ones. In fact, there is a solution: if 'part' is completely randomly extracted from the node, when a certain sample size is reached, the 'full' meaning can be statistically expressed. The whole consensus process is then divided into several steps. In each step, a committee composed of several nodes is randomly elected, and the consensus is completed by this committee. The next step is the random election of another committee, in a longer time span, for fairness, but also for the goal of efficient consensus. However, because of the complexity, the per-formance of random consensus in the actual network needs to be verified [28].

## 11.5.2 Privacy protection

Blockchain is a distributed ledger, which has the advantages of openness, trans-parency, non-tampering, and so on. However, when blockchain is applied to the real business world, new problems are required to be addressed. First of all, privacy protection needs to be handled. In detail, how to solve the contradiction between openness, transparency, and privacy protection has been an important direction of the development of blockchain technology.

Bitcoin has good anonymity because the account address of Bitcoin is obtained by series of operations with the public key of asymmetric key. All transactions that Bitcoin transmits online are public. There is no privacy in Bitcoin system. Ethereum also has exposed privacy protection problems. If someone records someone else's privacy information on the public chain of the Ethereum in the form of additional information to the transaction information, no one can delete the information, which exists permanently on the public chain of the Ethereum [29].

For data encryption on the chain, only the parties involved in the transaction can decrypt, which can solve most of the privacy protection problems. However, the blockchain system must directly face such a problem: how to achieve multiparty checksum under the condition of data encryption on the chain?

Homomorphic encryption, which processes ciphertext directly, is the same as encrypting the processing result after processing plaintext [30]. From the point of view of abstract algebra, it maintains homomorphism. At present, there is only addition homomorphism technology, which can reach the commercial level of homomorphism encryption technology. The top technology companies in the world are also developing full homomorphism encryption schemes. However, because the performance of multiplication homomorphism encryption is still poor, there is no visible commercial product that supports full homomorphism encryption.

### 11.5.3    *Application of cross-blockchain GIS*

Blockchain brings us tamper proof, decentralized, irreversibility, smart contract, and other valuable features that we can use as a separate blockchain system to build a perfect distributed ledger. However, it is also very necessary to interconnect multiple blockchains. Different GIS applications may work on different block-chain. Since their data are maintained on different blockchains, with interconnection, participants can perform their internal transactions in parallel, resulting in higher performance. To perform communication between different applications, one approach is to use cross-chain swap operation. Through designing a trust mechanism between blockchain systems, one blockchain can receive and verify transactions on another blockchain. A cross-chain transaction contains multiple sub-transactions.

CAPER was introduced in [25], a permissioned blockchain system to support both internal and cross-application transactions of collaborating distributed applications. In CAPER, the blockchain ledger is formed as a directed acyclic graph where each application accesses and maintains only its own view of the ledger, including its internal and all cross-application transactions.

## 11.6    Conclusion

The incumbent GIS systems are facing a number of challenges, including hetero-geneity, geospatial data sharing, privacy, and security vulnerability. The block-chain technologies essentially offer a solution to the issues with the enhanced data sharing capability, privacy, security, traceability, and reliability.

In this chapter, we have investigated integrating blockchain with GIS. We analysed the characteristics of blockchain and GIS and discussed the opportunities of blockchain GIS. The architecture of blockchain GIS is depicted. Furthermore, we have discussed the potential applications of blockchain GIS and outlined the challenges and opened research directions in blockchain GIS.

# References

[1] Pan, S., Xiong, L., Xu, Z., Chong, Y., and Meng, Q. (2018). A dynamic replication management strategy in distributed GIS. Computers & Geosciences, 112, 1–8.

[2] Zheng, Z., Xie, S., Dai, H. N., Chen, X., and Wang, H. (2018). Blockchain challenges and opportunities: A survey. International Journal of Web and Grid Services, 14(4), 352–375.

[3] Maesa, D. D. F. and Mori, P. (2020). Blockchain 3.0 applications survey. Journal of Parallel and Distributed Computing, 138, 99–114.

[4] Abolghasem S. N. and Choi S. M. (2020). A survey of marker-less tracking and registration techniques for health & environmental applications to augmented reality and ubiquitous geospatial information systems, Sensors, 20, 2997–3023.

[5] Zhang J. Q., Xu L. R., Zhang Y., and Liu G. (2019). An on-demand scalable model for geographic information system (GIS) data processing in a cloud GIS, International Journal of Geo-Information, 8, 392–407.

[6] Helmi, A. M., Farhan, M. S., and Nasr, M. M. (2018). A framework for integrating geospatial information systems and hybrid cloud computing. Computers & Electrical Engineering, 67, 145–158.

[7] Jones, M. T., Rohlf, J., and McClendon, B. (2020). U.S. Patent Application No. 16/659,811.

[8] Johnson, D., Menezes, A., and Vanstone, S. (2001). The Elliptic Curve Digital Signature Algorithm (ECDSA). International Journal of Information Security, 1(1), 36–63.

[9] Dolgui, A., Ivanov, D., Potryasaev, S., Sokolov, B., Ivanova, M., and Werner, F. (2020). Blockchain-oriented dynamic modelling of smart contract design and execution in the supply chain. International Journal of Production Research, 58(7), 2184–2199.

[10] Christidis, K. and Devetsikiotis, M. (2016). Blockchains and smart contracts for the Internet of Things. IEEE Access, 4, 2292–2303.

[11] Casino, F., Dasaklis, T. K., and Patsakis, C. (2019). A systematic literature review of blockchain-based applications: Current status, classification and open issues. Telematics and Informatics, 36, 55–81.

[12] Bartoletti, M., Carta, S., Cimoli, T., and Saia, R. (2020). Dissecting Ponzi schemes on Ethereum: Identification, analysis, and impact. Future Generation Computer Systems, 102, 259–277.

[13] Cachin, C. (2016, July). Architecture of the hyperledger blockchain fabric. In Workshop on Distributed Cryptocurrencies and Consensus Ledgers (Vol. 310, No. 4).

[14] Liang, W., Tang, M., Long, J., Peng, X., Xu, J., and Li, K. C. (2019). A secure fabric blockchain-based data transmission technique for industrial Internet-of-Things. IEEE Transactions on Industrial Informatics, 15(6), 3582–3592.

[15]   Lu, Q. and Xu, X. (2017). Adaptable blockchain-based systems: A case study for product traceability. IEEE Software, 34(6), 21–27.

[16]   Gatteschi, V., Lamberti, F., Demartini, C., Pranteda, C., and Santamaría, V. (2018). Blockchain and smart contracts for insurance: Is the technology mature enough? Future Internet, 10(2), 20.

[17]   Behnke, K. and Janssen, M. F. W. H. A. (2020). Boundary conditions for traceability in food supply chains using blockchain technology. International Journal of Information Management, 52, 101969.

[18]   Mendi, A. F. and Çabuk, A. (2020). Blockchain applications in geographical information systems. Photogrammetric Engineering & Remote Sensing, 86(1), 5–10.

[19]   Nanni, M., Andrienko, G., Boldrini, C., et al. (2020). Give more data, awareness and control to individual citizens, and they will help COVID-19 containment. arXiv preprint arXiv:2004.05222, 2020.

[20]   Jelokhani-Niaraki, M. (2018). Knowledge sharing in Web-based collaborative multicriteria spatial decision analysis: An ontology-based multi-agent approach. Computers, Environment and Urban Systems, 72, 104–123.

[21]   Aguilar, R., Flacke, J., and Pfeffer, K. (2020). Towards supporting collaborative spatial planning: Conceptualization of a maptable tool through user stories. ISPRS International Journal of Geo-information, 9(1), 29.

[22]   Jelokhani-Niaraki, M. and Malczewski, J. (2012). A web 3.0-driven collaborative multicriteria spatial decision support system. Cybergeo.

[23]   Mahmood, T., Fulmer, W., Mungoli, N., Huang, J., and Lu, A. (2019, October). Improving information sharing and collaborative analysis for remote geospatial visualization using mixed reality. In 2019 IEEE International Symposium on Mixed and Augmented Reality (ISMAR) (pp. 236–247). IEEE.

[24]   Pirotti, F., Guarnieri, A., and Vettore, A. (2010). Road safety analysis using WEB-BASED collaborative GIS. In ISPRS Conference (Vol. 34).

[25]   Amiri, M. J., Agrawal, D., and Abbadi, A. E. (2019). Caper: A cross-application permissioned blockchain. Proceedings of the VLDB Endowment, 12(11), 1385–1398.

[26]   Thakkar, P., Nathan, S., and Viswanathan, B. (2018, September). Performance benchmarking and optimizing hyperledger fabric blockchain platform. In 2018 IEEE 26th International Symposium on Modeling, Analysis, and Simulation of Computer and Telecommunication Systems (MASCOTS) (pp. 264–276). IEEE.

[27]   Wang, J. and Wang, H. (2019). Monoxide: Scale out blockchains with asynchronous consensus zones. In 16th USENIX Symposium on Networked Systems Design and Implementation (NSDI 19) (pp. 95–112).

[28]   Feng, J., Zhao, X., Chen, K., Zhao, F., and Zhang, G. (2020). Towards random-honest miners selection and multi-blocks creation: Proof-of-negotiation consensus mechanism in blockchain networks. Future Generation Computer Systems, 105, 248–258.

[29]  Feng, Q., He, D., Zeadally, S., Khan, M. K., and Kumar, N. (2019). A survey on privacy protection in blockchain system. Journal of Network and Computer Applications, 126, 45–58.

[30]  Liang, W., Zhang, D., Lei, X., Tang, M., Li, K. C., and Zomaya, A. (2020). Circuit copyright blockchain: blockchain-based homomorphic encryption for IP circuit protection. IEEE Transactions on Emerging Topics in Computing. http://doi.acm.org/10.1109/TETC.2020.2993032.

## Chapter 12

# Blockchain application in remote sensing big data management and production

*Jining Yan[1], Lizhe Wang[1], Feng Zhang[1], Xiaodao Chen[1], Xiaohui Huang[1] and Jiabao Li[1]*

In the field of Earth observation (EO), the main challenges in remote sensing big data management and production include the detection of data tampering, process recording, process accuracy evaluation, and data protection. These challenges result in low data utilization and unreliable decision-making. Blockchain technology presents a possible solution to these problems due to its openness, transparency, decentralization, traceability, and tamper resistance. In this chapter, we present a prospective study on blockchain-based strategies for remote sensing big data management and production. Specifically, (1) we propose remote sensing big data management rules that when metadata enters the chain, image files remain in the original storage and watermarking is added to maintain on-chain and off-chain consistency; (2) we establish a unified metadata model (UMM) to solve the problem of heterogeneous metadata in multisource data integration; (3) we devise a data block structure containing metadata identification, image encryption paths, and other information and propose technical solutions for multisource remote sensing data integration, chain entry, and sharing; (4) we establish the specific steps and technical details of the blockchain-based remote sensing big data production; (5) and construct a logical blockchain-based system serving remote sensing big data management and production under a multi-satellite data center scenario. This prospective study will definitely provide practical guidance for blockchain technology to truly serve remote sensing big data management and product production.

## 12.1 Introduction

The development of EO technology has caused the rapid growth of remote sensing data volume and the continuous expansion of its application fields; this also brings great challenges for data management and production [1]. The ability

[1]School of Computer Science, China University of Geosciences, Wuhan, China

to effectively track the collection, storage, processing, and application chains of various data sources while ensuring tamper resistance is one of the most urgent challenges in current remote sensing big data management [2]. Tracing the precise source of remote sensing products at all levels is also a critical issue in this regard [3]. For remote sensing data processing and production, the processing accuracy of remote sensing data sources at various levels directly determines the resulting decision value. For example, the level 2 remote sensing data distributed by each satellite ground station must undergo accurate geometric correction [4], atmospheric correction [5], and other processes before it can be applied to surface parameter inversion and information extraction. However, evaluating the accuracy of processes such as geometric and atmospheric correction to ensure that the value-added products [6] obtained by subsequent processing are of high quality, and ultimately obtain high-credibility decision-making knowledge, is one of the main problems facing remote sensing data processing and production. In addition, in the context of the era of big data [7], fusing multisource remote sensing data for feature extraction has become the current technical trend [8]. However, how extracting hidden ground observation information from nonpublic remote sensing data to study global change while protecting its privacy is another important issue faced by the current remote sensing data processing and production.

Blockchain is a data structure composed of data blocks in a chronological order similar to a linked list and cryptographically ensures a non-tamperable and unforgeable distributed decentralized ledger, which can safely store the simple and sequential related data that can be verified within the system [9,10]. The blockchain uses proof-of-work [11], proof-of-stake (PoS) [12], or other consensus mechanisms, as well as encryption technology, to change an untrusted network into a trusted one in which all participants can agree on a certain aspect without trusting a single node. Blockchain technology can record the full life cycle of data processing, thereby solving the traceability problem of various remote sensing data [13], and can use the features of openness, transparency, traceability, non-tampering, and consensus mechanisms to solve the problems of data copyright protection and public trust [14].

Therefore, we present a prospective study on the application of blockchain technology in remote sensing big data management and production, propose key technology solutions, and build a blockchain-based logical system architecture for data management and production to provide technical support and suggestions for the comprehensive application of blockchain technology in remote sensing.

The remainder of this chapter is organized as follows. In the next section, we discuss in detail the main problems and challenges for remote sensing big data management and product production. In Sections 12.3 and 12.4, we propose solutions for remote sensing big data management and production based on blockchain technology. In Section 12.5, we propose logical system architecture based on blockchain technology for remote sensing data management and production. Finally, in Section 12.6, we summarize this study identifying areas of focus for future work.

## 12.2   Challenges in remote sensing big data management and production

At present, the main challenges in remote sensing big data management and production are as follows:

- It is impossible to detect whether the remote sensing data have been tampered with during transmission and sharing, and the quality of the data obtained by the user cannot be guaranteed. From data collected in satellite ground stations to serve the public, remote sensing data sources require the union services of remote sensing data collectors, primary data processors, data providers, data servicers, and data sharing parties. However, ensuring that the data have not been tampered with arbitrarily [15] in the collecting–storage–transferring–sharing chain [16] and that the remote sensing data obtained by the user are indeed a product directly processed by the data collector is one of the main challenges in remote sensing data management.
- It is impossible to trace what processes were performed on the remote sensing data in the entire life cycle, and there is a lack of credible data processing accounting books. Once collected in the satellite ground station, the remote sensing data that obtained by the user must undergo data unpacking, cloud detection, system geometric correction, system radiation correction, geometric precision correction, radiation correction, atmospheric correction, etc. [17]. In general, processing from raw data to the digital number (DN) product is completed by the processing system of the satellite ground station. However, from processing DN product to surface reflectance product, as well as various levels of value-added products, should be performed by remote sensing data servers or users themselves. Nonetheless, accurately recording the processing of the data throughout the entire data–information–knowledge lifecycle [18], increasing the transparency in the process of realizing the value of remote sensing data, and providing users with true and reliable data sets are the other major problems for remote sensing big data management.
- It is impossible to evaluate the accuracy of the processing steps of remote sensing data in the entire lifecycle, which results in final decision-making knowledge that is not credible. From raw data to value-added products, remote sensing data must undergo a variety of algorithms or model processing [19]. However, each step of the processing algorithm may have multiple choices or require the adjustment of multiple parameters. Ensuring that the parameter settings of each step of data processing are completely correct, that the value-added products [20] obtained by each processing step are of high quality, and that the decision-making knowledge obtained is credible are the main challenges faced by remote sensing production.
- It is impossible to produce multisource remote sensing products on the premise of ensuring the privacy of nonpublic data. In the context of the current big data era, the use of multiple remote sensing data sources for information extraction has become a major trend. However, as a data set reflecting the physical

parameters of the Earth's surface, the production process of remote sensing data often consumes significant human resources manpower, financial resources, and computing power; that is, remote sensing data have certain commodity attributes [21]. In addition, some remote sensing data are often secret due to problems such as temporal and spatial resolution and cannot be freely disclosed or given. Therefore, considering the constraints of laws, regulations, and other factors, the production of remote sensing value-added products is carried out without the disclosure of private data, which is another important challenge for remote sensing production.

In view of the aforementioned challenges, this study proposes to use blockchain technology to overcome challenges to data tampering detection, process recording, process accuracy evaluation, and privacy protection.

## 12.3    Blockchain-based remote sensing big data management

Blockchain-based remote sensing big data management mainly uses the blockchain's open, transparent, decentralized, traceable, and non-tamperable features to accurately record the processes undergone in the collection, storage, processing, and application of remote sensing data, thereby solving the problems of the low-quality and unreliable decision-making knowledge caused by arbitrary data tampering.

At present, various remote sensing data sources are distributed and stored in separate data centers and use independent data storage containers. For example, a land satellite data center stores Landsat series satellite data, and the Fengyun (FY) satellite center mainly stores FY series satellite data. Considering the large volume of remote sensing images archived in various data centers and their diverse storage formats, it is unrealistic to directly record the original remote sensing images in the blockchain. Therefore, based on the UMM [22], this study intends to integrate the metadata of the remote sensing images of each data center and record the metadata identification, image hash values, and image storage paths into the blockchain, while the original images remain in the local or cloud storage of each data center. In addition to preventing the recorded remote sensing from being modified offline, each remote sensing image will be marked with a digital watermark during the integration process to ensure the consistency of both the on-chain and off-chain data storage.

According to the processes of data integration, storage, blockchain entry, and sharing, the blockchain-based remote sensing big data management technology mainly involves distributed data integration, data entering the blockchain, distributed data storage and digital watermarking, and data sharing.

### 12.3.1    Distributed data integration

Distributed data integration ingests the metadata of remote sensing images from each data center through active or passive modes to realize the unified discovery and access of the distributed storage multisource remote sensing data. This includes metadata standardization, metadata integration, metadata identification establishment, and data entering the blockchain.

### 12.3.1.1 Metadata standardization

Remote sensing image metadata, which are the descriptive information of remote sensing images, include information about the image identification, image collection time, image collection location, product level, image quality, spatial reference system, and other characteristics of the image. At present, the metadata standards of remote sensing images adopted by various satellite data centers are different, typically including the directory interchange format (DIF) 10 [23], earth observing systems Clearinghouse (ECHO) metadata model [24,25], and ISO (International Standardization Organization) 19115 standards.

The DIF is simply the "container" for the metadata elements that are maintained in the Committee on Earth Observation Satellite International Directory Network database. It is used to create directory entries that describe a group of data. The ECHO metadata standards, which were originally used in the Independent Information Management System project that originated in 1998, are used for the integration, retrieval, and acquisition of ground observation data in distributed data centers to provide users with a unified multicenter data query service. ISO 19115, which is the geographic information-metadata standard issued by the ISO Technical Committee-211, mainly defines the metadata model used to describe geographic information and services and provides other attribute information such as identification, quality, space, time, content, spatial reference system, and distribution of geographic information and services. ISO 19115-2, which is an extension of image and grid data of the ISO 19115, provides information on remote sensing data acquisition and band description.

With the continuous development of EO technology, the amount of remote sensing images received and archived in satellite data centers around the world is exploding; the worldwide integration and sharing of remote sensing data has become an inevitable trend. However, different remote sensing metadata standards pose great difficulties for data integration and management. Therefore, a widely accepted UMM must be developed, and the remote sensing metadata of each distributed satellite data center must be converted to a standard format before data integration. Referring to NASA's Common Metadata Repository [26] metadata standard, we established the UMM and formulated specific mapping rules for DIF 10, ECHO 10, and ISO 19115-2: 2009 (Table 12.1).

In this study, the metadata standardization process is performed using the smart contract method [27] on the blockchain. The smart contract is stored and synchronized at each node of the blockchain, and the blockchain will automatically perform verification based on the code on the smart contract. Because the execution process of smart contracts is open and transparent, both it and the execution results are auditable. This will ensure high availability, improve the integration efficiency of multisource remote sensing images, and ensure that no single point of failure will occur in the data integration system.

*Table 12.1  The mapping rules for DIF 10, ECHO 10, and ISO 19115-2: 2009 with UMM (part)*

| DIF 10 | ECHO 10 | ISO19115-2:2009 | UMM |
|---|---|---|---|
| /DIF/Platform | /Collection/Platforms /Platform | /gmi:MI Metadata<br>/gmi:acquisitionInformation/gmi:MI AcquisitionInformation/<br>gmi:platform<br>/eos:EOS Platform | Platform |
| /DIF/Platform /Instrument | /Collection/Platforms /Platform/Instruments /Instrument | /gmi:MI Metadata/gmd:identificationInfo/gmd:MD DataIdentification/gmd:descriptiveKeywords | Instrument |
| /DIF/Project | /Collection/Campaigns /Campaign | /gmi:MI Metadata<br>/gmi:acquisitionInformation/gmi:MI AcquisitionInformation/<br>gmi:operation<br>/gmi:MI Operation | Project |
| /DIF/Spatial Coverage | /Collection/Spatial | /gmi:MI Metadata<br>/gmd:identificationInfo<br>/gmd:MD DataIdentification | SpatialExtent |
| /DIF/Temporal Coverage/ Range DateTime | /Collection/Temporal | /gmi:MI Metadata /gmd:identificationInfo/gmd:MD DataIdentification | TemporalExtent |

### 12.3.1.2    Metadata integration

Metadata integration is achieved through the smart contract on the blockchain to aggregate the remote sensing metadata distributed in various satellite data centers [28]. Smart contracts for metadata integration on the blockchain mainly comprise remote sensing metadata extraction scripts, file ingestion scripts, file transmission scripts, file identification scripts, and file entering blockchain scripts.

First, the remote sensing metadata extraction script (metadataCrawler) automatically and repeatedly executes the metadata extraction process within a certain time interval for each satellite data type. At the same time, the extracted remote sensing metadata are converted into the standard metadata format according to the UMM and stored in the staging area of each data center.

Next, the file ingestion script (fileIngestion) will automatically and repeatedly scan the metadata staging area of each data center within a certain time interval. At the same time, the pre-ingestion process begins, and the hash value verification method [29] is used to compare whether the blockchain data center has integrated the remote sensing image metadata of each data center. If the metadata of the remote sensing image already exist in the blockchain data center, the comparison process of the next image metadata is entered. Otherwise, the file transfer script (fileTransfer) transfers the metadata information to the file buffer of the blockchain data center and waits to enter the blockchain.

Finally, the file entering blockchain script (fileintoBlock) will automatically scan the file cache container of the blockchain data center at regular intervals. At the same time, to prevent the repeated ingestion of the metadata that has been added to the blockchain, the file blockchain entry script (fileintoBlock) still compares whether the metadata of a remote sensing image have been added to the blockchain through the pre-ingestion process. If the metadata are not in the blockchain, the file encoding script (fileEncoding) performs metadata identification establishment, and the file entering blockchain script (fileintoBlock) initiates a data entering request to the blockchain data center.

The remote sensing metadata integration process is shown in Figure 12.1.

### 12.3.1.3    Metadata identification establishment

As with typical spatial data, the use of multiple terms such as "satellite platform+sensor+collection time+spatial range+product level" is unavoidable in remote sensing data retrieval. Therefore, to realize the integrated remote sensing data retrieval, these multiple elements must be used to establish unified identification for each integrated data.

In this study, unified metadata identification is composed of the codings of retrieval requiring multiple terms. The encoding rules for multiple elements used in remote sensing data retrieval are as follows:

- Satellite platform and sensor encoding rules: Encoding satellite platform and sensor of string type into 8-bit binary digits.
- Collection time encoding rule: Unified encoding as eight decimal digits.

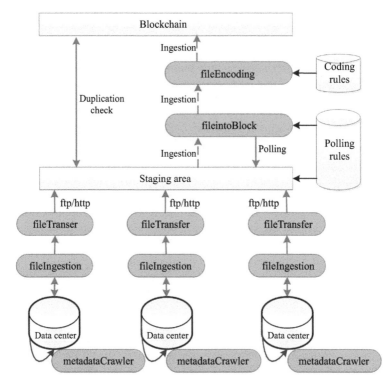

*Figure 12.1    The schematic diagram of remote sensing metadata integration*

- Spatial encoding rule: As a spatial grid coding algorithm, GeoHash [30] can convert two-dimensional latitude and longitude coordinates into a simple string that can be sorted and compared, effectively reducing the dimension of spatial attribute parameters. Thus, the center-point latitude and longitude of the remote sensing image are used for GeoHash spatial coding as the spatial attribute part of the metadata identification.
- Product level encoding rule: According to the conventional grading standards, remote sensing products can be divided into four levels, from bottom to top are the original image, fine processing products, inversion index products, and thematic products [31]. Each level of products can also be divided into multiple sublevels, and there are hierarchical relationships between the four levels and each sublevel product. The specific encoding rules for these four levels and sublevels are as follows: (1) the first-layer coding contains two binary numbers (0 and 1), and the original image, fine processing products, inversion index products, and thematic products will be coded as 00, 01, 10, and 11, respectively. (2) The second-layer coding is mainly aimed at each sublevel products, in which 3-bit binary numbers are used to encode as many levels as possible. (3) The third-layer coding uses four binary digits to encode the product name (Table 12.2).

*Table 12.2 The coding rules of remote sensing products (part)*

| Classify | Level 1 | Level 2 | Level 3 | Typical product |
|---|---|---|---|---|
| Original image | 00 | 000 | 0000 | Digital number |
| | 01 | 000 | 0000 | Accurate geometric correction product |
| Fine processing products | 01 | 000 | 0001 | Atmospheric correction product |
| | 01 | 000 | 0010 | Mosaic product |
| | 01 | 000 | 0011 | Fusion product |
| | 10 | 000 | 0000 | Surface reflectance |
| Inversion index products | 10 | 001 | 0000 | Normalized difference vegetation index (NDVI) |
| | 10 | 010 | 0000 | Leaf area index (LAI) |
| | 10 | 011 | 0000 | Photosynthetically active radiation (PAR) |
| | 10 | 100 | 0000 | Fraction of photosynthetically active radiation (FPAR) |
| | 10 | 101 | 0000 | Net primary productivity (NPP) |
| Thematic products | 11 | 000 | 0000 | Agricultural product |
| | 11 | 000 | 0001 | Forest product |
| | 11 | 000 | 0010 | Marine product |
| | 11 | 000 | 0011 | Mineral product |
| | 11 | 000 | 0100 | City product |

*Table 12.3 The coding samples of Landsat8-OIL-NDVI*

| Terms | Example | Example encoding |
|---|---|---|
| Satellite | Landsat8 | |
| Sensor | OLI | 00010010 |
| Collection time | 2015-01-01 | 20150101 |
| Spatial location | 116.389550,39.928167 | wx4g0e |
| Product level | NDVI | 100010000 |

Following this, the unified metadata identification of each remote sensing image can be obtained. For example, the metadata identification of normalized vegetation index (NDVI) products, which is generated from Landsat8-OLI data collected at the central point (116.389550,39.928167) on January 1, 2015, can be established as "0001001020150101wx4g0e100010000," as shown in Table 12.3.

## 12.3.2 Data entering blockchain

After the metadata integrated and the identification established, the metadata identification, image hash value, and image storage path can be recorded into the blockchain.

### 12.3.2.1   Entry steps

Once the original remote sensing image (DN) is registered to the blockchain by each satellite data center, the genesis block of the blockchain is constructed. Next, for the data processing, transformation, product production, and other data modification processes, they must adhere to the following block entry steps (Figure 12.2):

- Transaction (entering chain application) initiation

  If user A in the blockchain wants to modify the ocean satellite data in data center C, they must use the private key of the data center to digitally sign the ocean data to be entered into the chain and append the digital signature to the end of the application (transaction) of this chain to create the entry-chain application form (transaction form) $T_{AC}$.

- Transaction (entering chain application) broadcast

  User A in the blockchain broadcasts the entry-chain application form (transaction form) $T_{AC}$ to nodes B and D in the blockchain network. Both B and D will collect many unverified entry-chain applications (transaction) into their respective blocks.

- Block generation

  If node B, which did not participate in the transaction in the blockchain, completes the verification of the consensus mechanism first, node B will become a miner node. The miner node will generate, sign, and time-stamp a new block b. To reduce potential risks, the consensus mechanism in this study stipulates that miner nodes cannot process transactions involving themselves.

  The generation of miner node B is implemented using the delegated PoS (DPoS) [32] consensus mechanism. The basic idea of the DPoS consensus mechanism is similar to the board decision approach. Specifically, each shareholder node in the system can grant its shareholder's equity as a vote to a representative, and the top 101 nodes that receive the most votes and are willing to become representative nodes (miner node) will enter the "Board of Directors." The Board takes turns packaging and settling transactions in accordance with the established schedule and signs new blocks. Before each block is signed, it must be verified that its predecessor has been signed by a trusted representative node. The authorized representative node of the board can obtain reward points (i.e., incentives) from each transaction. To become an authorized representative node, a certain amount of reward points must be paid; the number of points is equivalent to 100 times the reward points obtained by generating a new block.

  The authorized representative node must be responsible to other shareholder nodes. If it misses signing the corresponding block, the shareholder will withdraw the votes and vote the node out of the Board. Therefore, authorized representative nodes must usually guarantee more than 99% of online time to achieve profitability goals. In the DPoS consensus mechanism, each node can independently determine its trusted authorized nodes and these nodes take turns in accounting to generate new blocks. Thus, the number of nodes

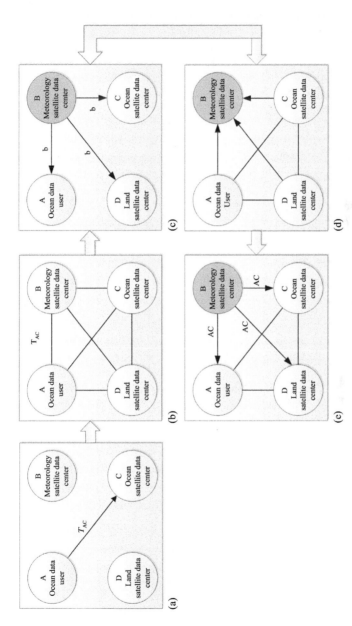

Figure 12.2 The process of metadata entering blockchain: (a) transaction initiation, (b) transaction broadcast, (c) block generation, (d) block verification, and (e) blockchain synchronization

participating in verification and accounting is greatly reduced, and rapid consensus verification is achieved.
- Block verification
  Miner node B will propagate the newly generated block to all nodes (A, C, D) in the network through the peer-to-peer [33] networks for full node verification. Other nodes will confirm the validity of the transaction contained in the block and confirm that it has not been doubly spent (repetitive consumption) and has a valid digital signature. They will then accept the block and feed back to miner node B.
- Blockchain synchronization
  After the newly generated block b is verified by other nodes in the entire network, it will be officially linked to the blockchain by miner node B to generate a new blockchain AC, which cannot be tampered with. Next, other nodes in the network will be synchronized to obtain the latest state of the blockchain at the current moment [34]. In order to ensure the stability of the system, the computing power of the entire network changes continuously with the block creation time, thereby preventing the newly created remote sensing data or products being barred from the chain due to calculation efficiency problems.

## 12.3.2.2 Structure of the data block

The structure of the data block generally includes a block header and a block body (Figure 12.3) [35].

1. The block header encapsulates the predecessor block hash value, the random number set of the current block, the signature set of participating transaction nodes, the time stamp, the Merkle root [36], and other information.
   (i) The predecessor block hash value is used to verify whether the current transaction is correct. Specifically, according to the hierarchical relationship of remote sensing products, the same products recorded in the current block should be generated from the data sources recorded in the previous block. Therefore, only if the predecessor block hash value is verified, it can be guaranteed that the remote sensing product recorded in the current block originates from the data sources recorded in the previous block, thereby preventing data from being tampered with arbitrarily.
   (ii) The random number set of the current block consensus process is mainly determined by the data key distributed by the key center of the blockchain. In other words, the nodes (remote sensing data users) that have obtained the data download or data modification key (the right random number set) and have been verified by all miners will have the data download or data modification rights of the current block.
   (iii) The signature set of participating transaction nodes is mainly used to ensure that the current transaction has passed the authentication of all nodes; that is to say, since the original remote sensing data are added to the blockchain by

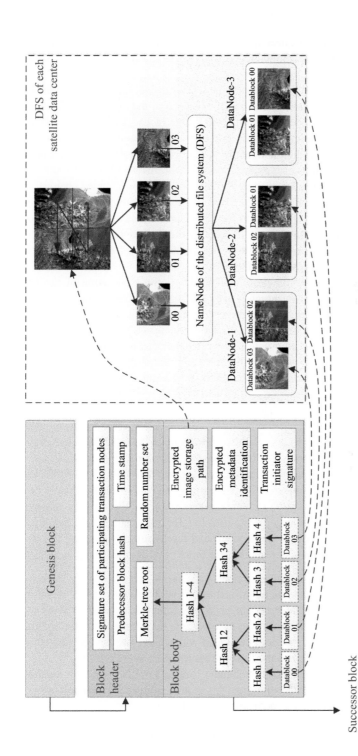

*Figure 12.3    The structure of block for remote sensing big data management*

the satellite data center, subsequent data processing must be certified by all nodes. Thus, the true and high-quality characteristics of the data products are guaranteed.

(iv)   The time stamp indicates the time when the data are written into the block, which can be used as a proof of existence of the block data. This helps to form a non-tamperable and non-forgeable blockchain database, which lays the foundation for the application of the blockchain in time-sensitive fields such as notarization and intellectual property registration. The stamping of the time stamp enables the blocks on the main chain to be arranged in chronological order, thereby forming an infinitely extended chain structure starting from the genesis block, which records the complete history of the development and change of the data source. Thus, the list structure of the blockchain can provide the traceability functions of remote sensing products of various levels, thereby allowing the detection of data tampering during collection, processing, and application.

(v)   The Merkle root in the block header is the hash value of the remote sensing image file, which is used to ensure the integrity of the image file.

(vi)   The block body includes the established metadata identification and its corresponding image file storage path, transaction initiator signature, and all verified transaction records generated during the block creation process. These records will generate a unique Merkle tree root through the hashing process of the Merkle tree and record it into the block header.

In this study, each transaction record is a data block of remote sensing image if the data storage containers adopt the distributed file system (DFS) of each satellite data center. In the DFS, such as HDFS (Hadoop Distributed File System) and GFS (Google File System), each file can be divided into 128 MB of data blocks and stored in distributed data nodes. This file splitting mechanism can not only be able to store large image files, thereby saving storage space, but also greatly improve the transmission efficiency of large image files [37,38]. Otherwise, if the satellite data center uses the NFS (network file system) and the Lustre object-based file system [39], the image file contains only one data block; that is, the block body contains only one transaction record.

(i)   The established metadata identification is mainly used to data retrieval, but it must be encrypted before it can be stored in the block.

(ii)   The image file storage path is used to point to the access address of the remote sensing image. But it should be signed with the private key distributed in the satellite data center, i.e., the file path information is encrypted.

(iii)   The signature of the transaction initiator is mainly used to verify the authenticity of this transaction. In other words, this modification of the remote sensing data was indeed done by the node who obtained the key.

(iv)   The Merkle tree usually contains the underlying database of the block body (transaction), the root hash value of the block header (the Merkle root), and all branches along the underlying block data to the root hash. The main function of the Merkle tree is to quickly summarize and verify the existence and integrity of block data. The Merkle tree calculation process is generally for grouping the block data and inserting the new hash value into the Merkle tree so that the recursion recorded only until the last root hash value is given as the Merkle root of the block header.

The Merkle tree has many advantages. First, it greatly improves the operating efficiency and scalability of the blockchain so that the block header only needs to contain the root hash value without having to encapsulate all the underlying data. This allows the hash operation [40] to efficiently run on smartphones and even Internet of Things devices [41,42]. Second, the Merkle tree can support the simplified payment verification protocol [43]; that is, it can verify transaction data without running a complete blockchain network node. For example, we need to transmit the large remote sensing image shown in the upper right side of Figure 12.3, which contains four data blocks. To improve the data transmission efficiency, the four data blocks can be transmitted separately. Next, the hash value of each received data block is calculated and compared with the hash values of all the original downloaded data blocks. If the hash values are consistent, the transmission is considered completed; otherwise is incomplete. With the Merkle tree, there is no need to download the hash values of all the original data blocks. For example, to verify whether the data block 4 has been transmitted, we can request a hash sequence from the hash value of transaction 4 along the Merkle tree to the block header root hash (hash nodes 4, 3, 34, 12, 1234) to quickly confirm the existence and correctness of the transaction. In general, the algorithm complexity of confirming any transaction in a block composed of $N$ transactions is only $\log_2 N$ [44]. This considerably reduces the bandwidth and verification time required for the operation of the blockchain and makes it possible for lightweight clients to save only part of the relevant blockchain data.

## 12.3.3 Distributed data storage and digital watermarking

After the metadata of the remote sensing images distributed in each data center is ingested, the image file will be distributed by the key center to a private key and digitally signed [45] using the smart contract script (dataEncryption). This signature adds digital watermarking, making it clear that the metadata have indeed entered the blockchain. Once the off-chain images change, their corresponding digital watermarking will change to ensure the consistency of both on-chain and off-chain data.

In addition, the image file path recorded on the chain is signed with the private key distributed in the respective data center; that is, the file path information is encrypted. Because the distributed ledger of the blockchain is public [46], anyone can search or browse all the remote sensing data that have been integrated. However, some remote sensing data need require payment to download. Therefore, this study encrypts the image file path recorded in the blockchain, meaning the user needs to provide the private key as the identity authentication along with the decryption key. Only when the correct signature is matched, the encrypted image file path will be shown to an authorized user. Next, the data interaction system accesses the storage container of the satellite data center where the image file is stored and returns the required remote sensing image to the authorized user. Here, the private keys of users are distributed by the key center according to the type of registered users, such as paid users and free users.

### 12.3.4   Data sharing

The essence of blockchain-based remote sensing data sharing is to share the image file path through a consensus mechanism, thereby establishing a virtual mapping from the satellite data center to the shared user storage directory [47]. Each virtual mapping is associated with a user ID, different users are isolated from each other, and the data sharing processes do not affect one another. Each user's renaming, moving, and deleting of remote sensing image files are used only for the modification of the virtual mapping, and the storage files in the distributed data centers are not substantially altered. Finally, the virtual mapping information is digitally signed by the user's private key and stored in the blockchain, thus ensuring the privacy of the user's personal information (Figure 12.4).

## 12.4   Blockchain-based remote sensing big data production

Remote sensing products, which are generated by one or more original ground observation data through processing, transformation, information extraction, and other steps, are a set of remote sensing data that can reflect physical parameters

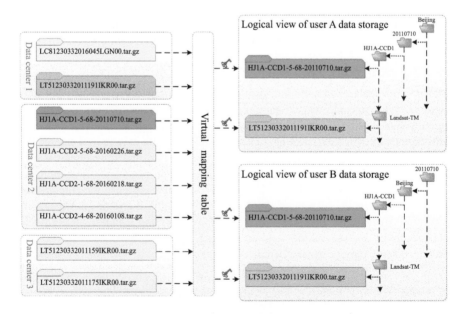

*Figure 12.4   Blockchain-based data sharing*

such as land, ocean, and weather [48]. According to incomplete statistics, there are currently up to 11,000 kinds of remote sensing products widely used. There is often a serious hierarchical dependency relationship between various remote sensing products. In other words, the production of a remote sensing product often requires multiple original remote sensing images (i.e., DN) or other low-level products.

However, if the accuracy of low-level remote sensing products is low, it directly affects the accuracy of remote sensing products at all subsequent levels, which leads to unreliable decision-making knowledge. In addition, if the remote sensing data sources needed to produce high-level products cannot be arbitrarily disclosed or shared, meaning the remote sensing data sources are nonpublic, it will directly affect the generation of the products. Thus, effectively evaluating the accuracy of various levels of remote sensing products and generating them without revealing privacy data are the main problems that this study seeks to solve.

### 12.4.1   Advantages

The blockchain-based remote sensing product generation can fully mobilize the enthusiasm of data centers, remote sensing professionals, and industry departments and utilize their respective professional advantages to produce high-quality and high-reliable remote sensing value-added products. This provides sufficient and reliable decision-making knowledge for global change research, environmental protection, and land planning.

In addition, the blockchain's linked list storage structure, decentralization, and other features ensure high reliability of the entire system (no single point of failure) and that no third party can tamper with blockchain data without permission. Moreover, the verification process of the data entry chain is completely transparent, which ensures the high-quality characteristics of the remote sensing products at all levels in the block-chain and solves the problem of unreliable decision-making knowledge.

### 12.4.2   Implementation process

The specific implementation process of the blockchain-based remote sensing product generation is as follows (Figure 12.5):

- The data provider adds the remote sensing original image into the blockchain to create a genesis block and encrypts the access path of the data set using the key distributed by the key center. This process is data entering blockchain, which was discussed in the previous section.
- The product generators use the smart contract script "orderAnalysis" to determine the required computing nodes, data sets, and intermediate products through order analysis of the production task. Next, the smart contract script "productionFlow" is used to build the product generation flow. The original data set and intermediate products required for product generation are derived from the remote sensing product hierarchy relationship using the smart contract script "productsDatabase." The computing node is determined by the data center where the data sources required for product generation are located. For example,

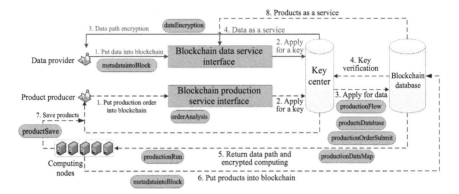

*Figure 12.5    The logical flow of blockchain-based remote sensing products production*

suppose that one wants to produce an NDVI monthly product with a spatial resolution of 30 m. The original data required by order analysis are HJ-1A/B data stored in the land satellite data center [49]. The computing nodes are the computing clusters where the land satellite data center is connected to the blockchain, and all production tasks are executed in these computing clusters.

• Next, the product generator uploads the constructed production flow to the blockchain using the smart contract script "productionOrderSubmit." The blockchain key center will use the smart contract script "productionDataMap" to match and encrypt the production flow and return the processing result to the product generator computing nodes.

• The computing nodes receive the encryption processing order fed back by the key center and use the smart contract script "productionRun" to perform data processing and production. All data scheduling and resource scheduling performed in the entire calculation process are encrypted.

• Once the production task on the computing nodes is complete, the generated products will be saved in the distributed storage of the data center with the computing nodes using the smart contract script "productSave." The corresponding metadata will be uploaded to the blockchain database by the smart contract script "metadataintoBlock." The process of recording the remote sensing products into the blockchain is the same as that of data entering blockchain, which was discussed in the previous section. The blockchain key center also distributes the product keys and uses the smart contract script "dataEncryption" to encrypt its storage path.

## 12.5    Blockchain-based remote sensing big data management and production system

Based on the strategies proposed earlier, we constructed a blockchain-based remote sensing big data management and production system. Its logical architecture, from

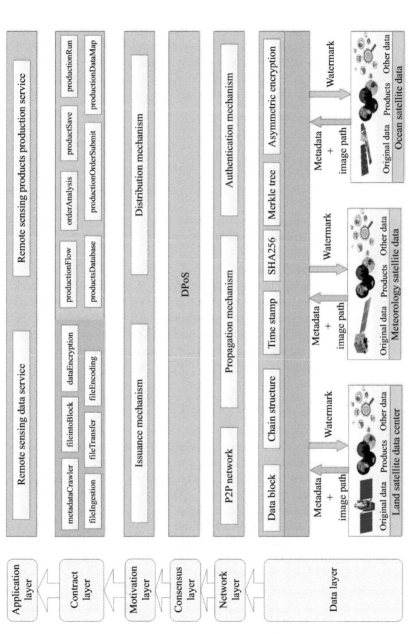

Figure 12.6 The logical architecture of the blockchain-based remote sensing big data management and production system

bottom to top, can be divided into the data, network, consensus, incentive, contract, and application layers (Figure 12.6).

1. Data layer

   The data layer encapsulates the data blocks and related data encryption, digital watermarking, and time-stamping technologies constructed using the physical data from each data center and the generated products. This includes distributed data integration, data entering the blockchain, distributed data storage and digital watermarking, and data sharing; these were discussed in detail in the previous section.

2. Network layer

   The network layer encapsulates elements such as the networking methods, message propagation protocols, and data verification mechanisms of the blockchain system. Through designing a specific propagation protocol and data verification mechanism, each node in the blockchain system can participate in the block data verification and accounting processes in the actual applications. Only when the block data passes the verification of most nodes in the entire network, it is recorded into the blockchain.

3. Consensus layer

   The consensus layer encapsulates the consensus mechanism of each node of the blockchain to become a miner. In this study, it specifically refers to the DPoS consensus mechanism. Only once verified by the DPoS consensus mechanism enables miners to obtain accounting authority. The construction of the consensus mechanism in the blockchain can enable each node to efficiently reach consensus on the validity of block data in a decentralized system with highly dispersed decision-making power.

4. Incentive layer

   By aggregating the computing resources of large-scale consensus nodes, the blockchain consensus process can achieve data verification and accounting for shared blockchain ledgers. Thus, the blockchain consensus process is essentially a task crowdsourcing process between consensus nodes. In a decentralized system, the consensus node is self-interested, and maximizing its own revenue is the fundamental goal of its participation in data verification and accounting. Therefore, it is necessary to design a reasonable crowdsourcing mechanism, so that the individual tendency of the consensus node to maximize its own profits is consistent with the overall goal of ensuring the safety and effectiveness of the decentralized blockchain system. By designing a moderate economic incentive mechanism and integrating with the consensus process, the blockchain system brings together large-scale nodes to participate and form a stable consensus on the blockchain. In this study, the incentive mechanism specifically refers to the reward of miners' points. Each node that enters the chain needs to earn enough points to become a node of the "Board of Directors," which provides the opportunity to obtain the accounting authority of the blockchain.

5. Contract layer

The data layer, network layer, and consensus layer are viewed as the underlying "virtual machine" of the blockchain, respectively, undertaking the functions of data representation, data propagation, and data verification. Thus, the contract layer is the business logic and algorithm built on the underlying "virtual machine," which is the basis for the flexible programming and operation data of the blockchain system. The contract layer encapsulates various scripts, algorithms, and more complex smart contracts generated by the blockchain system. In this study, the contract layer primarily encapsulates two types of scripts [50], data management and product generation, which are responsible for the integration, in-chain, downloading, sharing, and product generation of remote sensing big data.

6. Application layer

The application layer encapsulates various application scenarios and use cases of the blockchain. In this study, it provides the application interface of remote sensing big data retrieval, sharing, downloading, product generation, and other application cases.

## 12.6  Conclusions

The rise of blockchain technology provides new ideas for remote sensing big data management and production and overcomes challenges to data tampering detection, process recording, process accuracy evaluation, and private data protection. The introduction of blockchain technology into remote sensing big data management and production will surely give full play to the value of remote sensing data sources and provide increasingly credible decision-making knowledge for global change research. Therefore, we carried out a prospective study on blockchain-based strategies for remote sensing big data management and product generation. Specifically, we proposed remote sensing big data management rules for metadata entering chain, image files remaining in the original storage, and watermarking to maintain consistency on-chain and off-chain. In addition, we established the UMM to solve the problem of heterogeneous metadata in multisource data integration and constructed a data block structure containing metadata identification, image encryption paths, and other information. We proposed technical solutions for multisource remote sensing data integration, chain entry, and sharing and established the specific steps and technical details of the blockchain-based product production. Finally, we constructed a logical blockchain-based system serving remote sensing big data management and product generation under a multi-satellite data center scenario.

The application of blockchain technology to remote sensing big data management and product production is still in its preliminary stage, and the technical level in all aspects is not sufficiently mature. We performed a prospective study on a theoretical level. A blockchain system that serves remote sensing big data management and product generation has not been completed. Thus, future work will focus on the implementation details of blockchain infrastructure, software system construction, and smart contract code writing.

In addition, there are still a number of problems to be solved in the block-chain's own storage requirements, privacy and security, and scalability and inter-operability [51]. The existing mainstream blockchains such as Bitcoin [52], Ethereum [53], and Hyperledger [54] cannot meet the needs of remote sensing big data management and product production. For this reason, the design of a highly scalable, highly interconnected blockchain suitable for remote sensing big data management and product generation needs a critical area of focus for future work.

# References

[1]    Ma Y, Wu H, Wang L, *et al.* Remote sensing big data computing: Challenges and opportunities. Future Generation Computer Systems. 2015;51:47–60.
[2]    Zhang L, Gao Y, Chen J, *et al.* Research on remote sensing data sharing model based on blockchain technology. In: Proceedings of the 2019 2nd International Conference on Blockchain Technology and Applications; 2019. p. 59–63.
[3]    Lu Y, Wang X, Wei R, *et al.* Design of transaction system for remote sensing cloud service based on blockchain. In: Proceedings of the 2019 2nd International Conference on Blockchain Technology and Applications; 2019. p. 81–85.
[4]    Moreno JF, and Melia J. A method for accurate geometric correction of NOAA AVHRR HRPT data. IEEE Transactions on Geoscience and Remote Sensing. 1993;31(1):204–226.
[5]    Wei J, Lee Z, Garcia R, *et al.* An assessment of Landsat-8 atmospheric correction schemes and remote sensing reflectance products in coral reefs and coastal turbid waters. Remote Sensing of Environment. 2018;215:18–32.
[6]    Vuolo F, Żółtak M, Pipitone C, *et al.* Data service platform for Sentinel-2 sur-face reflectance and value-added products: System use and examples. Remote Sensing. 2016;8(11):938.
[7]    Deng X, Liu P, Liu X, *et al.* Geospatial big data: New paradigm of remote sensing applications. IEEE Journal of Selected Topics in Applied Earth Observations and Remote Sensing. 2019;12(10):3841–3851.
[8]    He C, Gao B, Huang Q, *et al.* Environmental degradation in the urban areas of China: Evidence from multi-source remote sensing data. Remote Sensing of Environment. 2017;193:65–75.
[9]    Zheng Z, Xie S, Dai HN, *et al.* Blockchain challenges and opportunities: A survey. International Journal of Web and Grid Services. 2018;14(4):352–375.
[10]   De Aguiar EJ, Faiçal BS, Krishnamachari B, *et al.* A survey of blockchain-based strategies for healthcare. ACM Computing Surveys (CSUR). 2020;53(2):1–27.
[11]   Vukolić M. The quest for scalable blockchain fabric: Proof-of-work vs. BFT replication. In: International Workshop on Open Problems in Network Security. Springer; 2015. p. 112–125.

[12] Kiayias A, Russell A, David B, *et al.* Ouroboros: A provably secure proof-of-stake blockchain protocol. In: Annual International Cryptology Conference. Springer; 2017. p. 357–388.

[13] Liu X, Wang W, Guo H, *et al.* Industrial blockchain based framework for product lifecycle management in industry 4.0. Robotics and Computer-Integrated Manufacturing. 2020;63:101897.

[14] ESA. Blockchain and Earth observation: a white paper. 2019.

[15] Tian Z, Li M, Qiu M, *et al.* Block-DEF: A secure digital evidence framework using blockchain. Information Sciences. 2019;491:151–165.

[16] Li S, Dragicevic S, Castro FA, *et al.* Geospatial big data handling theory and methods: A review and research challenges. ISPRS Journal of Photogrammetry and Remote Sensing. 2016;115:119–133.

[17] Liu J, Xue Y, Ren K, *et al.* High-performance time-series quantitative retrieval from satellite images on a GPU cluster. IEEE Journal of Selected Topics in Applied Earth Observations and Remote Sensing. 2019;12(8):2810–2821.

[18] Khayat MG and Kempler S. Life cycle management considerations of remotely sensed geospatial data and documentation for long term preservation. Journal of Map and Geography Libraries. 2015;11(3):271–288.

[19] Liu P, Di L, Du Q, *et al.* Remote sensing big data: Theory, methods and applications. Remote Sensing. 2018;10:711.

[20] Albrecht F, Blaschke T, Lang S, *et al.* Providing data quality information for remote sensing applications. ISPRS – International Archives of the Photogrammetry, Remote Sensing and Spatial Information Sciences. 2018;42(3):15–22.

[21] Kumar MN and Namratha D. An agent based distributed scheduler for remote sensing information products generation. 2013.

[22] Cantrell S, Stevens T, Rincione J, *et al.* New metadata capabilities within NASA's Common Metadata Repository (CMR). 2018.

[23] Mende V, Ritschel B, Freiberg S, *et al.* Directory interchange format (DIF) metadata and handling at the German Research Center for Geosciences' Information System and Data Center. In: Geoinformatics 2008—Data to Knowledge; 2008. p. 42.

[24] Mitchell A, Ramapriyan H, and Lowe D. Evolution of web services in EOSDIS—Search and order metadata registry (ECHO). In: 2009 IEEE International Geoscience and Remote Sensing Symposium. vol. 5. IEEE; 2009. p. V–371.

[25] Ramapriyan H. Development, operation and evolution of EOSDIS–NASA's major capability for managing Earth science data. In: CENDI/NFAIS Workshop on Repositories in Science & Technology: Preserving Access to the Record of Science. vol. 30; 2011. p. 2011.

[26] Gilman JA and Shum D. Making metadata better with CMR and MMT. 2016.

[27] Christidis K and Devetsikiotis M. Blockchains and smart contracts for the internet of things. IEEE Access. 2016;4:2292–2303.

[28] Fan J, Yan J, Ma Y, *et al.* Big data integration in remote sensing across a distributed metadata-based spatial infrastructure. Remote Sensing. 2018;10(1):7.

[29] Khezr S, Moniruzzaman M, Yassine A, *et al.* Blockchain technology in healthcare: A comprehensive review and directions for future research. Applied Sciences. 2019;9(9):1736.

[30] Liu J, Li H, Gao Y, *et al.* A geohash-based index for spatial data management in distributed memory. In: 2014 22nd International Conference on Geoinformatics. IEEE; 2014. p. 1–4.

[31] Yan J, Ma Y, Wang L, *et al.* A cloud-based remote sensing data production system. Future Generation Computer Systems. 2017;86:1154–1166.

[32] Zhou T, Li X, and Zhao H. DLattice: A permission-less blockchain based on DPoS-BA-DAG consensus for data tokenization. IEEE Access. 2019;7:39273–39287.

[33] Li J, Wu J, and Chen L. Block-secure: Blockchain based scheme for secure P2P cloud storage. Information Sciences. 2018;465:219–231.

[34] Saberi S, Kouhizadeh M, Sarkis J, *et al.* Blockchain technology and its relationships to sustainable supply chain management. International Journal of Production Research. 2019;57(7):2117–2135.

[35] Pilkington M. Blockchain technology: Principles and applications. In: Research Handbook on Digital Transformations. Edward Elgar Publishing; 2016.

[36] Li H, Lu R, Zhou L, *et al.* An efficient Merkle-tree-based authentication scheme for smart grid. IEEE Systems Journal. 2013;8(2):655–663.

[37] Huang W, Meng L, Zhang D, *et al.* In-memory parallel processing of massive remotely sensed data using an apache spark on Hadoop YARN model. IEEE Journal of Selected Topics in Applied Earth Observations and Remote Sensing. 2016;10(1):3–19.

[38] Lin FC, Chung LK, Wang CJ, *et al.* Storage and processing of massive remote sensing images using a novel cloud computing platform. GIScience & Remote Sensing. 2013;50(3):322–336.

[39] Chen L, Ma Y, Liu P, *et al.* A review of parallel computing for large-scale remote sensing image mosaicking. Cluster Computing. 2015;18(2):517–529.

[40] Li P, and Ren P. Partial randomness hashing for large-scale remote sensing image retrieval. IEEE Geoscience and Remote Sensing Letters. 2017;14 (3):464–468.

[41] Ruiz-Fernández D, Marcos-Jorquera D, Gilart-Iglesias V, *et al.* Empowerment of patients with hypertension through BPM, IoT and remote sensing. Sensors. 2017;17(10):2273.

[42] Gubbi J, Buyya R, Marusic S, *et al.* Internet of Things (IoT): A vision, architectural elements, and future directions. Future Generation Computer Systems. 2013;29(7):1645–1660.

[43] Ray PP, Kumar N, and Dash D. BLWN: Blockchain-based lightweight simplified payment verification in IoT-assisted e-healthcare. IEEE Systems Journal. 2020.

[44]  Yuan Y and Wang FY. Towards blockchain-based intelligent transportation systems. In: 2016 IEEE 19th International Conference on Intelligent Transportation Systems (ITSC). IEEE; 2016. p. 2663–2668.

[45]  Ma Z, Jiang M, Gao H, *et al.* Blockchain for digital rights management. Future Generation Computer Systems. 2018;89:746–764.

[46]  Ølnes S, Ubacht J, and Janssen M. Blockchain in Government: Benefits and Implications of Distributed Ledger Technology for Information Sharing. Elsevier; 2017.

[47]  Zhou L, Chen N, Chen Z, *et al.* ROSCC: An efficient remote sensing observation-sharing method based on cloud computing for soil moisture mapping in precision agriculture. IEEE Journal of Selected Topics in Applied Earth Observations and Remote Sensing. 2016;9(12):5588–5598.

[48]  Zheng Z, Molotch NP, Oroza CA, *et al.* Spatial snow water equivalent estimation for mountainous areas using wireless-sensor networks and remote-sensing products. Remote Sensing of Environment. 2018;215:44–56.

[49]  Singha M, Wu B, and Zhang M. Object-based paddy rice mapping using HJ-1A/B data and temporal features extracted from time series MODIS NDVI data. Sensors. 2017;17(1):10.

[50]  Song J. Programming Bitcoin: Learn How to Program Bitcoin from Scratch. O'Reilly Media; 2019.

[51]  Kolb J, AbdelBaky M, Katz RH, *et al.* Core concepts, challenges, and future directions in blockchain: A centralized tutorial. ACM Computing Surveys (CSUR). 2020;53(1):1–39.

[52]  Nakamoto S. Bitcoin: a peer-to-peer electronic cash system. 2008.

[53]  Wood G. Ethereum: A secure decentralised generalised transaction ledger. Ethereum Project Yellow Paper. 2014;151(2014):1–32.

[54]  Cachin C. Architecture of the hyperledger blockchain fabric. In: Workshop on Distributed Cryptocurrencies and Consensus Ledgers. vol. 310; 2016. p. 4.

# Index